iOS 12 Programming for Beginners
Third Edition

An introductory guide to iOS app development with Swift 4.2 and Xcode 10

Craig Clayton

BIRMINGHAM - MUMBAI

iOS 12 Programming for Beginners
Third Edition

Commissioning Editor: Amarabha Banerjee
Acquisition Editor: Larissa Pinto
Content Development Editor: Flavian Vaz
Technical Editor: Akhil Nair
Copy Editor: Safis Editing
Project Coordinator: Kinjal Bari
Proofreader: Safis Editing
Indexer: Rekha Nair
Graphics: Alishon Mendonsa
Production Coordinator: Jyoti Chauhan

First published: October 2016
Second edition: October 2017
Third edition: December 2018

Production reference: 1201218

Published by Packt Publishing Ltd.
Livery Place
35 Livery Street
Birmingham
B3 2PB, UK.

ISBN 978-1-78934-866-8

www.packtpub.com

mapt.io

Mapt is an online digital library that gives you full access to over 5,000 books and videos, as well as industry leading tools to help you plan your personal development and advance your career. For more information, please visit our website.

Why subscribe?

- Spend less time learning and more time coding with practical eBooks and videos from over 4,000 industry professionals

- Improve your learning with Skill Plans built especially for you

- Get a free eBook or video every month

- Mapt is fully searchable

- Copy and paste, print, and bookmark content

Packt.com

Did you know that Packt offers eBook versions of every book published, with PDF and ePub files available? You can upgrade to the eBook version at www.packt.com and, as a print book customer, you are entitled to a discount on the eBook copy. Get in touch with us at customercare@packtpub.com for more details.

At www.packt.com, you can also read a collection of free technical articles, sign up for a range of free newsletters, and receive exclusive discounts and offers on Packt books and eBooks.

Contributors

About the author

Craig Clayton is a self-taught, senior iOS engineer at Adept Mobile, specializing in building mobile experiences for NBA and NFL teams. He also volunteered as the organizer of the Suncoast iOS meetup group in the Tampa/St. Petersburg area for three years, preparing presentations and hands-on talks for this group and other groups in the community. He has also launched Cocoa Academy online, which specializes in bringing a diverse list of iOS courses, ranging from building apps to games for all programming levels, to the market.

About the reviewer

Kevin Munc (@muncman) is a programming veteran with 20+ years' experience in a variety of areas, ranging from mainframes to mobile, from web to blockchain, and from enterprise to startup. Along the way, he's reviewed books on Objective-C, watchOS, RFP, UIAutomation, SpriteKit, JavaFX, and Vim.

> *I would like to thank all of the people who have helped me sharpen my reviewing skills over the years. I'm also grateful for the ongoing support of my family as I continue to seek to grow as a developer.*

Packt is searching for authors like you

If you're interested in becoming an author for Packt, please visit `authors.packtpub.com` and apply today. We have worked with thousands of developers and tech professionals, just like you, to help them share their insight with the global tech community. You can make a general application, apply for a specific hot topic that we are recruiting an author for, or submit your own idea.

Table of Contents

Preface

In this book, we will build a restaurant reservation app called *Let's Eat*. We will start the book off by exploring Xcode, our programming environment, which is also known as the Interface Development Environment (IDE). Next, you will start learning the foundations of Swift, the programming language used in iOS apps. Once we are comfortable with the basics of Swift, we will dig deeper to build a more solid foundation.

Once we have a solid foundation of using Swift, we will start creating the visual aspects of our *Let's Eat* app. During this process, we will work with storyboards and connect our app's structure together using segues. With our UI complete, we will go over the different ways in which we can display data. To display our data in a grid, we will use `Collection Views`, and to display our data in a list, we will use `Table Views`.

We will also look at how to add basic and custom annotations on to a map. Finally, it's time to get real data; we will look at what an Application Programming Interface (API) is and how we can get actual restaurant data into our `Collection Views`, `Table Views`, and `Map`.

We now have a complete app, but how about adding some bells and whistles? The first place where we can add a feature will be the restaurant detail page, where we can add restaurant reviews. Here, users will be able to take or choose a picture and apply a filter to their picture. They will also be able to give the restaurant a rating as well as a review. When they are done, we will save this data using `Core Data`.

Since we built our app to work on both iPhone and iPad, we should add the ability to make our app support iPad multitasking. Doing this will allow our app to be open alongside another app at the same time.

If we want to be able to send our reservation to a friend, we can create a custom UI for iMessages, which will send them the details for the reservation along with the app it came from. The one thing missing from our app is the ability to notify the user with a custom notification to alert when they have an upcoming reservation.

Finally, let's create quick access by using SiriKit and Siri to request money and send reservations. Now that we have added some bells and whistles, let's get this app to our friends using TestFlight, and finally get it into the App Store.

Who this book is for

This book is for you if you are completely new to Swift, iOS, or programming and want to make iOS applications. However, you'll also find this book useful if you're an experienced programmer looking to explore the latest iOS 12 features.

What this book covers

Chapter 1, *Getting Familiar with Xcode*, takes you through a tour of Xcode and talks about all the different panels that we will use throughout the book.

Chapter 2, *Building a Foundation with Swift*, deals with the basics of Swift.

Chapter 3, *Building on the Swift Foundation*, teaches us to build on our Swift foundation and learn some further basics of Swift.

Chapter 4, *Digging Deeper into Swift*, talks about ranges and control flow.

Chapter 5, *Digging into Swift Collections*, talks about the different types of collections.

Chapter 6, *Starting the UI Setup*, is about building the *Let's Eat* app. We will focus on getting our structure set up using storyboards.

Chapter 7, *Setting Up the Basic Structure*, deals with working on our *Let's Eat* app in a storyboard.

Chapter 8, *Building Our App Structure in Storyboard*, is about adding more to our app structure in a storyboard.

Chapter 9, *Finishing Up Our App Structure in Storyboard*, concludes the discussion of our app structure in a storyboard.

Chapter 10, *Designing Cells*, is about designing the table and collection view cells in a storyboard.

Chapter 11, *Getting Started with the Grid*, concerns working with `Collection Views` and how we can use them to display a grid of items.

Chapter 12, *Getting Data into Our Grid*, concerns the incorporation of data into our `Collection Views`.

Chapter 13, *Getting Started with the List*, teaches us to work with `Table Views` and takes an in-depth look at dynamic `Table Views`.

Chapter 14, *Where Are We?*, deals with working with MapKit and learning how to add annotations to a map. We will also create custom annotations for our map.

Chapter 15, *Working with an API*, involves learning how to use a JSON API within our app.

Chapter 16, *Displaying Data in Restaurant Detail*, teaches you how to pass data using segues.

Chapter 17, *Foodie Reviews*, talks about working with the phone's camera and library.

Chapter 18, *Working with Photo Filters*, takes a look at how to apply filters to our photos.

Chapter 19, *Understanding Core Data*, teaches us the basics of using core data.

Chapter 20, *Saving Reviews*, wraps up reviews by saving them using core data.

Chapter 21, *Universal*, deals with multitasking on the iPad, and how we can get an update to be supported on all devices.

Chapter 22, *iMessages*, is about building a custom message app UI. We will also create a framework to share data between both apps.

Chapter 23, *Notifications*, provides instruction on how to build basic notifications. Then, we will look at embedding images into our notifications as well as building a custom UI.

Chapter 24, *SiriKit*, teaches the reader how to use Siri to create money requests.

Chapter 25, *Beta and Store Submission*, concerns how to submit apps for testing as well as submitting apps to the App Store.

To get the most out of this book

You need to have Xcode 9 installed on your system. To download Xcode 9, visit https://developer.apple.com/xcode/.

Download the example code files

You can download the example code files for this book from your account at www.packt.com. If you purchased this book elsewhere, you can visit www.packt.com/support and register to have the files emailed directly to you.

You can download the code files by following these steps:

1. Log in or register at www.packt.com.
2. Select the **SUPPORT** tab.
3. Click on **Code Downloads & Errata**.
4. Enter the name of the book in the **Search** box and follow the onscreen instructions.

Once the file is downloaded, please make sure that you unzip or extract the folder using the latest version of:

- WinRAR/7-Zip for Windows
- Zipeg/iZip/UnRarX for Mac
- 7-Zip/PeaZip for Linux

The code bundle for the book is also hosted on GitHub at https://github.com/ PacktPublishing/iOS-12-Programming-for-Beginners-Third-Edition. In case there's an update to the code, it will be updated on the existing GitHub repository.

We also have other code bundles from our rich catalog of books and videos available at https://github.com/PacktPublishing/. Check them out!

Download the color images

We also provide a PDF file that has color images of the screenshots/diagrams used in this book. You can download it here: https://www.packtpub.com/sites/default/ files/downloads/9781789348668_ColorImages.pdf.

Conventions used

There are a number of text conventions used throughout this book.

CodeInText: Indicates code words in text, database table names, folder names, filenames, file extensions, pathnames, dummy URLs, user input, and Twitter handles. Here is an example: "Mount the downloaded WebStorm-10*.dmg disk image file as another disk in your system."

A block of code is set as follows:

```
states.insert("Ohio", at:1) states.insert(contentsOf:["North
Carolina", "South Carolina", "Nevada"],at:3)
```

Bold: Indicates a new term, an important word, or words that you see on screen. For example, words in menus or dialog boxes appear in the text like this. Here is an example: "Hit **Next** and then **Create**."

 Warnings or important notes appear like this.

 Tips and tricks appear like this.

Get in touch

Feedback from our readers is always welcome.

General feedback: If you have questions about any aspect of this book, mention the book title in the subject of your message and email us at customercare@packtpub.com.

Errata: Although we have taken every care to ensure the accuracy of our content, mistakes do happen. If you have found a mistake in this book, we would be grateful if you would report this to us. Please visit www.packt.com/submit-errata, selecting your book, clicking on the Errata Submission Form link, and entering the details.

Piracy: If you come across any illegal copies of our works in any form on the internet, we would be grateful if you would provide us with the location address or website name. Please contact us at copyright@packt.com with a link to the material.

If you are interested in becoming an author: If there is a topic that you have expertise in, and you are interested in either writing or contributing to a book, please visit authors.packtpub.com.

Reviews

Please leave a review. Once you have read and used this book, why not leave a review on the site that you purchased it from? Potential readers can then see and use your unbiased opinion to make purchase decisions, we at Packt can understand what you think about our products, and our authors can see your feedback on their book. Thank you!

For more information about Packt, please visit `packt.com`.

Getting Familiar with Xcode

So, you want to get into iOS development? I was in your shoes on January 27, 2010, when Apple first announced the iPad. As soon as the conference was over, I knew that I wanted to learn how to create apps for the iPad. I signed up for the Apple Developer website and paid my $99 annual fee. But then, I realized that I did not know where to begin. A large variety of instructional books or videos did not exist, especially since the iPad hadn't released. I had previous programming experience; however, I had no idea how to write Objective-C (the original programming language for iOS). Therefore, I had to teach myself the basics. In this book, we will learn what it takes to become an iOS developer together.

If you are new to programming, take your time. You should understand the lessons that are provided in one chapter before moving on to the next. These essential skills will set you up with a solid foundation in iOS development. If you have previous programming experience, you should still review the earlier chapters, as they will be a refresher for you.

Throughout this book, we will work in Xcode, specifically Xcode 10 (and Swift 4, which we will tackle later in this book). Xcode is known as an **Integrated Development Environment** (**IDE**). Using Xcode gives us everything we will need to build apps for iOS, tvOS, macOS (formerly, OS X), and watchOS. In this chapter, we will explore Xcode to help you get more comfortable using it. If you are not on Xcode 10, make sure to update Xcode, as the code in this book will not run correctly otherwise.

Our focus in this book will be on creating a universal iOS app (an app for both the iPhone and iPad). The best way to do this is to create a project to familiarize yourself with where everything is and how to find what you need. So first, let's first download and install Xcode.

Getting started

To download Xcode, launch the App Store on your Mac and then type `Xcode` into the search bar in the upper-right corner:

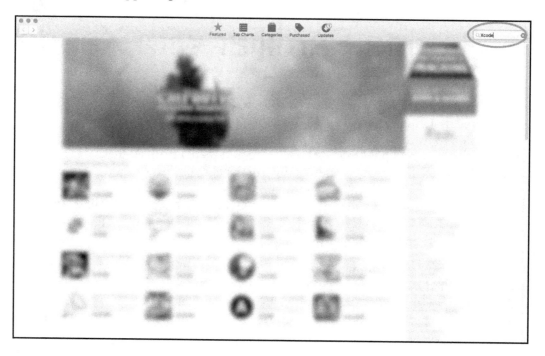

 For enhanced image quality, download the graphics bundle from `https://www.packtpub.com/sites/default/files/downloads/9781789348668_ColorImages.pdf`.

Next, click on **INSTALL**:

Once installed, launch Xcode, and you should see the following **Welcome to Xcode** screen:

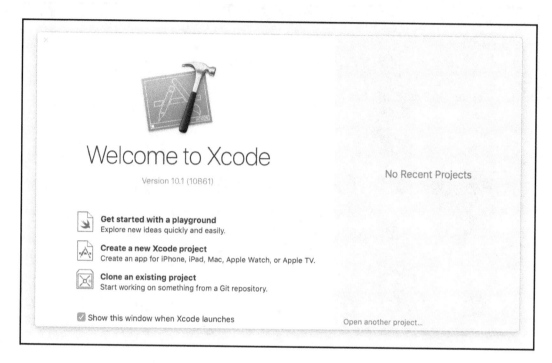

If this is the first time you have launched Xcode, then you will see **No Recent Projects** in the right-hand panel. If you have previously created projects, then you will see those listed to the right. To get started, we are going to click on **Create a new Xcode project** in the left-hand panel of the welcome screen. You will see the new project screen, as follows:

Across the top of this screen, you can select one of the following items: **iOS**, **watchOS**, **tvOS**, **macOS**, and **Cross-platform**. Since we are creating apps for iOS, make sure that you have iOS selected. Then, choose **Single View App** and click on **Next**. Now, you will see an options screen for a new project:

This option screen has the following seven items to complete or choose:

1. **Product Name**: The product name is your app. We are going to set ours as `ExploringXcode`.
2. **Team**: The team connects to your Apple account. We are going to ignore this for now, because we do not need the Team for this chapter. If you already have a team set up, leave it as is. We will cover this in greater detail later in this book.

3. **Organization Name**: You can set the organization name to your company name, or just use your name.

4. **Organizer Identifier**: You will set the organizer identifier to be your domain name in reverse. For example, my website URL is cocoa.academy, and therefore, my identifier is academy.cocoa. Since URLs are unique, it will ensure that no one else will have your identifier. If you do not have a domain, then use your first and last names for now. However, you will eventually have to purchase a domain if you want to submit your app to the Apple Store.

5. **Bundle Identifier**: When you create a new project, Apple will combine your **Product Name** with your **Organizer Identifier** to create your unique bundle identifier. So, even if 10,000 people create this project, each person will have a different bundle identifier.

6. **Language**: Set language to **Swift**.

7. **Checkboxes**: You can uncheck **Use Core Data**, **Include Unit Tests**, and **Include UI Tests**, as these are things that we will not use in this chapter.

Now, select **Next**, and Xcode will prompt us to save our project. I have a dedicated folder for all my projects, but you can save it on your desktop for easy access.

The Xcode interface

Your project is now open, and it is time for us to get familiar with all of the panels. If this is your first time in Xcode, then it will probably be a bit overwhelming for you. Therefore, we will break it down into six parts:

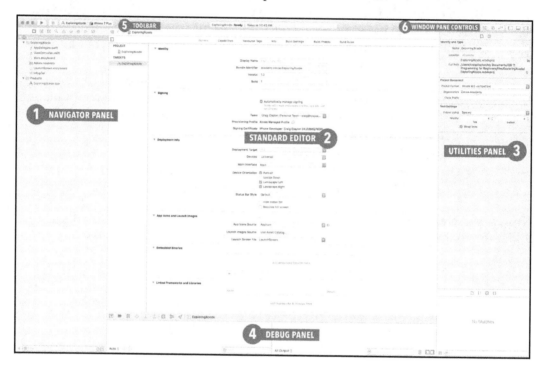

- NAVIGATOR PANEL
- STANDARD EDITOR
- UTILITIES PANEL
- DEBUG PANEL
- TOOLBAR
- WINDOW PANE CONTROLS

Navigator panel

The primary use of the navigator panel is to add new files and select existing files. The other icons are used from time to time; we will cover them as we need them.

Standard editor

The standard editor is a single panel view that's used to edit files. The standard editor area is the primary area in which you will work. In this area, we can view storyboard files, see our Swift files, or view our project settings.

Utilities panel

The utilities panel can be a bit confusing when you first use Xcode because this menu changes based on what you have selected in the standard editor. When we start building an app, we will dig deeper into this. For now, know that the utilities panel is made up of the inspector pane at the top and the library pane at the bottom. The inspector pane allows you to change the attributes or properties of things you put in your storyboard; the library pane enables you to insert objects, image assets, and code snippets into your app.

Debug panel

The debug panel will allow us to see log messages from our app. You will become very familiar with this panel by the time you finish this book. The debug panel is one of the most excellent tools for getting feedback on what your app is doing or not doing.

Toolbar

Next, we look at the toolbar, which is demonstrated as follows:

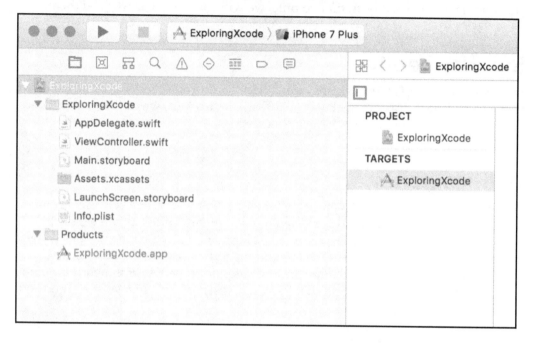

First, we have a play button, which is how we launch our app (or use *command + R*). Next, you will see a stop button, which will not be active until you run your app. This stop button (or *command + .*) is used to stop your app from running. To the right of the stop button, you will see your target (your project name), along with the current simulator that has been selected. If you click on your project name, you will see a screen similar to this:

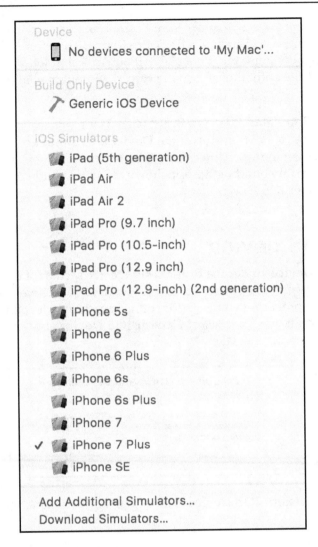

This drop-down menu, which we will call the **Device** and **iOS Simulators** drop-down menu, allows you to change your simulator type. For our project, select **iPhone7 Plus** as your simulator and then click on the play icon (or use *command + R*) to run your app.

Now, let's return to Xcode and select the stop button (or use *command + .*).

If you use the keyboard shortcut, make sure Xcode is in focus; otherwise, this shortcut will not work. I work on a 15-inch MacBook Pro Retina. Therefore, when I am working on an app, I will use the iPhone X or iPad Air 2 simulator in landscape mode. They both fit nicely on my screen without me having to resize either.

In addition to the **Simulator**, there is a **Build Only Device** as well as a **Device** section, both of which can be found at the top of the **Device** and **Simulator** drop-down menu that was shown earlier in this chapter. Note that, for our purposes, you will only need a simulator while we are building the app; however, you can add an iOS device if you would like (see under **iOS Device**).

Generic iOS device

The **Generic iOS Device**, under the **Build Only Device** section of the **Device** and **Simulator** drop-down menu, is used for when you need to archive your app, which means that you are preparing your app for submission to Apple (either to the App Store or Test Flight). If you try to select **Generic iOS Device** now and run the app, you will get the following message:

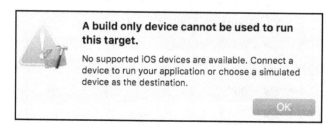

Therefore, change **Generic iOS Device** to an actual simulator, and then you will be able to continue.

iOS device

If you do not have a device connected to the computer, you will see **No devices connected** under the **Device** section of the **Device** and **Simulator** drop-down menu.

As noted earlier, when we start building the *Let's Eat* app, you will have the option of using the simulator or connecting a device to Xcode. Using a device is slower; however, the simulator will not perform in the same way as a device will.

In the past, you needed to have a paid account to build your app on a device. Nowadays, you do not need a developer account to run the app on your device. Note that, if you decide to connect your device instead of using a simulator, you will need iOS 12 installed on it. Xcode 10 introduced the capability of connecting your phone wirelessly. We will look at the traditional way first and then we will go over how you can connect your phone wirelessly.

The following steps are only intended for those of you who do not want to pay for the Apple Developer Program at this time:

1. Connect your iOS device via USB.
2. In the drop-down menu, select your device (here, I have chosen **Xclusive iPhone 6 Plus**):

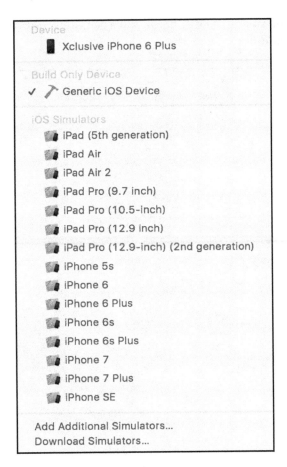

3. Wait for Xcode 10 to finish indexing and processing. The indexing and processing may take a bit of time. Once complete, the status will say **Ready**.

4. Run the project by hitting the Play button (or use *command + R*).

You will get two errors that state the following:

- Signing for `ExploringXcode` requires a development team. Select a development team in the project editor.
- Code signing requires a product type application in SDK iOS 12.0.

Ignore the specifics of these errors as they indicate that we need to create an account and add our device to that account.

5. Now, in the standard editor, you will see under **Signing** that you need to add an account:

6. Click on **Add Account**. If a **Sign into Xcode with your Apple ID** dialog box does not pop up, inside the **Accounts** screen on the bottom left, click on the + and select **Apple ID**:

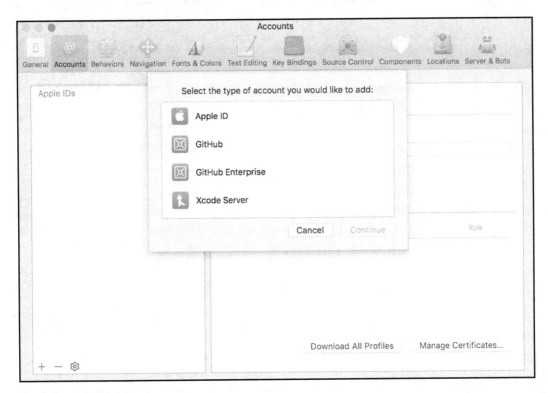

7. Then, when you click on **Create Apple ID**, you will be asked to enter your birth date, name, email, and password, along with a number of security questions. Make sure that you verify your email before you answer the security questions, otherwise you will have to come back to this screen and add your **Apple ID** again.

8. Once you have finished all of the steps, you will see your account, as follows:

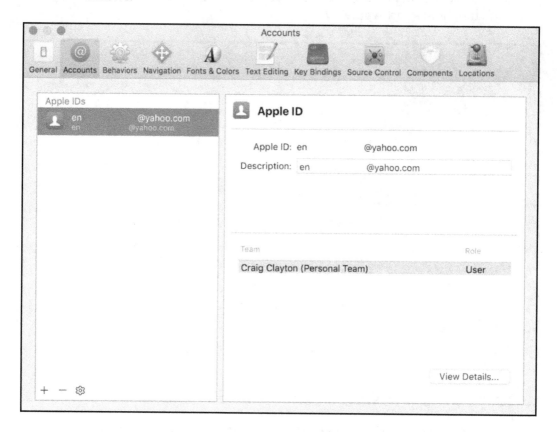

If you already have an account, then instead of seeing **Add Account**, you will see a drop-down menu with your account listed. If your device is not connected to this account, you might see a message asking if you would like to add your device to your account. Adding your device to an account is for testing purposes only.

Connecting wirelessly

Now that you have your phone and account connected, you can quickly get your phone set up to run wirelessly. With your device already connected via USB, go to **Window | Devices**, and then **Simulators**. Click on the checkbox marked **Connect via network**:

Make sure that your phone and your computer are connected to the same Wi-Fi network.

When I first connected to my device, I saw a globe icon in Xcode that lets you know that your device is connected via the network, as demonstrated in the following screenshot:

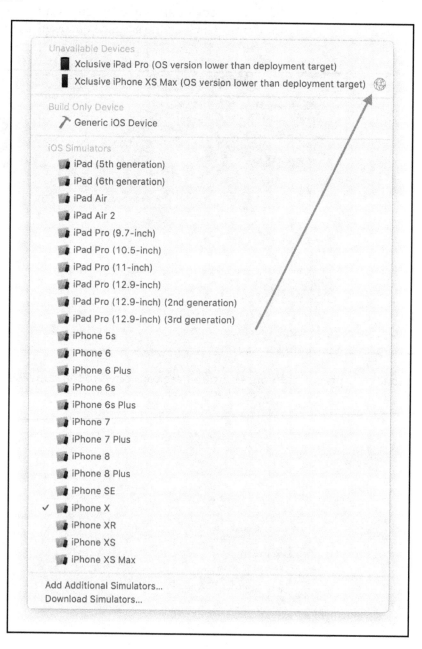

After a short time, the globe went away. Even if you do not see the icon, you can disconnect the USB, and your device should still be connected to Xcode (as long as it is connected to the same Wi-Fi network).

You will not need to use a device for this book, but it is always good to run your app in an actual device before you submit it to the store.

Before we get to the right-hand side of the toolbar, select the `Main.storyboard` file in your navigator panel. This file is used to display all of your visual setup for your entire app. We will cover this in detail later in this book. After you select the file, you should see the following:

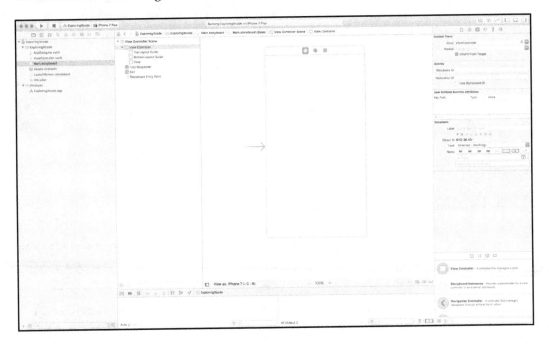

Window pane controls

The following screenshot shows the window pane controls:

Moving on to the window pane controls, you will see two groups of icons. The first group is called the Editor Mode, and the second group is called the View. Let's look at the functions of the Editor Mode icons:

Editor Mode icons	Function
	This icon controls the standard editor (which is the center panel in the earlier screenshot of the Main.storyboard file in the navigator panel).
	This icon splits the Standard editor into two panels, where you will see the ViewController.swift file on the right. We will use this split screen throughout this book.
	This icon is the Version editor. We will not address the Version editor in this book since it is a more advanced feature.

At this point, you might be thinking that there are way too many panels open, and I would agree with you! The last panel is where the previous group of View icons in the toolbar comes in handy.

Let's look at these icons and their functions in the following table:

View Mode icons	Function
	This icon will toggle (hide or show) the navigator panel (or use *command* + O).
	This icon will toggle (hide or show) the debug panel (or use *command* + *shift* + *Y*).
	This icon will toggle (hide or show) the utilities panel (or use *command* + *alt* + O).

Summary

Congratulations! You have finished exploring the basics of Xcode. When we start building our app, we will cover the more essential parts of Xcode in depth. In the next few chapters, we will begin learning about the Swift programming language. We will use the latest Swift version, and this will be a basic intro into the programming language. If you are familiar with Swift, feel free to skip ahead to Chapter 6, *Starting the UI Setup*. Even if you are familiar with Swift, it is always good to go back through the basics as a refresher. So, let's get started!

2
Building a Foundation with Swift

Now that we have had a short tour of Xcode, it is time to start learning about Swift. Remember, if you are new to programming, things will be very different for you, so take your time. The essential skills that you learn here will set you up with a solid foundation in iOS development. If you have previous programming experience, you should still review this chapter, as it can only enhance your programming skills and act as a refresher for you.

On June 2, 2014, Apple changed the game for iOS development, because this was the day they announced Swift to the world. With this announcement, everybody was put on an even playing field, because they had to learn a new programming language. Swift has brought a more modern approach to developing apps and has seen a massive influx of new developers of all ages wanting to build iOS apps. However, enough about history! Let's dig in and look at what you are going to learn about.

The following topics will be covered in this chapter:

- Playgrounds
- Data types
- Variables and constants
- Debug and `print()`
- Comments

Playgrounds – an interactive coding environment

Before we jump into building the app that we will be creating in later chapters, called *Let's Eat*, we need to understand the basics of Swift. An easy way to experiment with Swift is to use **Playgrounds**. It is an interactive coding environment that evaluates your code and displays the results. Using Playgrounds gives us the ability to work with Swift without needing to create a project. It is great for prototyping a particular part of your app. So, whether you are learning or experimenting, Playgrounds are an invaluable tool. To create a Playground, we need to launch Xcode and click on **Get started with a playground**:

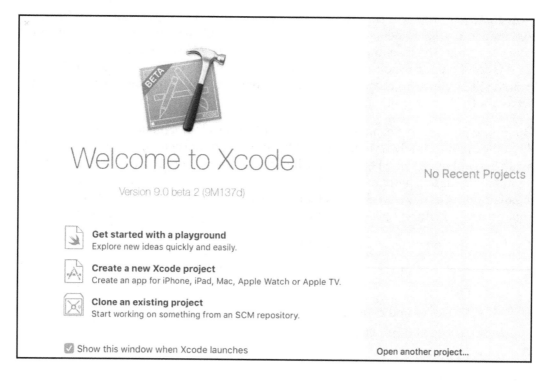

The **Playground** template screen appears. Make sure that you select **iOS**, and then choose **Blank** and hit **Next**:

You will be asked to give your project a name and a location to save the file; name your new project `Playground iOS11-Programming-for-Beginners-Ch2`. You can save the file anywhere that you like. Now, with the project saved, we can explore Playgrounds in a little more detail.

When you launch the app, you will see five distinct areas:

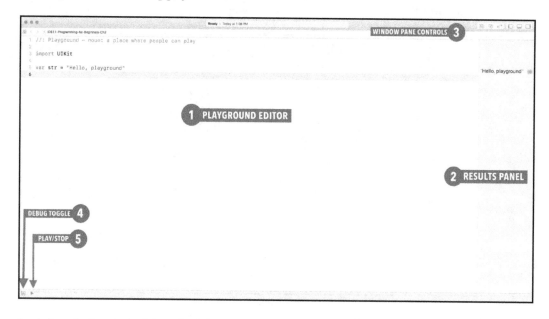

Let's break down each area in Playgrounds:

- **Playground Editor**: This area is where you write all of your code.
- **Results Panel**: The Results panel is a feature that's only found in Playgrounds and provides immediate feedback.
- **Window Pane Controls**: The Window Pane Controls have two groups of icons:

As we discussed earlier, the first group is called the **Editor Mode**, and the second group is called the **View**. Refer to the detailed description of these icons in the previous chapter for information about what each one does.

- **Debug Toggle**: This button allows you to hide and show the Debug panel and toggle on the Debug panel.
- **Play/Stop**: This button is used to make Playgrounds execute code or to stop Playgrounds from running. Typically, Playgrounds runs on its own, but sometimes you need to manually toggle this feature on when Playgrounds does not execute your code for you.

Now that we have the Xcode panels setup, delete all of the code in this file. Your Playground should have three open panels: your Playground Editor, the Results Panel, and the Debug Panel. Let's start digging into some code.

Data types – where it all starts

Swift offers a collection of built-in data types. Its data types are a string, an integer, floating-point numbers, and Booleans. These data types are found in most programming languages. Therefore, if you are not new to programming, you can skip this section and start at the *Variables and constants – where data is held* section later.

Let's walk through each data type for those of you who are new to programming or would like a refresher.

String

The first data type we will cover is a string. A series of characters represent a string. Strings are used to display text in an app. A string wrapped in quotes is known as a string literal. In programming, we cannot just add text to Playgrounds. So, to write a string, we must wrap our string inside quotes.

Let's add our name into Playgrounds, wrapped in quotes:

In Playgrounds, your values appear inside of your Results Panel. So, we now know that in order to create a string, we need to use quotes.

Integer data type

Integers (**Ints**) are whole numbers, such as 32 and −100. Integers are useful when you need to perform calculations (that is, adding, subtracting, multiplication, and so on). Let's add some numbers to Playgrounds. On the next line, under your name, type 32, and then, on the following line, −100, as demonstrated in the following screenshot:

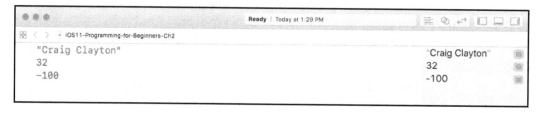

Again, you see both 32 and −100 in the Results Panel under your name.

Floating-point numbers

Floating-point numbers are numbers with a fractional component, such as 4.993, 0.5, and −234.99. Let's add these values to Playgrounds as well:

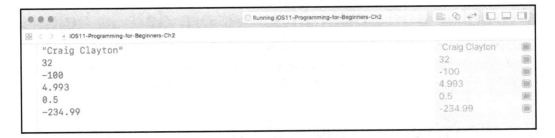

Booleans

Booleans (bools) are referred to as logical because they can either be true or false. Use Booleans when you need to determine whether some logic is true or false. For example, did the user log in? This statement would either be true—yes they did, or false—no they did not. So, in Playgrounds, add true and false:

Now, we have covered all of the primary data types in Swift. Right now, we have no way to use these data types. Using the data is where variables and constants come into play.

Variables and constants – where data is held

Variables and constants are like containers that contain any data. When you want to declare a variable, you have to use the var keyword. Let's declare each of the data types we did earlier, but, this time, using variables and constants instead.

Creating a variable with a string

First, delete what you have entered in Playgrounds already, and let's declare our first variable, named `fullName`, and set it to your name:

```
var fullName = "Craig Clayton"
```

The preceding code says that we have a variable named `fullName` and that it is holding a string value of `Craig Clayton`. Your Results Panel shows your actual name as its data:

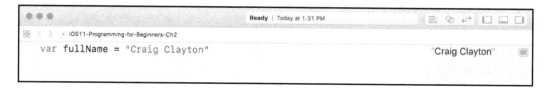

Creating a variable with an integer (int)

Now, let's create a variable with an int called age and set it to our age (or whatever you want your age to be) by adding the following:

```
var age = 40
```

Our program now knows that age is an int. You should see both your name and age in the Results Panel, just like you did previously:

Debug and print() – detecting your bugs

We can use the Debug panel (at the bottom of the following screenshot)
using print(). So, let's see how print() works by printing both our name and age.
We can do this by adding the following:

```
print(fullName)
print(age)
```

It should appear on your screen as follows:

You should now see the output in both the **Results** and **Debug Panels**. Using `print()` allows us to see things in our Debug Panel and therefore verify expected results. Using `print()` is a handy debugging tool.

Adding floating-point numbers

Now let's add floating-point numbers, using the `let` constant, in Playground:

```
let gradeAvg = 2.9
let version:Float = 1.1
```

This is demonstrated in the following screenshot:

```
var fullName = "Craig Clayton"          "Craig Clayton"
var age = 40                             40

print(fullName)                          "Craig Clayton\n"
print(age)                               "40\n"

let gradeAvg = 2.9                       2.9
let version:Float = 1.1                  1.1
```

You will notice that a couple of things are different. First, we are using the `let` keyword. Using `let` tells our program that this is a constant. Constants are variables that cannot change once they are set (as opposed to a non-constant variable, which can change after being set).

The other thing you might have noticed is that we explicitly set our `version` to `Float`. When dealing with a floating-point number, it can be a `Double` or a `Float`. Without getting too technical, a `Double` is much more precise than a `Float`. The best way to explain this is to use pi as an example. Pi is a number in which the digits go on forever. Well, we cannot use a number that goes on forever; however, a `Double` and `Float` handle how precise that number is. Let's look at the following diagram to see what I mean by precise:

Double vs Float

let lessPrecisePI = Float("3.14")
let morePrecisePI = Double("3.1415926536")

So, in the preceding example, you can see that `Float` only displays `3.14`, whereas `Double` gives you a much more accurate number. In Swift, a `Double` is preferred. Therefore, if you do not explicitly set the floating-point number to a `Float`, Swift defaults to a `Double`. To set `version` to a `Float`, you must purposely set it that way.

Creating a Boolean

Now, it is time to create a `Bool`. Let's make it a constant. Enter the following code:

```
let isConstant:Bool = true
```

This is demonstrated in the following screenshot:

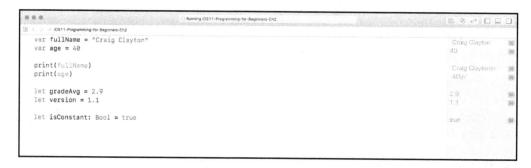

Since `isConstant` is set, let's make it `false` by adding this:

```
isConstant = false
```

On the same line as what you just entered, you will now see a red circle with a white dot in the middle. The red circle means that there is an error. The white circle inside of it indicates that Xcode can fix the error for you (most of the time):

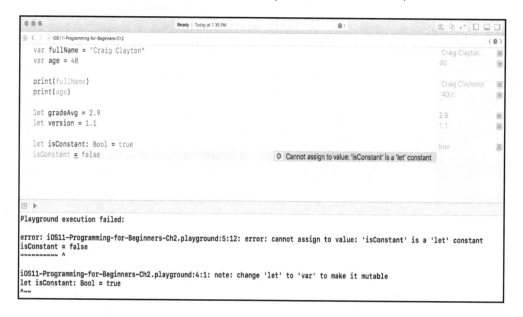

You will also notice an error in your Debug Panel, which is just a more detailed version of the error. This error is telling us that we are trying to change the value of a constant when we cannot do so.

If you tap on the circle, you will see that Playgrounds suggests that you change the `let` to a `var` since you cannot assign a value to a constant:

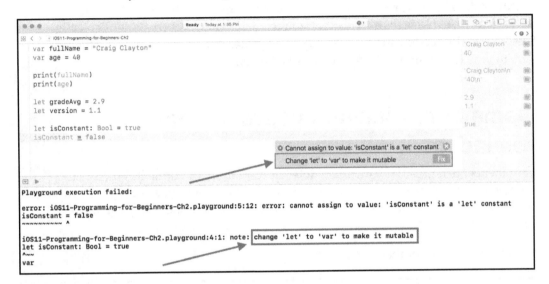

Since we want it to remain a constant, let's delete the line `isConstant = false`. We have covered basic data types, but there are some other programming basics we should discuss as well.

Why constants versus variables?

You might be asking yourself "Why would you ever want to make something constant?". Since constants cannot change after you run your app, they keep you from accidentally breaking a value that should not change. Another excellent use for constants is for base URLs, as you would not want these to change. When you are getting data, you do not want to change the value midway through your app accidentally. Apple recommends that you use `let` whenever possible. Typically, I use `let` until Xcode warns me that a `var` is preferable. If I change the value from `let` to `var`, then I am verifying that this is the behavior I want.

Comments – leaving yourself notes or reminders

Comments are a great way to create notes or reminders to yourself. When you comment code, it means that it will not execute when your code runs. There are two types of comment used: `//` or `/* */`. `//` is used for a one-line comment and `/**/` is used for a block of text.

Let's see what both of these look like:

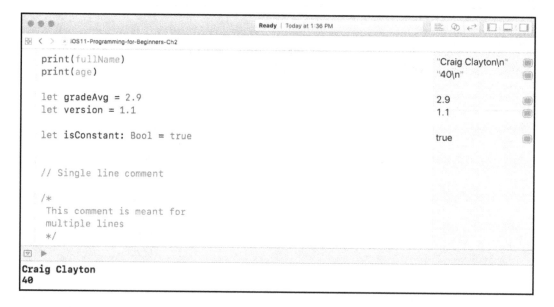

Type safety and type inference

Swift is a type-safe language, which means that you are encouraged to be clear about the value types with which your code works. Type inference means that, before your code runs, it quickly checks to ensure that you did not set anything to a different type. If you do, Xcode gives you an error. Why is this good? Let's say that you have an app in the store and that you set one of your variables as a `String` in one part of your code, but then accidentally set the same variable as an `Int` in another part of your code. This error may cause some bad behavior in your app that could cause it to crash. Finding these kinds of errors is like finding a needle in a haystack. Therefore, type checking helps you write safer code by helping you to avoid errors when working with different types.

We have now looked at data types and know that strings are for textual data, `Int` is for integer, `Bool` is for Boolean, and `Double` and `Float` are for floating-point numbers. Let's look a bit deeper into data types and see how we can do more than assign them to variables.

Concatenating strings

String concatenation is the result of combining multiple string literals to form an expression. So, let's create one by first entering two string literals:

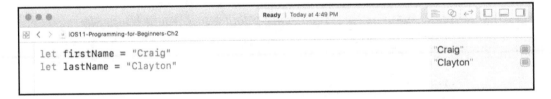

Combining these two gives us a string concatenation. We can combine strings by using the + operator, add the following:

```
let full = firstName + lastName
```

When you look in the Results Panel, you will notice that there is no space between our first and last names.

Also, if we just put the variables in quotes, they will revert to simple string literals and will no longer be variables.

String interpolation

To correct this, we can put these variables inside quotes, which is known as string interpolation, using a backslash and parentheses around each of our variables inside the string interpolation. Let's update our name variable to the following, and you will see the space in the name in the Results Panel:

```
let full = "\(firstName) \(lastName)"
```

After adding the preceding line, our code should look something like this:

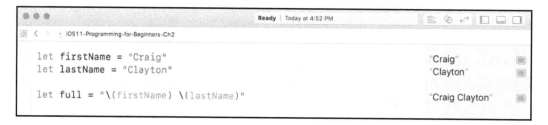

Now that we know about using variables inside quotes, we can do the same inside `print()`. Let's put the `firstName` and `lastName` variables inside `print()`, as follows:

```
print("\(firstName) \(lastName)")
```

The `print` statements are great for checking to see whether you are getting the value you want:

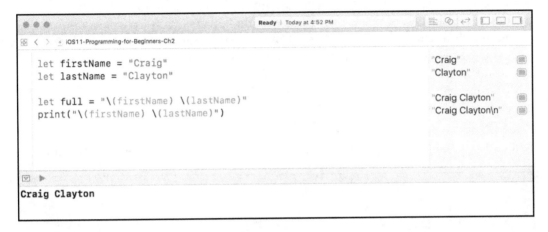

Bam! Now, we have a way to view multiple variables inside of `print()` and to create string interpolation by combining multiple strings. We can do much more with `Strings`, and we will cover that later in this book.

Operations with our integers

In our Playground, we know that age is an int, but with `Int`, we also can write arithmetic expressions using numbers, variables/constants, operators, and parentheses. Let's start with addition, subtraction, multiplication, and division. Add the following into Xcode:

So, sum added two integers (+ operator) together, totaling 43 in our preceding example. Then, we subtracted (– operator) sum from 32 to create a result (–11, in our example). After that, we took the result and multiplied (* operator) it by 5 (see –55 in the Results Panel). All of this is pretty basic math; however, you may have noticed something different with our division equation (/ operator). When you divide two integers, the result is the third integer. So, instead of –55 divided by 10 equals –5.5, our result was –5. To get the correct floating-point value of –5.5, we need to make our division value a Double. Therefore, let's add the following:

```
let divide2 = Double(total) / 10
```

After adding the preceding line of code, your code should look something like this:

```
// (+) operator
let sum = 23 + 20                                          43
// (-) operator
let result = 32 - sum                                      -11
// (*) operator
let total = result * 5                                     -55
// (/) operator
let divide = total / 10                                    -5
let divide2 = Double(total) / 10                           -5.5
```

All of these operations might look familiar to you, but there is one with which you might not be familiar, and that is the remainder operator. The remainder operator returns the remainder when a number is divided by another.

So, for example, 7 divided by 3 equals 2.33. When we apply the remainder operator, we get back 1. Add the following to Playgrounds:

```
let mod = 7 % 3
```

Now, your code should look something like this:

```
// (+) operator
let sum = 23 + 20                        43
// (-) operator
let result = 32 - sum                    -11
// (*) operator
let total = result * 5                   -55
// (/) operator
let divide = total / 10                  -5
let divide2 = Double(total) / 10         -5.5
let mod = 7 % 3                          1
```

Increment and decrement

There are times when you need to increment (increase) or decrement (decrease) a value. There are two ways you can accomplish this. Add the following into Playgrounds:

```
var count = 0                   0

// Option #1
count = count + 1               1
count = count - 1               0

// Option #2
count += 1                      1
count -= 1                      0
```

Both of these options do the same thing, but option #2 is in shorthand. The preferred way is to use option #2, which is += (addition assignment operator) and -= (subtraction assignment operator), but the choice is yours.

Comparison operators

We can also compare different numerical variables. These might be familiar to you from math class. Let's enter these in to Playgrounds:

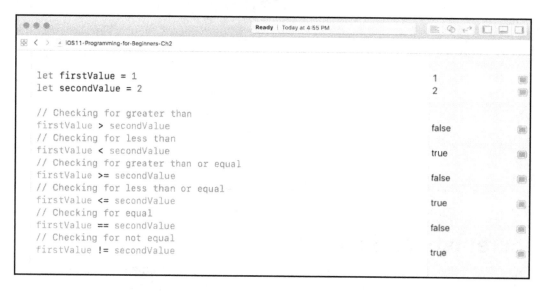

As you can see in the Results panel, these comparison entries result in true or false based on the values that you enter (here, these are 1 and 2).

Summary

We have hit the basics and, from this point, if you are new to programming, it is a good idea to make sure that you understand each topic we cover. As the chapters progress, we will cover more and more, so take your time and make sure that you are comfortable with all of the topics covered in this chapter.

3
Building on the Swift Foundation

In the last chapter, we went through the basics of understanding data types and how to create variables and constants. Now that we are comfortable with those topics, let's look at adding more building blocks. This chapter will build on what we learned in the previous chapter and get us a bit closer to understanding Swift better.

The following topics will be covered in this chapter:

- Type safety and type inference
- Operations with integers
- `if` statements
- Optionals and optional bindings
- Functions

Data types are good, but we will need to add some logic to our app. For example, we want to be able to control whether someone should see a login screen when they launch the app, or whether they should go right into the app. You will use logic a lot, so let's look at what an `if` statement is and how to use it.

Creating a Playground project

As you learned earlier, launch Xcode and click on **Get started with a playground**:

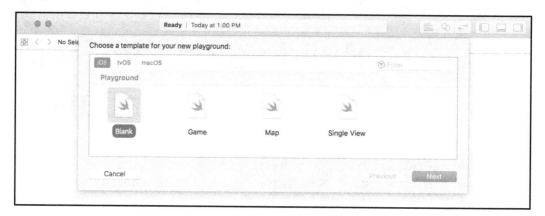

The Playground template screen will appear. Make sure that you select **iOS** and then choose **Blank** and hit **Next**. You will be asked to give your project a name and a location to save the file; name your new Playground `iOS11-Programming-for-Beginners-Ch3`. You can save the file anywhere you like. Now, with the project saved, we can explore Playgrounds a bit.

The if statements – having fun with logic statements

Let's add our first piece of logic using an `if` statement. An `if` statement is a simple statement to determine whether or not a statement is `true`. Input the following into Xcode:

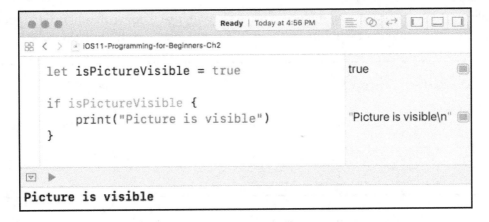

```
Picture is visible
```

In the first line of the preceding code, we created a constant named `isPictureVisible`, and we set it to `true`. The next line starts our `if` statement and reads as follows: if `isPictureVisible` is `true`, then print `Picture is visible`. When we write `if` statements, we must use the curly braces to enclose our logic. It is a good practice to put the opening curly brace (`{`) on the same line as the `if` statement and the closing curly brace (`}`) on the line immediately after your logic.

When writing `if` statements using a `bool`, you are always checking for `true`; however, if you wanted to check for `false`, you would do the following:

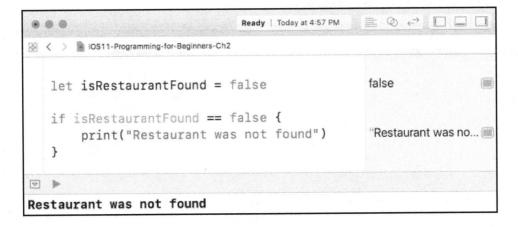

```
Restaurant was not found
```

Bools work great with `if` statements, but we also can use them with other data types. Let's try an `if` statement with an `Int` next. Write the following in Playgrounds:

```
let drinkingAgeLimit = 19                                          19

if drinkingAgeLimit < 21 {
    print("Since we cannot offer you an adult beverage – would you     "Since we cannot offer you a..."
        like a water or soda to drink?")
}
```
```
Since we cannot offer you an adult beverage – would you like a water or soda to drink?
```

In the preceding example, we first created another constant with our `Int` set to `19`. The next line says: if the `drinkingAgeLimit` is less than `21`, then print `Since we cannot offer you an adult beverage – would you like water or soda to drink?` When you are using `Int` within `if` statements, you will use the comparison operators (<, >, <=, >=, ==, or !=). However, our last `if` statement feels incomplete because we are not doing anything for someone over 21. When you need to cover the contradictory statement, this is where you will utilize an `if...else` statement. You enter an `if...else` statement precisely as you do with an `if` statement, but, at the end, you add the word else.

You can add else to both of the `if` statements we have inputted so far, but, for now, add it to the end of our last `if` statement:

```
let drinkingAgeLimit = 19                                          19

if drinkingAgeLimit < 21 {
    print("Since we cannot offer you an adult beverage – would you     "Since we cannot offer you a..."
        like a water or soda to drink?")
} else {
    print("What type of beverage would you like? We have adult
        beverages along with water or soda to drink.")
}
```
```
Since we cannot offer you an adult beverage – would you like a water or soda to drink?
```

With else added to the end of our `if` statement, it turns into an `if...else` statement, which now reads: if the `drinkingAgeLimit` is less than 21, then print `Since we cannot offer you an adult beverage – would you like water or soda to drink?` Otherwise (or `else`), print `What type of beverage would you like? We have adult beverages along with water or soda to drink.`

Now, our `if...else` statement can handle both conditions. Based on the value 19 for our `drinkingAgeLimit`, we can see the following in the Debug Panel: `Since we cannot offer you an adult beverage – would you like water or soda to drink?` If we change `drinkingAgeLimit` to 30, our Debug Panel says `What type of beverage would you like? We have adult beverages along with water or soda to drink.` Go ahead and change 19 to 30 in Playgrounds:

```
let drinkingAgeLimit = 30                                          30

if drinkingAgeLimit < 21 {
    print("Since we cannot offer you an adult beverage – would you
        like a water or soda to drink?")
} else {
    print("What type of beverage would you like? We have adult     "What type of beverage wou...
        beverages along with water or soda to drink.")
}

What type of beverage would you like? We have adult beverages along with water or soda to drink.
```

Note that we got the behavior we wanted in the Debug Panel.

So far, we have covered using an `if` statement with a `bool` and an `Int`. Let's take a look at one more example using a string. Add the following bit of code to Playgrounds:

```
●●●                                    Ready | Today at 4:58 PM

⊠ ❬ ❭  iOS11-Programming-for-Beginners-Ch2

let restaurantName = "La Bamba"                      "La Bamba"

if restaurantName == "La Bamba" {
    print("I've only been to La Bamba II!")          "I've only been to L...
}
else {
    print("Oh! I've never heard of that restaurant")
}

I've only been to La Bamba II!
```

In programming, we use equals (=) when setting data to variables. However, to compare two data types, we must use the double equals (==) sign. Therefore, when we write an if statement that compares two strings, we must use double equals (==) instead of a single equal (=) to determine equality.

An if...else statement only lets us check two conditions, whether they are true or not. If we wanted to add more conditions, we would not be able to use just an if...else statement. To accomplish this, we would use what is called an if...else...if...else statement. This statement gives us the ability to add any number of else-if inside our if...else statement. We will not go overboard, so let's add one. Update your last if...else statement to the following:

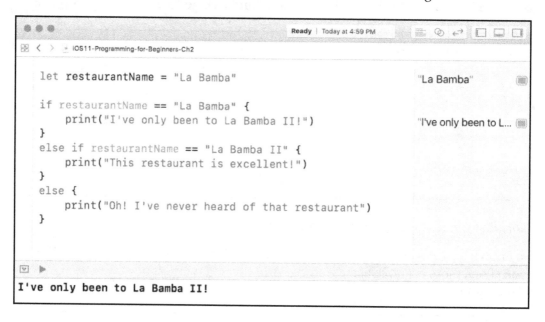

In this example of an if...else...if...else statement, we are checking whether restaurantName equals La Bamba, then print I've only been to La Bamba II!, else if restaurantName equals La Bamba II, then print This restaurant is excellent!, else print Oh! I've never heard of that restaurant.

Using if, if...else, and if...else if...else statements helps you to create simple or complex logic for your app. Being able to use them with Strings, bools, Ints, and floating-point numbers give you more flexibility.

Optionals and optional bindings

Use optionals when a value cannot be set. Think of optionals as containers that can take either a value or nil. Optionals gives us the ability to check whether the value is nil or not. To create an optional value, you will have to provide it with a data type followed by a question mark (?). Before we do that, let's create a string that is not an optional. Add the following to Playgrounds:

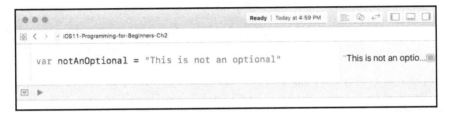

Now, let's add an optional to Playgrounds:

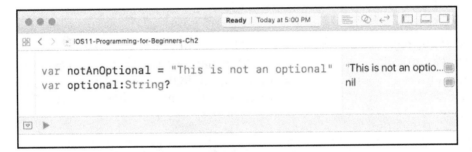

In this example, we created a string optional, and, if you notice in the Results Panel, it is nil. But for our `notAnOptional`, we see `"This is not an optional"`. Now, on the next line, let's set `optional` equal to `"This is an optional"`:

```
var notAnOptional = "This is not an optional"     "This is not an optional"
var optional:String?                              nil

optional = "This is an optional"                  "This is an optional"
```

In our Results Panel, we see "`This is an optional`". Now let's print both `notAnOptional` and `optional`, as you will see a difference between the two:

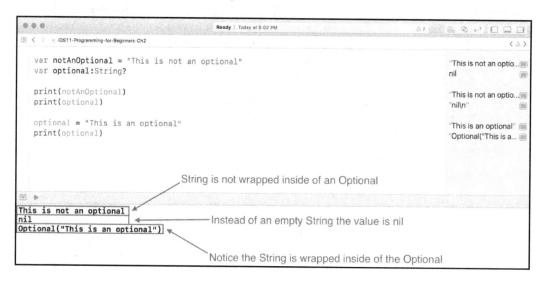

Note that our `notAnOptional` variable looks fine, but `optional` has an optional ("") wrapped around the `String`. The ("") means that, in order for us to access the value, we must unwrap the optional. One way we could do this is by force-unwrapping the optional using an (!). Let's update our `print` statement and change it to the following:

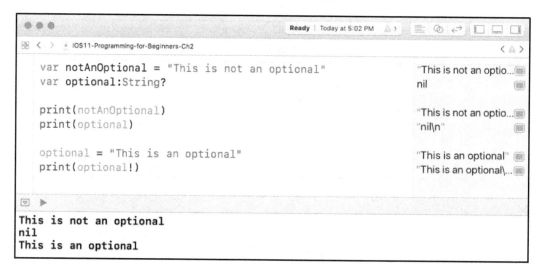

We force-unwrapped our optional, but this method is not recommended. If you force-unwrap an optional and there is no value, your app will crash, so avoid this. We should use what is called **optional binding**, which is the safe way to access the value using an `if...let` statement. Remove the (!) from the `print` statement and instead write the following optional binding:

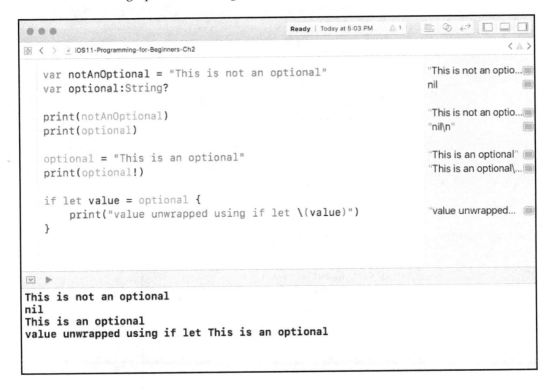

This `if...let` statement is saying that if the optional is not nil, set it to `value`, but, if this optional is nil, ignore it and do nothing. Now, we do not have to worry about anything regarding setting our value and causing our app to crash.

Why optionals?

So, now, you are probably asking yourself: "Why do you have to do this?". Trust me, when I first learned about optionals, I felt the same way. Using optionals helps to protect your code. For now, understand that when you see a data type followed by a question mark, this variable is an optional. As we work with optionals more and more throughout this book, it will become more evident to you.

Functions

Now, it is time to get into an enjoyable part of programming and learn how to write functions. Functions are self-contained pieces of code that you want to run on something. In Swift 3, Apple made a change to how you should write functions. All of the functions we will write in this chapter will perform an action (think of verbs). Let's create a simple function called `greet()`:

```swift
func greet() {
    print("Hello")
}
```

This example is a basic function with a `print` statement in it. In programming, functions do not run until you call them. We call a function by merely calling its name. So, let's call `greet`, as follows:

```swift
greet()
```

Once we add this to the code, this is what we'll see on screen:

```swift
func greet() {
    print("Hello")                    "Hello\n"    ▣
}

greet()
```
```
Hello
```

That's it! We just created our first function and called it. However, functions can do so much more. We can add what is called a parameter to a function. A parameter allows us to accept data types inside our parentheses. Doing this will enable us to build more reusable chunks of code. So, let's update our `greet()` function to accept a parameter called `name`:

```swift
func greet(name:String) {
    print("Hello")
}
```

After you update the function, you will get the following error:

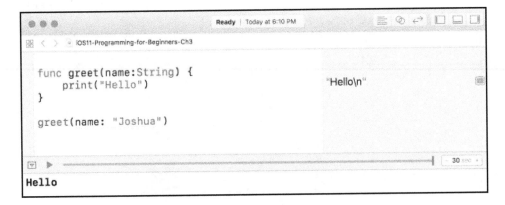

We received this error because we updated our function, but we did not update the line where we called it. Let's update where we call it. Let's update where we call `greet()` to the following:

```
greet(name: "Joshua")
```

When you are done you should see the following:

```
func greet(name:String) {
    print("Hello")
}

greet(name: "Joshua")
```

The preceding code looks good; however, the Debug Panel shows us that we are not using the name in our greeting. Earlier, you learned how to create a string interpolation. So, we need to append our variable name inside our `print` statement, as follows:

```
print("Hello \(name)")
```

This is how your code will now look:

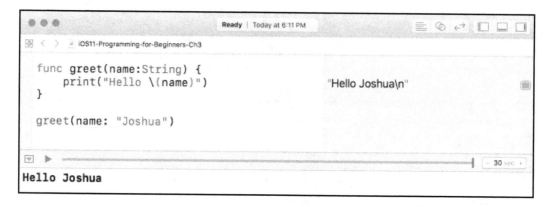

Functions can take multiple parameters, so let's create another `greet()` function that takes two parameters, a first name, and a last name:

```
func greet(first:String, last:String) {
 print("Hello \(first) \(last)")
 }
```

Now, your code and its output should look as shown in the following screenshot:

```
        func greet(name:String) {
            print("Hello \(name)")                        "Hello Joshua\n"
        }

        greet(name: "Joshua")

        func greet(first: String, last: String) {
            print("Hello \(first) \(last)")
        }

Hello Joshua
```

We also need to update where we called `greet()` in order to accept multiple parameters as well:

```
greet(first: "Craig", last: "Clayton")
```

Now, your code and output screen should look something like this:

```
func greet(name:String) {
    print("Hello \(name)")                         "Hello Joshua\n"
}

greet(name: "Joshua")

func greet(first: String, last: String) {
    print("Hello \(first) \(last)")                "Hello Joshua Clayton\n"
}


greet(first: "Joshua", last: "Clayton")
```
```
Hello Joshua
Hello Joshua Clayton
```

We now have a function that takes multiple parameters.

Functions can perform an action, but they can also run an action, and then, when it is done, return back some type of data. Whenever we want our function to return something, we need to use a noun as a way to describe what our function will do. We just created a function called `greet()` that takes a first and last name and creates a full name.

Now, let's create another function called `greeting()`, which will return a full name with a greeting. Let's see what this looks like:

```
func greeting(first:String, last:String) -> String {
    return "Hello \(first) \(last)"
}
```

The following is how your code and output screen should appear:

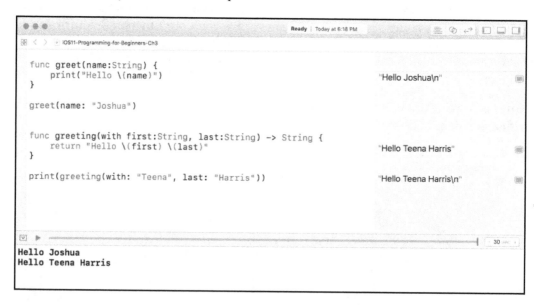

This function is almost the same as the previous one, but with a couple of new things. First, -> `String` tells the function that we want to return a string. Inside our function, we return "Hello \(first) \(last)." Since we said that we want to return something after our parentheses, we have to do just that. Now, let's look at how we can do this. Enter the following code:

```
print(greeting(first:"Teena", last:"Harris"))
```

Now, this is how your code and output screen should look:

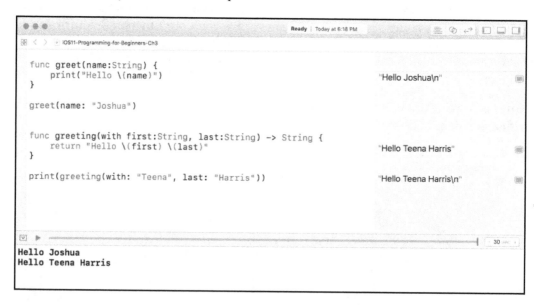

As you may have noticed, in the Debug Panel, we now have our full name with `Hello` added to the beginning. As you start to build on functions, you start to see the power.

These are just the basics of functions. We will cover more advanced functions throughout our *Let's Eat* app. The main thing novice programmers forget is that functions should be small. Your function should do one thing and one thing only. If your function is too long, then you need to break it up into smaller chunks. Sometimes, longer functions are unavoidable, but you should always be mindful of keeping them as small as possible. Nice work!

Let's work

We covered a lot in this chapter, and now it is time to put everything we covered into practice. Here are two challenges. If you are comfortable with them, then work on them on your own. Otherwise, go back into this chapter, where you can follow along with me and see how you can do each one:

- **Challenge 1**: Write a function that accepts and returns a custom greeting (other than `Hello`, which we addressed earlier in this chapter), along with your first and last name
- **Challenge 2**: Write a function that will take two numbers and add, subtract, multiply, or divide those two numbers

Summary

In this chapter, we learned about operations with integers, as well as working our way through `if` statements. Finally, we discussed the power of optionals and learned about what functions are and how to use them.

In the next chapter, we will move on to some more Swift basics by digging into Swift collections.

4
Digging Deeper

When I first started programming, I was in my mid-twenties. I started a lot older than most, but I will say that grasping the basics took me a bit longer than most, too. I remember when I bought my first programming book, and I read and re-read chapters over and over again until the concepts made sense to me. I found that a lot of books talked to me like I had majored in computer science. As you progress through this book, take your time and, if you need to go back, it is okay to do so. No one is going to care that it took you an extra day to understand a concept. It is more important that you fully understand that concept.

One tip I would give you is to not copy and paste the code. No matter where you find the code and no matter how long it takes, it benefits you to type it out. Doing this benefited me, as I eventually started to remember the code, and it became second nature to me.

In the last chapter, we went over the basics of Swift to get you warmed up. Now, we will dig deeper and learn about some more programming concepts. These concepts will build on what you have already learned. In this chapter, we will cover the following topics:

- Ranges
- Control flow

Let's begin by creating a new Playground project.

Creating a Playground project

As you learned earlier, launch Xcode and click on **Get started with a playground**:

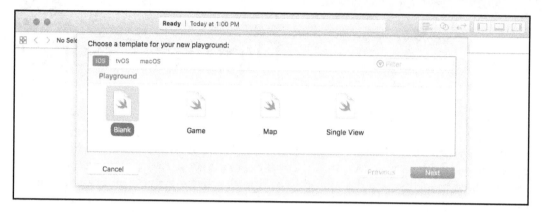

The Playground template screen will appear. Make sure that you select **iOS** and then choose **Blank** and hit **Next**. You will be asked to give your project a name and a location to save the file; name your new Playground `iOS11-Programming-for-Beginners-Ch4`. You can save the file anywhere you like. Now, with the project saved, we can explore Playgrounds a bit.

Next, delete everything inside your file and toggle on the Debug panel using the toggle button (*command* + *shift* + *Y*). You should now have a blank screen with the Results Panel on the right, and the Debug Panel opened at the bottom.

We focused on the basics earlier, and now we will build upon those skills. Ranges are one such data type that we should learn about. These are very useful and can come in handy for a variety of reasons. Let's take a look at what ranges are and then start to understand the difference between a *closed range,* a *half-closed range,* and a *one-sided range.*

Ranges

Ranges are generic data types that represent a sequence of numbers. Let's look at the following diagram to understand this:

| 10 11 12 13 14 15 16 17 18 19 20 |

Closed range

Notice that, in the preceding diagram, we have numbers ranging from **10** to **20**. Rather than having to write each value, we can use ranges to represent all of these numbers in shorthand form. To do this, let's remove all of the numbers in the diagram except for **10** and **20**:

Now that we have removed those numbers, we need a way to tell Swift that we want to include all of the numbers that we just deleted. All the numbers in-between are where the range operator (...) comes into play. Therefore, in Playgrounds, let's create a constant called range and set it equal to `10...20`:

```
let range = 10...20
```

You should see the following:

The range that we just entered says that we want the numbers between `10` and `20`, as well as both `10` and `20` themselves. This type of range is known as a closed range.

Inside Playground, in the result, you will see a Show Result icon:

If you hover over the result, you will also see quick look:

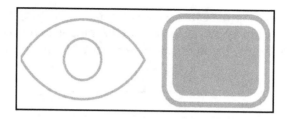

Select the Show Result icon so that you can see the result:

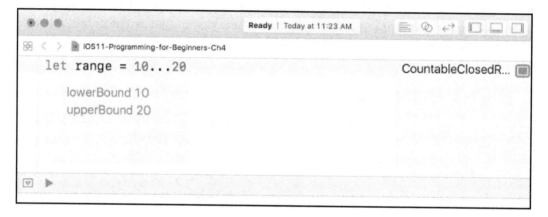

We also have what is called a half-closed range.

Half-closed range

Let's make another constant that is known as a half-closed range and set it equal to `10 < 20`. Add the following to Playgrounds:

```
let halfClosedRange = 10..<20
```

Your code should now look like this:

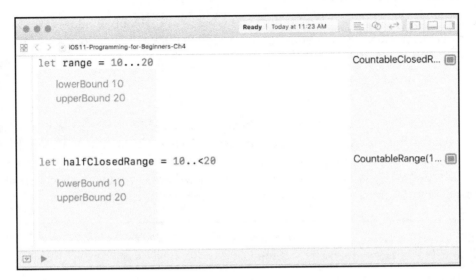

A half-closed range is the same as a closed range, except that the end value is not included. In this example, this means that 10 through 19 are included, and 20 will be excluded.

At this point, you will notice that your Results Panel shows you `CountableClosedRange(10...20)` and `CountableRange(10..<20)`. We cannot see all of the numbers within the range. To see all of the numbers, we need to use a loop.

Control flow

In programming, control flow is the order in which your code executes. When working with Swift, we can use a variety of control statements. Loops, in particular, are useful for when you want to repeat a task multiple times. Let's take a look at a few different types of loop.

The for...in loop

One of the most common control statements is a for...in loop. It allows you to iterate over each element in a sequence. Let's see what a for...in loop looks like:

```
for <value> in <sequence> {
 // Code here
 }
```

We start the for...in loop with for, which is proceeded by <value>. <value> is a local constant (only the for...in loop can access it) and can be any name you like. Typically, you will want to give this value an expressive name. Next, we have in, which is followed by <sequence>. <sequence> is where we want to provide it with our sequence of numbers. Let's write the following into Playgrounds:

Notice that, in our Debug Panel, we can see all of the numbers we wanted in our range.

Let's do the same for our `halfClosedRange` variable by adding the following:

```
for index in halfClosedRange {
    print("half closed range - \(index)")
}
```
(10 times)

```
half closed range - 10
half closed range - 11
half closed range - 12
half closed range - 13
half closed range - 14
half closed range - 15
half closed range - 16
half closed range - 17
half closed range - 18
half closed range - 19
```

In our Debug Panel, we can see that we get the numbers **10** through **19**. One thing to note is that these two `for...in` loops have different variables. In the first loop, we used the `value` variable, and in the second one, we used the `index` variable. You can make these variables whatever you choose them to be.

Also, in the two preceding examples, we used constants, but we could just use the ranges within the loop. As a next step, you need to add the following:

```
for index in 0...3 {
    print("range inside - \(index)")
}
```
(4 times)

```
range inside - 0
range inside - 1
range inside - 2
range inside - 3
```

Now, you will see **0** to **3** print inside the Debug Panel.

What if you wanted the numbers to go in reverse order? Let's input the following `for...in` loop:

```
for index in (10...20).reversed() {
    print("reversed range - \(index)")
}
```
(11 times)

```
reversed range - 20
reversed range - 19
reversed range - 18
reversed range - 17
reversed range - 16
reversed range - 15
reversed range - 14
reversed range - 13
reversed range - 12
reversed range - 11
reversed range - 10
```

One-sided range

A one-sided range operator allows you to use ranges that continue as far as possible in one direction. If you want the range to continue, then this is what you would use. Let's look at a one-sided range by adding the following:

```
let names = ["Craig", "Teena", "Jason", "Joshua", "Myah", "Tiffany",
"Kim", "Veronica", "Mikki(KK)", "Milan", "Shelby", "Kaysey"]

for name in names[2...] {
    print(name)
}
```

You will see that all the names print in the console:

As a next step, let's add the following:

```
for name in names[...6] {
 print(name)
}

// Craig
// Teena
// Jason
// Joshua
// Myah
// Tiffany
// Kim
```

You should now see in the console how this update changes what is in the console:

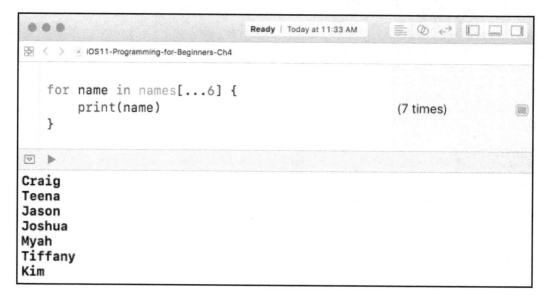

Another useful loop is the `while` loop. Let's take a look at how the `while` loop is used.

The while loop

A `while` loop executes a Boolean expression at the start of the loop, and the set of statements run until a condition becomes `false`. It is important to note that `while` loops can execute zero or more times. Here is the basic syntax of a `while` loop:

```
while <condition> {
 // statement
 }
```

Let's write a `while` loop in Playgrounds and see how it works. You have to add the following:

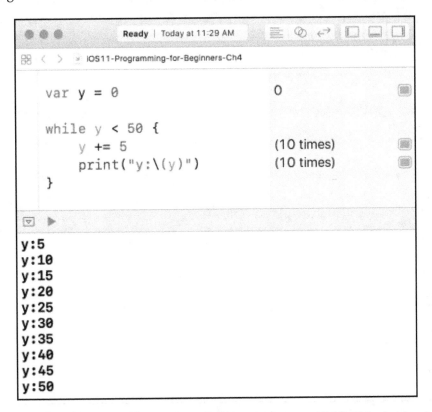

So, this `while` loop starts with a variable that begins at zero. Before the `while` loop executes, it checks to see whether y is less than 50, and, if so, it continues into the loop. Using the += operator, which we covered earlier, we increment y by five each time. Our `while` loop will continue to do this until y is no longer less than 50. Now, let's add the same `while` loop after the one we created and see what happens:

```
while y < 50 {
    y += 5
    print ("y: \(y)")
}
```

When you are done, you should see the following:

```
var y = 0                                               0

while y < 50 {
    y += 5                                        (10 times)
    print("y:\(y)")                               (10 times)
}

while y < 50 {
    y += 5
    print("y:\(y)")
}
```

```
y:5
y:10
y:15
y:20
y:25
y:30
y:35
y:40
y:45
y:50
```

You will notice that the second `while` loop never runs. This may not seem like it is essential until we look at our next type of loop.

The repeat...while loop

The `repeat...while` loop is pretty similar to a `while` loop in that it continues to execute the set of statements until a condition becomes `false`. The main difference is that the `repeat...while` loop does not evaluate its bool condition until the end of the loop. Here is the basic syntax of a `repeat...while` loop:

```
repeat {
// statement
} <condition>
```

Let's write a `repeat...while` loop in Playgrounds and see how it works. Add the following to Playgrounds:

```
var x = 0

repeat {
    x += 5
    print("x: \(x)")
} while x < 100

print("repeat completed x: \(x)")
```

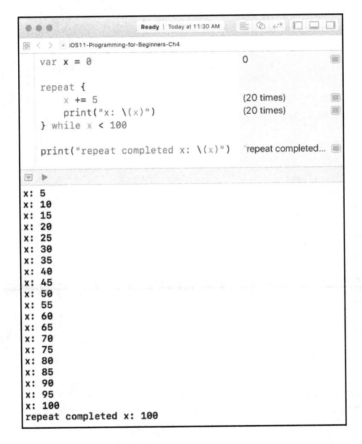

You will notice that our `repeat...while` loop executes first and increments x by 5, and after, as opposed to checking the condition like it did before, as with a `while` loop, it checks to see whether x is less than 100. This means that our `repeat...while` loop will continue until the condition hits 100. Here is where it gets interesting.

Let's add another `repeat...while` loop after the one we just created:

```
repeat {
    x += 5
    print("x: \(x)")
} while x < 100
```

```
var x = 0                                          0

repeat {
    x += 5                                         (20 times)
    print("x: \(x)")                               (20 times)
} while x < 100

print("repeat completed x: \(x)                    "repeat completed...

repeat {
    x += 5                                         105
    print("x: \(x)")                               "x: 105\n"
} while x < 100
```

```
x: 5
x: 10
x: 15
x: 20
x: 25
x: 30
x: 35
x: 40
x: 45
x: 50
x: 55
x: 60
x: 65
x: 70
x: 75
x: 80
x: 85
x: 90
x: 95
x: 100
repeat completed x: 100
x: 105
```

Now, you can see that our `repeat...while` loop incremented to 105 instead of 100, like the previous `repeat...while` loop. This happens because the bool expression does not get evaluated until after it is incremented by 5. Knowing this behavior will help you to pick the correct loop for your situation.

Summary

So far, we have looked at three loops: the `for...in` loop, the `while` loop, and the `repeat-while` loop. We will use the `for...in` loop again, but first, we need to talk about collections.

In the next chapter, we will focus on what collections are and how to use them when working with data. Make sure that you fully understand loops, because we will build on them in the next chapter and throughout this book. Therefore, review as much as you need so that you feel confident that you are proficient in the topics contained in this chapter.

Digging into Collections

5

In the last couple of chapters, we reviewed the basics of Swift to get you warmed up. Before we start building our app, we need to look at one more programming concept—collections. In Swift, we have three primary collection types, which we will cover in this chapter:

- Arrays
- Dictionaries
- Sets

We will dig deeper into each one, but we will start with the most common collection type—arrays.

Arrays

Arrays are ordered collections of values and can hold any number of items, for example, a list of strings, ints, and floating-point values. Arrays are stored in an ordered list, starting at 0. Let's look at a diagram:

0	Florida
1	Ohio
2	California
3	North Carolina
4	Colorado
5	Nevada
6	New York

0	45
1	66
2	23
3	10
4	88

0	Florida
1	California
2	32
3	New York
4	99
5	true
6	9.0

Starting from left to right in the preceding examples, we first have an array that holds a collection of strings. In the second example, we have another array that holds a collection of ints. In our third example, we have an array that holds a collection of mixed data values.

Now, let's review the following diagram, which is a mixed array:

0	Florida
1	California
2	32
3	New York
4	99
5	true
6	9.0

Since this example contains mixed data types, such as strings, ints, and bools, we would have to name this an array type of Any. This means that we can have mixed data types inside our array. Until you are genuinely comfortable with arrays, I would not recommend using mixed data arrays. Try to stick to arrays with the same data type because you will know the exact data type of each element.

An array can hold any data type, but making the array strongly typed means that every element in it must be of the same type.

Creating an empty array

Now let's create a few arrays in Playgrounds.

Sometimes, you may want to remove your prior entries from your Playground so that it is easier for you to see each new `print` statement. Do that now and input the following:

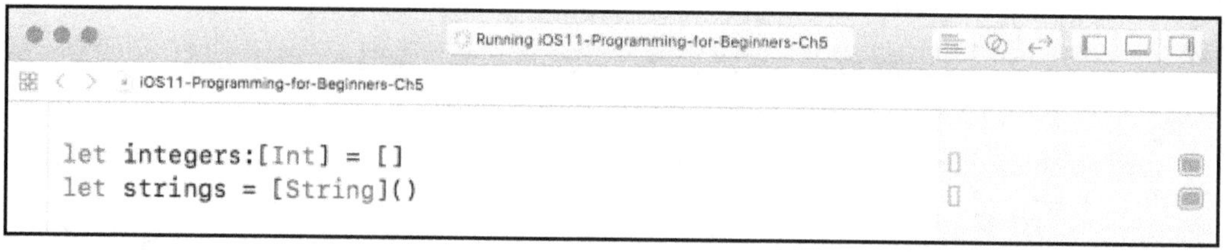

```
let integers:[Int] = []
let strings = [String]()
```

We just created our first two arrays. The reason for two different syntaxes is because you can create it in two different ways. Regarding the first example, you will see me create arrays throughout this book.

The data types within each set of brackets tells Swift what type of array we want to create. The first array (`integers`) we created has a data type of ints, and our second array (`strings`) has a data type of strings.

Creating an array with initial values

Arrays can have initial values when they are created. Let's see how this would look by entering the following in Playgrounds:

```
let integers2 = [54, 29]
```

Your code will now look like this:

The array that we just entered uses type inference to declare the data type of the array using its initial values. In this case, Swift understands that it is an array of ints because the values we entered are integers. In addition, when we use a constant (`let`) on an array, we are telling Swift that the array is an immutable array, which means that the contents or size cannot change once it is instantiated.

Creating a mutable array

It is a best practice to make all arrays (and, for that matter, collections) immutable, but there are some cases where you will need to create an array that is mutable. Let's have some fun and create a mutable array:

```
var states:[String] = []
```

As an aside, when creating a mutable array (or any variable), note that each variable must be unique.

One use of a mutable array is so that we can add to the array. Let's look at some ways in which we can do this.

Adding items to an array

Let's add some data to our array. There are a few different convenience methods for adding data to an array.

A convenience method is, just as its name implies, a method that makes things convenient. A method is a function that lives inside a class. We will discuss classes later in this book. If this is starting to get overwhelming, that's understandable. You do not need to worry about every single detail at this time. We will cover this again, and things will slowly start to click at some point. Everyone learns differently, so there is no reason to worry if someone else understands something more quickly. Just go at your own pace.

The first convenience method we will look at is the `append()` method:

```
states.append(23)
```

Your code and the output window should now look like this:

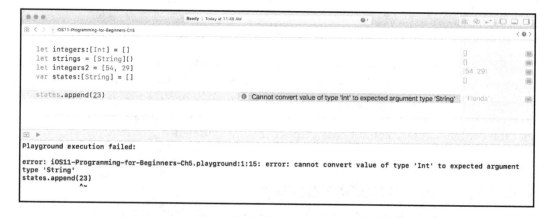

Houston, we have a problem! You will see that we are getting an error. I did this for a couple of reasons, because getting errors is normal and common. Most people who start out coding are afraid to make a mistake or get scared about getting or seeing errors. Trust me, I have been coding for years, and I make mistakes all the time. The error is telling us that we tried to add an int into an array that can only hold strings.

For every developer, whether they are a beginner or a veteran, there will come a time when they encounter an error that they cannot figure out. This error might get you frustrated to the point where you want to throw the computer across the room (I have been there a few times). The best advice my boss ever gave me was to take a walk for 10-15 minutes or do something to take your mind off it. Sometimes, this helps, and you will come up with an idea after you walk away. Even if you come back and it still takes you hours to figure out what is wrong, this is still part of the process. The best errors are the ones where you overlooked the simplest thing and had to spend hours trying to figure it out. You might have lost time, but you will have learned a great lesson. Lessons like these will stay with you forever, and you will never forget the error the next time you encounter it. So, if your coding results in an error, even in this book, embrace the challenge, because there is no greater feeling than figuring out a challenging error.

So, let's correct what we just did by revising the array to show the following:

```
states.append("Florida")
```

The following is how your code should now look:

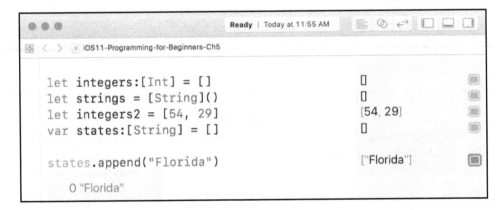

In the Results Panel, you will see the contents of our corrected array.

Since an array can hold any number of items, let's add some more. Earlier, I mentioned that we have a variety of ways to add items to an array. The `append()` method allows us to add only one item at a time. To add multiple items, we can use the convenience called `append(contentsOf:)`.

Add the following to Playgrounds:

```
states.append(contentsOf:["California", "New York"])
```

Now, your code should look like this:

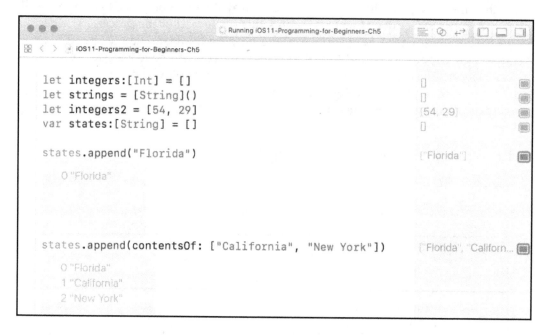

We added two more items to our array, but, so far, every example we have utilized has added items at the end of our array. We have two convenience methods that allow us to add items at any index position that is available in the array.

The first method we can utilize to do this is called insert(at:), which allows us to add a single item at a specific index position. We also have insert(contentsOf:at:), which enables us to add multiple items into an array at a certain index position. Let's use them both and add Ohio after Florida and then North Carolina, South Carolina, and Nevada in front of New York:

```
states.insert("Ohio", at:1)
states.insert(contentsOf:["North Carolina", "South Carolina",
"Nevada"],at:3)
```

Now, your code should look like this:

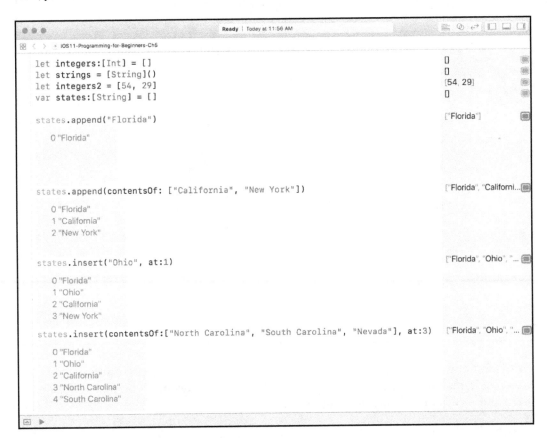

We just added items to our array using append(contentsOf:), but there also is a shorthand version of this, which is done by using the += operator. As a next step, let's add the following:

```
states += ["Texas", "Colorado"]
```

Now, your code should look like this:

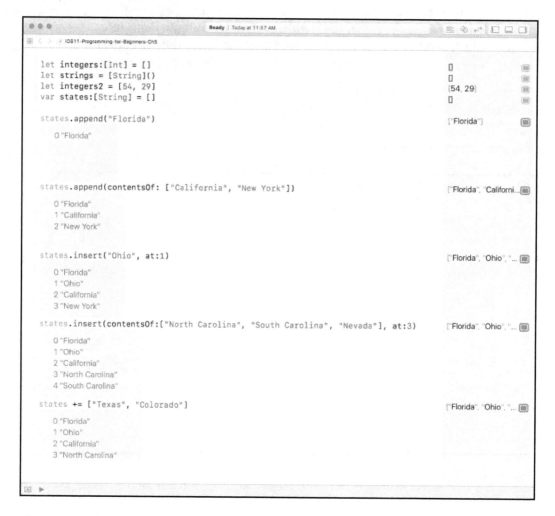

This technique for adding items is much more concise and is my preferred way of inserting items into an array. Writing less code is not always better but, in this case, using the += operator is my go-to method.

Checking the number of elements in an array

If you are keeping track, we now have nine items in our array. Luckily, we do not have to keep track of how many items are in our array because we have a property called `count`. This property will keep track of the current item count and give us the total count of our array when we want to check. Let's look at the count for states:

```
states.count
```

Your code will now look like this:

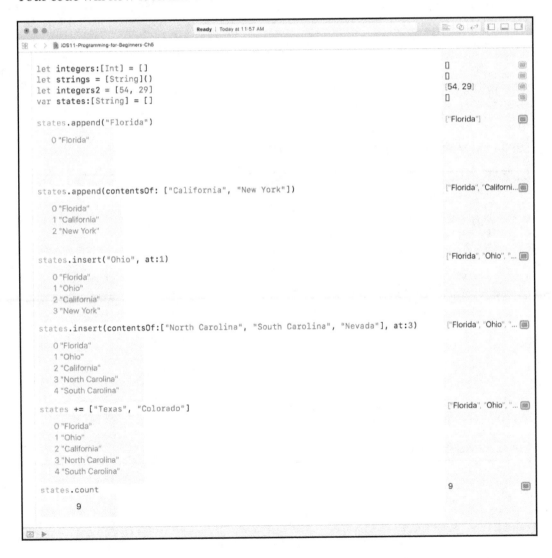

Checking for an empty array

The count property is not the only property we can use to calculate how many items are in an array. The most commonly used property for an array is called isEmpty. This property uses the count property by checking to see whether the count is greater than 0. This method will return true or false, depending on whether there are any items within our array. Since you learned that if...else statements work well with bools, let's use this isEmpty property in an if...else statement.

Add the following to Playgrounds:

```
if states.isEmpty {
   print("There are no items in the array")
}
else {
   print("There are currently \(states.count) total items in our
array")
}
```

Now, your code and output should look like this:

```
let integers:[Int] = []                                                      □
let strings = [String]()                                                     □
let integers2 = [54, 29]                                                     [54. 29]
var states:[String] = []                                                     □

states.append("Florida")                                                     ["Florida"]
states.append(contentsOf: ["California", "New York"])                        ["Florida", "Californ...
states.insert("Ohio", at:1)                                                  ["Florida", "Ohio", "...
states.insert(contentsOf:["North Carolina", "South Carolina", "Nevada"], at:3)  ["Florida", "Ohio", "...
states += ["Texas", "Colorado"]                                              ["Florida", "Ohio", "...
states.count                                                                 9


if states.isEmpty {
    print("There are no items in the array")
}
else {
    print("There are currently \(states.count) total items in our array")    "There are currentl...
}
```

There are currently 9 total items in our array

Now, our Debug panel prints the following: `There are currently total 9 items in our array.`

One thing to remember in programming is that occasionally, there are multiple ways of writing a piece of code. It is not shocking to meet someone who will approach the same problem differently to you. To me, this is why programming is so amazing. Ultimately, all that matters is that it works as expected, especially when you are new to programming.

All programming languages have what is known as a style guide, which is a preferred way of writing code, and it is no different in Swift. Using the preferred style means a suggested method, but even then, you will notice that most preferred methods differ on certain things. For now, you do not need to worry about different style guides, other than to know that they exist. In this book, we will follow a style that I have incorporated into my code.

Once you get comfortable, I recommend that you start to look at style guides and adapt them into your code. Knowing different styles helps you to know your options as well as to understand what others are doing with their code, even if you do not agree with how they write something. If you write your code with a defined structure or style throughout a project, it will make it easier for you to come back to your code if you, for instance, had to take a break for some reason, such as starting another project, or just taking some time off.

Retrieving a value from an array

We discussed creating arrays as well as adding items to an array. Now, let's turn to retrieving a value from an array. Since arrays are stored by their index, we can use their index to retrieve values. By way of an example, let's retrieve California:

```
let state = states[3]
```

Now, your code should look like this:

```
let integers:[Int] = []                                                              []
let strings = [String]()                                                             []
let integers2 = [54, 29]                                                             [54, 29]
var states:[String] = []                                                             []

states.append("Florida")                                                             ["Florida"]
states.append(contentsOf: ["California", "New York"])                                ["Florida", "Californi...
states.insert("Ohio", at:1)                                                          ["Florida", "Ohio", "...
states.insert(contentsOf:["North Carolina", "South Carolina", "Nevada"], at:3)       ["Florida", "Ohio", "...
states += ["Texas", "Colorado"]                                                      ["Florida", "Ohio", "...
states.count                                                                         9


if states.isEmpty {
    print("There are no items in the array")
}
else {
    print("There are currently \(states.count) total items in our array")           "There are currently...
}

let state = states[3]                                                                "North Carolina"

    North Carolina
```

The Results Panel shows North Carolina and not California. Remember, arrays start at 0, not 1. Therefore, for us to get California, we would actually need to use the index position of 2. Let's make that update in Playgrounds as follows:

```
let state = states[2]
```

When you are done, you should see that we get `"California"`:

```
let integers:[Int] = []                                                    []
let strings = [String]()                                                   []
let integers2 = [54, 29]                                                   [54, 29]
var states:[String] = []                                                   []

states.append("Florida")                                                   ["Florida"]
states.append(contentsOf: ["California", "New York"])                      ["Florida", "Californi...
states.insert("Ohio", at:1)                                                ["Florida", "Ohio", "...
states.insert(contentsOf:["North Carolina", "South Carolina", "Nevada"], at:3)  ["Florida", "Ohio", "...
states += ["Texas", "Colorado"]                                            ["Florida", "Ohio", "...
states.count                                                               9


if states.isEmpty {
    print("There are no items in the array")
}
else {
    print("There are currently \(states.count) total items in our array")  "There are currently...
}

let state = states[2]                                                      "California"
    California
```

There we go!

We now have this great list of states, but someone told you that Arizona is also amazing. Instead of just adding Arizona to our list, you decide that you'd actually prefer to replace South Carolina with Arizona. We could simply look at our array and see in which index South Carolina is located. This would not be helpful, however, if it were to change, or if the state for which you were searching did not exist. So, the safe way to code this is to check the array for an item, and, if that item is found, then Swift will give us its current index position. The index(of:) method is what we will use to get the index position of South Carolina:

```
if let index = states.index(of:"South Carolina") {
    print("Current index position is \(index)")
}
```

This is how our code and output should now appear:

```
let integers:[Int] = []                                              []
let strings = [String]()                                             []
let integers2 = [54, 29]                                             [54, 29]
var states:[String] = []                                             []

states.append("Florida")                                             ["Florida"]
states.append(contentsOf: ["California", "New York"])                ["Florida", "Californi...
states.insert("Ohio", at:1)                                          ["Florida", "Ohio", "...
states.insert(contentsOf:["North Carolina", "South Carolina", "Nevada"], at:3)   ["Florida", "Ohio", "...
states += ["Texas", "Colorado"]                                      ["Florida", "Ohio", "...
states.count                                                         9

if states.isEmpty {
    print("There are no items in the array")
}
else {
    print("There are currently \(states.count) total items in our array")      "There are currently...
}

let state = states[2]                                                "California"
    California

if let index = states.index(of: "South Carolina") {
    print("Current index position of South Carolina is \(index)")    "Current index posi...
}
```

```
There are currently 9 total items in our array
Current index position of South Carolina is 4
```

Now that we have the position, we can replace South Carolina with Arizona, as follows:

```
if let index = states.index(of:"South Carolina") {
  states[index] = "Arizona"
}
```

This is how our code should now look:

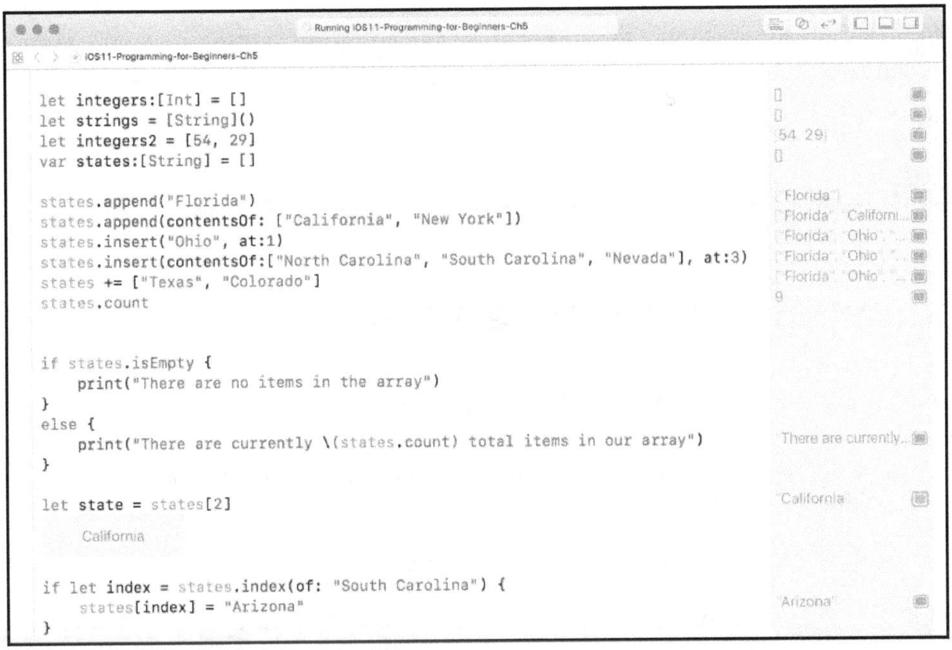

Iterating over an array

It would be nice if we could see a list of states in our array. Earlier, you learned that `for...in` loops work with sequences. Since our array is a sequence, we can use `for...in` loops to loop through each element. When working on a project that has arrays, it is helpful to use a `print` statement inside a `for...in` loop. This lets us print every item in our array to the Debug Panel. So, let's use a `for...in` loop to look at the contents of our array:

```
for state in states {
  print(state)
}
```

This is how our code and output should now look:

```
for state in states {
    print(state)                        (9 times)
}
```

```
Florida
Ohio
California
North Carolina
Arizona
Nevada
New York
Texas
Colorado
```

Removing items from an array

Now, it is time to start deleting items from our array. Let's delete the first item from our list. We have a convenience method for removing items from an array, called `removeFirst()`. This method will remove the first item from our array, which, in our case, is Florida. Let's remove Florida and add this line above our `for...in` loop:

```
let updatedStates = states.removeFirst()

for state in states {
    print(state)
}
```

This is how our code and output should now look:

```
let updatedStates = states.removeFirst()            "Florida"

for state in states {
    print(state)                                    (8 times)
}
```

```
Ohio
California
North Carolina
Arizona
Nevada
New York
Texas
Colorado
```

Since we removed Florida, all of our states' index positions will be updated to move one position closer to the top of the array. But what if we wanted to remove an item that was not first? To do this, we can use the remove(at:) convenience. So, let's remove North Carolina and New York, which are sitting at positions 2 and 4, respectively. We will add the following above our for...in loop:

```
states.remove(at:2)
states.remove(at:4)
```

This is how our code and output should now look:

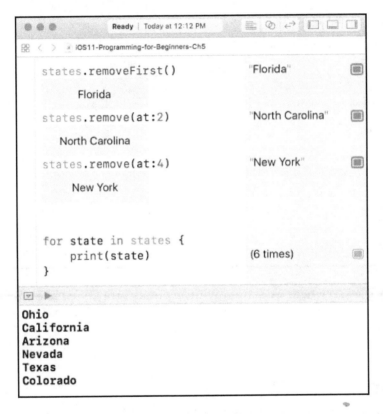

Now, both North Carolina and New York have been removed. You will see that California and Ohio did not move, but Colorado and Nevada moved up closer to the top of the list. To remove the remaining six items, we could use remove(at:) for each one, but instead we will use the simpler method of removeAll(). So, let's use removeAll() in Playgrounds:

```
states.removeAll()
```

Now, your code should look something like this:

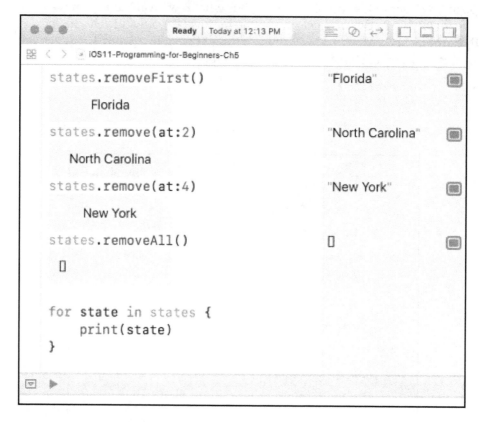

Now, we are back to where we started with an empty array. We have only scratched the surface of arrays. We will do more with arrays later in this book, but we first need to look at the next collection type: dictionaries.

Dictionaries

A dictionary is an unordered collection of values, with each one accessed through a unique key. Let's look at the following diagram:

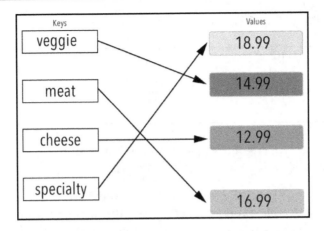

In our diagram, we have a dictionary of pizzas (**keys**) with their prices (**values**). To find something inside a dictionary, we must look it up according to its key. Let's look at a dictionary syntax:

```
Dictionary<Key, Value>
```

Now, that we understand what a dictionary is and its syntax let's look at how we can use it by creating our first dictionary.

Creating a dictionary

The traditional way of creating a dictionary is to first declare it as a dictionary and then, inside angle brackets, declare a type for the key and value. Let's create our first dictionary inside Playgrounds:

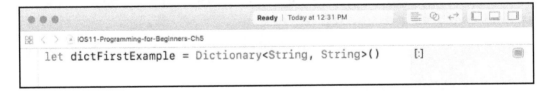

The immutable dictionary we created earlier has a string data type for both its key and value. We have multiple ways to create a dictionary. Let's look at another by adding the following to Playgrounds:

```
let dictSecondExample = [String: Int]()
```

Your code should now look like this:

```
let dictFirstExample = Dictionary<String, String>()
let dictSecondExample = [String: Int]()
```

In this latest example, we created another immutable dictionary, with its key having a string data type and its value having an int data type.

If we wanted to use our pizza diagram, the key would have a string data type and the value would have a double data type. Let's create this dictionary in Playgrounds, but, this time, we will make it a mutable dictionary and give it an initial value:

```
var dictThirdExample = Dictionary<String, Double>(dictionaryLiteral:
("veggie", 14.99), ("meat", 16.99))
```

Your code should now look like this:

```
let dictFirstExample = Dictionary<String, String>()
let dictSecondExample = [String: Int]()

var dictThirdExample = Dictionary<String, Double>(dictionaryLiteral: ("veggie", 14.99), ("meat", 16.99))
  ► (key "meat", value 16.99)
  ► (key "veggie", value 14.99)
```

The preceding example is just one way of creating a dictionary for our pizza diagram example. Let's look at a much more common method using type inference:

```
var dictPizzas = ["veggie": 14.99]
```

Once you add this to your code, your code should look something like this:

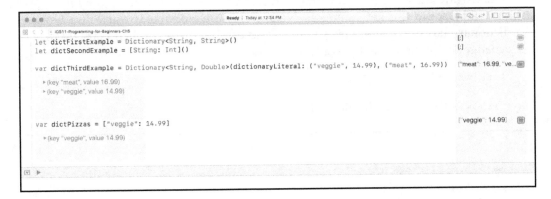

The preceding is a much simpler way of creating a dictionary with an initial value. When initializing a dictionary, it can have any number of items. In our case, we are starting off with just one.

Now, let's look at how we can add more pizzas to our dictionary.

Adding and updating dictionary elements

Let's add another item to our `dictPizzas` dictionary:

```
dictPizzas["meat"] = 17.99
```

Once you add this line of code, your code snippet should look like this:

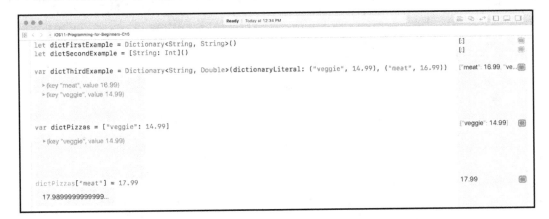

This is the shorthand method for adding an item to a dictionary. After the dictionary variable, we add the key inside the brackets. Since the key for this dictionary is strings, we must put this key in quotes. Next, we assign a double to our value. Now, our dictionary has two items. This syntax is also used to update a dictionary item. Let's change the price of meat pizza to `16.99`:

```
dictPizzas["meat"] = 16.99
```

Have a look at the code. It should look like this:

Instead of using the shorthand syntax, you can use the `updateValue(_:forKey:)` method. This method does almost the same thing as the shorthand syntax. If the value does not exist, it creates the item; if it does exist, it will update the item. The only difference is that, when using the `updateValue(_:forKey:)` variable, it actually returns the old value after performing the update. Using this method, you will get an optional value because it's possible that no value exists in the dictionary. Now, let's change the value from `16.99` to `15.99`:

```
if let oldValue = dictPizzas.updateValue(15.99, forKey: "meat") {
    print("old value \(oldValue)")
}
```

Your code should now look like this:

Since we do not need the old value, we will just use the shorthand syntax to add a couple more pizzas:

```
dictPizzas["specialty"] = 18.99
dictPizzas["chicken"] = 16.99
```

Your code and output should now look like this:

Now that we have some data inside our dictionary, let's see how we can access that data.

Accessing an item in a dictionary

When trying to access an item inside a dictionary, you will always receive an optional value. The reason for this is that you could potentially receive `nil` if the value does not exist. So, you should always use an `if...let` statement to safeguard your code:

```
if let numChickenPrice = dictPizzas["chicken"] {
  print(numChickenPrice)
}
```

Your code should now look like this:

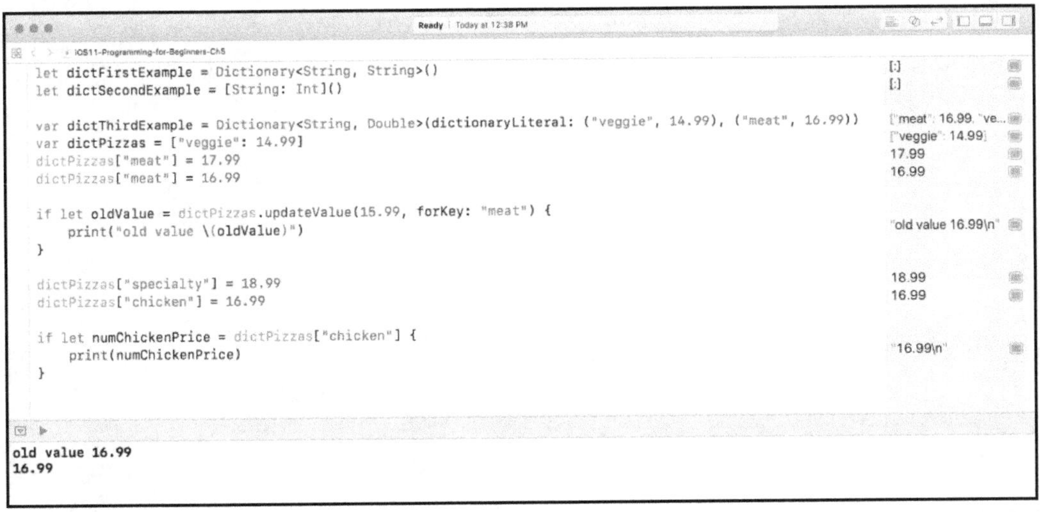

Iterating over dictionary values

Just like an array, we can iterate through our dictionary. However, there are a few differences. Since a dictionary is unordered, each time you loop through, the values will never be in the same order. With dictionaries, you can loop through both the values and keys.

Let's iterate over a dictionary's values using a `for...in` loop. Add the following to Playgrounds:

```
for value in dictPizzas.values {
  print(value)
}
```

Your code should now look like this:

```
let dictFirstExample = Dictionary<String, String>()
let dictSecondExample = [String: Int]()

var dictThirdExample = Dictionary<String, Double>(dictionaryLiteral: ("veggie", 14.99), ("meat", 16.99))
var dictPizzas = ["veggie": 14.99]
dictPizzas["meat"] = 17.99
dictPizzas["meat"] = 16.99

if let oldValue = dictPizzas.updateValue(15.99, forKey: "meat") {
    print("old value \(oldValue)")
}

dictPizzas["specialty"] = 18.99
dictPizzas["chicken"] = 16.99

if let numChickenPrice = dictPizzas["chicken"] {
    print(numChickenPrice)
}

for value in dictPizzas.values {
    print(value)
}
```

```
old value 16.99
16.99
16.99
15.99
14.99
18.99
```

Iterating over dictionary keys

To iterate over a dictionary's keys using a `for...in` loop, add the following to Playgrounds:

```
for key in dictPizzas.keys {
  print(key)
}
```

Your code and output should now look like this:

```
let dictFirstExample = Dictionary<String, String>()                                    [:]
let dictSecondExample = [String: Int]()                                                 [:]

var dictThirdExample = Dictionary<String, Double>(dictionaryLiteral: ("veggie", 14.99), ("meat", 16.99))   ["meat": 16.99, "ve...
var dictPizzas = ["veggie": 14.99]                                                      ["veggie": 14.99]
dictPizzas["meat"] = 17.99                                                              17.99
dictPizzas["meat"] = 16.99                                                              16.99

if let oldValue = dictPizzas.updateValue(15.99, forKey: "meat") {
    print("old value \(oldValue)")                                                      "old value 16.99\n"
}

dictPizzas["specialty"] = 18.99                                                         18.99
dictPizzas["chicken"] = 16.99                                                           16.99

if let numChickenPrice = dictPizzas["chicken"] {
    print(numChickenPrice)                                                              "16.99\n"
}

for value in dictPizzas.values {
    print(value)                                                                        (4 times)
}

for value in dictPizzas.keys {
    print(value)                                                                        (4 times)
}
```

```
old value 16.99
16.99
16.99
15.99
14.99
18.99
chicken
meat
veggie
specialty
-----------
meat
veggie
specialty
```

Iterating over dictionary keys and values

When you need to iterate over both dictionary keys and values using a `for...in` loop, you use the following:

```
for (key, value) in dictPizzas {
    print("\(key): \(value)")
}
```

Your code and output should now look like this:

```
let dictFirstExample = Dictionary<String, String>()                                    []
let dictSecondExample = [String: Int]()                                                []

var dictThirdExample = Dictionary<String, Double>(dictionaryLiteral: ("veggie", 14.99), ("meat", 16.99))   ["meat": 16.99, "ve...
var dictPizzas = ["veggie": 14.99]                                                     ["veggie": 14.99]
dictPizzas["meat"] = 17.99                                                             17.99
dictPizzas["meat"] = 16.99                                                             16.99

if let oldValue = dictPizzas.updateValue(15.99, forKey: "meat") {
    print("old value \(oldValue)")                                                     "old value 16.99\n"
}

dictPizzas["specialty"] = 18.99                                                        18.99
dictPizzas["chicken"] = 16.99                                                          16.99

if let numChickenPrice = dictPizzas["chicken"] {
    print(numChickenPrice)                                                             "16.99\n"
}

for value in dictPizzas.values {
    print(value)                                                                       (4 times)
}

for value in dictPizzas.keys {
    print(value)                                                                       (4 times)
}

for (key, value) in dictPizzas {
    print("\(key): \(value)")                                                          (4 times)
}
```

```
old value 16.99
16.99
16.99
15.99
14.99
18.99
chicken
meat
veggie
specialty
chicken: 16.99
meat: 15.99
veggie: 14.99
specialty: 18.99
```

We have successfully looked at how to loop through a dictionary.

Checking the number of items in a dictionary

In addition to keys and values, we have other useful properties. We can see the number of items in a dictionary using the `count` property. Let's try that by adding the following:

```
print("There are \(dictPizzas.count) total pizzas.")
```

Now, your code and output should look like this:

```
let dictFirstExample = Dictionary<String, String>()                                              [:]
let dictSecondExample = [String: Int]()                                                          [:]

var dictThirdExample = Dictionary<String, Double>(dictionaryLiteral: ("veggie", 14.99), ("meat", 16.99))   ["meat": 16.99, "ve...
var dictPizzas = ["veggie": 14.99]                                                               ["veggie": 14.99]
dictPizzas["meat"] = 17.99                                                                       17.99
dictPizzas["meat"] = 16.99                                                                       16.99

if let oldValue = dictPizzas.updateValue(15.99, forKey: "meat") {
    print("old value \(oldValue)")                                                               "old value 16.99\n"
}

dictPizzas["specialty"] = 18.99                                                                  18.99
dictPizzas["chicken"] = 16.99                                                                    16.99

if let numChickenPrice = dictPizzas["chicken"] {
    print(numChickenPrice)                                                                       "16.99\n"
}

for value in dictPizzas.values {
    print(value)                                                                                 (4 times)
}

for value in dictPizzas.keys {
    print(value)                                                                                 (4 times)
}

for (key, value) in dictPizzas {
    print("\(key): \(value)")                                                                    (4 times)
}

print("There are \(dictPizzas.count) total pizzas.")                                             "There are 4 total pi...
```

```
old value 16.99
16.99
16.99
15.99
14.99
18.99
chicken
meat
veggie
specialty
chicken: 16.99
meat: 15.99
veggie: 14.99
specialty: 18.99
There are 4 total pizzas.
```

Along with a count, we can check whether a dictionary is empty. Let's use this in an
if...else statement by adding the following:

```
if dictPizzas.isEmpty {
  print("there are no pizzas")
}
else {
  print("There are \(dictPizzas.count) total pizzas.")
}
```

Now, your code and output should look like this:

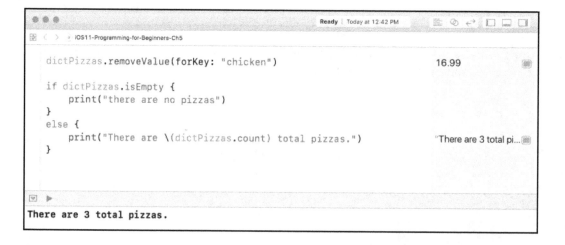

```
if dictPizzas.isEmpty {
    print("there are no pizzas")
}
else {
    print("There are \(dictPizzas.count) total pizzas.")        "There are 4 total pi...
}
```

```
There are 4 total pizzas.
```

This kind of logic is helpful when you want to display something back to the user or hide a UI.

Removing items from a dictionary

Next, let's learn how to remove an item from a dictionary. When deleting items from a dictionary, we have two primary ways of doing this. The first uses `removeValue(forKey:)`. Let's add this right above our `if...else` statement that checks whether the dictionary is empty:

```
dictPizzas.removeValue(forKey: "chicken")
```

Your code should now look like this:

```
dictPizzas.removeValue(forKey: "chicken")                       16.99

if dictPizzas.isEmpty {
    print("there are no pizzas")
}
else {
    print("There are \(dictPizzas.count) total pizzas.")        "There are 3 total pi...
}
```

```
There are 3 total pizzas.
```

Let's look at the second way of removing dictionary items, which is by using the shorthand syntax. Add the following to Playgrounds, following on from the `removeValue(forKey:)` variable:

```
dictPizzas["meat"] = nil
```

Your code should now look like this:

```
dictPizzas.removeValue(forKey: "chicken")          16.99
dictPizzas["meat"] = nil                           nil

if dictPizzas.isEmpty {
    print("there are no pizzas")
}
else {
    print("There are \(dictPizzas.count) total pizzas.")   There are 2 total pi...
}
```

There are 2 total pizzas.

Notice that, just like with `updateValue(_:forKey:)`, `removeValue(forKey:)` will return you the value before it is removed. If you do not need the value, the shorthand syntax is the preferred method.

So far, we have covered arrays and dictionaries, and now we will review one last collection: sets.

Sets

A set stores unique values of the same type in a collection without a defined order. Let's look at the following diagram:

In the preceding diagram, we have two circles, both of which represent a set. On the left, we have Craig's favorite movies, and on the right, we have Gabe's favorite movies.

Creating an empty set

Before we create these sets, let's create an empty set and see what that looks like:

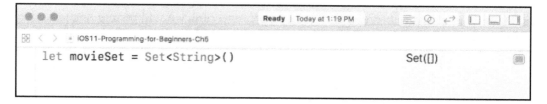

In this first set, after the equals sign, we create the set and give it a string data type. Then, we use the parentheses to initialize the set.

Creating a set with an array literal

Our first set was an empty string set, but we can create a set using an array literal.
Let's add the following to Playgrounds:

```
let numberSet = Set<Int>([])
```

Your code should now look like this:

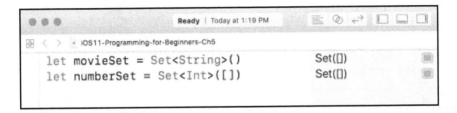

This preceding immutable set has an `int` data type, but, in the parentheses, we
passed an empty array literal when we used the brackets.

Creating a mutable set

Now that we are familiar with the way sets are created, let's create a mutable set for
Craig's favorite movies and one for Gabe's favorite movies. Add the following to
Playgrounds:

```
var craigsFavMovieSet = Set<String>([])
var gabesFavMovieSet = Set<String>(["Fight Club", "Matrix", "Evil
Dead", "Big Trouble in Little China", "Aliens", "Winter Solider", "The
Illusionist", "Predator"])
```

Be aware that if you copy and past this code into Xcode, you might see a number of errors due to line breaks and book formatting.

Now, your code should look like this:

We now have two mutable sets. The first set is created with an empty array literal, and the second set is created with some initial values. Let's add some more items to both sets.

Adding items to a set

To add an item to a set, we have to use the `insert()` method. Let's use that to add another movie to Gabe's favorite movies:

```
gabesFavMovieSet.insert("Terminator")
gabesFavMovieSet
```

Your code should now look like this:

Now, Gabe has nine films, and Craig still has none. We added the `gabeFaveMovieSet` variable again so that we can see the contents update in the Results Panel. To add multiple items to a set, we can use an array literal.

Let's add ten films to Craig's list, as follows:

```
craigsFavMovieSet = ["The Pianist", "The Shawshank Redemption", "Dark
Knight", "Black Swan", "Ip Man", "The Illusionist", "The Silence of
the Lambs", "Winter Solider", "Green Mile", "Se7en"]
```

Your code should now look like this:

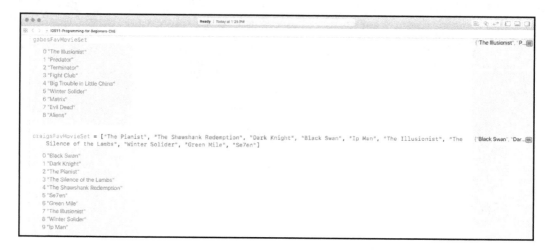

Craig's set now has ten films. Next, let's look at how we can work with sets.

Checking whether a set contains an item

The first thing we can do with sets is check whether a set includes an item. Let's see whether Craig's movie list includes the movie `Green Mile`:

```
if craigsFavMovieSet.contains("Green Mile") {
  print("Green Mile found")
}
```

Your code should now look like this:

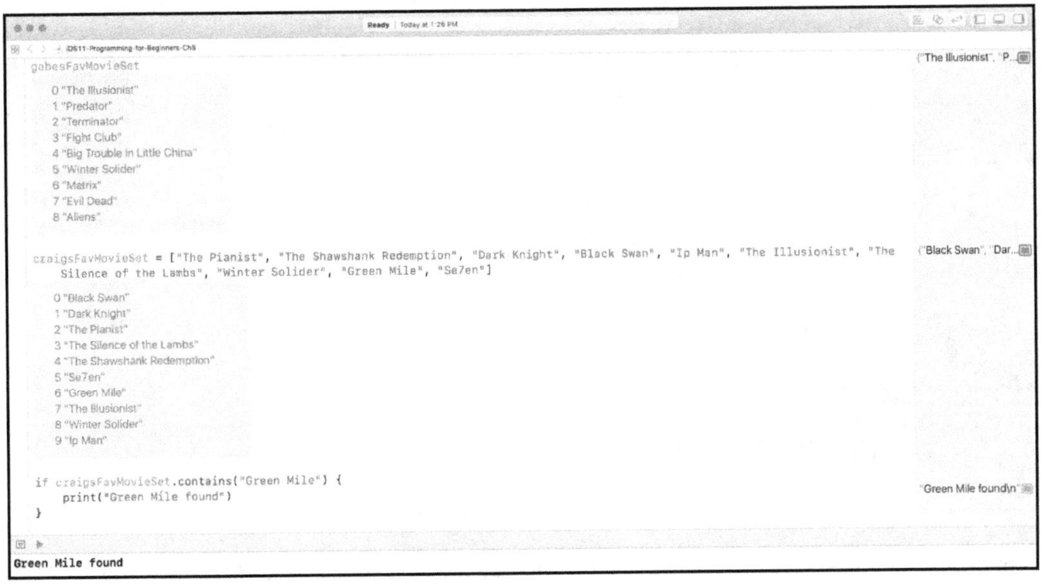

```
gabesFavMovieSet

    0 "The Illusionist"
    1 "Predator"
    2 "Terminator"
    3 "Fight Club"
    4 "Big Trouble in Little China"
    5 "Winter Solider"
    6 "Matrix"
    7 "Evil Dead"
    8 "Aliens"

craigsFavMovieSet = ["The Pianist", "The Shawshank Redemption", "Dark Knight", "Black Swan", "Ip Man", "The Illusionist", "The
    Silence of the Lambs", "Winter Solider", "Green Mile", "Se7en"]

    0 "Black Swan"
    1 "Dark Knight"
    2 "The Pianist"
    3 "The Silence of the Lambs"
    4 "The Shawshank Redemption"
    5 "Se7en"
    6 "Green Mile"
    7 "The Illusionist"
    8 "Winter Solider"
    9 "Ip Man"

if craigsFavMovieSet.contains("Green Mile") {
    print("Green Mile found")
}
```
Green Mile found

In the preceding example, we used the `contains()` method to discover whether an item is in the set.

Iterating over a set

If we want a list of all the movies in Gabe's list, we can use a `for...loop`. Let's see how that works:

```
for movie in gabesFavMovieSet {
  print("Gabe's movie - \(movie)")
}
```

Your code should now look like this:

```
let movieSet = Set<String>()                                                Set([])
let numberSet = Set<Int>([])                                                Set([])

var craigsFavMovieSet = Set<String>([])                                     Set([])
var gabesFavMovieSet = Set<String>(["Fight Club", "Matrix", "Evil Dead", "Big Trouble in Little China", "Aliens", "Winter    ["The Illusionist", "P...
    Solider", "The Illusionist", "Predator"])
gabesFavMovieSet.insert("Terminator")                                       inserted true, mem...
gabesFavMovieSet                                                            ["The Illusionist", "P...

craigsFavMovieSet = ["The Pianist", "The Shawshank Redemption", "Dark Knight", "Black Swan", "Ip Man", "The Illusionist", "The   ["Black Swan", "Dar...
    Silence of the Lambs", "Winter Solider", "Green Mile", "Se7en"]

if craigsFavMovieSet.contains("Green Mile") {
    print("Green Mile found")                                               "Green Mile found\n"
}

for movie in gabesFavMovieSet {
    print("Gabe's movie - \(movie)")                                        (9 times)
}
```
```
Gabe's movie - The Illusionist
Gabe's movie - Predator
Gabe's movie - Terminator
Gabe's movie - Fight Club
Gabe's movie - Big Trouble in Little China
Gabe's movie - Winter Solider
Gabe's movie - Matrix
Gabe's movie - Evil Dead
Gabe's movie - Aliens
```

Now that we have seen a `for...in` loop for all three collections, that is, arrays, dictionaries, and sets, you can see that there are a lot of similarities. Remember, since sets come unordered, every time we run our `for...in` loop, we will get a list in a different order. The way around this is to use the `sorted()` method. Using `sorted()` will ensure that every time we loop through our list, it will always be in the same order. Let's do that with Craig's movie list:

```
for movie in craigsFavMovieSet.sorted() {
  print("Craig's movie - \(movie)")
}
```

Your code should now look like this:

```
let movieSet = Set<String>()                                                      Set([])
let numberSet = Set<Int>([])                                                      Set([])

var craigsFavMovieSet = Set<String>([])                                           Set([])
var gabesFavMovieSet = Set<String>(["Fight Club", "Matrix", "Evil Dead", "Big Trouble in Little China", "Aliens", "Winter   ["The Illusionist", "P...
    Solider", "The Illusionist", "Predator"])
gabesFavMovieSet.insert("Terminator")                                             (inserted true, mem...
gabesFavMovieSet                                                                  ["The Illusionist", "P...

craigsFavMovieSet = ["The Pianist", "The Shawshank Redemption", "Dark Knight", "Black Swan", "Ip Man", "The Illusionist", "The   ["Black Swan", "Dar...
    Silence of the Lambs", "Winter Solider", "Green Mile", "Se7en"]

if craigsFavMovieSet.contains("Green Mile") {
    print("Green Mile found")                                                     "Green Mile found\n"
}

for movie in gabesFavMovieSet {
    print("Gabe's movie - \(movie)")                                             (9 times)
}

for movie in craigsFavMovieSet.sorted() {
    print("Craig's movie - \(movie)")                                            (10 times)
}
```

```
Craig's movie - Black Swan
Craig's movie - Dark Knight
Craig's movie - Green Mile
Craig's movie - Ip Man
Craig's movie - Se7en
Craig's movie - The Illusionist
Craig's movie - The Pianist
Craig's movie - The Shawshank Redemption
Craig's movie - The Silence of the Lambs
Craig's movie - Winter Solider
```

Now that we have our set sorted, let's look at the real power of using sets.

Intersecting two sets

In the following diagram, we can see that, where both sets intersect, we should get a list of any movies they have in common:

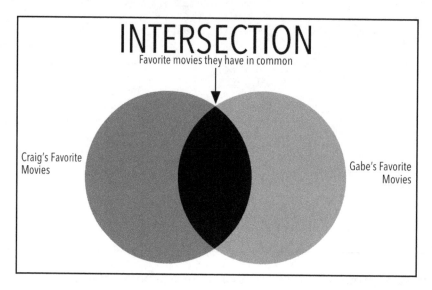

We can do the same using the `intersection()` method in our code. Let's intersect both movie lists and see what happens:

```
craigsFavMovieSet.intersection(gabesFavMovieSet)
```

Your code and output should now look like this:

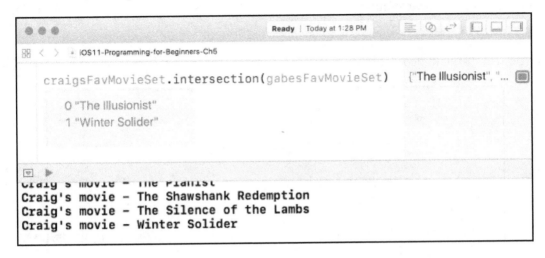

We can see that the only two movies that these sets have in common are *The Illusionist* and *Winter Solider*. In addition to seeing which movies the two sets have in common, we can also join the lists to get one consolidated list of the movies from both sets.

Joining two sets

If you look at the following diagram, you will see the two sets joined together:

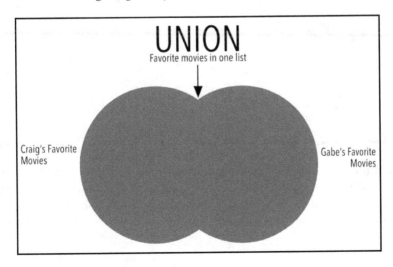

Using the `union()` method, we get a consolidated list of items with no duplicates. Let's try this in Playgrounds:

```
craigsFavMovieSet.union(gabesFavMovieSet)
```

Your code should now look like this:

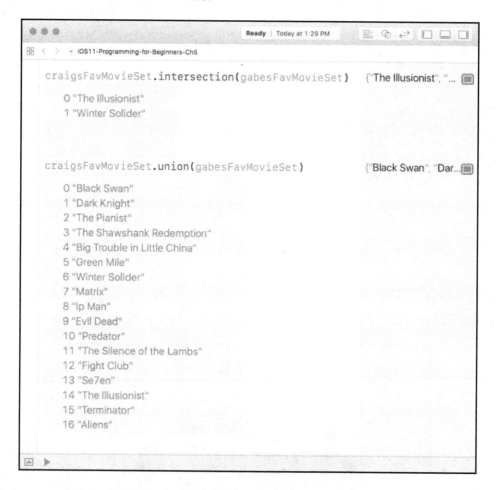

We have a combined list of movies that includes all of the movies that the two sets did not have in common, along with the two movies that were in common but listed only once. As you can see, sets are really powerful, and you can use them to manipulate data. Finally, we need to look at how we can remove items from a set.

Removing items from a set

To remove an item from a set, we can use the `remove()` method. When we use this method, we input the item we want to remove in the parentheses. Let's remove *Winter Solider* from Craig's movie list:

```
craigsFavMovieSet.remove("Winter Solider")
```

Your code should now look like this:

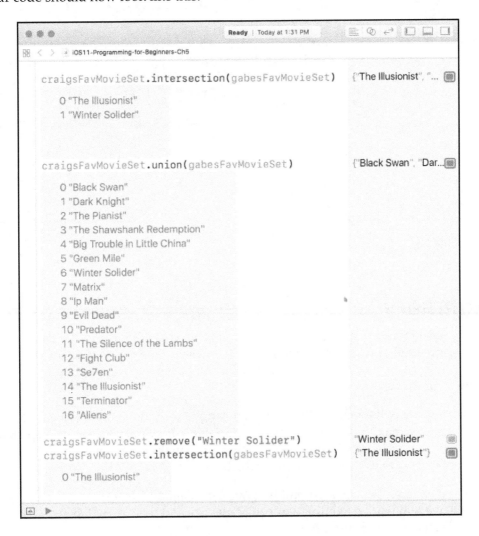

If you tried to remove more than a single item from a set (for instance, all of the items), then you can use the `removeAll()` method or give it an empty array literal:

```
craigsFavMovieSet.removeAll()
gabesFavMovieSet = []
```

Your code should now look like this:

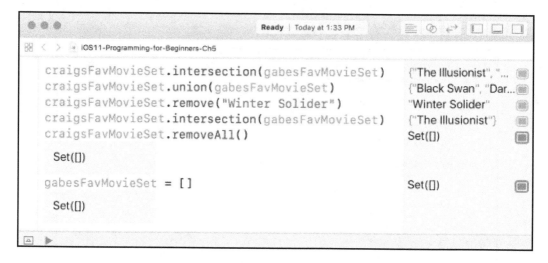

Now, both sets are empty.

Summary

We covered a lot in this chapter. We are now comfortable with using collections. Now that you are familiar with arrays, dictionaries, and sets, take the time to practice and work with them as much as you can. Collections are used a lot in programming, so getting comfortable is very important.

Even though we will touch on these things throughout the creation of the *Let's Eat* app, it is best to make sure that you are comfortable with what we covered here. So, please review the material as often as is necessary to make sure you feel that you are proficient in the topics contained in this chapter.

In the next chapter, we will start building our *Let's Eat* app. Over the next two chapters, we will work on getting our project set up, and then we will begin working on the visual aspects of our app.

6
Starting the UI Setup

Now that you have learned Swift, which will help you to understand a lot of the boilerplate code you will see later, it's time to start building our *Let's Eat* app. Let's begin by getting an overview of what we are going to build. We will review the finished product and then get into how to create this app. Before we start, there will be a lot of new terms and things with which you may or may not be familiar. Learn as much as you can, and do not let the finer details stop you from progressing.

We will cover the following topics in this chapter:

- Useful terms
- App tour
- Project setup
- Storyboards
- Creating a custom title view

Useful terms

Before we dig in and start getting our UI set up, we need to take a few minutes to introduce (or re-introduce) you to some terms that you should understand while we build our app:

- **View Controller**
- **Table View Controller**
- **Collection View Controller**
- **Navigation Controller**
- **Tab Bar Controller**
- **Storyboard**
- **Segue**
- **Stack Views**
- **Auto layout**
- **Model View Controller** (MVC)

View Controllers

View Controllers (`UIViewControllers`) are blank scenes that you can use to hold other UI elements. They give you the ability to create a custom interface.

Table View Controllers

A Table View Controller (`UITableViewController`), which inherits from `UIViewController`, is one of the most common UI elements and is used to display a list of items. For example, Apple's **Settings** screen uses a Table View Controller to display the list of settings a user can access and change:

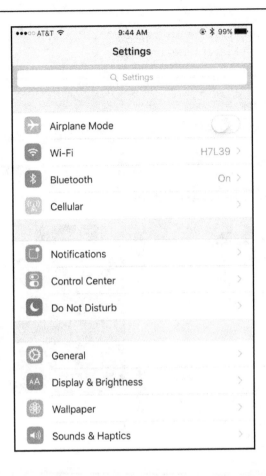

Collection View Controllers

Collection View Controllers (`UICollectionViewControllers`) are typically used when you want to display elements within a grid. They are highly customizable and, because of that, are becoming more popular in non-grid-based layouts.

The App Store, for example, currently uses `UICollectionViewControllers` for both its featured page and its app details page:

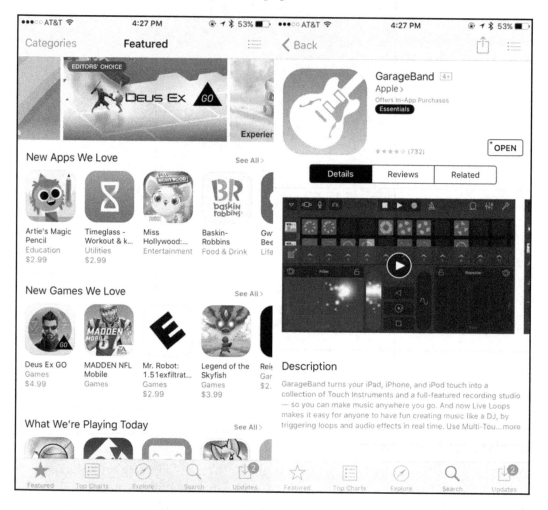

Navigation Controllers

A Navigation Controller (`UINavigationController`) is a UI element that allows you to build a drill-down interface for hierarchical content. When you embed a View Controller, Table View Controller, or Collection View Controller into a Navigation Controller, it manages navigation from one controller to another.

Tab Bar Controllers

The Tab Bar Controller (UITabBarController) manages an array of View Controllers. The *Let's Eat* app will use a Tab Bar Controller. This controller will give us the ability to have navigation for our app with minimal setup.

Apple has a few apps with which you might be familiar that use the Tab Bar Controller:

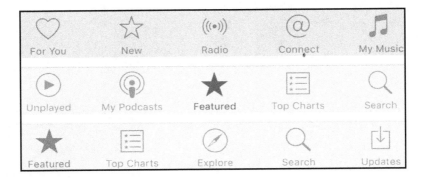

UITabBarController can only have five tabs on the iPhone. If your UITabBarController has more than five tabs on the iPhone, the fifth tab, and any after that, move underneath a **More** button:

Storyboards

A storyboard is a file that displays a visual representation of your app's UI. The following is what a storyboard looks like for an app:

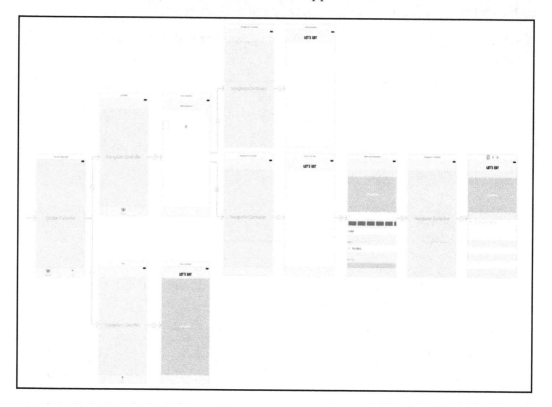

Storyboards let you create your entire app visually using View Controllers, Table View Controllers, and Collection View Controllers as scenes. Along with building your app visually, you can connect scenes and set up transitions between scenes using segues.

Segues

Segues are used to connect one controller to another. In the storyboard, segues are represented by an arrow with an icon:

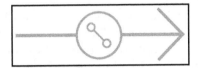

Segues also give you the ability to specify a transition from one scene to another, with very little to no programming.

Stack Views

Stack Views are a great way to stack different components either horizontally or vertically. We will cover Stack Views in this book because they are a great way to easily organize components with equal spacing.

Auto Layout

Auto layout is an excellent tool that allows you to support different screen sizes and device-rotation. With auto layout, you can set different constraints on UI elements for it to adjust to changes in size and rotation. Using auto layout in your app allows you to use one storyboard for all devices.

Model View Controller (MVC)

MVC is a standard software design pattern, which is a solution for commonly occurring problems within software design. Apple has built iOS apps on the MVC design pattern. This pattern divides our app into three camps, known as the Model, View, and Controller. We will cover this in detail later in this book.

App tour

The *Let's Eat* app that we are building is a restaurant reservation app that allows users to find restaurants in a specific area and create reservations from within the app (although our app does not book those reservations). I chose a restaurant reservation app for the lessons in this book because most of the new iOS 12 features work well together in such an app. The app covers a lot of different aspects, from maps to iMessage extensions. Let's take a look at the overall flow of the app, so that, as we build, you have a good idea of the direction we are heading in:

The Explore tab

When the app launches, you will see the **Explore** tab. This tab allows users to search for a particular cuisine and to set their location. Let's break down each component in this view:

For this screen, we will work with an empty View Controller, which is where all of our UI components live. As you can see, this view in our app is designed to be a grid so that we will be using a Collection View Controller. We will be setting up this Collection View Controller ourselves.

When I build apps, I typically start with a blank Collection View or Table View, because it gives me more flexibility in my code as well as with my user interface.

Locations

The Locations view is a list of cities accessed from the **Explore** tab. We load a list of cities from a local file and, when the user selects a city, the app loads all of the restaurants from that area:

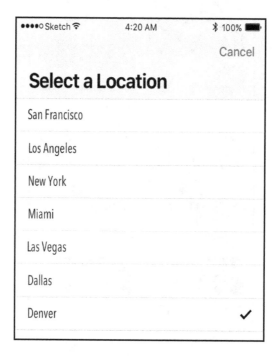

For this Locations view, we will be working with a View Controller that uses a Table View.

Restaurant listings

In Restaurant listings, we can see restaurants in the area by the selected cuisine:

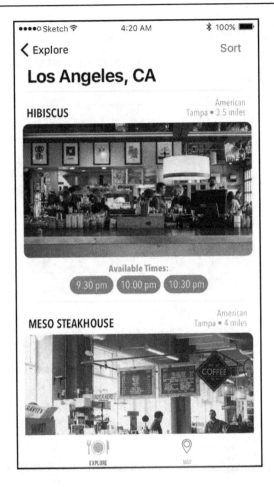

We will be covering both UICollectionViews and UITableViews in this book, but, as an introduction, you should know that UICollectionViews are very powerful—this is because you can customize them to look how you want. For example, the App Store detail is a custom UICollectionView.

One great feature when using UICollectionView is that, when you are building a universal app such as this one, you can make your view look like a list for the iPhone, but appear as a grid on the iPad with minimal effort.

Restaurant detail

Our Restaurant detail has more information about the restaurant. This view is built using a `UITableView` that uses static cells:

The Map tab

Our **Map** tab is a View Controller with a map that has pins dropped on it from a specific location, denoting all of the restaurants in the area:

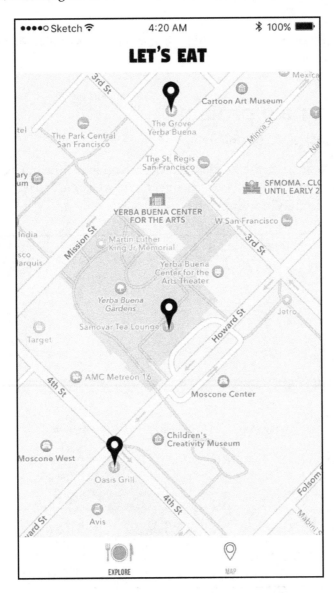

Project setup

Now that we have gotten a tour of the app, we are going to build the *Let's Eat* app. First, we need to create the app, then work on the UI and, lastly, design our app in a storyboard.

For the initial setup of the app, we will look at some basics of iOS, starting with creating a new project.

Creating a new project

To create a new project, do the following:

1. Open Xcode and the Xcode welcome screen will appear. Click on **Create a new Xcode project** in the left panel of the welcome screen.
2. Select **Single View App** and click on **Next**:

3. In the options screen that will appear, there will be a number of items to complete or choose. Add the following into that options screen and then hit **Next**:

- **Product Name**: LetsEat
- **Team**: Your account, or leave blank
- **Organization Name**: Your name/company name
- **Organization Identifier**: Your domain name in reverse order
- **Language**: Swift
- **Use Core Data**: Unchecked
- **Include Unit Tests**: Unchecked
- **Include UI Tests**: Unchecked

Your screen should look like the following screenshot:

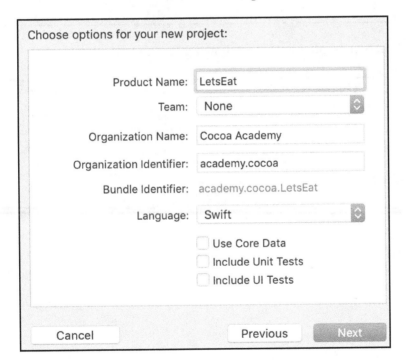

4. Choose where to save your project, and then hit **Create**:

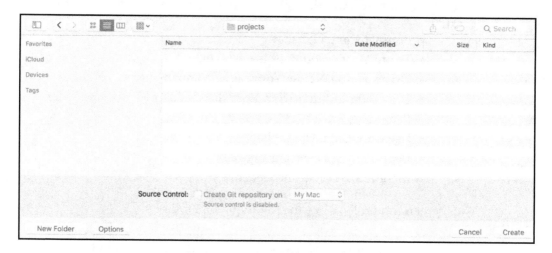

5. You're presented with the following screen:

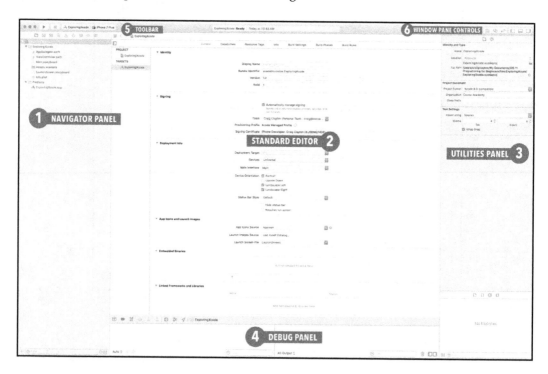

Your project is created, and we can start working on building our first iOS app.

Summary

In this chapter, we covered useful terms that we will use throughout this book. We also looked at what we are going to build within the app, and now we have a good idea of what the app will look like when we are done.

Next, we'll start working inside the storyboard and getting the UI of the application set up. Once we have everything set up, we will focus on code throughout the rest of the book. If you are familiar with working with storyboards or do not want to learn the design aspect of iOS, please skip to `Chapter 11`, *Getting Started with the Grid*.

7
Setting Up the Basic Structure

Typically, before I write any code when working on a project, I like to set up my storyboard, which allows me to focus on coding without having to go back and forth from storyboard to code. In this book, we will do some of our layouts in code to show you how to do that. But first, as I mentioned earlier, my preference is to set up as much as I can inside of the storyboard.

The following will be covered in this chapter:

- Creating a Tab Bar Controller
- Tab Bar buttons
- Launch screens
- Navigation Controllers

In the last chapter, we created our project, and now we are going to continue with that by building a Tab bar Controller from scratch. Although there is a Tab Bar Controller template that has everything you need, I find that starting from scratch is an excellent way to learn. Also, I find that it is easier to start to clean, rather than fix or update, the template. However, you may want to utilize the template to begin your project in the future. Let's start setting up our app.

Starting from scratch

We will be creating all of our files from scratch, so we will delete the existing files in our project and recreate them in the coming chapters. The reason for this is so you can become comfortable with a project and understand how it was set up.

To delete the `ViewController.swift` file, do the following:

1. Select the `ViewController.swift` file in the **NAVIGATOR PANEL**:

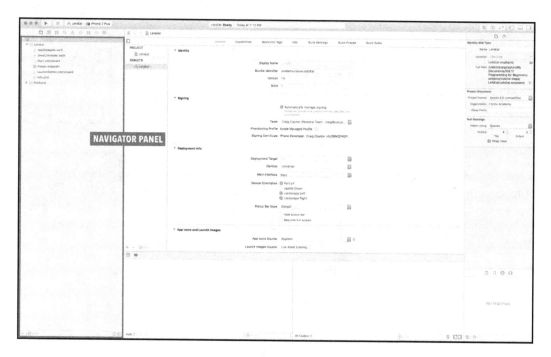

2. With the file selected, hit the *Delete* or *Backspace* key. You will get the following message:

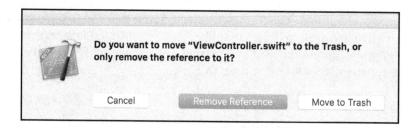

3. Select **Move to Trash**.

Now, we can continue with the setup of the storyboard.

Storyboard setup

Let's get familiar with the UI setup. To update your Main.storyboard, do the following:

1. Select the Main.storyboard file in the Navigator panel:

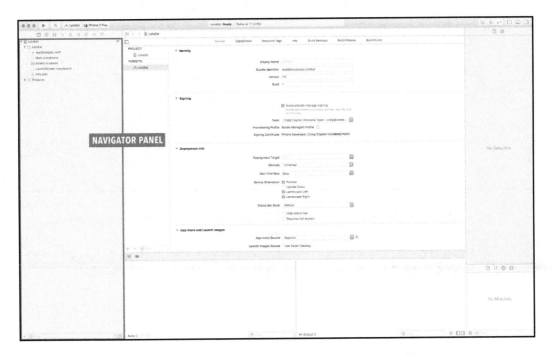

2. In this storyboard file, select **View Controller scene** in the **OUTLINE VIEW**:

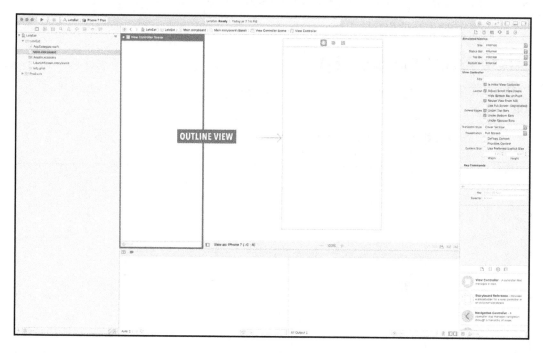

3. With the scene selected, press the *Delete* or *Backspace* key, and now your `Main.storyboard` file will be empty.

4. In your **UTILITIES PANEL**, in the bottom pane, you will see the **LIBRARY SELECTOR BAR**. In the bar, select the object library:

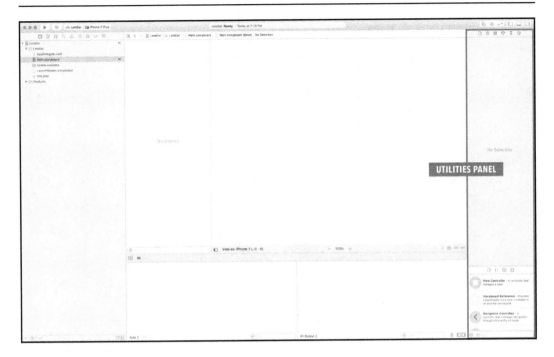

5. Pull up on the **LIBRARY SELECTOR BAR** to view more of the object library:

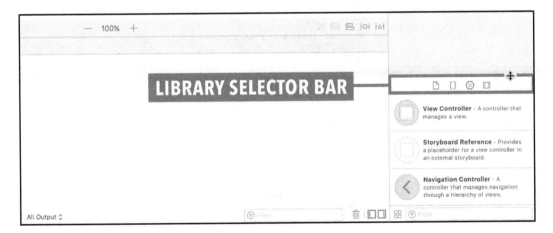

6. Find the **Tab Bar Controller**:

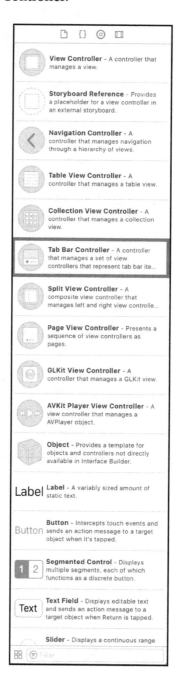

7. Drag the **Tab Bar Controller** out onto the canvas:

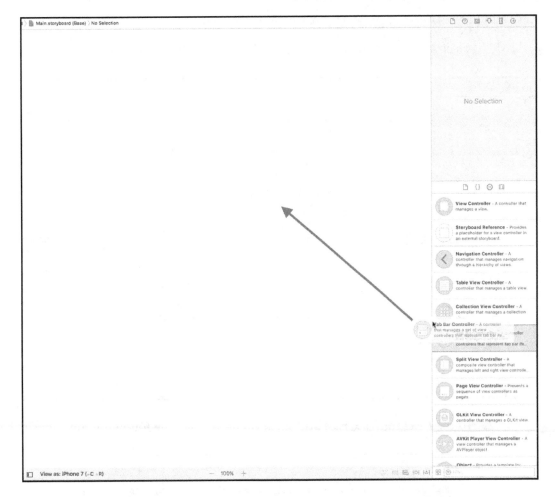

We now have our **Tab Bar Controller**, which will only have two tabs.

Next, we will get our app assets set up so that we can give our tabs image icons.

Adding our app assets

Let's add images into our project by performing the following:

1. Select the `Assets.xcassets` folder in the **NAVIGATOR PANEL**:

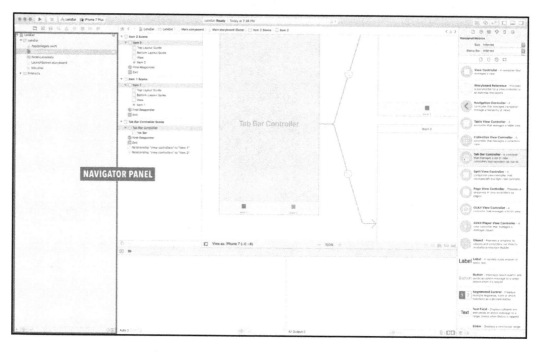

2. Hit the *Delete* or *Backspace* button, and you will get the following message:

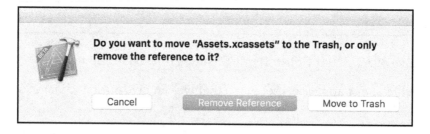

3. Select **Move to Trash**.

4. Open the project's `assets` folder that you downloaded from Packt's website or GitHub. Open `Chapter_07`. Drag the `Assets.xcassets` folder into your project in the Navigator Panel:

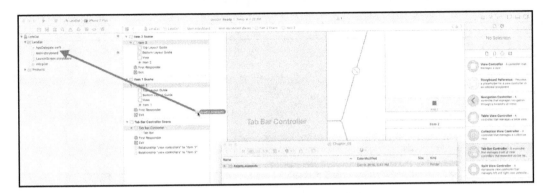

5. When you drop the folder, you will get the following message:

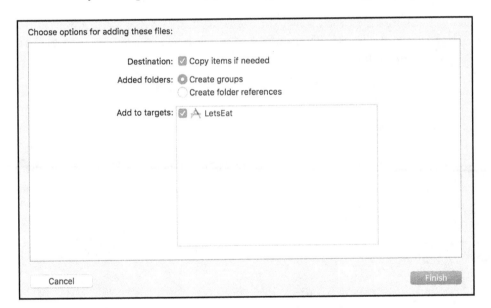

6. Make sure that both **Copy items if needed** and **Create groups** are selected. Then, hit **Finish**.

If you open the `Assets.xcassets` folder, you will now see all the assets for your entire project:

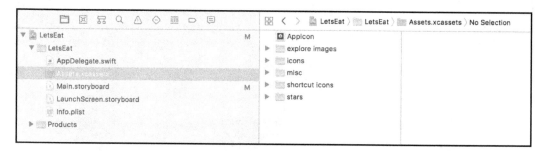

When you explore the assets, you will notice that we will be using both PNGs and PDFs.

Using PDFs allows us to support multiple device resolutions with only one image. Therefore, Xcode can handle supplying assets for all resolutions.

7. Select `Main.storyboard` again, and, in the Outline view, select both disclosure arrows for `Item 1 Scene` and `Item 2 Scene`, to have them face downwards:

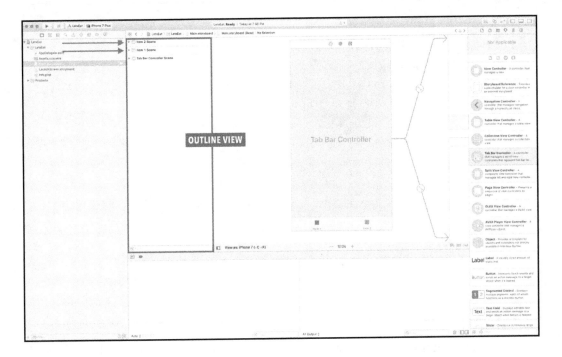

8. Select both disclosure arrows for **Item 1** under `Item 1 Scene` and **Item 2** under `Item 2 Scene`. Both should be downward-facing:

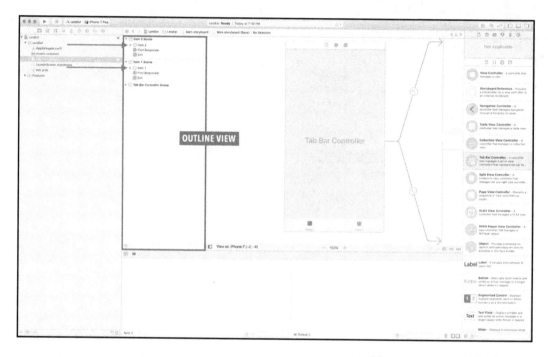

9. Select **Item 1** with the blue star to the left of it, and then select the Attributes inspector in the **UTILITIES PANEL**:

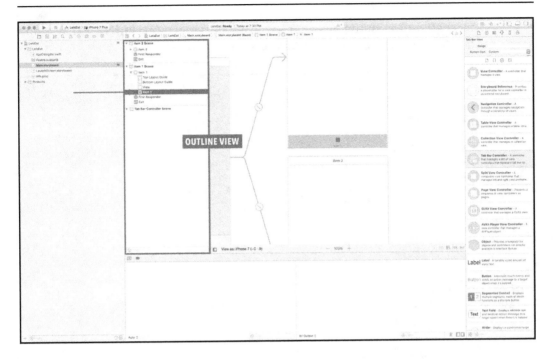

10. In the panel, use the following values to update your first tab icons:

- In the **Tab Bar Item**, enter the following details:
  - **Badge**: Leave this field blank
  - **System Item**: Select **Custom** from the drop-down list
  - **Selected Image**: icon-explore-on
  - **Title Position**: Select **Default Position** from the drop-down list

- In the **Bar Item**, enter the following details:
  - **Title**: Type Explore in this field
  - **Image**: icon-explore-off
  - **Tag**: Enter 0 in this field
  - **Enabled**: This checkbox should be checked

11. Select **Item 2** with the blue star to the left of it in the **OUTLINE VIEW**, and the Attributes inspector should already be open:

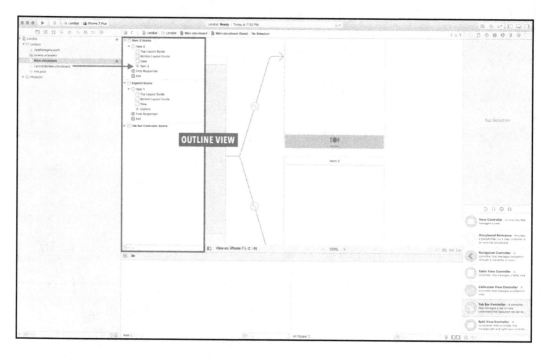

12. Add the following to the panel:

- In the **Tab Bar Item**, enter the following details:
    - **Badge**: Leave this field blank
    - **System Item**: Select **Custom** from the drop-down list
    - **Selected Image**: icon-map-on
    - **Title Position**: Select **Default Position** from the drop-down list
- In the **Bar Item**, enter the following details:
    - **Title**: Type Map in this field
    - **Image**: icon-map-off
    - **Tag**: Enter 0 in this field
    - **Enabled**: This checkbox should be checked

13. Run the project by hitting the play button (or use *command* + *R*) to see where we are:

As you may have noticed, this screen does not look like an app. Since we are building a Tab Bar Controller from scratch, we need to add an entry point. So, close the simulator, and continue with the steps.

14. Select `Main.storyboard` again in the **OUTLINE VIEW**, and make sure that the disclosure arrow is down for `Tab Bar Controller Scene`:

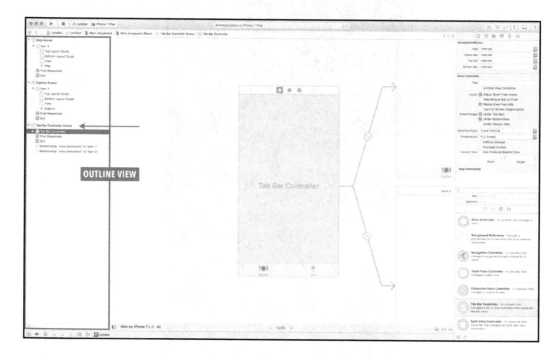

15. Select `Tab Bar Controller` **under** `Tab Bar Controller Scene`, and, in the **UTILITIES PANEL**, make sure that the Attributes inspector is selected:

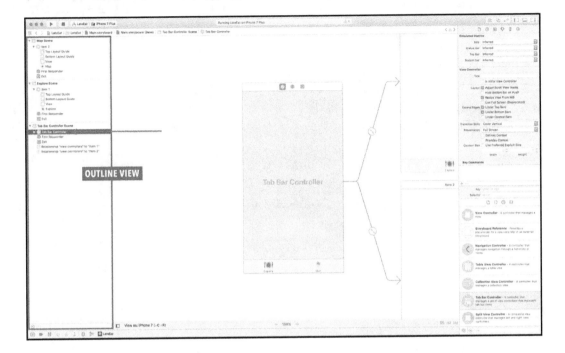

16. Under the **View Controller** section, you will need to check the box for **Is Initial View Controller**:

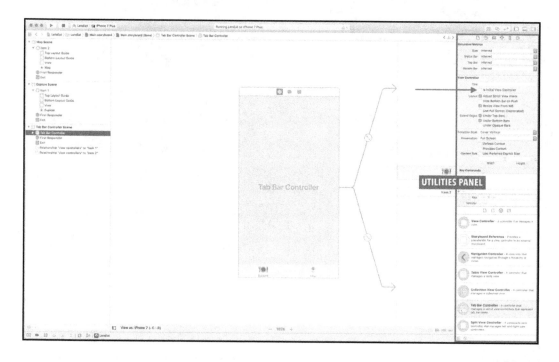

17. Once you set the initial **View Controller**, there will be an arrow pointing to the **Tab Bar Controller**. This arrow signifies the entry point of our app:

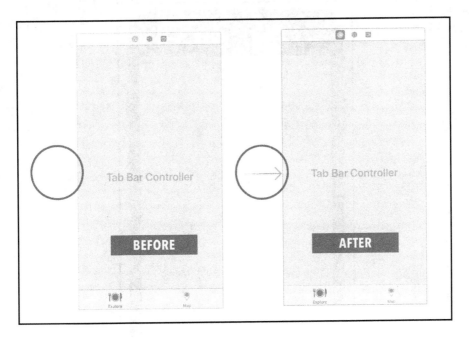

18. Let's rerun the project by hitting the play button (or use *command + R*):

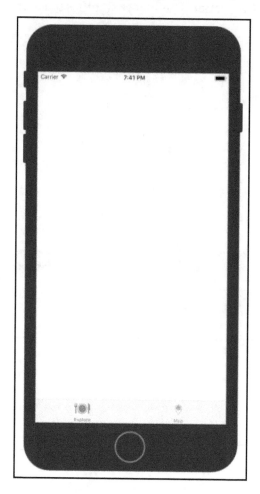

Perfect! Now, with our basic structure established, we can start adding more specific elements to our views.

Storyboards

Before we do that, let's update `LaunchScreen.storyboard`. This storyboard is used when our app first launches.

Creating our launch screen

Launch screens can use images, but that would mean that you would have to create images for every device and device orientation. Using LaunchScreen.storyboard gives us the ability to create just one asset for all devices and orientations:

1. Select the LaunchScreen.storyboard file, and, in the Outline view, make sure that the disclosure arrows for View Controller Scene and View Controller are collapsed. Then, select View under View Controller:

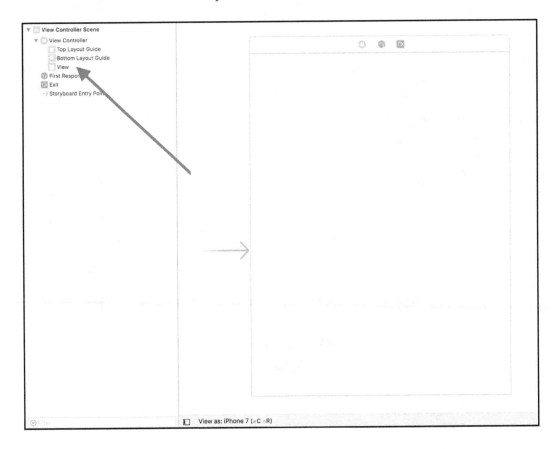

2. In the **UTILITIES PANEL** panel, select the Attributes inspector, and click on the white **Background** bar:

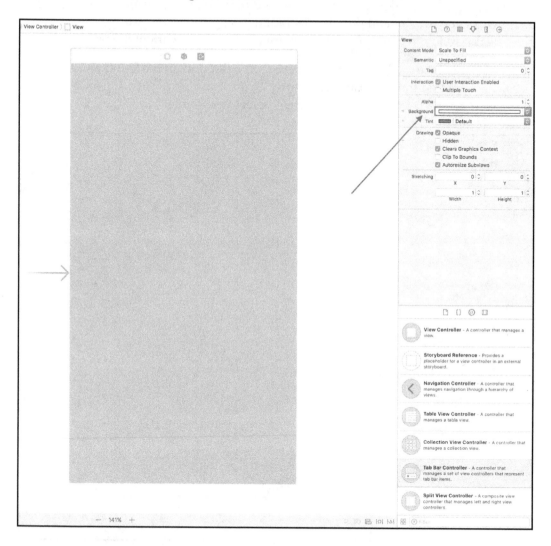

3. A **Colors** panel will appear. Select the second tab, which is called the **Color Slider**:

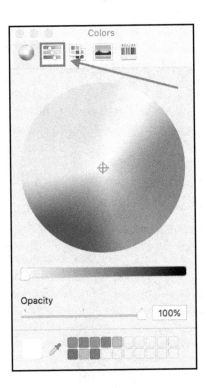

4. Under **RGB Sliders**, **Hex Color** #, update the value from FFFFFF to 4A4A4A. This should change your background color from white to a dark gray:

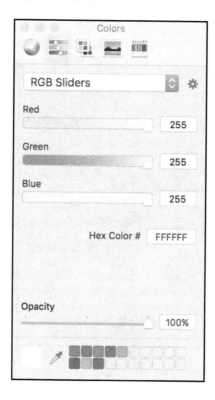

5. You might have to select the background color a second time. If so, select the **Background** bar in the Attributes inspector again, which should change the **Hex Color** # back to FFFFFF. Then, change it again to 4A4A4A. You can now close the **Color** panel, and you should see the background color update in your Standard Editor panel:

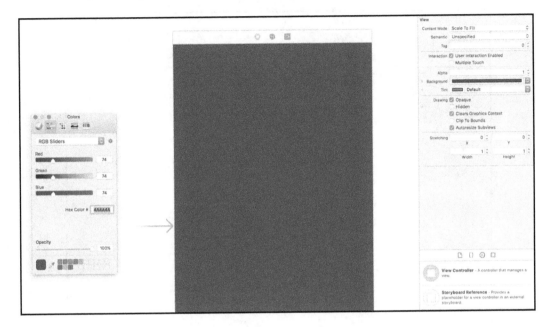

Next, we need to bring the app logo onto the screen:

1. While still in `LaunchScreen.storyboard`, launch the Media Library (*command + Shift + M*). You can also access the library if you long-press the object library, but the shortcut is much faster:

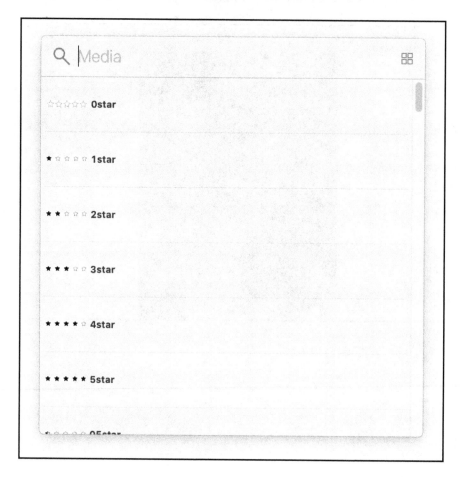

The Media Library allows us to access our image assets, and it will place them inside a `UIImageView` for us.

2. In the filter, at the bottom of the Library pane, type `detail-logo`. Once that appears, drag and drop the logo onto `LaunchScreen.storyboard`:

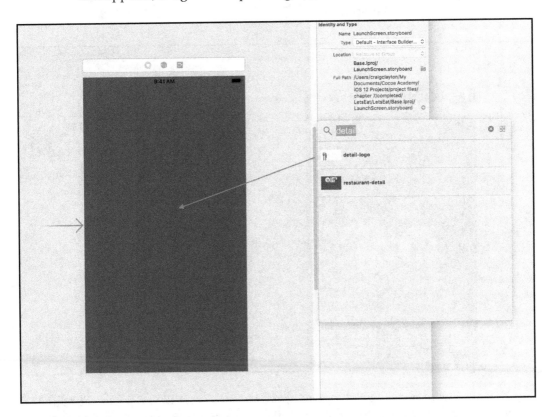

 There might be a bug in Xcode and, therefore, sometimes when you drag the logo out, the width and height will not be set, and you will need to enter the width and height manually.

3. If your logo does not drag out to size, do this step: with the logo selected, open the **SIZE INSPECTOR** in the **UTILITIES PANEL**, and set the width and height to the following:

- **Width**: 220
- **Height**: 112

4. We want our *Let's Eat* logo to appear in the center of the screen. For our logo to appear in the center for all devices, we need to apply auto layout. Select detail-logo, and then select the **ALIGN** icon, which is to the left of the **PIN** icon:

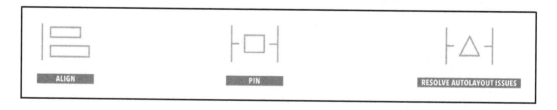

5. Check the following boxes that appear:

- Horizontally in container
- Vertically in container

6. Click on **Add 2 Constraints**.

When you are done, you will see the following:

Our launch screen is now set up for all devices. If you rerun the project, you will now see the launch screen with the **LET'S EAT** logo and new background color.

Let's move on to adding some detail to our **Explore** tab, since this is the first thing a user will see after the app launches.

Adding a Navigation Controller

We first need to add a Navigation Controller to our **Explore** tab. The Navigation Controller will allow us to do a few things, such as adding a button to the title bar of the navigation to present our cities list:

1. Select `Main.storyboard`, and, in the **OUTLINE VIEW**, select `Explore` with the blue star to the left of it, under `Item 1` in `Explore Scene`:

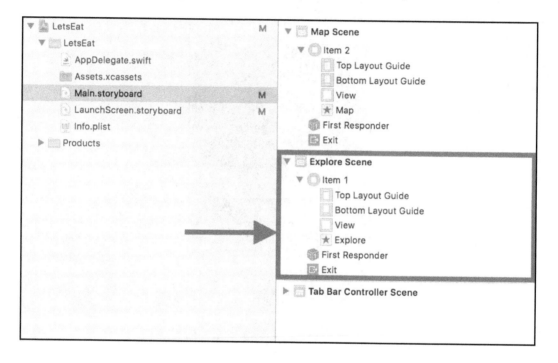

2. Navigate to **Editor** | **Embed In** | **Navigation Controller**:

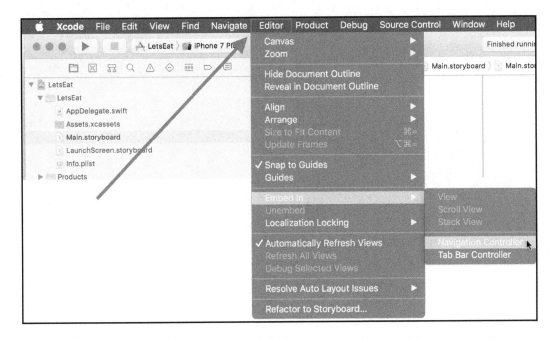

3. Our View Controller has a **Navigation Controller**:

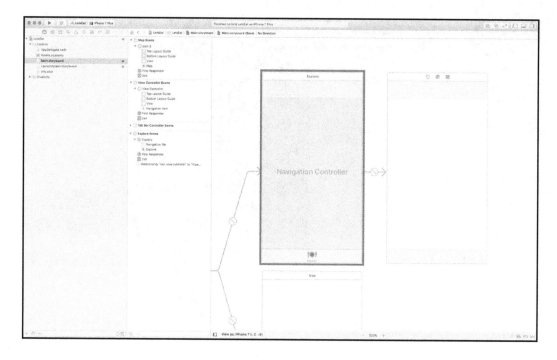

4. Run the project by hitting the Play button (or use *command + R*):

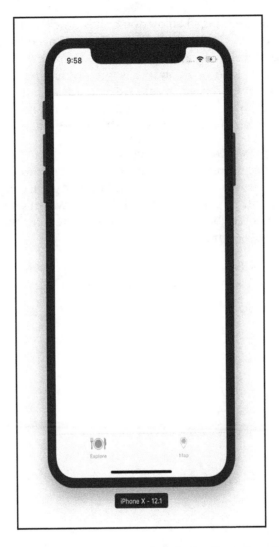

Repeat steps 1 to 4 from the *Adding a Navigation Controller* subsection for the **Map** tab. Now that we have added both Navigation Controllers, in the next chapter, we will continue to create other View Controllers.

Summary

Storyboarding is one of the things I enjoy doing. It is quick and easy to set up your UI with storyboards. Being able to drag and drop what you need onto the canvas is such an efficient method of developing app storyboards. There are times when you will need to code, but being able to work on things without having to write any code is an excellent capability. My preference is to use storyboards as much as possible, but many developers prefer to work in code. If you come from another programming language, try to keep an open mind and learn storyboarding.

When you work on a project that uses storyboards, you can get a high-level overview of the project. When everything is written in code, it takes more time to get a basic idea of how the app is structured, and its overall flow. Again, some people love to code their UI, and we will do some of that in this book. My main point is that you have to find what works for you. This book leans more toward the storyboard side versus the coding side of setting up your UI.

In the next chapter, we will continue setting up our UI, and become familiar with more of the UI elements that you have seen in many iOS apps.

8
Building Our App Structure in Storyboard

In the previous chapter, we created our Tab Bar Controller. In this chapter, we will be creating other View Controllers that we need in our app. Our goal for the end of this chapter is to be able to navigate through the app with the least code required.

The following will be covered in this chapter:

- Collection View
- Outlets
- Modals

Before we begin setting up our Collection View Controller, you will need to add two files, `ExploreViewController` and `RestaurantViewController`, which you'd have downloaded from Packt's website or GitHub. By combining these files and then a bit of code, we will be able to focus on the design of our app.

Later in the book, we will delete these files, and create them ourselves. But, for this chapter, let's add these two files into our project:

1. Open the `assets` project folder that you downloaded from Packt's website or GitHub. Open `Chapter_08` and drag the two files in the folder into your project in the Navigator panel:

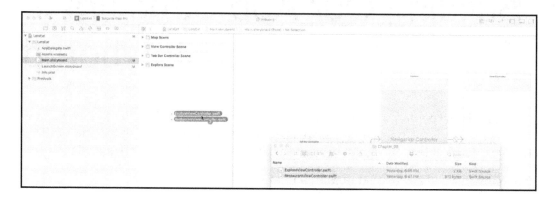

2. When you drop the folder, you will get the following message:

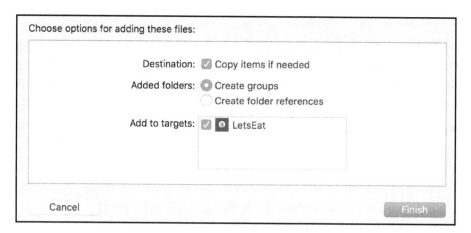

3. Make sure you have both **Copy items if needed** and **Create groups** selected, then hit **Finish**.

4. Add code to these new files, which will allow us to dismiss modals that we will create later in this chapter. A modal is a container that opens on top of the current content showing in an app and allows you to take more action without opening up all of the information on the viewed screen.

Let's add the code to enable us to dismiss modals. Open the `ExploreViewController.swift` file and, under where it says `// Add Unwind here` at the bottom of the file, add the following code:

```
@IBAction func unwindLocationCancel(segue:UIStoryboardSegue)
{}
```

If we look at our app design, which we reviewed earlier in this book, in our first tab, the **Explore** tab, we show a grid of food cuisines as well as a list of locations. First, we will set up our grid.

Adding a Collection View Controller

As we discussed earlier in the book, Collection View Controllers allow us to display elements within a grid. Let's set up our **Collection View**:

1. Select the `Main.storyboard` file, making sure that you are zoomed out and can see all of your scenes. In the Utilities Panel (*command + Shift + L*), ensure that you have the object library tab selected.
2. In the filter field, type `collec`:

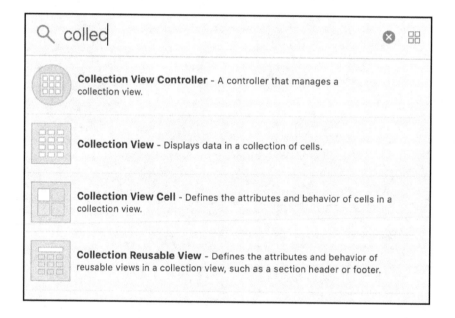

3. Click on and drag **Collection View**, and drop it onto the **Explore View Controller**:

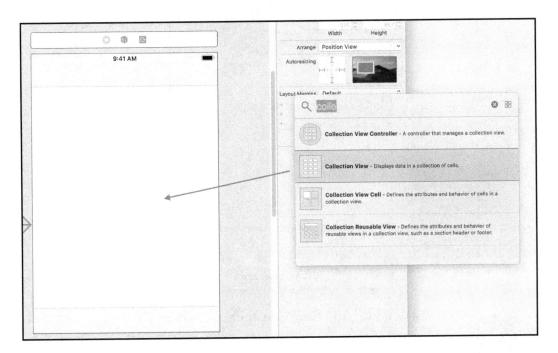

4. You will see small boxes around the entire **Collection View** component. Select the Pin icon, and enter the following values:

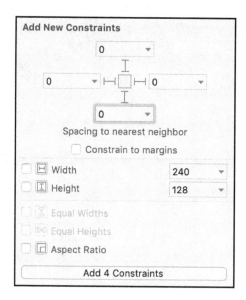

 All values under **Add New Constraints** are set to 0.

5. Click on **Add 4 Constraints**.

We now have our **Collection View** component set up for our **Explore** tab.

Hooking up our outlets

Let's now link our file, ExploreViewController, to our UIViewController in the storyboard:

1. While still in the Main.storyboard file, select the UIViewController with the **Collection View** that we just created, by clicking on the leftmost icon at the top of that controller:

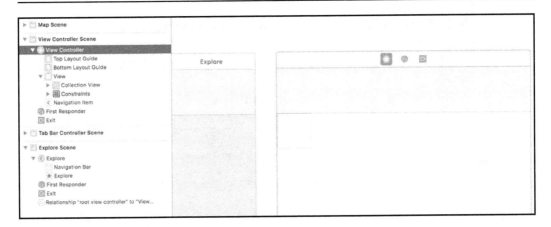

2. In the Utilities Panel, select the Identity Inspector, which is the third icon from the left:

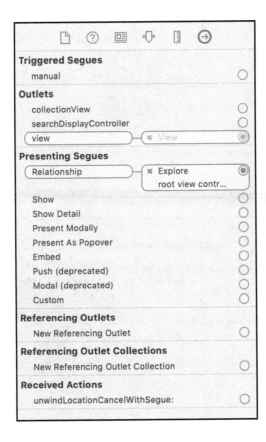

3. Under **Custom Class**, in the **Class** drop-down menu, choose
   `ExploreViewController` and hit the *Enter* key.

4. Select the **Connections Inspector**, the last icon on the right, in the Utilities
   Panel.

5. Under **Outlets**, you will see **collectionView** and an empty circle:

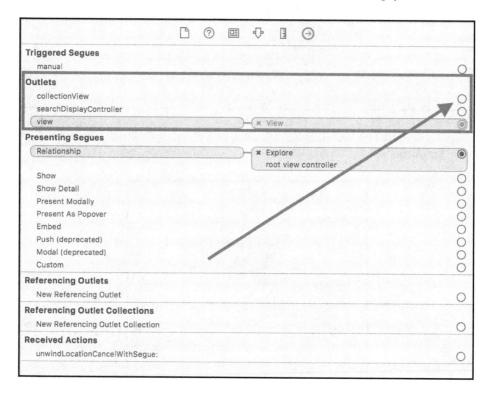

 `IBOutlet` is a way to connect to a UI element. We have a **Collection
View** on our `UIViewController`; now, we are hooking into that
variable. Later in the book, you will learn how to create these
variables.

6. Click on the **collectionView** circle, and click-drag from the circle in the Connections inspector to the **Collection View** that we just added inside of the `UIViewController`:

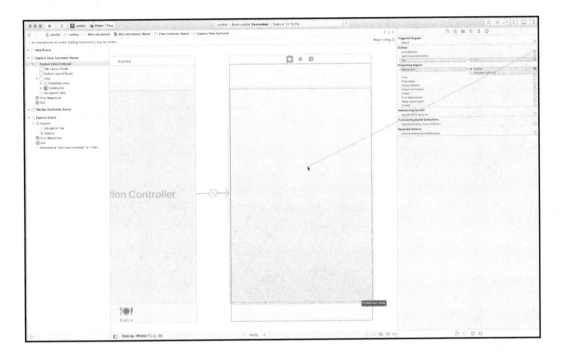

7. Release it and you will see the circle become filled:

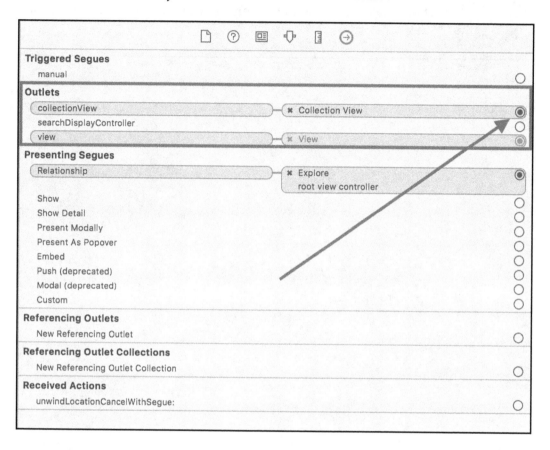

We need to hook up the data source and delegate. The delegate and data source allow us to pass data to our **Collection View**, and to know when our **Collection View** has some kind of interaction.

The `dataSource` property is what is used to supply the data for our **Collection View**, so we need to pass whatever data we have to this property. On the other hand, the `delegate` property, which supplies the behavior, does not require us to provide anything, as it receives interactions that happen within our **Collection View**.

8. In your scene, select your **Collection View** and then, in the Utilities Panel, select the **Connections Inspector**.

9. Under the **Outlets** section, you will see two empty circles, `dataSource` and `delegate`:

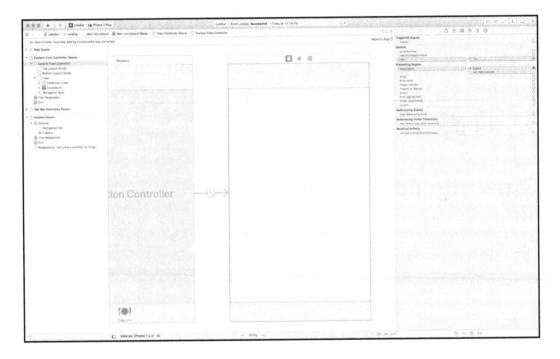

10. Click and drag from the empty circle of the `dataSource` property to the **Explore View Controller** in your Outline view, and then release:

11. Repeat for the `delegate` property:

Next, let's set up our **Collection View** prototype cell to have a color.

Creating a custom color

Let's add colors to your `Assets.xcassets` folder. Adding colors here is great when you want to have all your colors in one location. Before we update our explore cell, let's create a new color:

1. Open the `Assets.xcassets` file.

2. Right-click inside of `Assets.xcassets`, where you will see folders, and create a new folder called colors:

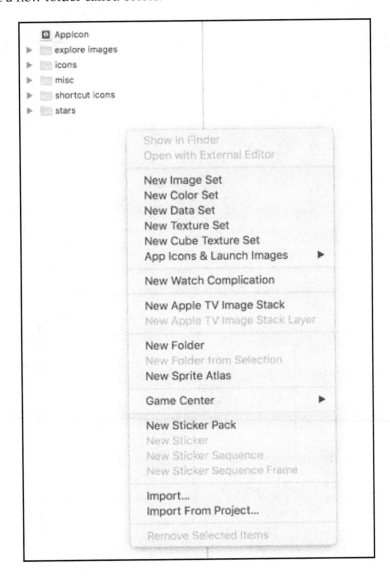

2. Right-click the `colors` folder, and, this time, select **New Color Set**. You will see a new color added to your folder. Select the Attributes inspector in the Utilities panel:

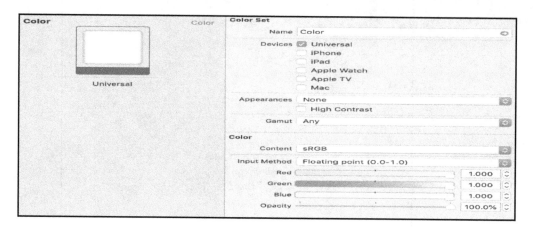

4. Under **Color** set, update the name to `Demo Grey`.
5. Under **Color**, click the **Input Method** dropdown:

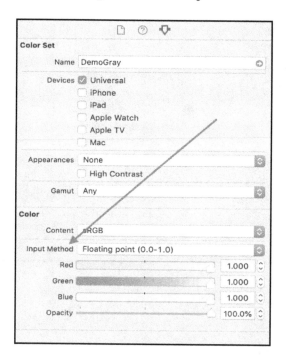

6. Select 8-bit Hexadecimal. Change the **Hex** # value to #AAAAAA. When you are done, you should see the following:

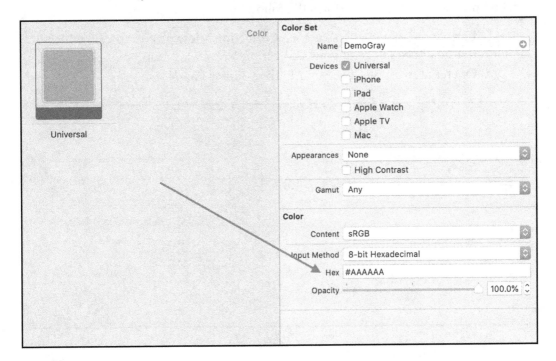

Now that we have a color, we will be able to find our new color in the **Color** dropdown, as you will see next.

Setting up our cell

To set up our cell, we need to perform the following steps:

1. In `Main.storyboard`, select the **Collection View** prototype cell, which is the small box inside of your **Collection View**.
2. Open the Attributes inspector in the Utilities Panel:

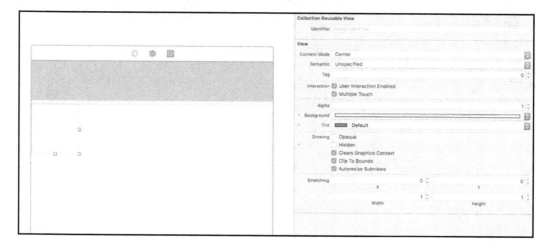

3. Update the following:

   - **Identifier**: `exploreCell`
   - **Background**: **Demo Grey**

4. To update the background, you will need to click on the drop-down arrow under **Background**. You will see that our **Demo Grey** is added:

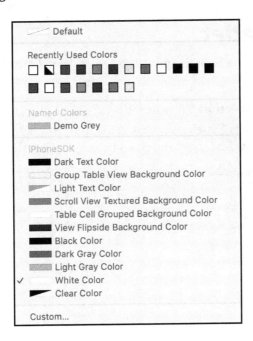

You should now see the following:

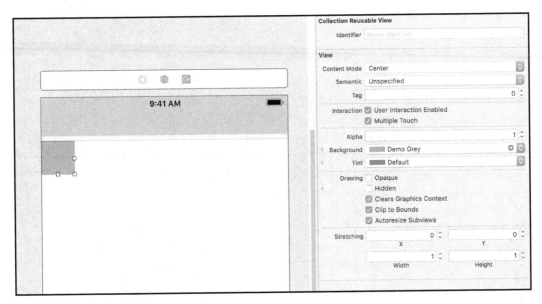

Next, we need to add a section header.

Section header

Our section header will include the page title, the selected location, and a button that we will use to see the locations:

1. Select the **Collection View** in the `Main.storyboard` outline.
2. In your Utilities Panel, select the Attributes inspector and, under **Collection View Accessories**, select the checkbox next to **section header**:

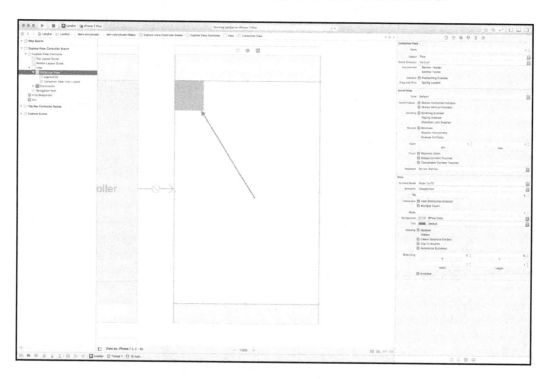

3. You will see a box appear above our **Demo Grey** cell, which is our new section header—select it:

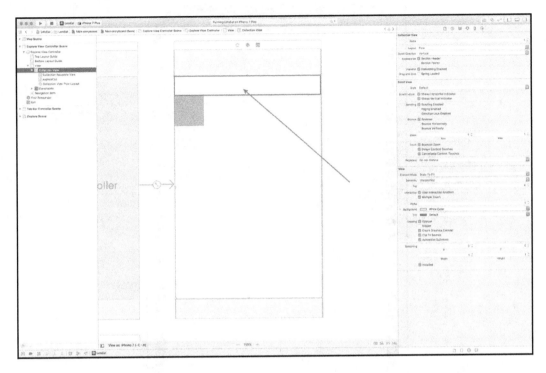

4. In the Attributes inspector in the Utilities Panel, update **Identifier** to **header**:

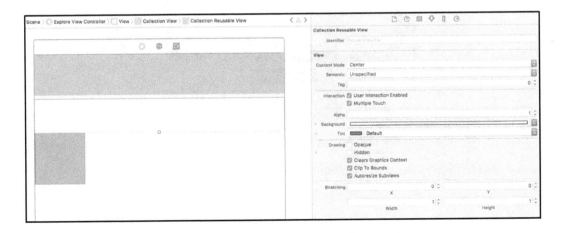

Let's build and run the project by hitting the Play button (or use *command + R*):

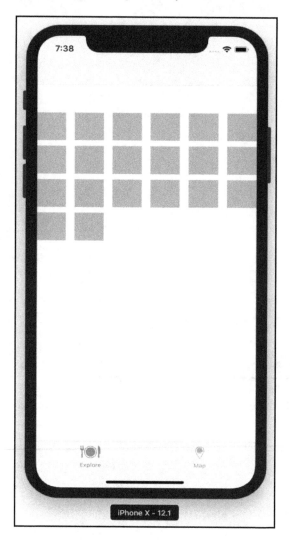

You will see that you now have a grid of boxes and some white space (the section header) near the top of the grid. Before we work on the section header, let's update our grid to match our design of two items per row with a particular cell size.

Updating the grid

To update our grid, we need to take the following steps:

1. Use *command + Shift + O* and, in the **Open Quickly** window, type `Main.storyboard`, and then hit the *Enter* key.
2. Select the **Collection View**, and then, in the Utilities Panel, select **Size Inspector**.
3. Update the following values, based on the simulator that you are currently using. These values may need to be changed so that your grid has two columns of cells, so feel free to alter the values.

For iPhone 7, use the following values:

Fields	Values			
Cell Size	Width: 176	Height: 195		
Min Spacing	For Cells: 0	For Lines: 7		
Section Insets	Top: 7	Bottom: 7	Left: 7	Right: 7

For iPhone 7 Plus, use the following values:

Fields	Values			
Cell Size	Width: 196	Height: 154		
Min Spacing	For Cells: 0	For Lines: 7		
Section Insets	Top: 7	Bottom: 7	Left: 7	Right: 7

For iPhone 4/iPhone SE/iPhone 5/iPhone 5s, use the following values:

Fields	Values			
Cell Size	**Width**: 150	**Height**: 154		
Min Spacing	**For Cells**: 0	**For Lines**: 7		
Section Insets	**Top**: 7	**Bottom**: 7	**Left**: 7	**Right**: 7

When you are done, this is what everything should look like:

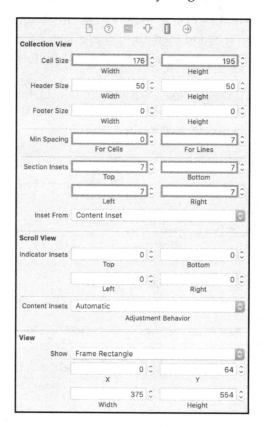

Challenge: If you are using iPhone XR, or iPhone Xs, try to see whether you can figure out how to make the grid work. For now, as we just did, we will use storyboard settings to get our cells set up. Later in the book, we will make this dynamic so that our widths and heights adjust with code. Next, we will work on our section header.

Adding a modal

Let's review the design for the section header:

Note that we have a **+ Location** button that will display our locations. Let's add that modal now:

1. While in the `Main.storyboard` file, select the object library and, in the filter field at the bottom of the Library pane, type `button`.

2. Drag and drop the `Button` component into the section header we created in our **Explore View Controller**:

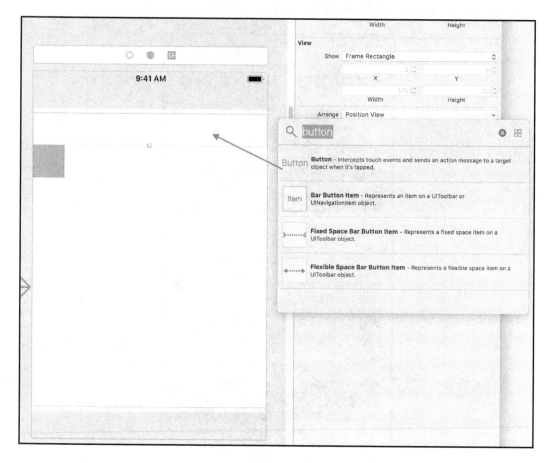

Ignore the layout warning. We will format the button later regarding location and size, and that will get rid of the warning.

Next, we need to add another View Controller to our storyboard:

1. In the filter, type `viewcontroller`, and drag and drop the `ViewController` component above the **Explore View Controller** in `Main.storyboard`.

2. With the **View Controller** selected, navigate to **Editor** | **EmbedIn** | **NavigationController**.

3. *Control* + drag from where it says **Button** in the View Controller, under the **Explore** tab, to the Navigation Controller that was just created (you can also do this within Outline view, by *Control* + dragging from the button to the new Navigation Controller you just created):

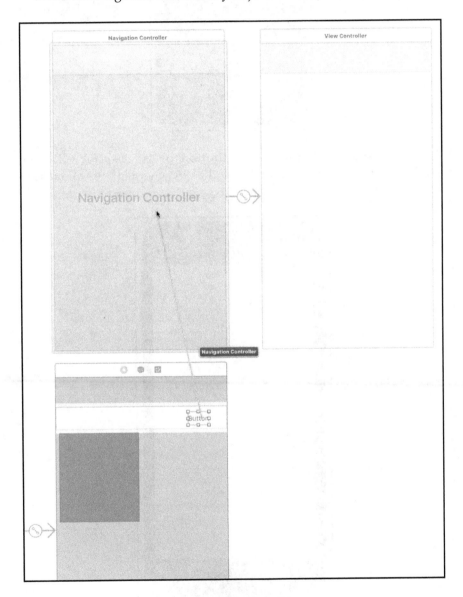

4. When you let go, you will be presented with the following menu, and you should select **Present Modally**:

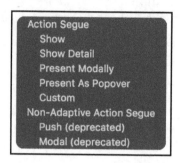

Now, let's run the project by hitting the Play button (or use *command + R*). You will see that our button now launches a modal. In the next chapter, we will make this button match our design:

Currently, as you can see in the preceding screenshot, we cannot dismiss this modal. Therefore, we need a cancel button and a done button to dismiss the view. Let's fix this:

1. Open `Main.storyboard` and then go to your **View Controller** (not the **Navigation Controller**) of your modal:

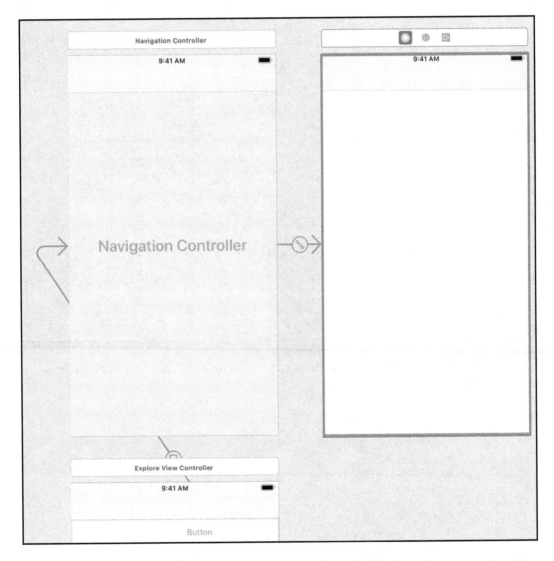

2. Open the object library (*command + Shift + L*) and type `bar button` into the filter area of the objects library in the Utilities Panel.

3. Drag and drop a **Bar Button Item** into the right-hand side of the **Navigation Bar** of your View Controller Scene:

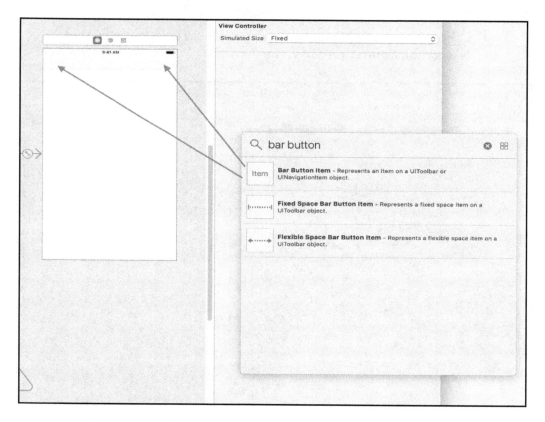

4. Drag another **Bar Button Item** into the left-hand side of the **Navigation Bar**.

5. You should have two **Bar Button Items** that both say **Item**:

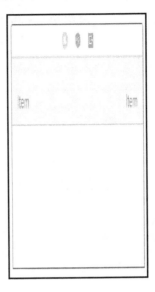

Updating Bar Button Items

Next, we need to update both of the **Bar Button Items** to say cancel and done:

1. Select the left-hand **Bar Button Item**, and, in the Utilities Panel, select the Attributes inspector.
2. Click on **System Item** and select **Cancel** in the drop-down menu.
3. Select the right-hand **Bar Button Item**, and, while still in the Attributes inspector in the Utilities panel, update **System Item** to **Done**.

Now, you should see **Cancel** on the left and **Done** on the right:

Unwinding our Cancel button

Now that we have our buttons, we want to dismiss the modal when a user hits **Cancel**.

In the `Main.storyboard`, *Control* + drag from the **Cancel** button to **Exit**:

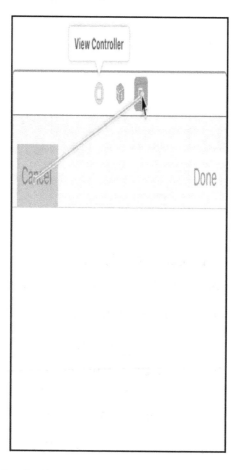

You can also do this in the Outline view.

You will see a window popup that says **Action Segue** and **unwindLocationCancelWithSegue**. Select `unwindLocationCancelWithSegue`:

Let's build and run the project by hitting the Play button (or use *command +R*), and test our **Cancel** button. It should now dismiss the View. We will update the **Done** button when we add code later.

Adding our first Table View

Now, let's add a `UITableView` into our `UIViewController`:

1. In the Utilities Panel of `Main.storyboard`, in the filter field, type `table`, then drag the Table View onto the scene:

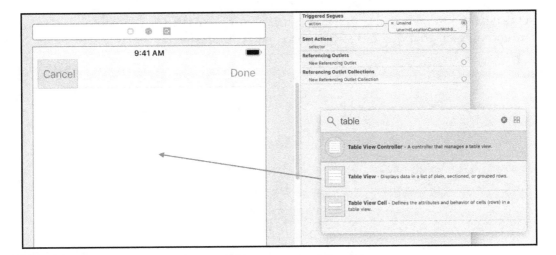

2. Select the Pin icon and enter the following values:

   - Set all values under **Add New Constraints** to 0.
   - The **Constrain to margins** checkbox should be unchecked.

3. Click on **Add 4 Constraints**.

If you build and run the project, and then launch the modal, you will see an empty Table View. We will complete this Table View later.

Summary

We are about halfway through the setup of our UI structure. In this chapter, we created our **Collection View** with a dummy cell. Dummy cells allow us to continue to work on the basic structure of our app and focus on the design of the app, getting all of the assets ready to go before we add code. We also added our first prototype header, as well as presenting a modal to the user.

In the next chapter, we will complete the rest of our basic structure, before concentrating on adapting our structure to match our design.

9
Finishing Up Our App Structure in Storyboard

The more we do storyboard work, the easier it gets. I remember that, when I started Xcode, it was a bit overwhelming because of all the panels, and it took me time to get comfortable. Any time I speak with someone looking to get into iOS, I always tell them to dedicate at least 10-15 minutes a day to it for the first six months. It seems like a lot, but it makes a difference when you are trying to learn. If you step away for a week and try to come back, it's like starting from square one; at least, it was for me. When I finally started to catch on was when I was in Xcode every day and was relentless.

In the previous chapter, we got our **Explore** and **Location** both set up. In this chapter, we are still working on just the structure, and in the next couple of chapters we will work on the design.

We will cover the following in this chapter:

- Restaurant View Controller
- Restaurant Detail View Controller
- Reviews View Controller
- The Map tab

Adding our Restaurant List View

Our restaurant list has the same basic setup as in the previous chapter. If you think you have a grasp of this, now is an excellent time to challenge yourself. If you think you still need more practice, keep reading and let's set up the restaurant list:

1. Select the `Main.storyboard` file, making sure that you are zoomed out and can see all of your scenes (depending on your screen resolution). Open the object library (*command + shift + L*).
2. Drag out a View Controller—it should be the first item in the list—put it next to Explore View Controller.
3. Open the object library (*Command + Shift + L*) and, in the filter field, type `collectionview`.
4. Click on and drag **Collection View** and drop it onto the new **View Controller** we just added, next to the Explore View Controller.
5. Select the **Pin** icon and enter the following values:

    - All values under **Add New Constraints** are set to 0.
    - Make sure to uncheck **Constrain to margins**.

6. Click on **Add 4 Constraints**.

We now have our **Collection View** component set up for our Restaurant list.

Hooking up our outlets

Let's now link our file, `RestaurantViewController`, to our new `UIViewController` in the storyboard:

1. Select the `UIViewController` with the **Collection View** that we just created.
2. In the Utility panel, select the Identity inspector. Under **Custom Class**, in the **Class** drop-down menu, select `RestaurantViewController` and hit the *Enter* key.
3. Select the **Connections Inspector** in the Utilities Panel.
4. Under **Outlets**, (just like we did earlier) click on the `collectionView` circle and drag from the circle to the **Collection View** that we just added inside of your `UIViewController`.

Now that we have our **Collection View** hooked up, we need to hook up the data source and delegate. The data source and delegate allow us to pass data to our **Collection View** as well as to know when our **Collection View** has some interaction. Let's do that now by doing the following:

1. In your scene, select your **Collection View**. In your Utilities Panel, select the **Connections Inspector**.
2. Click on and drag the `dataSource` property to the **Restaurant View Controller** in your Outline view.
3. Click on and drag the delegate property to the **Restaurant View Controller** in your Outline view.

Finally, let's set up our cell to have a color.

Setting up our cell

In `Main.storyboard`, select the small box inside of your **Collection View**. The small box is your **Collection View** prototype cell:

1. Open the Attributes inspector in the Utilities Panel.
2. Update the following:

    - **Identifier**: `restaurantCell`
    - **Background**: **Demo Grey**

3. *Control* + drag from the explore cell to Restaurant View Controller:

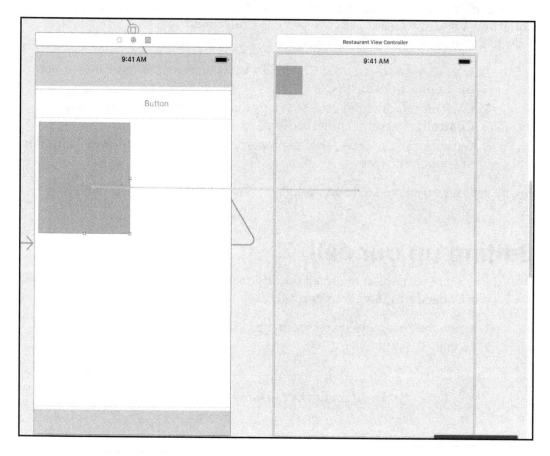

4. When you let go, you are presented with the following menu—select **Show**:

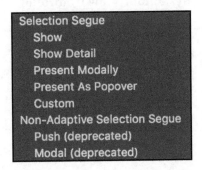

Now, let's run the project by hitting the Play button (or using *Command + R*). You will now be able to tap on an explore cell and see the following:

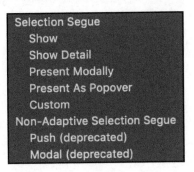

Next, we want the user to be presented with the restaurant's details when they touch a restaurant. We will use a static Table View Controller to do our detail. Using a static Table View allows us to create content without code. We will still have to hook up our data but, in the upcoming chapters, you will see how static Table Views come in handy. Let's set up the restaurant details:

1. Select the `Main.storyboard` file, making sure that you are zoomed out and can see all of your scenes (depending on your screen resolution). In the Utilities Panel, ensure that you have the object library tab selected.

2. In the filter field, type `tableviewcontroller` (make sure it's the controller—it will have a yellow icon). Drag this **Table View Controller** and put it next to **Restaurant View Controller**:

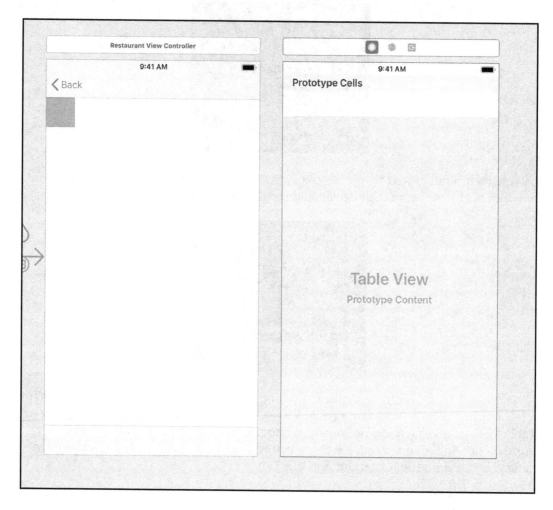

3. *Control*-drag from the restaurant cell button to the **Restaurant Detail Table View Controller.** When you let go, you are presented with the following menu, and you should select **Show**:

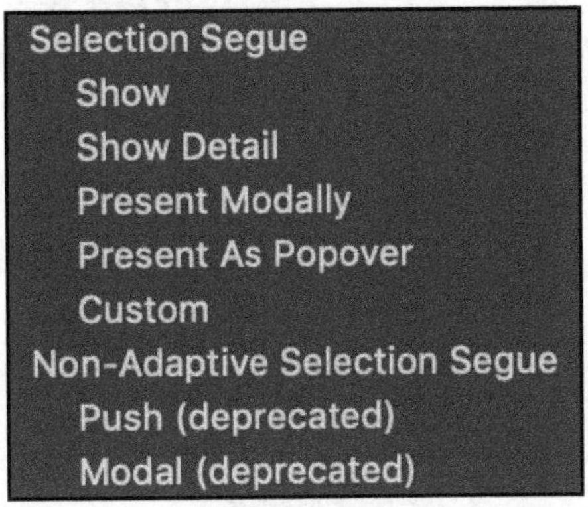

Selection Segue
  Show
  Show Detail
  Present Modally
  Present As Popover
  Custom
Non-Adaptive Selection Segue
  Push (deprecated)
  Modal (deprecated)

5. Click on the **Table View** inside of the Outline:

```
2018-11-20 10:25:11.339040-0500 LetsEat[59237:10190392] *** Assertion failure in -[UICollectionView
    _dequeueReusableViewOfKind:withIdentifier:forIndexPath:viewCategory:], /BuildRoot/Library/Caches/
    com.apple.xbs/Sources/UIKitCore_Sim/UIKit-3698.93.8/UICollectionView.m:5372
2018-11-20 10:25:11.344351-0500 LetsEat[59237:10190392] *** Terminating app due to uncaught exception
    'NSInternalInconsistencyException', reason: 'could not dequeue a view of kind: UICollectionElementKindCell
    with identifier restaurantCell - must register a nib or a class for the identifier or connect a prototype
    cell in a storyboard'
*** First throw call stack:
(
    0   CoreFoundation                      0x00000001056541bb __exceptionPreprocess + 331
    1   libobjc.A.dylib                     0x000000010397735 objc_exception_throw + 48
    2   CoreFoundation                      0x0000000105653f42 +[NSException raise:format:arguments:] + 98
    3   Foundation                          0x000000010369a877 -[NSAssertionHandler
        handleFailureInMethod:object:file:lineNumber:description:] + 194
    4   UIKitCore                           0x0000000107847706 -[UICollectionView
        _dequeueReusableViewOfKind:withIdentifier:forIndexPath:viewCategory:] + 2536
    5   UIKitCore                           0x0000000107847991 -[UICollectionView
        dequeueReusableCellWithReuseIdentifier:forIndexPath:] + 169
    6   LetsEat                             0x00000001033697db
        $S7LetsEat24RestaurantViewControllerC010collectionD0_13cellForItemAtSo012UICollectionD4CellCSo0kD0C_10F
        oundation9IndexPathVtF + 171
    7   LetsEat                             0x000000010336987c
        $S7LetsEat24RestaurantViewControllerC010collectionD0_13cellForItemAtSo012UICollectionD4CellCSo0kD0C_10F
        oundation9IndexPathVtFTo + 108
    8   UIKitCore                           0x00000001078312d8 -[UICollectionView
        _createPreparedCellForItemAtIndexPath:withLayoutAttributes:applyAttributes:isFocused:notify:] + 314
    9   UIKitCore                           0x0000000107831198 -[UICollectionView
        _createPreparedCellForItemAtIndexPath:withLayoutAttributes:applyAttributes:] + 31
    10  UIKitCore                           0x000000010783684f -[UICollectionView _updateVisibleCellsNow:] +
        6164
    11  UIKitCore                           0x000000010783c076 -[UICollectionView layoutSubviews] + 364
    12  UIKitCore                           0x000000001084c9795 -[UIView(CALayerDelegate)
        layoutSublayersOfLayer:] + 1441
    13  QuartzCore                          0x0000000109a51b19 -[CALayer layoutSublayers] + 175
    14  QuartzCore                          0x0000000109a569d3
        _ZN2CA5Layer16layout_if_neededEPNS_11TransactionE + 395
    15  QuartzCore                          0x00000001099cf7ca
        _ZN2CA7Context18commit_transactionEPNS_11TransactionE + 342
    16  QuartzCore                          0x0000000109a0697e _ZN2CA11Transaction6commitEv + 576
    17  UIKitCore                           0x0000000107fd9701 _UIApplicationFlushRunLoopCATransactionIfTooLate
        + 165
    18  UIKitCore                           0x00000001080d3569 __handleEventQueueInternal + 6874
    19  CoreFoundation                      0x00000001055b9721
        __CFRUNLOOP_IS_CALLING_OUT_TO_A_SOURCE0_PERFORM_FUNCTION__ + 17
    20  CoreFoundation                      0x00000001055b8f93 __CFRunLoopDoSources0 + 243
    21  CoreFoundation                      0x00000001055b363f __CFRunLoopRun + 1263
    22  CoreFoundation                      0x00000001055b2e11 CFRunLoopRunSpecific + 625
    23  GraphicsServices                    0x000000010d8551dd GSEventRunModal + 62
    24  UIKitCore                           0x0000000107fdf81d UIApplicationMain + 140
    25  LetsEat                             0x000000010336a927 main + 71
    26  libdyld.dylib                       0x0000000106aed575 start + 1
)
libc++abi.dylib: terminating with uncaught exception of type NSException
(lldb)
```

6. Make sure that you have the Attributes inspector opened in the Utilities Panel, then change the **Table View** content from **Dynamic Prototypes** to **Static Cells**:

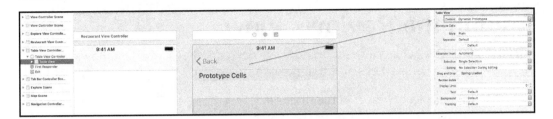

Now, let's run the project by hitting the Play button (or using *Command + R*). You will now be able to tap on a restaurant cell and see the following:

Adding the Reviews View

We have our static Table View set up now; we need another view that allows us to view restaurant reviews. Let's add that now:

1. In the object library, in the filter field, type `button`. Drag this button and put it next to one of the `tableview` cells:

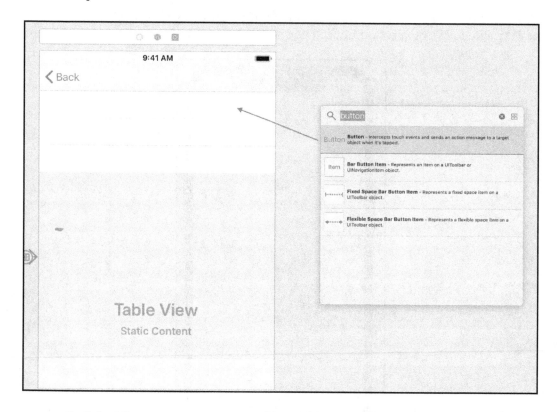

2. Select the `Main.storyboard` file, making sure that you are zoomed out and can see all of your scenes (depending on your screen resolution). In the Utilities panel, ensure that you have the object library tab selected.

3. In the filter field, type `viewcontroller`. Drag this **View Controller** and put it next to the **Restaurant Detail View Controller**.

4. In the filter field, type `label`.

5. Click on and drag **Label** and drop it onto the new **View Controller** we just added, next to the **Restaurant Detail View Controller**.

6. Double-click in the **Label** and add the `Reviews` text.

7. Select the **Align** icon that is to the left of the **Pin** icon and check the following boxes that appear:

   - Horizontally in container
   - Vertically in container

8. Click on **Add 2 Constraints**.

When you are done, you will see the following:

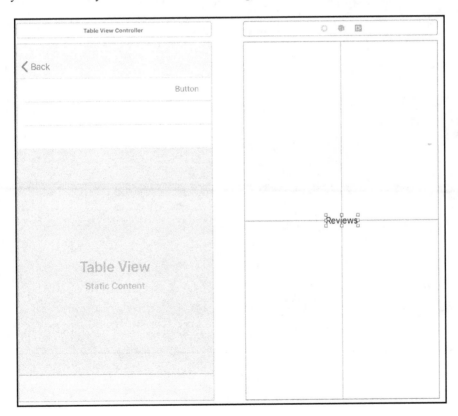

Viewing reviews

Now, we need to add a segue to be able to get to the Reviews View Controller:

1. *Control* + drag from the button to the **Review View Controller** that we added earlier.
2. When you let go, you are presented with a menu, and you should select **Show**:

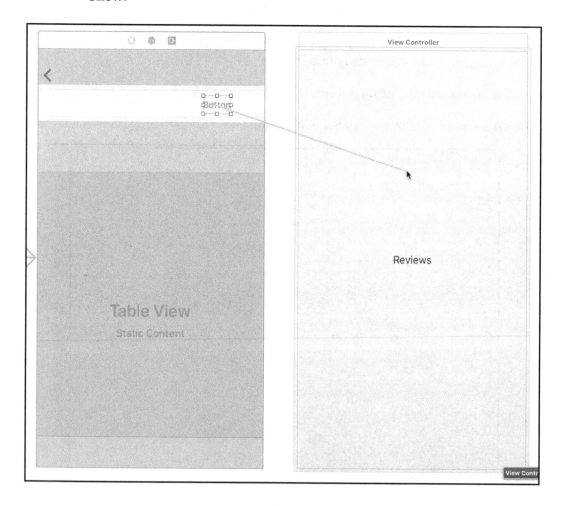

Let's run the project by hitting the Play button (or using *Command* + *R*). You will now be able to tap on the button in restaurant details and see the following:

Map Kit View

The last thing we need to do is to set up our **Map** tab. Select the `Main.storyboard` file and find the **View Controller** connected to the **Map** tab:

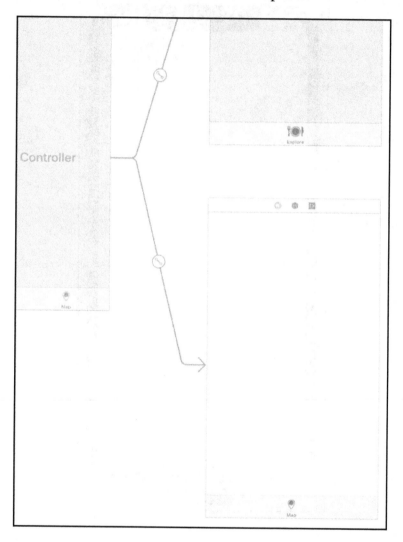

Let's get started:

1. Open the Object Library (*Command + shift + L*), then type map.
2. Drag and drop **Map Kit View** onto the **Map View Controller**:

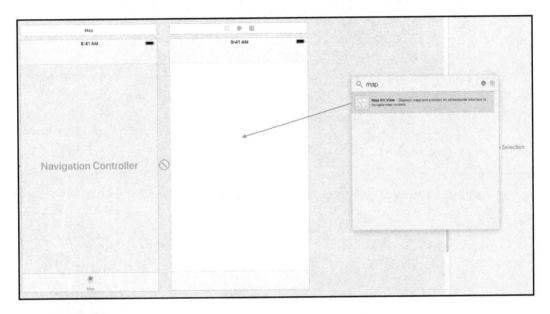

3. Select the **Pin** icon and enter the following values:
   - All values under **Add New Constraints** are set to 0.
   - Uncheck the **Constrain to margins** checkbox.
   - Click on **Add 4 Constraints**.

4. Your **View Controller** should look like the following when you are done:

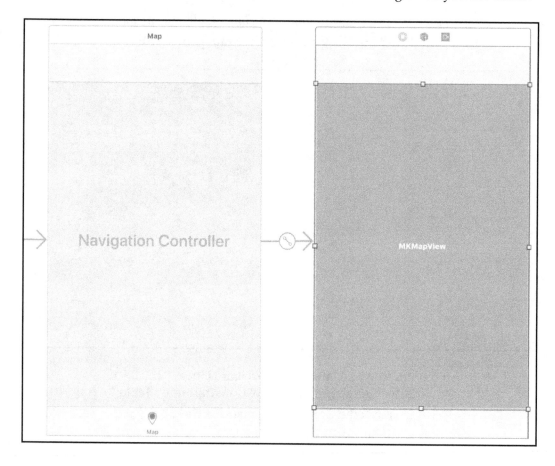

5. Run the project by hitting the Play button (or using *Command + R*) and selecting the **Map** tab:

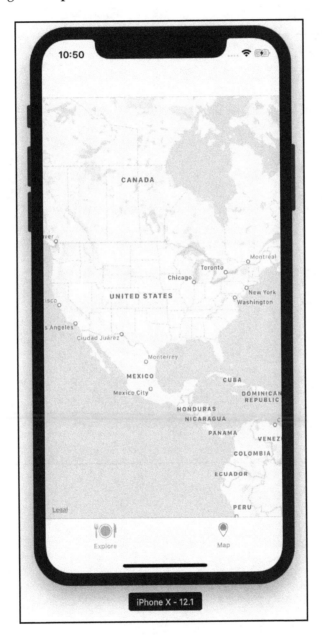

We now have both tabs set up, but, as we progress through the book, we will add more scenes to the storyboard. The following is what your `Main.storyboard` file should look like:

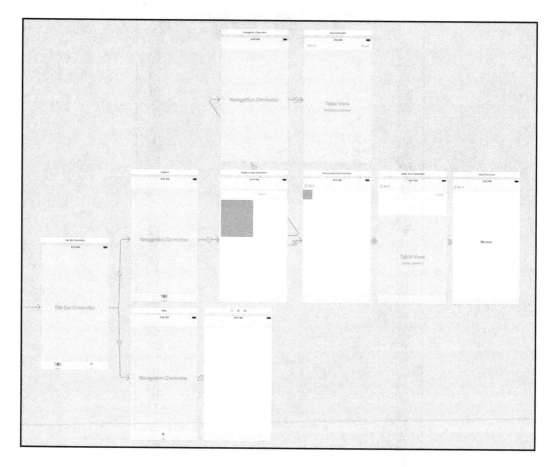

Summary

In this chapter, we finished the application structure. We hooked up our explore cell to a restaurant list. Then, we were able to connect a restaurant to a detail. Next, we added a button to our details, which allows us to see restaurant reviews. Lastly, we added a map to our **Map** tab.

At this point, a good challenge would be to see whether you can get back to this point. Try starting from when we created the project toward the end of Chapter 6, *Starting the UI Setup*, in the *Creating a new project* section. See whether you can get from that point to here without the book and without missing anything. This will help you, and it is something I like to do with those I mentor.

In the next chapter, we will start digging more into the design and getting our app to look like the design visually.

10
Designing Cells

In this chapter and throughout this book, we will adjust our app to match the design we reviewed earlier. However, the specifics of the design, such as custom fonts, are there as examples; you should feel free to change things to match your taste. By experimenting while learning, you should get a better understanding of how things work and become more comfortable using Xcode. I would recommend that you first thoroughly understand the lessons before experimenting; however, I highly encourage you to have fun and make the app your own.

In this chapter, we will be working with the following:

- Table View Cells
- Collection View Cells
- Auto Layout

Setting up the Explore header

Let's review the section header for the **Explore** tab:

In this header, we only have four elements: two `UILabels` (title and subtitle), a button, and a gray line underneath the title and button.

We already have the button in the prototype header (collection reusable view), which we created in `Chapter 8`, *Building Our App Structure in Storyboard*, and now we need to add the two `UILabels` and then revise all three elements so that they match our design:

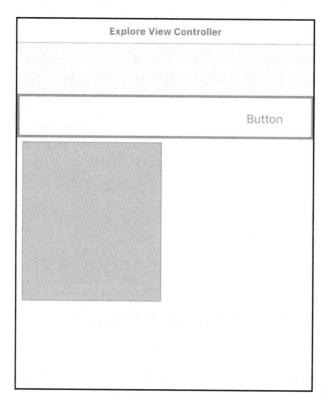

When working with multiple components in the same area, I like to put them into a view. The view acts as a container and allows me to keep my constraints down. Let's get started:

1. In `Main.storyboard`, select the prototype header and, in the Size inspector, update the following values:

   - **Width**: 0
   - **Height**: 100

   When you update the size, you might experience the following:

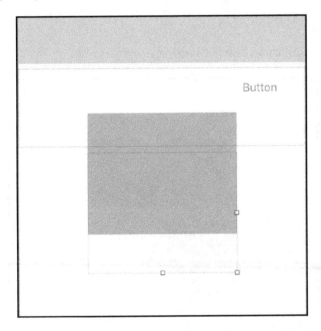

   If you do, click on a different file and come back; the storyboard should fix itself.

2. In the filter field of the object library, type `view`.

3. Drag out a **View** into the prototype header.

Make sure you use the outline view and move this below all the other elements using the Outline view. If you do not, it will cover everything.

4. In the Size inspector, update the following values:
   - **X**: 0
   - **Y**: 0
   - **Width**: 375
   - **Height**: 90

At this point, this view is covering up our button.

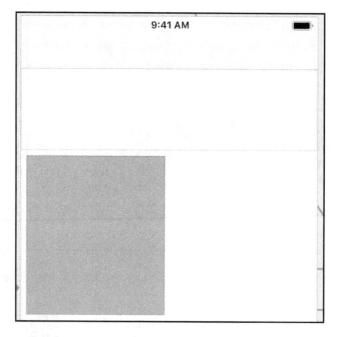

Let's fix this next.

5. Expand the Outline and you will see our newly added **View** and **Button**:

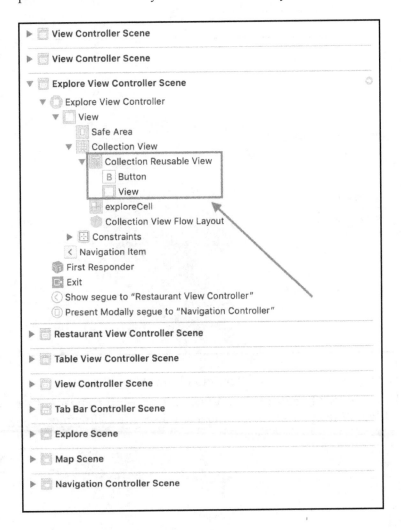

6. Select the **Button** in the Outline and drag it into the **View**. When you are done, it should look like the following:

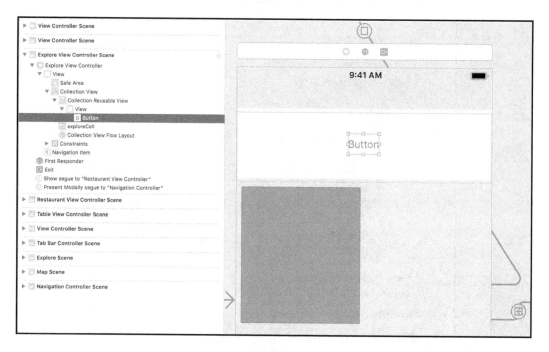

7. Next, type `label` in the filter field of the object library.

8. Drag out two **Labels** into the **View** of the prototype header that we just added. When you are done, you should see the following:

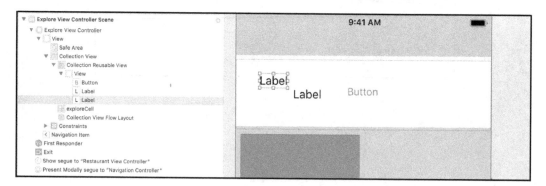

9. We are going to add a new color to our `Assets.xcassets` file. Name the color `LetsEat Light Grey` and set the **Hex Color** # to `AFAFB2`.

10. Let's rename `Demo Grey` to `LetsEat Dark Grey`. Our cells do not update to this new color, yet it does not break anything. We will change these colors later in the chapter.

11. Now, select one of the labels, which will be our subtitle, and, in the Attributes inspector, update the following values:

   - **Color**: `LetsEat Light Grey`
   - **Font**: `System Semibold 13`

10. In the Size inspector, update the following values:

   - **X**: `8`
   - **Y**: `24`
   - **Width**: `350`
   - **Height**: `21`

11. Select the other label, which will be our title, and, in the Attributes inspector, update the value of **Font** to `System Heavy 40.0`:

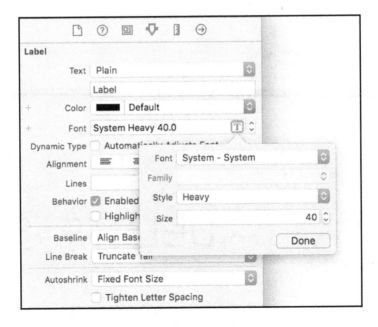

12. In the Size inspector, update the following values:

- **X**: 8
- **Y**: 45
- **Width**: 255
- **Height**: 37

13. Select the button (you might have to select it from the outline if the labels are covering it); then, in the Attributes inspector, update the following values:

- **Type**: Custom
- **Image**: btn-location
- Remove the text button

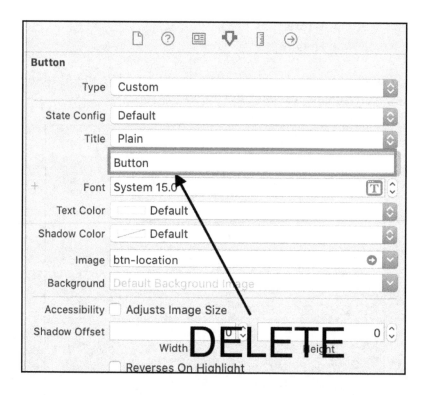

14. In the Size inspector, update the button to the following values:

- **X:** 271
- **Y:** 50

You should now have the following:

15. Type `view` in the filter field of the object library.
16. Drag a View into our view that we are using as a container.
17. Select the View (make sure you use the outline view and move this below all the other elements) and, in the Size inspector, update the following values:

- **X:** 8
- **Y:** 89
- **Width:** 359
- **Height:** 1

18. Now, with the View selected, in the Attributes inspector, update the value of **Background** to `LetsEat Light Grey`:

Now, with all of the elements placed into the prototype header, your cell should look as follows (inside your label, you should have the text **Label**):

To ensure that our cells adjust to the size of different devices, we must add Auto Layout constraints.

Adding Auto Layout to the Explore header

Working with Auto Layout can be very frustrating. If it does not work correctly, I recommend that you clear all the constraints and start over.

Let's begin by adding Auto Layout to our Label subtitle, which is where we should show the currently selected location:

1. Select the View, that we are using as a container and then the Pin icon. Enter the following value:

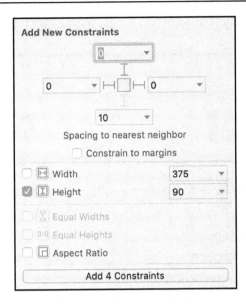

2. Click **Add 4 Constraints**.

3. Select the Label subtitle and then the Pin icon. Enter the following values:

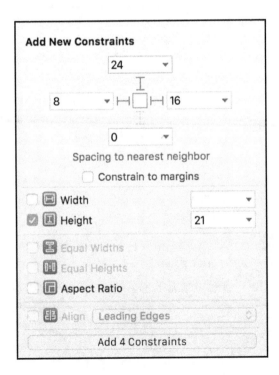

4. Click **Add 4 Constraints**. Your constraints should look like the following:

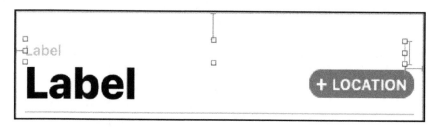

5. Next, select the **Location** button and then the Pin icon. Enter the following values:

- **Top**: 5
- **Right**: 8
- **Constrain to margins**: Unchecked
- **Width**: 96 (should be checked)
- **Height**: 25 (should be checked)

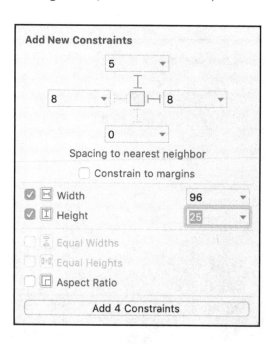

6. Click **Add 4 Constraints**. You should now see the following:

7. Now, select the grey line (it might be easier to use the outline to select the view) and then the Pin icon. Enter the following values:
   - **Right**: 8
   - **Bottom**: 0
   - **Left**: 8
   - **Constrain to margins**: Unchecked
   - **Height**: 1 (should be checked)

8. Click **Add 4 Constraints**. Your constraints should look like the following:

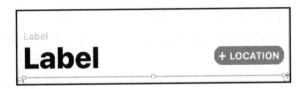

9. Select the **Label** (title) and then the Pin icon. Enter the following values:

   - **Top**: 0
   - **Right**: 8
   - **Left**: 8
   - **Height**: 37 (should be checked)
   - **Constrain to margins**: Unchecked

10. Click **Add 4 Constraints**. You should see the following when you are done:

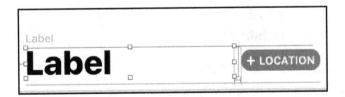

We have completed adding Auto Layout to the **Explore** tab header. If you want to check every constraint, feel free to look at Chapter 11, *Getting Started with the Grid*, starter project. Let's look at designing the Explore Cell next.

Setting up the Explore cell

Next, let's work on the Explore Collection View cell:

1. Select the prototype cell, called exploreCell, in the Attributes inspector, and update the background color to white. Then, in the Size inspector, change the Size from Default to Custom.
2. Then update the following values:

   - **Width**: 176
   - **Height**: 195

3. In the object library's filter field, type view.
4. Drag a View into the prototype cell.
5. Select the View and, in the Size inspector, update the following values:

   - **X**: 0
   - **Y**: 0
   - **Width**: 176
   - **Height**: 156

6. Type image in the filter field.
7. Drag an Image view into the View we just added.
8. With the Image view still selected, update the following values in the Size inspector:

   - **X**: 0
   - **Y**: 0
   - **Width**: 176
   - **Height**: 156

9. Type label in the filter field.
10. Drag a Label into the prototype cell (not the View).

11. With the Label selected, update the value of **Font** in the Attributes inspector to **Avenir Next Condensed Demibold 20**.

12. In the Size inspector, update the following values:

  - **X**: 8
  - **Y**: 165
  - **Width**: 160
  - **Height**: 21

`exploreCell` is now complete. Your cell should now look like the following:

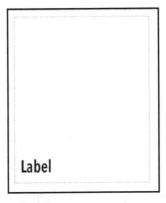

When setting up elements in storyboard, I like to get all my sizes set and then I use Auto Layout constraints to make sure it works for all devices. Let's add Auto Layout constraints before we move on to our Restaurant cell.

Adding Auto Layout to the Explore cell

1. In the Outline view, select the container View that is holding the Image view and then the Pin icon. Enter the following values:

  - **Top**: 0
  - **Right**: 0
  - **Left**: 0
  - **Constrain to margins**: Unchecked
  - **Height**: 156 (should be checked)

2. Click **Add 4 Constraints**.

3. Select the Image view and then the Pin icon. Enter the following values:

  - **Top**: 0
  - **Right**: 0
  - **Bottom**: 0
  - **Left**: 0
  - **Constrain to margins**: Unchecked

4. Click **Add 4 Constraints**.

5. Select the Label in this `exploreCell` and then the Pin icon. Enter the following values:

  - **Top**: 9
  - **Right**: 8
  - **Left**: 8
  - **Constrain to margins**: Unchecked
  - **Height**: 21 (should be checked)

6. Click **Add 4 Constraints**.

The Explore cell now has all the necessary constraints, and we can now set up the Restaurant cell.

Setting up the Restaurant cell

The Restaurant cell that we are setting up has many elements, so make sure to take your time. Make sure that you go to the Restaurant View Controller; let's get started:

1. Select the prototype cell, called `restaurantCell`, in the Attributes inspector, and update the background color to white. Then, in the Size inspector, change the **Size** from **Default** to **Custom**:

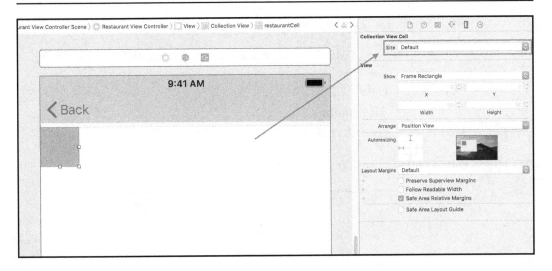

2. Then, update the following values:
   - **Width**: 375
   - **Height**: 312
3. In the filter field of the object library, type view.
4. Drag a View into the prototype cell.
5. With the View selected, update the following values in the Size inspector:

   - **X**: 75.5
   - **Y**: 245
   - **Width**: 224
   - **Height**: 56

6. Type label in the filter field.
7. Drag a **Label** into the **View** we just added.
8. With the Label selected, update the following values in the Size inspector:

   - **X**: 0
   - **Y**: 2
   - **Width**: 224
   - **Height**: 21

9. In the Attributes inspector, update the following values:

- **Text**: Add **Available Times** into the empty text field under the **Text**
- **Color**: `Black Color`
- **Alignment**: `Center`
- **Font: Avenir Next Condensed Bold 17**

When you are done, you should see the following:

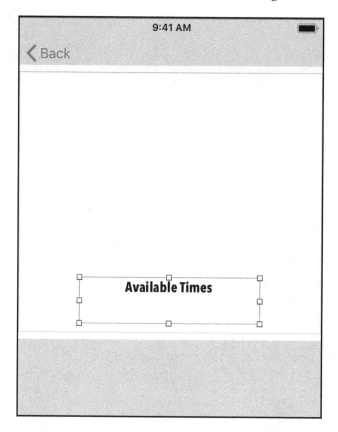

10. Next, in the filter field of the object library, type `button`.
11. From the Object library, drag the button from the into the View where we have the label.

12. With the button selected, update the following values in the Attributes inspector:

- **Type**: System
- **Title**: Plain and then add **7:30 pm** in the empty text field under the **Title**
- **Font**: **Avenir Next Condensed Regular 17**
- **Text Color**: White Color
- **Background**: time-bg

13. In the Size inspector, update the following values:

- **Width**: 68
- **Height**: 27

14. Select the button in the Outline view and hit *command* + *C* to copy.
15. Hit *command* + *V* twice to paste. You should now have three buttons.
16. Using the Outline view, *command* + click each button created and click on the **Embed in View** icon. The stack icon is two icons to the left of the Pin icon:

17. Select **Stack View** in the dropdown:

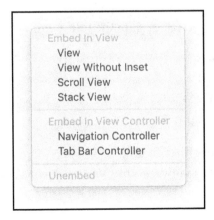

18. Select the stack view in the Outline view, and update the following values in the Attributes inspector:

    - **Axis**: **Horizontal**
    - **Alignment**: **Fill**
    - **Distribution**: **Equal Spacing**
    - **Spacing**: 10

19. In the Size inspector, set **X** to 0 and **Y** to 29.
    When you are done, you should see the following:

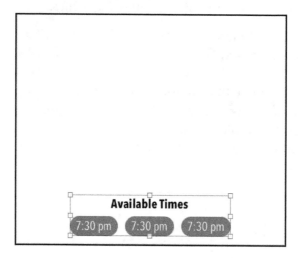

20. In the filter field of the Object library, type `view`.
21. Drag a View into the prototype cell.
22. With the View selected, update the following values in the Size inspector:

    - **X**: 11
    - **Y**: 42
    - **Width**: 353
    - **Height**: 200

23. Type `image` in the filter field.
24. Drag out an Image view into the View we just added.

25. Select the Image view in the Outline view and update the value of **Image** in the Attributes inspector with `american`. We are just using this image as a placeholder to see that our cells are set up correctly. Later, we will remove this and load the images using code.

26. With the Image view selected, update the following values in the Size inspector:

    - **X**: 0
    - **Y**: 0
    - **Width**: 353
    - **Height**: 200

27. Type `label` in the filter field.

28. Drag two Labels into the prototype cell.

29. Select one of the Labels and update the value of **Font** in the Attributes inspector with **Avenir Next Condensed Demi Bold 17**.

30. In the Size inspector, update the following values:

    - **X**: 10
    - **Y**: 3
    - **Width**: 355
    - **Height**: 19

31. Select the other Label and update the following values in the Attributes inspector:

    - **Color**: `LetsEat Dark Grey`
    - **Font: Avenir Next Condensed Regular 14**

32. In the Size inspector, update the following values:

    - **X**: 10
    - **Y**: 22
    - **Width**: 355
    - **Height**: 16

We have completed our Restaurant cell setup, and it now looks like the following:

Now we need to add Auto Layout to all of the elements.

Adding Auto Layout to the Restaurant cell

Since we have many elements in the Restaurant cell, it means that there are more chances for errors with Auto Layout. Although you may get frustrated when using Auto Layout, if you are a visual person like me, hopefully, you will eventually appreciate using it:

1. Select the top label and then enter the following values:

   - **Top**: 3
   - **Right**: 10
   - **Left**: 10
   - **Constrain to margins**: Unchecked
   - **Height**: 19 (should be checked)

2. Click **Add 4 Constraints**.

3. Select the Label right under the last label and then the Pin icon. Enter the following values:

   - **Top**: 0
   - **Right**: 10
   - **Left**: 10
   - **Constrain to margins**: Unchecked
   - **Height**: 16 (should be checked)

4. Click **Add 4 Constraints**.

5. Select the Image container and then the Pin icon. Enter the following values:

   - **Top**: 4
   - **Constrain to margins**: Unchecked
   - **Width**: 353 (should be checked)
   - **Height**: 200 (should be checked)

6. Click **Add 3 Constraints**.

7. Click on the Align icon and enter the value of **Horizontally in Container** as 0 (this should be checked).

8. Click **Add 1 Constraint**.

9. Select the Image inside of the container and then the Pin icon. Enter the following values:

   - **Top**: 0
   - **Right**: 0
   - **Bottom**: 0
   - **Left**: 0
   - **Constrain to margins**: Unchecked

10. Click **Add 4 Constraints**.

11. Select the container that is holding the stack view and the available time's label and then select the Pin icon. Enter the following values:

    - **Top**: 3
    - **Constrain to Margins**: Unchecked
    - **Width**: 224
    - **Height**: 56

12. Click **Add 3 Constraints**.
13. Click on the Align icon and enter the **Horizontally in Container** value as 0 (this should be checked).

14. Click **Add 1 Constraint**.
15. Select the stack view inside of the container and then the Pin icon. Enter the following values:

    - **Top**: 6
    - **Right**: 0
    - **Left**: 0
    - **Constrain to margins**: Unchecked
    - **Height**: 27

16. Click **Add 4 Constraints**.
17. Select the Label that is above the three buttons and then the Pin icon. Enter the following values:

    - **Top**: 2
    - **Left**: 0
    - **Right**: 0
    - **Constrain to margins**: Unchecked
    - **Height**: 21

18. Click **Add 4 Constraints**.
19. Click on the Align icon and enter the value of **Horizontally in Container** as 0 (this should be checked).

20. Click **Add 1 Constraint**.

Now, all of the Auto Layout for the Restaurant cell is set up. Before you run the project, select the collection view in the outline. Then, go to the Size inspector and update Cell Size **Width** to 375 and **Height** to 312 . These numbers are used for design purposes, and we will make these values dynamic depending on the device size later.

Let's build and run our project and go to the restaurant cell. You should now see the following:

The Locations cell

We now need to work on the Locations cell. Find the view we will use for our locations and, in your table view we need to update this cell, for this cell, we are using a predefined cell that Apple provides. Let's update our Table View by do the following:

1. Select the Table View, and update **Prototype Cells** to 1.
2. Select the prototype cell and enter the following values:

   - **Style**: **Basic**
   - **Identifier**: `locationCell`

That is all we need to do. Now, your cell should look as follows:

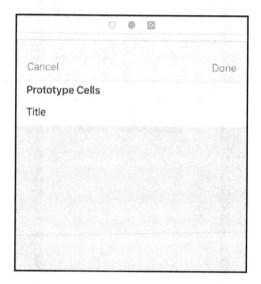

When you change the style from **Custom** to **Basic**, the word **Title** should appear in the cell. The word **Title** is just placeholder text. We have now finished designing our cell.

Summary

In this chapter, we formatted our cells to match our design and added Auto Layout constraints. Auto Layout can be complicated; however, as with anything, the more you practice, the easier it gets. You can write Auto Layout with code, but it is not what I prefer in a storyboard. If you would like to do it in code, there are plenty of tutorials that can help you with this.

We are now finished with the storyboard and design setup, so we can focus on the code side since our UI is pretty much set up. You should have a good idea of how our app should work. If you are struggling, there is nothing wrong with that. This stuff takes time to click, and. as I have said before, if you are struggling with anything that we have done, please go back. If you keep going when you are not comfortable, learning will get harder and harder. We will be covering a lot of new topics, so adding on to them when you are not ready is not recommended.

In the next chapter, we will learn what the Model View Controller is and how to work with it.

11
Getting Started with the Grid

I am a visual person; I prefer to start with the visuals and make sure that the app looks like the design. Starting with the UI helps me to identify the data structure and allows me to get familiar with the app, which means I can then focus my attention on the code.

In earlier chapters, we set up our app structure and developed a good understanding of the basics involved. In this chapter, you will learn about app architecture and how to create it for our *Let's Eat* app. For this chapter, please use the Chapter 11 project files, as I have added more design elements that you will need throughout the book.

We will cover the following in this chapter:

- Understanding the Model View Controller architecture
- Classes and structures
- Controllers and classes

Understanding the Model View Controller architecture

Apple built iOS apps to use what is known as the **Model View Controller (MVC)**, which is an architectural pattern that describes a way to structure the code in your app. In layman's terms, this just means breaking up our app into three distinct camps: Model, View, and Controller.

Here is a diagram of MVC to help you understand it:

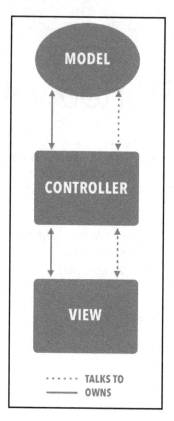

Let's discuss each camp:

- **Model**: The **Model** camp is responsible for an app's data and business logic. The Model's only job is to handle representations of data, data storage, and the operations performed on data.
- **View**: The **View** camp is responsible for all the things that you see on the screen. The View handles presenting and formatting data that results from the user's interactions.
- **Controller**: The **Controller** camp is the liaison or coordinator between the other two camps. The Controller handles a lot of setup and connections to the View. The Controller also interprets user interactions. Since the Controller is between both the View and the Model, the View and the Model should know nothing about each other.

In summary, the Controller takes user interactions and either responds back to the View or passes it onto the Model. When the Model completes a task, it passes it back to the Controller, and then the Controller talks with the View.

Getting familiar with the setup

For beginners, the MVC architecture can make you uncertain about where things should go. As we progress through the book, you will learn where to put things and why. So, you need not worry about where things should be placed as we work through this process together, step by step.

As your project grows, the MVC architecture places a lot of the responsibility on the Controller. Therefore, in this book, we tweak the MVC pattern to not put so much pressure on the Controller.

Before we continue with our coding, we need to discuss classes and structures.

Classes and structures

Classes and structures (also known as structs) are files that contain properties and methods. You use these properties and methods to add functionality. You have been working with structs since `Chapter 1`, *Getting Familiar with Xcode*. Strings, Ints, Bools, Arrays, Dictionaries, and Sets are all structs.

Earlier in the book, we created functions. As noted in `Chapter 6`, *Starting the UI Setup*, a method is a function that lives inside a class or struct.

Classes and structs are very similar; however, Swift handles each of them a bit differently. To get a better understanding of how classes and structs work, we create a new Playground project. Working in the Playground gives us the ability to learn how to create custom classes and structs and to gain an understanding of each of their positives and negatives.

Since we already have a project created, we can actually add a playground directly into our project. Right-click in the Project Navigator and create a new group called Playgrounds. When you are done, you should see the following:

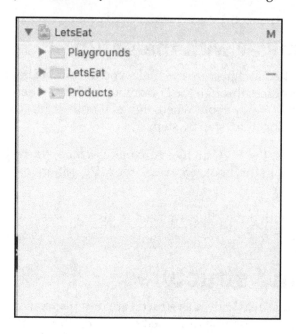

Next, right-click on the Playgrounds folder, go to **New File,** and do the following:

1. Scroll to the bottom of the template screen, select a **Blank** playground, and hit **Next.**

2. In the options screen that appears, name your new Playground `FunctionsStructs`, and make sure that your Platform is set to iOS. Hit **Next** and then **Create**. Now, let's delete everything inside your new Playground and toggle on the **Debug** Panel, using either the toggle button or *command + shift + Y*.

In your empty Playground, add the following:

```
class Cat {
}

struct Dog {
}
```

We just created our first class and struct and defined two new custom data types (known as **Swift types**), Cat and Dog. Since we have not yet given the class or struct a property (such as a name) or created an instance of either Cat or Dog, you see nothing in the **Results** or **Debug** Panels.

When you create classes and structs, it is best practice to start with a capital letter. Also, you must have different names for your class and your struct. Otherwise, you will get an error. Even though one is a class and the other is a struct, each of them needs a distinct name.

Now, we need to give names to our Cat class and our Dog struct. Therefore, let's give them both a property, called name:

```
class Cat {
  var name:String?
}

struct Dog {
  var name:String?
}
```

If you cannot set a property when it is created, then it is recommended that you set that property to an optional using the question mark (?). Using optional protects your code from trying to access the name if you never set it. You can also set your variable as an optional unwrapped. For example, you can also do the following:

```
var name:String!
```

With both `Cat` and `Dog` now having a property called `name`, let's create an instance of each of them:

```
let yellowCat = Cat()
yellowCat.name = "Whiskers"
print(yellowCat.name as Any)

var yellowDog = Dog()
yellowDog.name = "Bruno"
print(yellowDog.name as Any)
```

```
class Cat {
    var name:String?
}

struct Dog {
    var name:String?
}

let yellowCat = Cat()                    Cat
yellowCat.name = "Whiskers"              Cat
print(yellowCat.name as Any)            "Optional("Whiskers")\n"

var yellowDog = Dog()                    Dog
yellowDog.name = "Bruno"                 Dog
print(yellowDog.name as Any)            "Optional("Bruno")\n"
```

```
Optional("Whiskers")
Optional("Bruno")
```

So far, everything on the surface looks the same. We created both a `Cat` and a `Dog` and gave them each names. However, let's say `Whiskers` runs away and, a few weeks later, finds a home with a new family, who decide to change his name to `Smokey`. After `Whiskers` runs away, `Bruno` becomes lonely and decides to find him, but also gets lost. `Bruno` finds a new home as well, and this new family decides to name him `Max`.

In Playgrounds, we create a new constant called `yellowStrayCat` and set it equal to `yellowCat`, since it is still `Whiskers`. However, we change the name of `yellowStrayCat` to `Smokey`. We also create a new constant called `yellowStrayDog`, setting it equal to `yellowDog` and naming it `Max`:

```
let yellowStrayCat = yellowCat
yellowStrayCat.name = "Smokey"
print(yellowStrayCat.name)

var yellowStrayDog = yellowDog
yellowStrayDog.name = "Max"
print(yellowStrayDog.name)
```

Our **Results** Panel shows that the names of yellowStrayCat and yellowStrayDog, respectively, are now Smokey and Max. So, everything seems to be the same between our class and our struct, right? No, they are not the same. Let's print the name of yellowCat underneath the line where we have print(yellowStrayCat.name). In addition, let's do the same for the name of yellowDog underneath where we have print(yellowStrayDog.name). Your code should now look as follows:

```
let yellowStrayCat = yellowCat
yellowStrayCat.name = "Smokey"
print(yellowStrayCat.name)
print(yellowCat.name)

var yellowStrayDog = yellowDog
yellowStrayDog.name = "Max"
print(yellowStrayDog.name)
print(yellowDog.name)
```

In our **Results** Panel, you should notice an unexpected result. The yellowCat, Whiskers, now has the name Smokey, but the yellowDog is still Bruno. Without getting too technical, when you use a class and copy it as we did, it refers back to the original instance created. This is known as a **reference type**. However, when structs get copied, they create a new instance and the original is not affected. This is known as a **value type**.

Before we move on, let's look at one more difference between the two. In programming, we have what is called **inheritance**, which means that we can create another object with default values and other objects can inherit from those default values. Let's create an Animal class that is the base class immediately below our Cat class:

```
class Animal {
  var age:Int?
}
```

Now, let's update our `Cat` class to inherit from it, as shown in the following code:

```
class Cat:Animal {
    ...
}
```

Note that we are only updating what goes directly after `Cat`. The rest of the class in the curly brackets stays the same.

Since our class now inherits from `Animal`, we should have a new property called `age`. Underneath where we name `yellowCat` as `Whiskers` and above our `print` statement, enter the following after we set Whiskers' name:

```
yellowCat.age = 3
```

```
class Animal {
    var age:Int?
}

class Cat:Animal {
    var name:String?
}

struct Dog {
    var name:String?
}

let yellowCat = Cat()                                      Cat
yellowCat.name = "Whiskers"                                Cat
yellowCat.age = 3                                          Cat
print(yellowCat.name as Any)                               "Optional("Whiskers")\n"

var yellowDog = Dog()                                      Dog
yellowDog.name = "Bruno"                                   Dog
print(yellowDog.name as Any)                               "Optional("Bruno")\n"

let yellowStrayCat = yellowCat                             Cat
yellowStrayCat.name = "Smokey"                             Cat
print(yellowStrayCat.name as Any)                          "Optional("Smokey")\n"
print(yellowCat.name as Any)                               "Optional("Smokey")\n"

var yellowStrayDog = yellowDog                             Dog
yellowStrayDog.name = "Max"                                Dog
print(yellowStrayDog.name as Any)                          "Optional("Max")\n"
print(yellowDog.name as Any)                               "Optional("Bruno")\n"
```
```
Optional("Whiskers")
Optional("Bruno")
Optional("Smokey")
Optional("Smokey")
Optional("Max")
Optional("Bruno")
```

So, as expected, we were able to give `Whiskers` an `age`. Let's do the same for our `Dog` struct by adding `Animal` directly after `Dog`:

```
struct Dog:Animal {
  var name:String?
}
```

Once you have entered the preceding code snippet, you will see the following:

```
class Animal {
    var age:Int?
}

class Cat:Animal {
    var name:String?
}

struct Dog:Animal {          🔴 Non-class type 'Dog' cannot inherit from class 'Animal'
    var name:String?
}

let yellowCat = Cat()                                          Cat
yellowCat.name = "Whiskers"                                    Cat
yellowCat.age = 3
print(yellowCat.name as Any)                                   "Optional("Whiskers")\n"

var yellowDog = Dog()                                          Dog
yellowDog.name = "Bruno"                                       Dog
print(yellowDog.name as Any)                                   "Optional("Bruno")\n"

let yellowStrayCat = yellowCat                                 Cat
yellowStrayCat.name = "Smokey"                                 Cat
print(yellowStrayCat.name as Any)                              "Optional("Smokey")\n"
print(yellowCat.name as Any)                                   "Optional("Smokey")\n"

var yellowStrayDog = yellowDog                                 Dog
```

```
Optional("Whiskers")
Optional("Bruno")
Optional("Smokey")
Optional("Smokey")
Optional("Max")
Optional("Bruno")
```

A red error displays and informs you that `Non-class type 'Dog' cannot inherit from class 'Animal'`. Therefore, we need to create a struct called `AnimalB`, since structs cannot have the same name:

```
struct AnimalB {
  var age:Int?
}
```

Update your `Dog` struct from `Animal` to `AnimalB`:

```
struct Dog:AnimalB {
  var name:String?
}
```

Now, you should see an error, `Inheritance from non-protocol type 'AnimalB'`, which means that our struct cannot inherit from another struct:

```
class Animal {
    var age:Int?
}

class Cat:Animal {
    var name:String?
}

struct AnimalB {
    var age:Int?
}

struct Dog:AnimalB {          ⓘ  Inheritance from non-protocol type 'AnimalB'
    var name:String?
}

let yellowCat = Cat()                                              Cat
yellowCat.name = "Whiskers"                                        Cat
yellowCat.age = 3                                                  Cat
print(yellowCat.name as Any)                                       "Optional("Whiskers")\n"

var yellowDog = Dog()                                              Dog
yellowDog.name = "Bruno"                                           Dog
print(yellowDog.name as Any)                                       "Optional("Bruno")\n"

let yellowStrayCat = yellowCat                                     Cat
yellowStrayCat.name = "Smokey"                                     Cat
print(yellowStrayCat.name as Any)                                  "Optional("Smokey")\n"
print(yellowCat.name as Any)                                       "Optional("Smokey")\n"
```

```
Optional("Whiskers")
Optional("Bruno")
Optional("Smokey")
Optional("Smokey")
Optional("Max")
Optional("Bruno")
```

Inheritance is something that you can do with classes, but not with structs; this is another difference between classes and structs. There are a couple of other advanced technical differences but, for our purposes, the two described here are sufficient.

Controllers and classes

When working with `UIViewController`, `UICollectionViewController`, and `UITableViewController`, you need to create a class file for each of these elements. Each file handles all of the logic and interactions that the controller sends and receives. Along with interactions, the class file is responsible for receiving data. We can see what this looks like in Playground. Let's see how this works:

1. Right-click on the Playgrounds folder and go to **New File**.

2. Scroll to the bottom of the template screen, select a **Blank** playground, and hit **Next**.

3. In the options screen that appears, name your new Playground `CollectionViewBasics`, and make sure that your Platform is set to iOS. Hit **Next** and then **Create**. Delete the variable and leave the import statement, then toggle open/on the **Debug** Panel, using either the toggle button or *command + shift + Y*.

Now that we are set up, let's see how we can view the UI inside of playgrounds. Using Playgrounds really lets us focus on learning, instead of, having to worry about running our project every time we want to see changes.

Understanding Collection Views

The first thing we want to do is get access to all of the UI and Playground components that we will need. At the very top of the playground, please add the following import statements:

```
import UIKit
import PlaygroundSupport
```

The first import statement imports all of the UI elements we will need. The second import gives us access to Playground support, this will allow us to add our UI elements into playgrounds. Now let's create our first `UIViewController`, this setup is pretty much the same structure I like to use for all of my classes that are controllers. Add a line break and then add the following code:

```
class CollectionViewExampleController:UIViewController {
}
```

This code looks pretty similar to what we discussed earlier in this chapter. We created a class named `CollectionViewExampleController` and we subclass `UIViewController`. `UIViewController` is a class that Apple provides us with, and it gives us access to a lot of things. Going into all of them would take a chapter in itself, but throughout the book, we will slowly introduce you to new things we can access. Next, we need to create `UICollectionView`, so let's do that next by adding the following code inside of our curly brackets:

```
var collectionView:UICollectionView?
```

After you add the variable, your complete code should look like the following:

```
class CollectionViewExampleController:UIViewController {
    var collectionView:UICollectionView?
}
```

This is the variable we will use for our `UICollectionView`. The question mark signifies that we are making it an Optional value, just as we discussed earlier. The next thing we should do is the `UICollectionViewDataSource` protocol. This protocol has many methods that we can use, but there are two that are required to use `UICollectionView`. This protocol allows us to tell `collectionView` how many items we have in each section of `collectionView`, as well as creating a cell for each item we want to display in our collection view. Update your class to conform to `UICollectionViewDataSource` by adding it after the subclassing of `UIViewController`. In order to add it after, we must add a comma after `UIViewController`. When you are done, you should have the following:

```
class CollectionViewExampleController:UIViewController,
UICollectionViewDataSource {
    var collectionView:UICollectionView?
}
```

We now understand what this means, but we have an error:

```
1  //: Playground - noun: a place where people can play
2
3  import UIKit
4  import PlaygroundSupport
5
6  class CollectionViewExampleController : UIViewController, UICollectionViewDataSource {    ⊙ Type 'CollectionViewExampleController' does not conform t...
7
8      var collectionView:UICollectionView?
9
10 }
```

This error is telling us that we are missing the required methods for `UICollectionViewDataSource`. Click on the red dot with the white circle in it:

```
1  //: Playground - noun: a place where people can play
2
3  import UIKit
4  import PlaygroundSupport
5
6  class CollectionViewExampleController : UIViewController, UICollectionViewDataSource {    ⊙ Type 'CollectionViewExampleController' does not conform t...
7
8      var collectionView:UICollectionView?
9
10 }
```

When we click on the error, it lets us see more details:

```
1  //: Playground - noun: a place where people can play
2
3  import UIKit
4  import PlaygroundSupport
5
6  class CollectionViewExampleController : UIViewController, UICollectionViewDataSource {
7                                          Type 'CollectionViewExampleController' does not conform to protocol 'UICollectionViewDataSource'
8      var collectionView:UICollectionView?
9                                          Do you want to add protocol stubs?                                    Fix
10  }
```

We can either add the functions ourselves or we can click on the Fix button and it will add them for us.

Let's do that and we will see that we now have the two required methods needed for `UICollectionView`. Your code should look like the following:

```
1  //: Playground - noun: a place where people can play
2
3  import UIKit
4  import PlaygroundSupport
5
6  class CollectionViewExampleController : UIViewController, UICollectionViewDataSource {
7
8      func collectionView(_ collectionView: UICollectionView, numberOfItemsInSection section: Int) -> Int {
9          code                                    Editor placeholder in source file
10     }                                            Missing return in a function expected to return 'Int'
11
12     func collectionView(_ collectionView: UICollectionView, cellForItemAt indexPath: IndexPath) -> UICollectionViewCell {
13         code                                    Editor placeholder in source file
14     }                                            Missing return in a function expected to return 'UICollectionViewCell'
15
16
17     var collectionView:UICollectionView?
18
19  }
```

As you see, we have the new methods, but now we have more errors.

NOTE: Whenever you use the fix button, it adds the code to the top of your file. When coding, I like to have my variables at the top of my file and my functions after them.

Move the `collectionView` variable above the newly added functions. Inside each function, you should see the word code:

```
func collectionView(_ collectionView: UICollectionView, numberOfItemsInSection section: Int) -> Int {
    code  ◄
}
```

Inside the `numberOfItemsInSection` method, delete the word and replace the code with the following:

```
func collectionView(_collectionView:UICollectionView,
numberOfItemsInSectionsection:Int) -> Int {
    return 1
}
```

The `return 1` that we added tells our `UICollectionView` that we want to display 1 item.

Next, we need to fix our last method, `cellForItemAt`. Again, this method is responsible for displaying cells in our `UICollectionView`. Let's update this method to display a red box for every item we have in our `collectionView`. Add the following code:

```
func collectionView(_collectionView:UICollectionView,
cellForItemAtindexPath:IndexPath) -> UICollectionViewCell {
    let cell =
collectionView.dequeueReusableCell(withReuseIdentifier:"BoxCell",for:i
ndexPath)
    cell.backgroundColor = .red
    return cell
}
```

In the first line of the code we just added, we create a reusable cell with an identifier name of `"BoxCell"` and we pass the index path of the of the collection view to the reusable cell. Next, we set the background color to red, and then we return the cell we created to `UICollectionView`. This method is run for every item we need, and in our case, we are returning 1 cell because we set our `numberOfItemsInSection` to 1.

When you are done with both of these methods, your entire file should look like the following:

```
import UIKit
import PlaygroundSupport

class CollectionViewExampleController:UIViewController,
UICollectionViewDataSource {
    var collectionView:UICollectionView?
    func collectionView(_collectionView:UICollectionView,
numberOfItemsInSectionsection:Int) -> Int {
        return 1
    }
    func collectionView( _collectionView:UICollectionView,
cellForItemAtindexPath:IndexPath) -> UICollectionViewCell {
```

```
        let cell =
collectionView.dequeueReusableCell(withReuseIdentifier:"BoxCell",
for:indexPath)
        cell.backgroundColor = .red
        return cell
    }
}
```

All of your errors are now gone, but right now, nothing will run because we need to add a couple more things. We have a collectionView, but it actually needs to be created before we can use it. Typically, when working, I like to create a method that will create or set up my collectionView depending on what I am doing. Let's add the following code after our collectionView variable:

```
func createCollectionView() {
    self.collectionView = UICollectionView(frame:CGRect(x:0 , y:0,
width:self.view.frame.width, height:self.view.frame.height),
collectionViewLayout:UICollectionViewFlowLayout())
    self.collectionView?.dataSource = self
    self.collectionView?.backgroundColor = .white
    self.collectionView?.register(UICollectionViewCell.self,
forCellWithReuseIdentifier:"BoxCell")
    self.view.addSubview(self.collectionView!)
}
```

In the first line of this method, we create an instance of UICollectionView and we set the frame and layout. The frame sets its x and y positions, as well as, the width and height. Our width and height will match the size of the view we are using. In the next line, we set the data source to self, and we already added all of the methods that go with the data source when we set up our UICollectionViewDataSource. In the next line, we set the background color of our collection view to white. Then, we register our cell in the next line. In order for the collection view to know about our cell, we have to register it. Finally, we add the collection view to our view. Nothing too complicated here, but it is new and will take a bit of time to get used to. Now we just need to make sure that we call the createCollectionView method. Every UIViewController has an entry point, and the one that we will use is a method called viewDidLoad(). Add the following code above createCollectionView:

```
override func viewDidLoad() {
    super.viewDidLoad()
    createCollectionView()
}
```

Here, we are overriding the method viewDidLoad() so that we can use it to call methods we need too. Inside this method, we are calling the new method we just created—createCollectionView(). We will still not be able to see our collectionView, because when you are working inside of your app, this is all the code you would need. Since we are in Playgrounds, we have to do one more thing in order for it to be displayed inside of Playgrounds. After the very last curly bracket, add the following code:

```
// Present the view controller in the Live View window
PlaygroundPage.current.liveView = CollectionViewController()
```

Your entire class should look like the following:

```
import UIKit
import PlaygroundSupport

class CollectionViewExampleController:UIViewController,
UICollectionViewDataSource {
    var collectionView:UICollectionView?
    override func viewDidLoad(){
        super.viewDidLoad()
        createCollectionView()
    }
    func createCollectionView() {
        self.collectionView = UICollectionView(frame:CGRect(x:0, y:0,
width:self.view.frame.width,
        height:self.view.frame.height),
collectionViewLayout:UICollectionViewFlowLayout())
        self.collectionView?.dataSource = self
        self.collectionView?.backgroundColor = .white
self.collectionView?.register(UICollectionViewCell.self,forCellWithReu
seIdentifier:"BoxCell")
        self.view.addSubview(self.collectionView!)
    }
    func collectionView( _collectionView:UICollectionView,
numberOfItemsInSectionsection:Int) -> Int {
        return 1
    }
  func collectionView( _collectionView:UICollectionView,
cellForItemAtindexPath:IndexPath) -> UICollectionViewCell {
        let cell =
collectionView.dequeueReusableCell(withReuseIdentifier:"BoxCell",for:i
ndexPath)
        cell.backgroundColor = .red
        return cell
    }
}
```

```
// Present the view controller in the Live View window
PlaygroundPage.current.liveView = CollectionViewExampleController()
```

Now, you are probably wondering why you still cannot see anything, and that is because we need to open up the Assistant Editor. Click the following icon to do so:

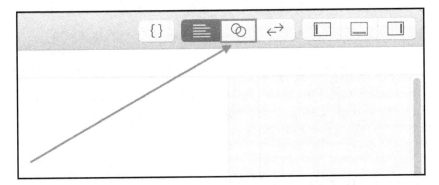

When you do this, you will see your collection view and 1 red box on the screen:

```
//: A UIKit based Playground for presenting user interface

import UIKit
import PlaygroundSupport

class CollectionViewExampleController : UIViewController,
    UICollectionViewDataSource {

    var collectionView:UICollectionView?

    override func viewDidLoad() {
        super.viewDidLoad()

        createCollectionView()
    }

    func createCollectionView() {
        self.collectionView = UICollectionView(frame: CGRect(x: 0, y:
            0, width: self.view.frame.width, height:
            self.view.frame.height), collectionViewLayout:
            UICollectionViewFlowLayout())
        self.collectionView?.dataSource = self
        self.collectionView?.backgroundColor = .white
        self.collectionView?.register(UICollectionViewCell.self,
            forCellWithReuseIdentifier: "BoxCell")
        self.view.addSubview(self.collectionView!)
    }

    func collectionView(_ collectionView: UICollectionView,
        numberOfItemsInSection section: Int) -> Int {
        return 1
    }

    func collectionView(_ collectionView: UICollectionView,
        cellForItemAt indexPath: IndexPath) -> UICollectionViewCell {
        let cell =
            collectionView.dequeueReusableCell(withReuseIdentifier:
            "BoxCell", for: indexPath)
        cell.backgroundColor = .red

        return cell
```

Note that you might have to click the play button at the bottom of your code to get it to show up:

```
32  }
33  // Present the view controller in the Live View window
34  PlaygroundPage.current.liveView =
        CollectionViewExampleController()
    ⊙ ◄───────────────────────────────
```

Now that we have covered the basics, let's go back to our app and set up a Collection View using a storyboard. Using Playgrounds is a great way to work things out with your code before coding them in your app.

Creating our controller

Now that we better understand how to create `UICollectionView`, let's add one to our project. Open your project and do the following steps:

1. Right-click inside of the `LetsEat` folder and select **New File**.
2. Inside of the **Choose a template for your new file** screen, select **iOS** at the top, and then **Cocoa Touch Class**. Then, hit **Next**:

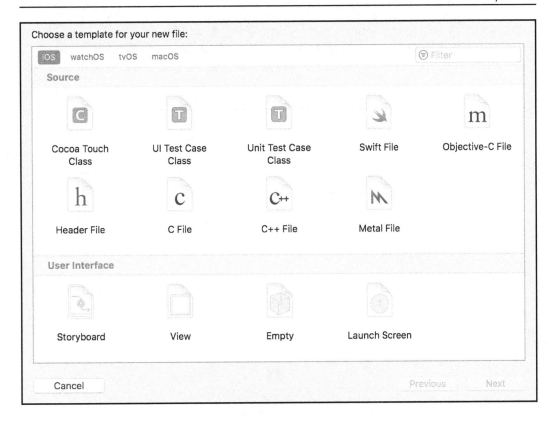

3. You should see an options screen. Add the following:

New file:

- **Class**: `ExploreViewController`
- **Subclass**: `UIViewController`
- **Also create XIB**: Unchecked
- **Language**: `Swift`

4. Upon hitting **Next**, you are asked to create this file. Select **Create** and then your file should look like mine.

Let's review this `ExploreViewController` class file and also do some maintenance inside of the file. We created this file to use with the `UIViewController` that we created when we initially set up our UI.

Note that there are three methods in this file: `viewDidLoad()`, `didReceiveMemoryWarning()`, and `prepare()` (which is commented out). Let's delete both `didReceiveMemoryWarning()` and `prepare()`, as we do not need them at this time:

```
import UIKit

class ExploreViewController: UIViewController {

    override func viewDidLoad() {
        super.viewDidLoad()
        // Do any additional setup after loading the view.    ⊗ DELETE
    }

    override func didReceiveMemoryWarning() {
        super.didReceiveMemoryWarning()
        // Dispose of any resources that can be recreated.
    }

    /*
    // MARK: - Navigation

    // In a storyboard-based application, you will often want to do a little preparation before navigation
    override func prepare(for segue: UIStoryboardSegue, sender: Any?) {
        // Get the new view controller using segue.destinationViewController.
        // Pass the selected object to the new view controller.
    }
    */

}
```

⊗ DELETE

```
import UIKit

class ExploreViewController: UIViewController {

    override func viewDidLoad() {
        super.viewDidLoad()
    }

}
```

⊕ UPDATED

What remains is `viewDidLoad()`; this method is called only once during the life of the View Controller. Let's see what this means by updating `viewDidLoad()` to the following:

```
func viewDidLoad() {
    super.viewDidLoad()
    print("Hello Explore View Controller")
}
```

Now, run the project by hitting the Play button (or using *command + R*). You should now only see `Hello Explore View Controller` inside of the Debug panel.

Understanding Collection View controllers and Collection View cells

As noted earlier in the book, Collection View Controllers allow us to display our data in a grid. The individual items inside of Collection Views are called cells, and these cells are what show our data. This data can be anything from an image to text, or both an image and text. You have complete control over what your Collection View cell can display. Our Collection View Controller is responsible for making sure the correct number of cells is displayed.

Let's now connect our file, `ExploreViewController`, with our `UICollectionView` in the storyboard. To do this, we use the Assistant Editor (or split screen), which we access by doing the following:

1. Open `Explore.storyboard`.
2. Close the Navigator panel using the hide Navigator toggle or *command + O*.
3. Close the Utilities panel by hitting the Utilities toggle or use *command + alt + O*.
4. Select the Assistant Editor or use *command + alt + enter*.

   You should now see `Explore.storyboard` on the left and `ExploreViewController.swift` on the right:

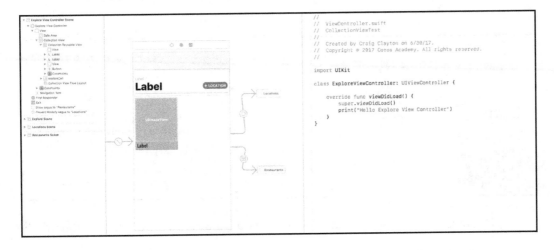

5. Add the following inside of your `ExploreViewController.swift` file on the line after the following code:

```
class ExploreViewController: UIViewController {
    @IBOutlet weak var collectionView:UICollectionView!
```

 `IBOutlet` is a way to a connect to the UI element. We have a Collection View on our `UIViewController`; now, we are creating a variable that allows us to hook into it.

6. After you create the variable, you should see a small circle to the left of the variable:

```
○        @IBOutlet weak var collectionView:UICollectionView!
```

7. When you hover over it, you should see a plus button appear inside of the circle:

```
⊕        @IBOutlet weak var collectionView:UICollectionView!
```

Click on it and drag this to your Collection View inside of your `UIViewController`:

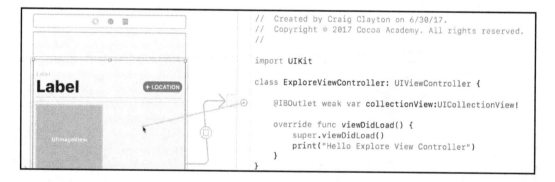

8. Once you release the mouse button, you should see the circle become filled:

```
◉        @IBOutlet weak var collectionView:UICollectionView!
```

9. Select the Standard Editor or use *command + enter*.

In your scene, select your Collection View. Then, in your Utilities Panel, select the Connections inspector, which is the last icon on the right. Under the **Outlets** section, we now add back `dataSource` and `delegate`, the same ones we removed earlier:

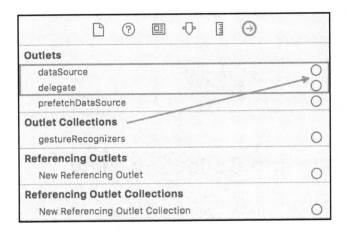

The `dataSource` property is what is used to supply the data for our Collection View, so we need to pass whatever data we have to this property. On the other hand, the `delegate` property, which supplies the behavior, does not require us to supply anything as it receives interactions that happen within our Collection View.

We need to update our data source for our Collection View; let's add this now:

10. Click and drag the `dataSource` property to the Explore View Controller in your Outline view:

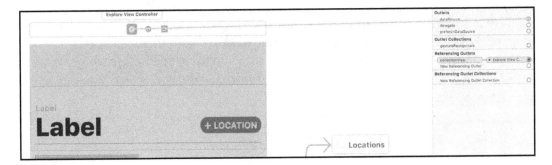

11. Click and drag the delegate property to the Explore View Controller in your Outline view:

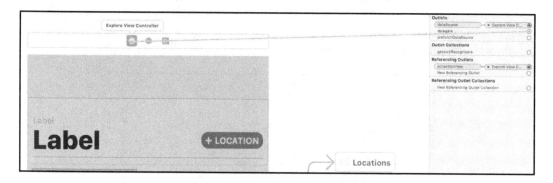

Getting data into Collection View

Having boxes is great, but having data with beautiful pictures is so much more appealing. Let's get some data displaying inside of our Collection View:

1. Use *command + shift + O*, which opens a small window called **Open Quickly**. Inside the window, type `ExploreView` and hit *enter* to select the `ExploreViewController.swift` file.

2. Update our class definition from the `ExploreViewController:UIViewController` class to the following:

```
class ExploreViewController:UIViewController,
UICollectionViewDataSource
```

Understanding the data source

Whenever we use Collection View to get data, we must conform to a protocol. A protocol is a set of methods to which we have access, and can either be required or optional. For Collection Views, we are required to implement three methods to get data into a Collection View. So, let's add the following four functions (each beginning with `func`) after the closing curly bracket of `viewDidLoad()`:

```
import UIKit

class ExploreViewController: UIViewController, UICollectionViewDataSource, UICollectionViewDelegate {

    @IBOutlet weak var collectionView: UICollectionView!

    override func viewDidLoad() {
        super.viewDidLoad()
        print("Hello Explore View Controller")
    }

    func collectionView(_ collectionView: UICollectionView, viewForSupplementaryElementOfKind kind: String, at indexPath: IndexPath) ->    A
        UICollectionReusableView {
        B   let headerView = collectionView.dequeueReusableSupplementaryView(ofKind: kind, withReuseIdentifier: "header", for: indexPath)
            return headerView
    }

    func collectionView(_ collectionView: UICollectionView, cellForItemAt indexPath: IndexPath) -> UICollectionViewCell {   C
    D       return collectionView.dequeueReusableCell(withReuseIdentifier: "exploreCell", for: indexPath)
    }

    func numberOfSections(in collectionView: UICollectionView) -> Int {   E
    F       return 1
    }

    func collectionView(_ collectionView: UICollectionView, numberOfItemsInSection section: Int) -> Int {   G
    H       return 20
    }

    // Add Unwind here
    I   @IBAction func unwindLocationCancel(segue:UIStoryboardSegue) {}
    }
}
```

Let's break down the code to better understand what we are doing:

- **Part A**: This first method is what we need to add a header to our Collection View:

  ```
  collectionView(_:viewForSupplementaryElementOfKind:at:)
  ```

- **Part B**: The identifier is what we added when we were designing in earlier chapters. This identifier helps Xcode know what view we are referring to:

  ```
  let headerView =
  collectionView.dequeueReusableSupplementaryView(ofKind: kind,
  withReuseIdentifier: "header", for: indexPath)
  return headerView
  ```

- **Part C**: Our next method gets called for every item we need. Therefore, in our case, it gets called 20 times:

  ```
  collectionView(_:cellForItemAt:)
  ```

- **Part D**: Here, we are creating a cell every time `collectionView(_:numberOfItemsInSection:)` is called. The identifier, `exploreCell`, is the name we gave it in the storyboard; so, this is the cell that is grabbed and used inside of our Collection View:

```
return collectionView.dequeueReusableCell(withReuseIdentifier:
"exploreCell", for: indexPath)
```

- **Part E**: This method tells our Collection View how many different sections we want to display:

```
numberOfSections(in collectionView: UICollectionView)
```

- **Part F**: Here, we are telling our Collection View that we only want one section:

```
return 1
```

- **Part G**: Our next method tells our Collection View how many different items we are going to display inside of the section we set up:

```
collectionView(_:numberOfItemsInSection:)
```

- **Part H**: We are telling our Collection View that we want to display 20 items:

```
return 20
```

- **Part I**: Finally, we add this line back as it was removed. We use this function to dismiss our location modal when you hit the **Cancel** button:

```
@IBAction func unwindLocationCancel(segue:UIStoryboardSegue)
{}
```

Let's build and run the project by hitting the Play button (or using *command + R*). We are now finished.

Summary

In this chapter, we covered quite a few new topics, as well as a lot of code. As long as you have a basic understanding of what we covered in this chapter, you will be OK to continue. A lot of these concepts and ideas will be covered again, as these are common design patterns in iOS.

We learned about the MVC architecture. Then, we covered classes and structures, along with their similarities and differences. Finally, we looked at Controllers and classes and how they work. We then created our Controller for our storyboard file.

In the next chapter, we will look at how to get local data into our app. We will also look at how to pass data from the **Explore** view to the restaurant list.

12
Getting Data into Our Grid

Working with data is very important but, when teaching beginners, I like to do it in steps so that this process is a bit easier. In this chapter, we are going to work with data that is stored on the device. Later in this book, we will work with data that we get from a feed. Feed data means it is coming from a website URL, and using data from a feed means you can update the data without having to update the app.

We will cover the following in this chapter:

- What is a model?
- What is a plist?
- How do we create a plist?
- Working with the manager class

In the last chapter, we got the **Explore** listing up, but we have no data. We need to create a model object that will represent the information that our cell can use to display data.

Model

Typically, when developing your model, the best way to start when you have design is to look at the data associated with your view. Let's look at our app design again:

The items (`UICollectionViewCell`) displayed in the grid are each supported by some data. Looking at the design, we see that each item needs an image and a name (cuisine). Therefore, we need to create a model, called `ExploreItem`, with two properties, specifically `image` and `name`.

In the model camp, we will create three files: `ExploreData.plist`, `ExploreItem.swift`, and `ExploreDataManager.swift`.

ExploreData.plist

The first file, `ExploreData.plist`, has already been created for you and can be found in your project inside of the `Explore` folder. This file contains all of the data we need for a list of cuisines. Create a new folder called `Model` and drag this file into it.

In the file, there is an array of dictionary items. Each item has a cuisine name and image for that particular cuisine. Let's take a look at the first few elements of this file:

▼ Root		Array	(31 items)
▼ Item 0		Dictionary	(2 items)
name	⊕ ⊖	String	All
image		String	all.png
▼ Item 1		Dictionary	(2 items)
name		String	Bistro
image		String	bistro.png
▼ Item 2	⊕ ⊖	Dictionary ⌄	(2 items)
name		String	Bar / Lounge / Bottle Service
image		String	bar.png
▼ Item 3		Dictionary	(2 items)
name		String	Brewery
image		String	brewery.png

We will load this file into our **Explore** list, and this is what we use to filter restaurants by a specific cuisine.

ExploreItem.swift

Next, we need to create a file to represent our data. Our **Explore** list displays an image and a name that match the corresponding image and name that we see in our `Explore.plist` file. Let's create this `ExploreItem` file now:

1. Right-click on the `Model` folder and select **New File**.
2. Inside the template screen, select **iOS** at the top and then **Swift File**, then hit **Next**.
3. Name the file `ExploreItem` and then hit **Create**.

The only thing in this file is an `import` statement.

 The `import` statement allows us to import other libraries into our file, giving us the ability to see inside of these libraries and use properties from them. Foundation is one of Apple's core frameworks, and it has a bunch of tools that we can use while we program.

Since we do not need to use inheritance, we are going to make this file a `struct`. Add the following to your file:

```
struct ExploreItem {
}
```

Now that we have declared it a `struct`, let's add the two properties we need for this file: an image and a name. For both of these properties, we are going to make them String data types. For the title, this makes sense, because it is text that we are displaying in our Collection View. However, for the image, using a String data type might not seem as obvious. The reason we are doing so is that, to get it, we have to access it by name. For example, `american.png` is the file name for the American cuisine image. Add the following to the inside of your curly brackets (`{  }`):

```
var name:String
var image:String
```

We have now added two properties, one for the image and one for the name, both of which are optional. Since we cannot give either of them an initial value, we have to make them optional.

Your file should look like the following:

```
struct ExploreItem {
   var name:String
   var image:String
}
```

We next need to add one more thing to this file.

We take the dictionary data we get from `plist` and create an `ExploreItem` for each item. Our dictionary now looks like the following:

```
["name": "All", "image": "all.png"]
```

We need to pass this dictionary object to our `ExploreItem`. When you are passing a dictionary object, you are required to create a custom initializer. Our initializer takes a dictionary object into it. Then, we can set each item from the dictionary to the data of both of our properties—image and name.

> When you create a struct, by default, you get an `init()` method that has all of the properties you created in the parameters.

For example, our `ExploreItem` will have a default initializer that looks like the following:

```
init(name:String, image:String)
```

Instead of using this initializer, we will create our own to pass a dictionary object into it.

To create a **custom initializer**, we are going to use what is called an **extension**, which gives us the ability to extend our code and add more functionality to it. Inside of your `ExploreItem` file, after the ending curly bracket, add the following:

```
extension ExploreItem {
}
```

Next, let's create our custom initializer, which takes a dictionary object into the parameters. Add the following between the curly brackets of the extension we just added:

```
init(dict:[String:Any Object]) {
}
```

We have now created an `init()` method in the parameters, which accepts a dictionary object. As stated in the preceding section, we know that our data looks like the following:

```
["name": "All", "image": "all.png"]
```

To pass each value, we need to use the following dictionary syntax:

```
dict["name"]
dict["image"]
```

Let's proceed by mapping the dictionary data to our two properties. Add the following inside of the `init()` method's curly brackets:

```
    self.name  = dict["name"] as! String
    self.image = dict["image"] as! String
}
```

 Since our dictionary value is `AnyObject`, we have to specify that our data is a String by using `as! String` at the end.

We now have our data item set up for our **Explore** view (cuisine list), and your file should look like the following:

```
extension ExploreItem {
  init(dict:[String:AnyObject]) {
    self.name  = dict["name"] as! String
    self.image = dict["image"] as! String
  }
}
```

Let's now focus on our data manager. We want our data manager to handle parsing the plist and giving us the data. Since our data will be coming from a plist, we need to have a method that will get the data from the plist first.

ExploreDataManager.swift

In our app, the data manager is responsible for communicating with a service (for example, the Yelp API), as well as manipulating the data from the service. Once the data from the service is received, the data manager will create model objects that we can use for our app.

In some apps, these two jobs are handled by the controller. However, rather than putting that responsibility on our controller, we limit the controller from talking to the manager so that it never knows anything about the service.

 As you get comfortable with programming, you will find that there are a few different types of architectures. We are sticking as closely as we can to MVC because it is what Apple uses to build iOS apps.

Let's create the `ExploreDataManager` file now:

1. Right-click on the `Model` folder and select **New File**.
2. Inside of the template screen, select **iOS** at the top and then **Swift File**, then hit **Next**.
3. Name this file `ExploreDataManager` and hit **Create**.

Since we need to define our class first, add the following under the `import` statement:

```
class ExploreDataManager {
}
```

Here, we used a `class` instead of a `struct`, because this is a file that we will inherit from later. You do not always necessarily know whether you are going to inherit from another class; therefore, you can default to a struct and then change to a class if you realize that you need to inherit from another class.

Now, we need to load data from the `ExploreData.plist` file. Add the following method to our `ExploreDataManager` class:

```
import Foundation

class ExploreDataManager {                    B                    C

   A—fileprivate func loadData() -> [[String: AnyObject]] {
        guard let path = Bundle.main.path(forResource: "ExploreData", ofType: "plist"),
            let items = NSArray(contentsOfFile: path) else {
                return [[:]]
        }                    E              D

      return items as! [[String : AnyObject]]——F
   }
}
```

Let's breakdown this method:

- **Part A**: This function starts with the `fileprivate` keyword. Think of `fileprivate` as a way to give your methods an access level. If you do not use `fileprivate`, it defaults to internal, which means anyone can access or use the method outside of the class:

  ```
  fileprivate
  ```

- **Part B**: Our `loadData()` function is returning something back. `->` states that our function has a return value. The return value for this method is an array of dictionary objects. Our dictionary will have a key to a String and the value will be `AnyObject`:

  ```
  [[String: AnyObject]]
  ```

  `AnyObject` lets us take any data type that comes back. Therefore, we can have one item give us an Int, while another gives us back a String.
  You can also use `Any`, which can represent an instance of any type at all, including functional types and optional types.

- **Part C**: Inside of the function, we are using what is known as a `guard` statement. A `guard` statement is designed to exit a method or function early when a given statement returns `false`. Our `guard` statement checks two statements and both need to return `true`:

  ```
  guard let path = Bundle.main.path(forResource: "ExploreData",
  ofType: "plist")
  ```

  The first statement checks to see whether the `ExploreData.plist` file exists in our app bundle. If the file is found, the statement returns `true`, and the file path is set to the constant path. Our next statement, which is separated by a comma, is discussed in *Part D*, as follows.

- **Part D**: In this statement, if the first statement returns `true`, we take the `path` constant, and then we check the contents inside of the file.

  ```
  let items = NSArray(contentsOfFile: path)
  ```

Let's take a look at the data in our file again:

Root	Array	(31 items)
▼ Root	Array	(31 items)
▼ Item 0	Dictionary	(2 items)
name	⊕⊖ String	All
image	String	all.png
▼ Item 1	Dictionary	(2 items)
name	String	Bistro
image	String	bistro.png
▼ Item 2	⊕⊖ Dictionary ↕	(2 items)
name	String	Bar / Lounge / Bottle Service
image	String	bar.png
▼ Item 3	Dictionary	(2 items)
name	String	Brewery
image	String	brewery.png

If you look at the root of this plist, you see that its type is an array. NSArray has a method that we can use to get the data out of our file and put it into an array with which we can work.

Typically, plists come in two types: an array or a dictionary. Currently, neither the standard Swift array nor dictionary gives us a method that allows us to get data out of a file, so we need to utilize NSArray (as we are here) or NSDictionary, respectively, to do that.

This statement now checks to verify that we are, indeed, working with an array, and then returns true if so. If both conditions return true, our array inside of our plist is given to us. The array is set to our constant items.

NSArray and NSDictionary come from Objective C (Apple's main programming language for building iOS apps); they have some extra features. Just know that they are similar to their Swift counterparts without the NS.

- **Part E**: Here, if any of the conditions are `false`, we return an array with an empty dictionary:

```
else { return [[:]] }
```

Otherwise, we run the following `return`.

- **Part F**: This `return` gives back an array of dictionary items. Once we have our data loaded out of the plist, we can create our `ExploreItem`. Therefore, we need a method so that we can access all of our **Explore** items and return an array of items:

```
return items as! [[String : AnyObject]]
```

Getting data

To get our data out of the plist, add the following method above `loadData()` inside of `ExploreDataManager`:

```
func fetch() {
  for data in loadData() {
    print(data)
  }
}
```

Our `fetch()` method is going to loop through our dictionary data from the plist. Here is what your file should look like now:

```
import Foundation

class ExploreDataManager {

    func fetch() {
        for data in loadData() {
            print(data)
        }
    }

    fileprivate func loadData() -> [[String: AnyObject]] {
        guard let path = Bundle.main.path(forResource: "ExploreData", ofType: "plist"),
            let items = NSArray(contentsOfFile: path) else {
            return [[:]]
        }

        return items as! [[String : AnyObject]]
    }
}
```

Inside of your `ExploreViewController.swift` file, delete the previous `print` statement that was inside your `viewDidLoad()` and replace it with the following:

```
let manager = ExploreDataManager()
manager.fetch()
```

Let's build and run the project by hitting the Play button (or use *command* + *R*). You will notice that, in the **Debug** Panel, every time our loop runs, it gives a dictionary object, such as the following:

```
["image": all.png, "name": All]
["image": bistro.png, "name": Bistro]
["image": bar.png, "name": Bar / Lounge]
["image": brewery.png, "name": Brewery]
["image": burgers.png, "name": Burgers]
["image": californian.png, "name": Californian]
["image": caribbean.png, "name": Caribbean]
["image": comfort.png, "name": Comfort Food]
["image": cuban.png, "name": Cuban]
["image": continental.png, "name": Continental]
["image": french.png, "name": French]
["image": international.png, "name": International]
["image": italian.png, "name": Italian]
["image": japanese.png, "name": Japanese]
["image": latin.png, "name": Latin American]
["image": mediterranean.png, "name": Mediterranean]
["image": mexican.png, "name": Mexican]
["image": organic.png, "name": Organic]
["image": panasian.png, "name": Pan-Asian]
["image": peruvian.png, "name": Peruvian]
["image": pizza.png, "name": Pizzeria]
["image": primerib.png, "name": Prime Rib]
["image": seafood.png, "name": Seafood]
["image": southamerican.png, "name": South American]
["image": southern.png, "name": Southern]
["image": spanish.png, "name": Spanish]
["image": steak.png, "name": Steakhouse]
["image": sushi.png, "name": Sushi]
["image": tapas.png, "name": Tapas / Small Plates]
["image": vietnamese.png, "name": Vietnamese]
["image": wine.png, "name": Wine Bar]
```

The above print statement is exactly what we want. Now, inside of `ExploreDataManager`, add the following above our `fetch` method:

```
fileprivate var items:[ExploreItem] = []
```

Next, inside of `fetch()`, update our `for...in` loop by replacing `print(data)` with the following:

```
items.append(ExploreItem(dict: data))
```

Your file should look like the following:

```
import Foundation

class ExploreDataManager {

    fileprivate var items:[ExploreItem] = []

    func fetch() {
        for data in loadData() {
            items.append(ExploreItem(dict: data))
        }
    }

    fileprivate func loadData() -> [[String: AnyObject]] {
        guard let path = Bundle.main.path(forResource: "ExploreData", ofType: "plist"),
            let items = NSArray(contentsOfFile: path) else {
            return [[:]]
        }

        return items as! [[String : AnyObject]]
    }
}
```

Let's build and run the project by hitting the Play button (or use *command* + *R*). In the **Debug** Panel, you should see an array of **Explore** items.

We currently have our data, and we have cells. However, we need to get our data to our cells so that we can see the image and name. Let's open up `Explore.storyboard` and update our `exploreCell`.

Connecting to our cell

Now that we have our cell set up, we need to create a file so that we can connect to our cells:

1. Right-click on the `Explore` folder and create a new group called `View` in the Navigator panel. Then, right-click on `View` and select **New File**.

2. Inside of the template screen, select **iOS** at the top, and then **Cocoa Touch Class**, then hit **Next**.

3. You should now see an options screen. Add the following:

   New file:

   - **Class**: `ExploreCell`
   - **Subclass**: `UICollectionViewCell`
   - **Also create XIB**: Unchecked
   - **Language**: `Swift`

4. Once you hit **Next**, you are asked to create this file. Select **Create** and your file should look like mine:

   ```
   import UIKit
   class ExploreCell: UICollectionViewCell {
   }
   ```

5. Open `Explore.storyboard` and select `exploreCell` in the Outline view.

6. In the Utilities Panel, select the Identity inspector and, under **Custom Class**, type `ExploreCell`, then hit *Enter*.

Hooking up our UI with IBOutlets

To access our UI elements, we need to connect them to `IBOutlets`. To do so, perform the following steps:

1. Open the `ExploreCell.swift` file in the Navigator panel (or use *command* + *Shift* + *O*, type `ExploreCell`, and then hit *Enter*).

2. Inside of the class declaration, add the following:

```
@IBOutlet var lblName:UILabel!
@IBOutlet var imgExplore:UIImageView!
```

3. Open `Explore.storyboard` and select your `exploreCell` again using the project Outline.

4. In the Utilities panel, select the Connection inspector. You should see both variables we just created, **lblName** and **imgExplore**, under **Outlets**:

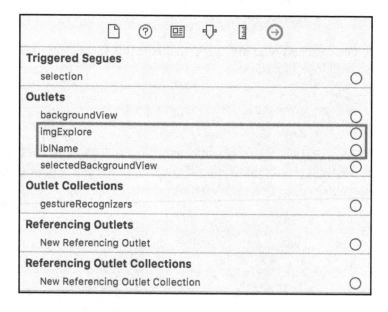

5. Click-drag from **imgExplore** to the **UIImageView** we put in our cell:

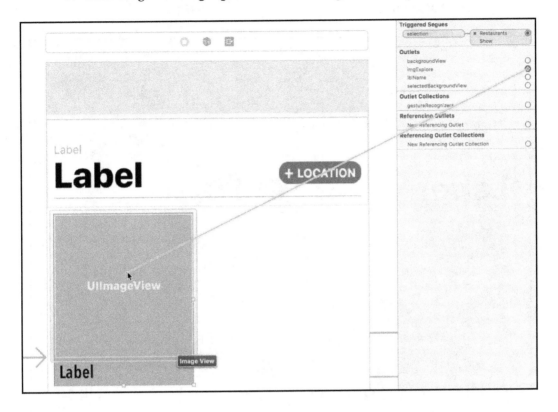

6. Repeat this step for **lblName** by click-dragging from **lblName** to the **UILabel** in our cell:

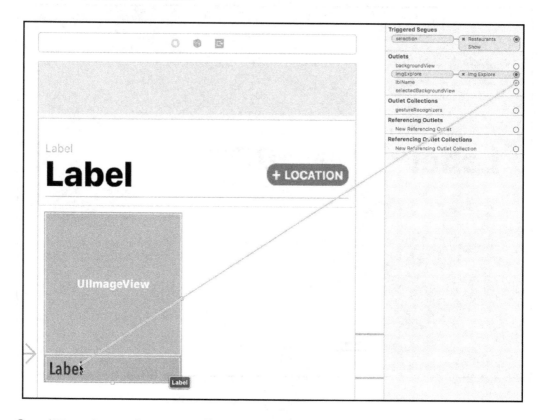

Great! Now that we have our cell set up, let's pull data into it. In our `ExploreDataManager,` add these two methods above the `loadData()` method:

```
func numberOfItems() -> Int {
   return items.count
}

func explore(at index:IndexPath) -> ExploreItem {
   return items[index.item]
}
```

We use the first method, `numberOfItems()`, to update the total number of items in our Collection View. The second method, `explore (at index:IndexPath)`, is called for each item we create in our Collection View. Then, we use this to pass the data to our cell to display the name and the image.

Now that we have these two methods added, let's open up our
`ExploreViewController` file. We currently have the following inside of our
`viewDidLoad()`:

```
let manager = ExploreDataManager()
manager.fetch()
```

Let's move `let manager` underneath our Collection View so that it is outside
`viewDidLoad()`; therefore, we can access it anywhere within the class as opposed to
only within the function. You should now have this before `viewDidLoad()`:

```
@IBOutlet var collectionView: UICollectionView!
let manager = ExploreDataManager()
```

Inside of `viewDidLoad()`, only `manager.fetch()` remains. Next, we need to update
`numberOfItemsInSection()` to say the following:

```
func collectionView(_ collectionView: UICollectionView,
numberOfItemsInSection section: Int) -> Int {
  return manager.numberOfItems()
}
```

Therefore, instead of returning 20, we are going to get the number of items from our
plist.

Finally, inside of `cellForItemAt()`, revise the `let` statement in the third required
method before the `return` cell by adding `as! ExploreCell`, as follows:

```
let cell = collectionView.dequeueReusableCell(withReuseIdentifier:
"exploreCell", for: indexPath) as! ExploreCell
```

Then, add the following after the code snippet you just added and before the `return`
cell:

```
let item = manager.explore(at: indexPath)
cell.lblName.text = item.name
cell.imgExplore.image = UIImage(named: item.image)
```

The preceding code gets an `ExploreItem` for each cell in our Collection View and
passes the data to the cell. Finally, for your return, add the following:

```
return cell
```

Let's build and run the project by hitting the Play button (or use *command + R*). You should now see your Collection View come to life with images and text:

The images are not perfect, but we will fix them later. Now that we have our cells displaying content, we need to make it so that, when you select a cell, it goes to our restaurant listing.

Let's build and run the project by hitting the Play button (or use *command + R*). You should now be able to select your cell, and it goes to what will be your restaurant listing page. This page will be empty for now, so let's work on this next.

Restaurant listing

Now that we have our **Explore** listing going to our restaurant listing, we need to get our Collection View connected to our `RestaurantListViewController`. To do so, perform the following steps:

1. Right-click inside of the `Restuaurants` folder and select **New File**.
2. Inside of the template screen, select **iOS** at the top and then **Cocoa Touch Class**, then hit **Next**. You should now see an options screen. Add the following under New file:

    - **Class**: `RestaurantListViewController`
    - **Subclass**: `UIViewController`
    - **Also create XIB**: Unchecked
    - **Language**: `Swift`

    After hitting **Next**, you will be asked to create this file.

4. Select **Create**.
5. Let's delete both `didReceiveMemoryWarning()` and `prepare()` (which has been commented out), as we do not need them at this time.
6. Open `Restaurants.storyboard`.
7. Select `UIViewController` in the Utility Panel, and select the Identity inspector, which is the third icon from the left.
8. Under **Custom Class**, and in the **Class** drop-down menu, select `RestaurantViewController` and hit *enter*.

Note that, when working with IBOutlets, it is easier to have the storyboard and View controller next to each other. In order to do this, we have to close a few windows:

- If your Navigator Panel is currently open, close it by clicking on the hide navigator toggle or *command + O*.
- If your Utilities Panel is currently open, close it by clicking on the Utilities toggle or use *command + Alt* or *Alt + O*.

9. Select the Assistant editor or use *command + Alt* or *Alt + Enter*.

10. You should now see `Restaurants.storyboard` on the left side and `RestaurantListViewController.swift` on the right. Add the following after the class declaration:

```
@IBOutlet var collectionView:UICollectionView!
```

12. Once you create the variable, you'll see a small circle to the left of the variable.

13. When you hover over it, you'll see a plus button appear inside of the circle. Click on it and drag this to your Collection View inside of your `UIViewController`.

14. Once you release it, you'll see the circle become filled:

```
⊚        @IBOutlet weak var collectionView:UICollectionView!
```

It's time to display something inside of our Collection View.

15. In your scene, select your Collection View. Then, in your Utilities panel, select the Connections inspector, which is the last icon on the right. Under the **Outlets** section, we now add back `dataSource` and `delegate`, which are the same ones we removed earlier:

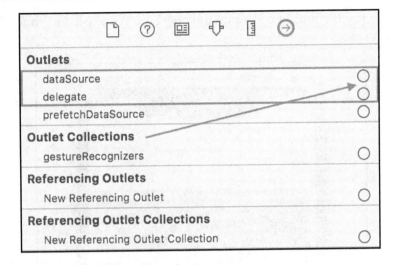

16. Update the class definition inside of RestaurantListViewController. You currently have RestaurantListViewController:UIViewController — update it to the following:

```
class RestaurantListViewController:UIViewController,
UICollectionViewDataSource
```

As you learned earlier with our **Explore** grid, we are required to implement numberOfSections(), numberOfItemsInSection(), and cellForItemAt() in order to use a Collection View. Therefore, add the following three methods inside of RestaurantListViewController:

```
func collectionView(_ collectionView: UICollectionView, cellForItemAt
indexPath: IndexPath) -> UICollectionViewCell {
    return collectionView.dequeueReusableCell(withReuseIdentifier:
"restaurantCell", for: indexPath)
}

func numberOfSections(in collectionView: UICollectionView) -> Int {
    return 1
}

func collectionView(_ collectionView: UICollectionView,
numberOfItemsInSection section: Int) -> Int {
    return 10
}
```

Let's build and run the project by hitting the play button (or use *command + R*) to see what happens:

Instead of having a grid, as we did for **Explore**, our restaurant list displays a column of cells. However, when the restaurant list displays on an iPad, it shows a grid instead. This is one of the flexibilities from which we benefit by using a Collection View. We will further set up our restaurant list cells along with displaying the data later in this book.

Summary

In this chapter, we learned how to create a model object and how to tie that data to a plist. We also looked at what a plist is. We learned how to create a plist as well as our first manager class, which takes care of the data. In our data manager, we covered getting data from a plist and how to represent that data as a model object.

In the next chapter, we will look at Table Views and how they are similar to—and yet different from—Collection Views.

Getting Started with the List **13**

When I started doing iOS development, I first worked with Table Views. At the time, Collection Views hadn't been introduced yet. As you progress in iOS development, you will work with a lot of Table and Collection Views. You'll begin with just the basics to allow you to use them, and then you'll slowly progress into more advanced Table and Collection Views.

The reason that I bring this up is that, by the end of this chapter, you may feel as though things are not clicking. This is perfectly normal. However, the more you go through the steps in these chapters, the more they will become second nature to you.

For those of you who've not done iOS development, Table Views are great for presenting a list of data. The iPhone's Mail app is an example of a Table View.

In this chapter, we are going to work with our first Table View. In our *Let's Eat* app, users select a specific location to look for restaurants.

In this chapter, we will cover the following topics:

- Understanding Table Views
- Creating our first property list (plist)
- Creating our location data manager
- Cleaning up our file structure

Understanding Table Views

The first thing we want to do is get access to all of the UI and Playgrounds' components that we will need. At the very top of the playground, please add the following two import statements:

```
import UIKit
import PlaygroundSupport
```

The first import statement imports all of the UI elements we will need. The second import gives us access to Playgrounds support; this will allow us to add our UI elements into Playgrounds. Now, let's create our first `UIViewController`. This setup is pretty much the same structure I like to use for all of my classes that are controllers. Add a line break and then add the following code:

```
class TableViewExampleController: UIViewController {

    }
```

This code looks pretty similar to what we did in the last chapter. We created a class named `TableViewExampleController` and we subclassed `UIViewController`. Next, we need to create a `UITableView` and an array of data to display in our `tableView`. Let's do that next by adding the following inside of our curly braces:

```
var tableView:UITableView?
var names:[String] = ["Deanna","Corliss","Deyvn"]
```

After you add the variable, your complete code should look like the following:

```
class TableViewExampleController: UIViewController {
    var tableView:UITableView?
    var names:[String] = ["Deanna","Corliss","Deyvn"]
}
```

This is the variable we will use for our `UITableView`. Here, we have an array with three names. The next thing we should do is create the `UITableViewDataSource` protocol. This protocol has many methods that we can use, but there are two we need that are required for us to be able to use a `UITableView`. This protocol allows us to tell the `tableView` how many items we have in each section of the `tableView`, as well as create a cell for each item we want to display in our `tableView`. Update your class to conform to `UITableViewDataSource` by adding it after the subclassing of `UIViewController`. To add it after, we must add a comma after `UIViewController`. When you are done, you should have the following:

```
class TableViewExampleController: UIViewController,
UITableViewDataSource {
    var tableView:UITableView?
    var names:[String] = ["Deanna","Corliss","Deyvn"]
}
```

We now understand what this is, but now we have an error:

```
1   import UIKit
2   import PlaygroundSupport
3
4   class TableViewExampleController : UIViewController, UITableViewDataSource {  ⊙ Type 'TableViewExampleController' does not conform to prot...
5
6       var tableView:UITableView?
7       var names:[String] = ["Deanna", "Corliss", "Deyvn"]
8
9   }
10
11
12
13
```

This error is telling us that we are missing the required methods for
`UITableViewDataSource`. Next, click on the red dot with the white circle in it:

```
1   import UIKit
2   import PlaygroundSupport
3
4   class TableViewExampleController : UIViewController, UITableViewDataSource {  ⊙ Type 'TableViewExampleController' does not conform to prot...
5
6       var tableView:UITableView?
7       var names:[String] = ["Deanna", "Corliss", "Deyvn"]
8
9   }
10
11
12
13
```

When you click on the error, it will give us the option to see more details:

```
1   import UIKit
2   import PlaygroundSupport
3
4   class TableViewExampleController : UIViewController, UITableViewDataSource {
5                                         ⊙ Type 'TableViewExampleController' does not conform to protocol 'UITableViewDataSource'      ⊗
6       var tableView:UITableView?        Do you want to add protocol stubs?                                                         Fix
7       var names:[String] = ["Deanna", "Corliss", "De
8
9
10  }
```

We can either add the functions ourselves, or we can click on the **Fix** button and it
will add them for us.

Let's do that. You will see that we now have the two required methods that are
needed for a `UITableView`. Your code should look like the following:

```
1   import UIKit
2   import PlaygroundSupport
3
4   class TableViewExampleController : UIViewController, UITableViewDataSource {
5       func tableView(_ tableView: UITableView, numberOfRowsInSection section: Int) -> Int {
6           code                                                                   ⚠ Editor placeholder in source file
7       }                                                                          ⊙ Missing return in a function expected to return 'Int'
8
9       func tableView(_ tableView: UITableView, cellForRowAt indexPath: IndexPath) -> UITableViewCell {
10          code                                                                   ⚠ Editor placeholder in source file
11      }                                                                          ⊙ Missing return in a function expected to return 'UITableViewCell'
12
13
14      var tableView:UITableView?
15      var names:[String] = ["Deanna", "Corliss", "Deyvn"]
16  }
17
```

As you can see, we have the new methods, but now we have more errors.

Whenever you use the **Fix** button, it adds the code to the top of your file. When coding, I like to have my variables at the top of my file and my functions after them.

Move the `tableView` and name variables above the newly added functions. Inside each function, you should see the word code:

```
func tableView(_ tableView: UITableView, numberOfRowsInSection section: Int) -> Int {
    code ←————————————————————————
}
```

Inside the `numberOfItemsInSection` method, delete the word 'code' and replace it with the following:

```
func tableView(_tableView:UITableView, numberOfRowsInSection
section:Int) -> Int {
    return names.count
}
```

The return tells our `UITableView` that we want to display in each cell and, since we have three names in our array, we should see three cells in our `tableView`.

Next, we need to fix our last method, `cellForItemAt`. Again, this method is responsible for displaying cells in our `UITableView`. Let's update this method so that it displays a red box for every item we have in our `tableView`. Add the following code:

```
func tableView(_tableView:UITableView,
cellForRowAtindexPath:IndexPath) -> UITableViewCell {
    let cell = tableView.dequeueReusableCell(withIdentifier:"cell",
for:indexPath) as UITableViewCell
    let name = names[indexPath.row]
    cell.textLabel?.text = name
    return cell
}
```

In the first line of the code we just added, we create a reusable cell with an identifier name of "cell", and we pass the index path of the `tableView` to the reusable cell. Next, we set the cell's label to the text in our array. Finally, we return the cell we created to the `UITableView`.

This method gets run for every item we need. In our case, we are returning three cells, which returns a name to each because our array has three items.

When you are done with both of these methods, your entire file should look like the following:

```
import UIKit
import PlaygroundSupport

class TableViewExampleController: UIViewController,
UITableViewDataSource {
    var tableView:UITableView?
    var names:[String] = ["Deanna","Corliss","Deyvn"]

    func tableView(_tableView:UITableView, numberOfRowsInSection
section:Int) -> Int{
        return names.count
    }
    func tableView(_tableView:UITableView,
cellForRowAtindexPath:IndexPath) -> UITableViewCell {
        let cell =
tableView.dequeueReusableCell(withIdentifier:"Cell",for:indexPath) as
UITableViewCell
        let name = names[indexPath.row]
        cell.textLabel?.text = name
        returncell
    }
}
```

All of your errors are now gone, but right now, nothing will run because we need to add a couple more things. We have a `tableView` variable, but it actually needs to be created before we can use it. Let's add the following code after our `tableView` variable:

```
func createTableView() {
    self.tableView = UITableView(frame:CGRect(x:0, y:0,
width:self.view.frame.width, height:self.view.frame.height))
    self.tableView?.dataSource = self
    self.tableView?.backgroundColor = .white
    self.tableView?.register(UITableViewCell.self,
forCellReuseIdentifier:"Cell")
    self.view.addSubview(self.tableView!)
}
```

In the first line of this method, we create an instance of an `UITableView` and we set up the frame and layout. The frame sets its x and y positions, as well as the width and height. Our width and height will match the size of the view we are using. In the next line, we set up the data source to self. We already added all of the methods that go with the data source earlier when we set up our `UITableViewDataSource`. In the next line, we set the background color our our `tableView` to white. Next, we register our cell in the next line. For the `tableView` to know about our cell, we have to register it. Finally, we add the `tableView` to our view. There's nothing too complicated here, but it is new and will take a bit of getting used to. Now, we just need to make sure that we call the `createTableView` method. Add the following code above `createTableView`:

```
override func viewDidLoad() {
    super.viewDidLoad()
    createTableView()
}
```

Here, we are overriding the method so that we can use it to call methods we need, too. Inside of this method, we are calling the new method we just created: `createTableView()`. We will still not be able to see our `tableView` because when you are working inside of your app, this is all the code you would need. However, since we are in Playgrounds, we have to do one more thing in order for it to be displayed inside of Playgrounds. After the very last curly brace, add the following code:

```
// Present the view controller in the Live View window
PlaygroundPage.current.liveView = TableViewExampleController()
```

Your entire class should look like the following:

```
import UIKit
import PlaygroundSupport

class TableViewExampleController:UIViewController,
UITableViewDataSource {
    var tableView:UITableView?
    var names:[String] = ["Deanna","Corliss","Deyvn"]
    override func viewDidLoad(){
        super.viewDidLoad()
        createTableView()
    }
    func createTableView(){
        self.tableView = UITableView(frame:CGRect(x:0, y:0,
width:self.view.frame.width,
height:self.view.frame.height))
```

```
        self.tableView?.dataSource = self
        self.tableView?.backgroundColor = .white
self.tableView?.register(UITableViewCell.self,forCellReuseIdentifier:"
Cell")
        self.view.addSubview(self.tableView!)
    }

    func tableView(_tableView:UITableView, numberOfRowsInSection
section:Int) -> Int {
        return names.count
    }
    func tableView(_tableView:UITableView,
cellForRowAtindexPath:IndexPath) -> UITableViewCell {
        let cell = tableView.dequeueReusableCell(withIdentifier:"Cell",
for:indexPath) as UITableViewCell
        let name = names[indexPath.row]
        cell.textLabel?.text = name
        return cell
    }
}

PlaygroundPage.current.liveView = TableViewExampleController()
```

Now, you are probably wondering why you still can not see anything, and that is because we need to open up the Assistant Editor. Click the following icon to do so:

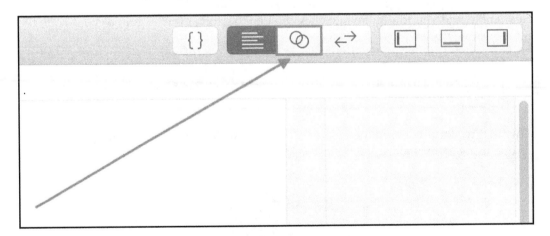

By doing this, you will see your `tableView` and the names we added to our array on the screen:

Please note that you might have to click the Play button at the bottom of your code to get it to show up:

```
36
37  PlaygroundPage.current.liveView = TableViewExampleController()
```

Now that we have covered the basics of Table View, let's go back to our app and set up one using a storyboard.

Creating our Location View Controller class

Now that we understand Table View more, we want to get locations displaying inside our Table View:

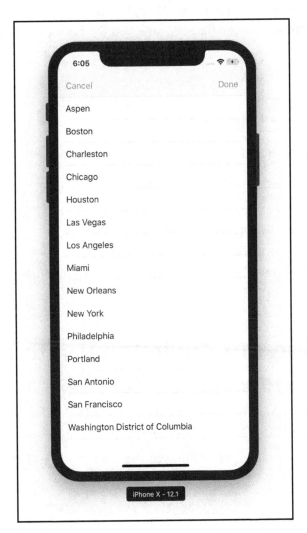

Before we start, create three new folders inside the Location folder – Controller, View, and Model. As we have previously done, right-click on the `Location` folder and hit **New Group** to create a new folder.

Next, we need to create a Location View Controller class that we can use with our `UIViewController`:

1. Right-click on the `Locations` folder inside of Controllers and select **New File**.
2. In the **Choose a template for your new file** screen, select **iOS** at the top and then **Cocoa Touch Class**. Then, hit **Next**.
3. In the **Options** screen that appears, add the following file after New file:

    - **Class**: `LocationViewController`
    - **Subclass**: `UIViewController`
    - **Also create XIB**: Unchecked
    - **Language**: `Swift`

4. Click on **Next** and then **Create**.

Next, we need to connect our View Controller with our class:

1. Select `Locations.storyboard`.
2. Then, select the **View Controller**
3. Now, in the **Utilities** Panel, select the Identity inspector.
4. Under **Custom Class**, in the **Class** drop-down menu, select `LocationViewController` and hit *Enter*.

Connecting our Table View with our Location View Controller

Currently, we have no way to communicate with our Table View and our Location View Controller. Let's see how we can connect these two:

1. Open the `LocationViewController.swift` file and add the following code after the class declaration:

    ```
    @IBOutlet weak var tableView:UITableView!
    ```

2. Save the file by hitting *command + S*. Your file should look like the following, with an empty circle next to the variable:

```
class LocationViewController: UIViewController {

    @IBOutlet weak var tableView:UITableView!
```

Before we get started, we are going to clean up our
`LocationViewController.swift` file. Delete everything after `viewDidLoad()`:

```
//
//   LocationViewController.swift
//   LetsEat
//
//   Created by Craig Clayton on 11/20/18.
//   Copyright © 2018 Cocoa Academy. All rights reserved.
//

import UIKit

class LocationViewController: UIViewController {

    @IBOutlet weak var tableView:UITableView!

    override func viewDidLoad() {
        super.viewDidLoad()

        // Do any additional setup after loading the view.
    }                               DELETE

    /*
    // MARK: - Navigation

    // In a storyboard-based application, you will often want to do a little
        preparation before navigation
    override func prepare(for segue: UIStoryboardSegue, sender: Any?) {
        // Get the new view controller using segue.destination.
        // Pass the selected object to the new view controller.
    }
    */
}
```

Next, let's connect our table view to the file:

1. Open `Locations.storyboard` again and make sure that you have the Location View Controller selected in the Outline view.

2. Then, in the Utilities Panel, select Connections inspector. Under the **Outlets** section, you will see an empty circle, **tableView**:

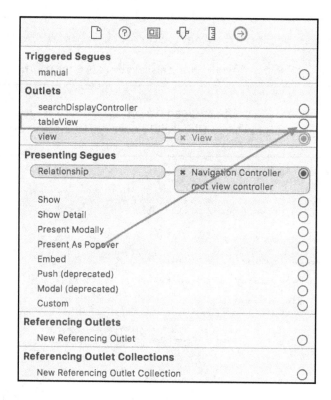

Click and drag the empty circle to the **Table View** in the storyboard:

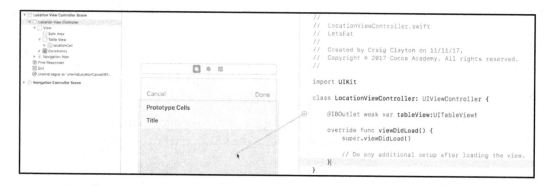

We have now connected our **Table View** to our **Location View Controller**.

Digging into our Table View code

To get data into our Table View, we must conform to a protocol, as we did with the Collection View. In this case, we must implement `UITableViewDataSource`:

1. First, we need to update our `class` declaration. We currently have the following:

   ```
   class LocationViewController: UIViewController
   ```

2. We now need to add `UITableViewDataSource`, as follows:

   ```
   class LocationViewController: UIViewController,
   UITableViewDataSource
   ```

Adding the data source and delegate

As discussed in the previous chapter, we need to add a data source and delegate to our Table View. Table View uses **dynamic cells**, which we are required to add:

1. Select **Table View** in the Outline view, and then Connections inspector in the Utilities Panel.

2. Click on and drag from `dataSource` to the **Location View Controller** in the Outline view:

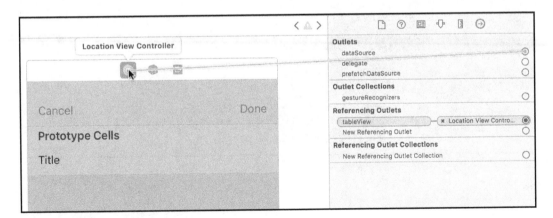

3. Repeat with the `delegate` property:

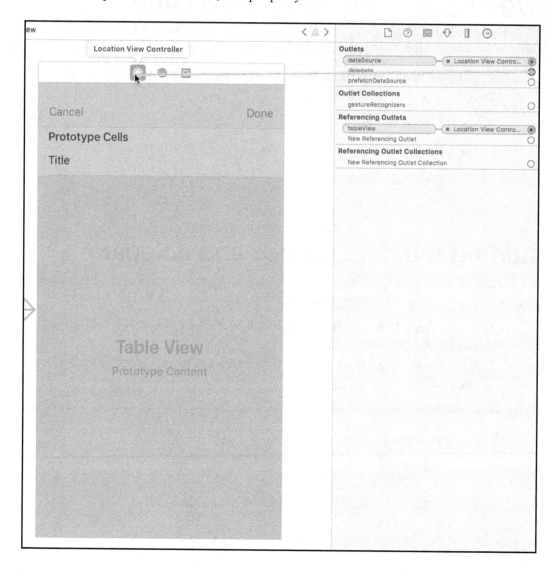

4. Now, select the Table View and then in the Utilities Panel, select the Attributes inspector, if not already selected, and make sure you have the following values:

- **Style**: `Basic`
- **Identifier**: `locationCell` (named for you)
- **Selection**: `Gray`
- **Accessory**: `Disclosure indicator`

Next, for us to display anything in `Tableview`, we need to add the `UITableViewDataSource` protocol. Our protocol requires that we implement the following three methods. Add the following after the closing curly brace of `viewDidLoad()`:

```
import UIKit

class LocationViewController: UIViewController, UITableViewDataSource {

    @IBOutlet weak var tableView:UITableView!


 A  func tableView(_ tableView: UITableView, numberOfRowsInSection section: Int) -> Int {
        return 15
    }       B
 C  func numberOfSections(in tableView: UITableView) -> Int {
        return 1
    }       D
 E  func tableView(_ tableView: UITableView, cellForRowAt indexPath: IndexPath) -> UITableViewCell {
        let cell = tableView.dequeueReusableCell(withIdentifier: "locationCell", for: indexPath) as UITableViewCell   F
        cell.textLabel?.text = "A cell"

        return cell
    }       G
}
```

Let's break down the code to understand what we are doing:

- **Part A**: This method tells our Table View how many rows we want to display:

    ```
    tableView(_:numberOfRowsInSection:)
    ```

- **Part B**: Here, we tell our Table View that we want to display 15 rows:

  ```
  return 15
  ```

- **Part C**: This method tells our Table View how many sections we want to display. Sections in Table Views are typically used as headers, but they can be used however you choose:

  ```
  numberOfSections(in:)
  ```

- **Part D**: We tell our Table View that we only want one section:

  ```
  return 1
  ```

- **Part E**: Our third and final method gets called for every item we need. Therefore, in our case, it gets called 15 times:

  ```
  tableView(_:cellForRowAt:)
  ```

- **Part F**: Here, we create a cell every time *Part E* is called, either by taking one from the queue, if available, or by creating a new cell. The identifier, locationCell, is the name we gave it in the storyboard. Therefore, we are telling our Table View that we want to use this cell. If we had multiple Table Views, we would reference the identifier for the row and section in which we want the cell to display:

  ```
  let cell = tableView.dequeueReusableCell(withIdentifier:
  "locationCell", for: indexPath) as UITableViewCell
  cell.textLabel?.text = "A cell"
  ```

  Since we do not have any data yet, we set our label to A cell. The textLabel variable is the default label we got when we selected a basic cell.

- **Part G**: Finally, after each time we create a new cell, we give the cell back to the Table View to display that cell:

  ```
  return cell
  ```

Let's build and run the project by hitting the Play button (or using *command + R*) to see what happens. You should now see A cell repeating 15 times:

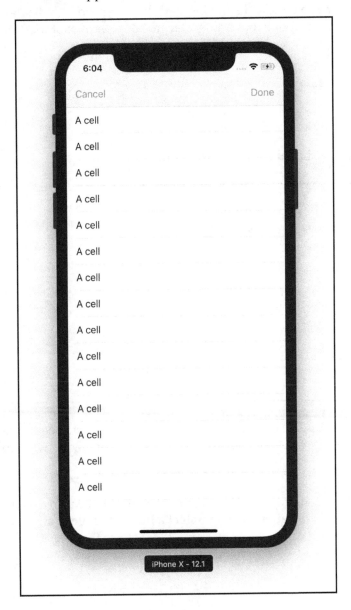

Adding locations to our Table View

We now have our Table View displaying data, but we need it to display a list of actual locations. Let's update our Table View to show our list of locations:

1. Directly under the `tableView` variable, add the following:

    ```
    let locations = ["Aspen", "Boston", "Charleston", "Chicago",
    "Houston", "Las Vegas", "Los Angeles", "Miami", "New Orleans",
    "New York", "Philadelphia", "Portland", "San Antonio", "San
    Francisco", "Washington District of Columbia"]
    ```

2. Your file should now look like mine:

```swift
import UIKit

class LocationViewController: UIViewController, UITableViewDataSource {

    @IBOutlet weak var tableView:UITableView!

    let locations = ["Aspen", "Boston", "Charleston", "Chicago", "Houston", "Las Vegas", "Los Angeles", "Miami", "New Orleans",
        "New York", "Philadelphia", "Portland", "San Antonio", "San Francisco", "Washington District of Columbia"]

    func tableView(_ tableView: UITableView, numberOfRowsInSection section: Int) -> Int {
        return 15
    }

    func numberOfSections(in tableView: UITableView) -> Int {
        return 1
    }

    func tableView(_ tableView: UITableView, cellForRowAt indexPath: IndexPath) -> UITableViewCell {
        let cell = tableView.dequeueReusableCell(withIdentifier: "locationCell", for: indexPath) as UITableViewCell
        cell.textLabel?.text = "A cell"

        return cell
    }
}
```

3. Next, to update our cell to display the locations, we need to replace the `cell.textLabel?.text = "A cell"` line with the following:

    ```
    cell.textLabel?.text = locations[indexPath.item]
    ```

Let's build and run the project by hitting the Play button (or using *command + R*). You should see the following after clicking **Select a location in your simulator**:

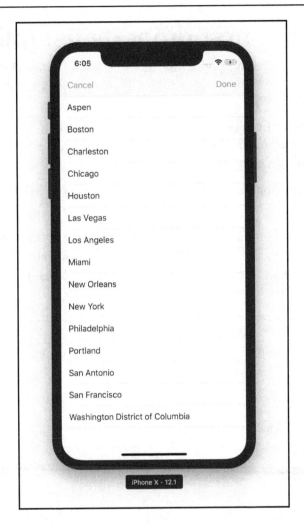

However, there are a couple of problems. If we add another location to the array, it crashes because we are manually setting the number of rows. Also, we are just loading this list from an array we built in the app. If we decide to add more locations, we would have to update our cell number count as well as our list of locations. Therefore, we should instead pull our locations from a plist, as we did in the last chapter. Plists provide a place where we can quickly add or remove a location from our list.

Creating our first property list (plist)

In the last chapter, we used a provided plist to load our cuisine list. We will do the same in this chapter, but now that you are familiar with what a plist is, we will create one from scratch together.

I use plists all the time, from creating menus to having a file that holds app settings such as colors or social media URLs. I find them very useful, especially if I need to come back later and update or change things.

Let's learn how to create a plist from scratch. To create a plist in Xcode, do the following:

1. Right-click on the `Locations` folder and create a **New Group** called `Model`. Then, right-click on this folder and select **New File**.

2. Under **Choose a template for your new file**, select **iOS** at the top, and then type **Property** in the filter field:

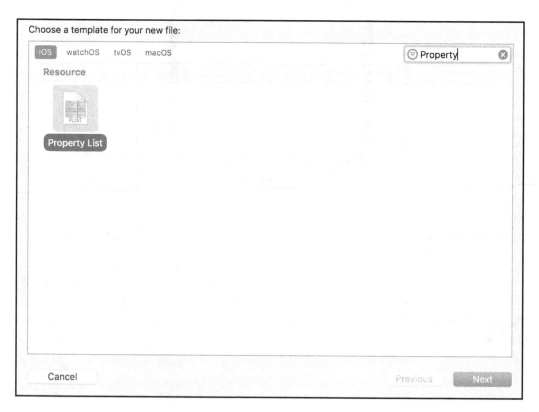

3. Select **Property List** and then hit **Next**.
4. Name the file **Locations** and hit **Create**.

You should now have a file that looks like mine:

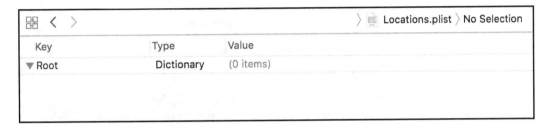

Adding data to our property list

As you learned in the previous chapter, our plist has a **Root**; for this new file, we created a **Dictionary** as our **Root** type. Since we are going to display a list of locations, we need our **Root** to be an **Array**:

1. Click on **Dictionary** in the plist and change it to **Array**:

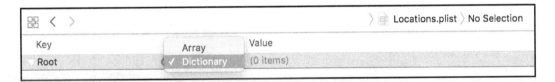

2. You should see a plus next to **Array** (if the plus button is not displaying, hover your mouse over that line item, and it will appear):

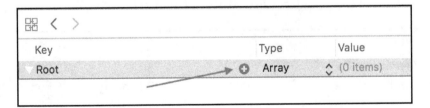

3. Click on the plus button, and it will add a new item with a String type. Change the type to **Dictionary**:

Key	Type	Value
▼ Root	Array	(1 item)
▼ Item 0	Dictionary	(0 items)

4. Click on the plus button that appears when you hover over **Item 0**.
5. We now need to update the **New Item.** Update the **Key** property to say state and update the **Value** property of the new item by entering **CO**:

Key	Type	Value
▼ Root	Array	(1 item)
▼ Item 0	Dictionary	(1 item)
state	String	CO

6. Next, click on the plus button when you hover over the state.
7. Update the **Key** property to say **city** and update the **Value** property of the new item by entering **Aspen**:

Key	Type	Value
▼ Root	Array	(1 item)
▼ Item 0	Dictionary	(2 items)
state	String	CO
city	String	Aspen

8. Next, click on the disclosure arrow for **Item 0** to close it:

Key	Type	Value
▼ Root	Array	(1 item)
▶ Item 0	Dictionary	(2 items)

9. Select **Item 0** and then hit *command* + C to copy and then *command* + V to paste:

Key	Type	Value
▼ Root	Array	(2 items)
▶ Item 0	Dictionary	(2 items)
▶ Item 1	Dictionary	(2 items)

10. Next, open up **Item 1** and update the **city** to **Boston** and the **state** to **MA**:

Key	Type	Value
▼ Root	Array	(14 items)
▼ Item 0	Dictionary	(2 items)
city	String	Aspen
state	String	CO
▼ Item 1	Dictionary	(2 items)
city	String	Boston
state	String	MA

11. Continue with the same process by adding the following cities and states:

Key	Type	City	State
Item 2	String	Charleston	NC
Item 3	String	Chicago	IL
Item 4	String	Houston	TX
Item 5	String	Las Vegas	NV
Item 6	String	Los Angeles	CA
Item 7	String	Miami	FL
Item 8	String	New Orleans	LA
Item 9	String	New York	NY
Item 10	String	Philadelphia	PA
Item 11	String	Portland	OR
Item 12	String	San Antonio	TX
Item 13	String	San Francisco	CA

When you are done, your file should look like mine:

Key	Type	Value
▼ Root	Array	(14 items)
▼ Item 0	Dictionary	(2 items)
city	String	Aspen
state	String	CO
▼ Item 1	Dictionary	(2 items)
city	String	Boston
state	String	MA
▼ Item 2	Dictionary	(2 items)
city	String	Charleston
state	String	NC
▼ Item 3	Dictionary	(2 items)
city	String	Chicago
state	String	IL
▼ Item 4	Dictionary	(2 items)
city	String	Houston
state	String	TX
▼ Item 5	Dictionary	(2 items)
city	String	Las Vegas
state	String	NV
▼ Item 6	Dictionary	(2 items)
city	String	Los Angeles
state	String	CA
▼ Item 7	Dictionary	(2 items)
city	String	Miami
state	String	FL
▼ Item 8	Dictionary	(2 items)
city	String	New Orleans
state	String	LA
▼ Item 9	Dictionary	(2 items)
city	String	New York
state	String	NY
▼ Item 10	Dictionary	(2 items)
city	String	Philadelphia
state	String	PA
▼ Item 11	Dictionary	(2 items)
city	String	Portland
state	String	OR
▼ Item 12	Dictionary	(2 items)
city	String	San Antonio
state	String	TX
▼ Item 13	Dictionary	(2 items)
city	String	San Francisco
state	String	CA

We just set up our data source. We now need to create a data manager similar to the one that we made in the previous chapter.

Creating our location data manager

Let's create the `LocationDataManager` file:

1. Right-click on the `Model` folder in the `Location` folder and select **New File**.
2. Under **Choose a template for your new file**, select **iOS** at the top, and then **Swift File**. Then, hit **Next**.
3. Name this file `LocationDataManager`, and then hit **Create**.
4. We need to define our class definition now, so add the following under the `import` statement:

```
class LocationDataManager {
}
```

5. Inside the class declaration, add the following variable to keep our array private, as there is no reason to have to access this outside the class:

```
private var locations:[String] = []
```

6. Now, let's add the following methods after our variable:

```
init() {
    fetch()
}

func fetch() {
    for location in loadData() {
        if let city = location["city"] as? String,
            let state = location["state"] as? String {
            locations.append("\(city), \(state)")
        }
    }
}

func numberOfItems() -> Int {
    return locations.count
}

func locationItem(at index:IndexPath) -> String {
    return locations[index.item]
```

```
    }

    private func loadData() -> [[String: AnyObject]] {
        guard let path = Bundle.main.path(forResource:
"Locations", ofType: "plist"), let items =
NSArray(contentsOfFile: path) else {
            return [[:]]
        }
        return items as! [[String : AnyObject]]
    }
}
```

These methods are the same as we had in `ExploreDataManager`, except that we are getting back an array of dictionary objects from our plist.

Working with our data manager

We now need to update our `LocationViewController`.

First, because we do not need it anymore, delete the following array that we created in the class:

```
let locations = ["Aspen", "Boston", "Charleston", "Chicago",
"Houston", "Las Vegas", "Los Angeles", "Miami", "New Orleans", "New
York", "Philadelphia", "Portland", "San Antonio", "San Francisco",
"Washington District of Columbia"]
```

Next, since we need to create an instance of our data manager in this class, add the following above `viewDidLoad()`:

```
let manager = LocationDataManager()
```

Inside `viewDidLoad()`, we want to fetch the data for the Table View, so add the following under `super.viewDidLoad()`:

```
manager.fetch()
```

Now, your `viewDidLoad()` should look like the following:

```
override func viewDidLoad()  {
    super.viewDidLoad()
    manager.fetch()
}
```

For the `numberOfRowsInSection()` method, instead of 15, we will use the following:

```
manager.numberOfItems()
```

Lastly, we need to update our `cellForRowAt`. Replace `cell.textLabel?.text = arrLocations[indexPath.item]` with the following:

```
cell.textLabel?.text = manager.locationItem(at:indexPath)
```

Your `cellForRowAt` should now look like this:

```
func tableView(_ tableView: UITableView, cellForRowAt indexPath:
IndexPath) -> UITableViewCell {
    let cell = tableView.dequeueReusableCell(withIdentifier:
"locationCell", for: indexPath) as UITableViewCell
    cell.textLabel?.text = manager.locationItem(at:indexPath)
    return cell
}
```

Let's build and run the project by hitting the Play button (or using *command* + R). We should still see our locations, but now they are coming from our plist.

Summary

In this chapter, we worked with a Table View that has dynamic cells, which allows the Table View to change based on the data. We looked at plists once more, learning how to create them from scratch, as well as how to add data to them. Finally, we created our locations data manager, which is responsible for giving data to the View Controller.

In the next chapter, we will work with a Table View that has static cells to build out our restaurant detail. Static cells are excellent for forms or detail views. We could build out the restaurant detail using a Collection View; however, a static Table View will work well and will be less complicated.

At this point, before moving on to the next chapter, you may want to download the starter project for this chapter and try to do it again without using the book as your guide. Going back helps solidify your understanding of what you have learned.

14
Where Are We?

We have all used a map at some point in our lives, be it an actual map or a map on our phone or other device. Apple Maps has come a long way from when it was first announced in 2012. Apple has made steady improvements to Apple Maps every year.

During this chapter, we will display our restaurant list using a map and custom pins. When users tap a pin on the map, they will be taken directly to the restaurant detail page that we created in the last chapter.

In this chapter, we will cover the following topics:

- What annotations are and how to add them to a map
- How to create custom annotations
- How to create a storyboard reference
- What extensions are and how to use them to clean up your code

Setting up map annotations

In our map, we are going to drop pins down at each restaurant location. These pins are called annotations, more specifically, `MKAnnotation`. MK stands for MapKit and is part of the MapKit framework. Since we are going to create multiple `MKAnnotation` protocols, we are going to create a class that conforms to `MKAnnotation`.

What is an MKAnnotation?

`MKAnnotation` is a protocol that provides us with information related to a map view. Protocols provide a blueprint for methods, properties, and other required functionalities. `MKAnnotation` will contain information, such as the coordinates (latitude and longitude), title, and subtitle of the annotation.

To drop a pin onto a map, we must subclass `MKAnnotation`. When we first looked at classes versus structs, we saw that classes could subclass or inherit from other classes, which means that we can get properties, methods, and additional requirements from the one that we are subclassing. Let's create an annotation that subclasses `MKAnnotation` and see how this works.

Creating a restaurant annotation

Before we jump into creating our file, we should first look at the data that we will be using. The data for the map view will be the same data that we use for our restaurant-listing page. Let's take a look at what the restaurant data will look like in plist format:

Key	Type	Value
▼ Root	Array	(5 items)
▼ Item 0	Dictionary	(16 items)
address	String	108 West 2nd Street #104
area	String	Los Angeles / Orange County
city	String	Los Angeles
▶ cuisines	Array	(2 items)
country	String	US
id	Number	104.173
image_url	String	https://www.opentable.com/img/restimages/104173.jpg
lat	Number	34.051061
long	Number	-118.244705
mobile_reserve_url	String	http://mobile.opentable.com/opentable/?restId=104173
name	String	Badmaash
phone	String	2132217466x
postal_code	String	90012
price	Number	2
reserve_url	String	http://www.opentable.com/single.aspx?rid=104173
state	String	CA
▶ Item 1	Dictionary	(16 items)
▶ Item 2	Dictionary	(16 items)
▶ Item 3	Dictionary	(16 items)
▶ Item 4	Dictionary	(16 items)

We need to create a file to represent this data for the map view, which will differ from the restaurant-listing page because we need to subclass `MKAnnotation`. Let's get started by creating this file now:

1. Right-click on the `Map` folder and create a new group called Model. Then, right-click this folder and select **New File**.
2. In the **Choose a template for your new file** screen, select **iOS** at the top and then **Cocoa Touch Class**. Then, hit **Next**.

3. In the **Options** screen that appears, add the following:

   New file:

   - **Class**: RestaurantItem
   - **Subclass**: NSObject
   - **Also create XIB**: Unchecked
   - **Language**: Swift

4. Click **Next** and then **Create**.
5. In this new RestaurantItem.swift file, under import UIKit, add import MapKit. We need this import statement so that Xcode knows where the files are that we are going to use.
6. Next, we need to update our class declaration to make our annotation. Since this is subclassing MKAnnotation, we need to change what we currently have (class RestaurantItem: NSObject) to the following:

```
class RestaurantItem: NSObject, MKAnnotation
```

You will see an error when you add the MKAnnotation. Just ignore it for now, as we will fix this error shortly.

Inside of the class declaration, add the following:

```
var name:String?
var cuisines:[String] = []
var lat:Double?
var long:Double?
var address:String?
var postalCode:String?
var state:String?
var imageURL:String?
```

When the user taps on the annotation, the name of the restaurant and the types of cuisine will appear, along with a detail icon. This detail icon will take the user to the restaurant detail page. Then, we will pass along all of this data and use it to populate the restaurant detail page we created in the last chapter.

We need to initialize all of the data that's been passed into the object. Therefore, let's create a custom `init()` method to which we can pass a dictionary object through its parameters:

```
class RestaurantItem: NSObject, MKAnnotation {        (O) Type 'RestaurantItem' does not conform to protocol 'MKAnnotation'
    var name: String?
    var cuisines:[String] = []
    var lat: Double?
    var long:Double?                         Ignore this error
    var address:String?
    var postalCode:String?
    var state:String?
    var imageURL:String?

    init(dict:[String:AnyObject]) {
        if let lat = dict["lat"] as? Double { self.lat = lat }
        if let long = dict["long"] as? Double { self.long = long }
        if let name = dict["name"] as? String { self.name = name }
        if let cuisines = dict["cuisines"] as? [String] { self.cuisines = cuisines }
        if let address = dict["address"] as? String { self.address = address }
        if let postalCode = dict["postal_code"] as? String { self.postalCode = postalCode }
        if let state = dict["state"] as? String { self.state = state }
        if let image = dict["image_url"] as? String { self.imageURL = image }
    }
}
```

This method is large, but it is nothing you have not seen before. We are using the `if...let` statement to check for data in each element. If something is missing, it will not be set.

Let's address this error now. The reason we are getting an error is because we are subclassing MKAnnotation and have not yet declared the coordinates, which is a required property. We also have two other optional properties—title and subtitle—that we are using for our map and that we need to declare. What we want to be able to do is pass the data that we have over to these three properties so that we can use them on our map.

To get rid of the error, we need to add the coordinates first. We need to set up the latitude and longitude, so add the following after the init() method:

```
var coordinate: CLLocationCoordinate2D {
  guard let lat = lat, let long = long else { return
CLLocationCoordinate2D() }
  return CLLocationCoordinate2D(latitude: lat, longitude: long )
}
```

`CLLocationCoordinate2D` is a class that is used by `MapKit` to set the exact location of a pin.

Note that we are using curly braces for this property. It is defined in `MKAnnotation`, and we are using the computed property to set the value. For the `coordinate` property, we will pass latitude and longitude to it using `CLLocationCoordinate2D`. In our `init()` method, we created the data that sets the latitude and longitude, and now, we are passing those coordinates over to the `coordinate` property.

Let's do the same with `subtitle` by adding the following above the variable coordinate:

```
var subtitle: String? {
    if cuisines.isEmpty { return "" }
    else if cuisines.count == 1 { return cuisines.first }
    else { return cuisines.joined(separator: ", ") }
}
```

The `subtitle` variable is a computed property, but this time we are using an `else...if` statement. We first check to see whether the array is empty; if so, nothing displays. If we only have one item in the array, we return that item. Finally, if we have multiple elements in our array, we take each item and put them in one string, separating each element with a comma. For example, if your array had the items `["American," "Bistro," "Burgers"]`, then we would create a string that looks like *American, Bistro, Burgers*.

Finally, we need to add the title. Enter the following above the `subtitle` variable:

```
var title: String? {
    return name
}
```

Your file should no longer have an error, and should now look as follows:

```swift
class RestaurantItem: NSObject, MKAnnotation {
    var name: String?
    var cuisines:[String] = []
    var lat: Double?
    var long:Double?
    var address:String?
    var postalCode:String?
    var state:String?
    var imageURL:String?

    init(dict:[String:AnyObject]) {
        if let lat = dict["lat"] as? Double { self.lat = lat }
        if let long = dict["long"] as? Double { self.long = long }
        if let name = dict["name"] as? String { self.name = name }
        if let cuisines = dict["cuisines"] as? [String] { self.cuisines = cuisines }
        if let address = dict["address"] as? String { self.address = address }
        if let postalCode = dict["postal_code"] as? String { self.postalCode = postalCode }
        if let state = dict["state"] as? String { self.state = state }
        if let image = dict["image_url"] as? String { self.imageURL = image }
    }

    var title: String? {
        return name
    }

    var subtitle: String? {
        if cuisines.isEmpty { return "" }
        else if cuisines.count == 1 { return cuisines.first }
        else { return cuisines.joined(separator: ", ") }
    }

    var coordinate: CLLocationCoordinate2D {
        guard let lat = lat, let long = long else { return CLLocationCoordinate2D() }
        return CLLocationCoordinate2D(latitude: lat, longitude: long )
    }
}
```

Next, we want to create a manager that will take our data and create annotations for our map.

Creating our Map Data Manager

In the next chapter, we will deal with data, but for now, we can mock up some data to set up our structure. We will use a plist to load our data, just like we did in the last chapter.

Let's create the `MapDataManager` file now:

1. Right-click on the `Model` folder inside of the `Map` folder and select **New File**.
2. In the **Choose a template for your new file** screen, select **iOS** at the top and then **Swift File**. Then, hit **Next**.
3. Name this file `MapDataManager` and then hit **Create**.
4. Next, we need to define our class definition, so add the following under the `import` statement:

```
class MapDataManager {}
```

5. Inside of the class declaration, add the following variables:

```
fileprivate var items:[RestaurantItem] = []

var annotations:[RestaurantItem] {
    return items
}
```

Note that we are keeping our array private since there is no reason to have to access this outside of the class.

6. Now, let's add the following methods inside of our class declaration, after our variables:

```
func fetch(completion: (_ annotations:[RestaurantItem]) -> ())
{

  if items.count > 0 { items.removeAll() }
        for data in loadData() {
            items.append(RestaurantItem(dict: data))
        }

        completion(items)
}

fileprivate func loadData() -> [[String:AnyObject]] {
        guard let path = Bundle.main.path(forResource:
"MapLocations", ofType: "plist"),
            let items = NSArray(contentsOfFile: path) else {
return [[:]] }
            return items as! [[String : AnyObject]]
}
```

Your file should now look as follows:

```
import Foundation

class MapDataManager {

    fileprivate var items:[RestaurantItem] = []

    var annotations:[RestaurantItem] {
        return items
    }

    func fetch(completion:(_ annotations:[RestaurantItem]) -> ()) {
        if items.count > 0 { items.removeAll() }

        for data in loadData() {
            items.append(RestaurantItem(dict: data))
        }
        completion(items)
    }

    fileprivate func loadData() -> [[String:AnyObject]] {
        guard let path = Bundle.main.path(forResource: "MapLocations", ofType: "plist"),
            let items = NSArray(contentsOfFile: path) else { return [[:]] }

        return items as! [[String: AnyObject]]
    }
}
```

7. The `fetch()` and `loadData()` methods are the same as those that we had in the `ExploreDataManager` file. However, the `fetch()` method here has something new inside of its parameters, specifically the following:

```
completion:(_ annotations:[RestaurantItem]) -> ()
```

The preceding code is called a **closure block**, which allows us to signify when we have completed the method, and it then dictates an action to occur (here, returning an array of annotations). We will use these annotations to load pins on our map. We are looping through the `for...in` loop; when we are done, we call `completion()`. When we get to our `MapViewController`, you will see how we can write this.

Now, let's take a look at our `MapLocations.plist` file:

Key	Type	Value
▼ Root	Array	(5 items)
▶ Item 0	Dictionary	(16 items)
▶ Item 1	Dictionary	(16 items)
▶ Item 2	Dictionary	(16 items)
▶ Item 3	Dictionary	(16 items)
▶ Item 4	Dictionary	(16 items)

This file has the same structure as our `ExploreData.plist` file. Our `Root` is an array, and each item inside of our `Root` is a dictionary item. There is an acronym that many programmers call **don't repeat yourself** (**DRY**). Since both plist files have an array of dictionary objects, we can update our code so that we can use the same method in multiple places.

Creating a base class

To keep us from repeating ourselves, we are going to create a base class. This base class will have a new method called `load(file name:)`, but we will add a parameter to pass the file name. Let's create a `DataManager` file now under our `Common` folder:

1. Right-click on the `Misc` folder and select **New File**.
2. In the **Choose a template for your new file** screen, select **iOS** at the top and then **Swift File**. Then, hit **Next**.
3. Name this file `DataManager`, and then hit **Create**.
4. In this new file, we need to define our class definition; therefore, add the following under the `import` statement:

   ```
   protocol DataManager {}
   ```

5. Inside of the protocol declaration, add the following method:

   ```
   func load(file name:String) -> [[String:AnyObject]]
   ```

6. Now, create an extension under the protocol:

   ```
   extension DataManager {}
   ```

7. Inside of the `extension` declaration, add the following:

   ```
   func load(file name:String) -> [[String:AnyObject]] {
       guard let path = Bundle.main.path(forResource: name,
   ofType: "plist"),  let items = NSArray(contentsOfFile: path)
   else { return [[:]] }
      return items as! [[String : AnyObject]]
   }
   ```

8. When you are done, your file should look like mine:

```
import Foundation

protocol DataManager {
    func load(file name:String) -> [[String:AnyObject]]
}

extension DataManager {
    func load(file name:String) -> [[String:AnyObject]] {
        guard let path = Bundle.main.path(forResource: name, ofType: "plist"),
            let items = NSArray(contentsOfFile: path) else { return [[:]] }

        return items as! [[String : AnyObject]]
    }
}
```

Other than changing the function name to include parameters, we created the same function as we have in our `Explore` and `Map Data Manager` files. However, this function here is no longer a `private` method, because we want it to be accessible to any class that wants to use it.

By creating a protocol, we are using what is known as protocol-oriented programming. We will not get too heavily into the detail of this since there are plenty of books and videos on this topic. The central concept that you will want to understand is that we can use this in any class we want and have access to the `load(name:)` method.

The preceding method is all we need to do in this file.

Refactoring code

Now that we have created this new protocol, we can access it from anywhere we need it. First, let's update our `MapDataManger` class to use our newly created protocol:

1. Delete the `loadData()` function, because we will not need it anymore. You will see an error after you delete the `loadData()` method. This error is happening because we need to give the `fetch()` method a filename to load whenever we call the `loadData()` method. We will fix this shortly.

2. Next, we need to update our class declaration to say the following:

   ```
   class MapDataManager: DataManager
   ```

3. We now have our `MapDataManager` class using our
   `DataManager` protocol, which means that we will use the `load(name:)`
   method from our `DataManager` inside of our `MapDataManager`.

4. Now, let's fix the error by updating our `fetch()` method from our data in
   `loadData()` to the following:

```
for data in load(file: "MapLocations")
```

Your updated file should now look like the following:

```swift
import UIKit
import MapKit

class MapDataManager: DataManager {

    fileprivate var items:[RestaurantItem] = []

    var annotations:[RestaurantItem] {
        return items
    }

    func fetch(completion:(_ annotations:[RestaurantItem]) -> ()) {
        if items.count > 0 { items.removeAll() }

        for data in load(file: "MapLocations") {
            items.append(RestaurantItem(dict: data))
        }

        completion(items)
    }

    func currentRegion(latDelta:CLLocationDegrees, longDelta:CLLocationDegrees) ->
        MKCoordinateRegion {
        guard let item = items.first else { return MKCoordinateRegion() }
        let span = MKCoordinateSpan(latitudeDelta: latDelta, longitudeDelta: longDelta)

        return MKCoordinateRegion(center: item.coordinate, span: span)
    }
}
```

We removed the error in our `MapDataManager`, but we need to do some refactoring
of our `ExploreDataManager` file to do the same.

Refactoring ExploreDataManager

Because our `loadData()` was written the same in both the `ExploreDataManager` and `MapDataManager` files, we need to update our `ExploreDataManager` in the same way that we just did for the `MapDataManager`. Open `ExploreDataManager` and do the following:

1. Delete the private `loadData()` function, because we will not need it anymore. Again, ignore the error, as we are going to fix this shortly.

2. Next, update our class declaration to now say the following:

   ```
   class ExploreDataManager: DataManager
   ```

3. Now, let's fix the error by updating our `fetch()` method from the data in `loadData()` to the following:

   ```
   for data in load(file: "ExploreData")
   ```

4. Your updated function should now look like the following:

   ```
   func fetch() {
       for data in load(file: "ExploreData") {
           items.append(ExploreItem(dict: data))
       }
   }
   ```

We have completed our files, and we can now use the same method any time we need to load a plist that has an array of dictionary items.

Refactoring is something you will become more comfortable with the more you write code. Understanding when to refactor is a bit harder when you first start out because you are still learning. The most prominent indicator that you need to refactor is when you have written something more than once. However, refactoring does not always work for everything; at times, writing the same code more than once can be unavoidable. Just being aware of when refactoring may be useful is a good sign and half the battle to a greater understanding of this method. I have been coding for years; there will be times when I copy and paste something I wrote to see if it works and then never refactor. Then, months later, I will wonder why I did not write a method to handle it in both places.

Creating and adding annotations

Now, we need to get our map hooked up and get the annotations displayed on the map. Then, we will customize our annotations to look like those in our design.

Creating our Map View Controller

We need to create our `MapViewController` file and then connect it with our `UIViewController` and map view in the storyboard. First, let's create this file:

1. In the Navigator panel, right-click on the `Controller` folder in the `Map` folder and select **New File**.
2. In the **Choose a template for your new file** screen, select **iOS** at the top and then **Cocoa Touch Class**. Then, hit **Next**.
3. Add the following to the **Options** screen that appears:

   New file:

   - **Class**: `MapViewController`
   - **Subclass**: `UIViewController`
   - **Also create XIB**: Unchecked
   - **Language**: `Swift`

4. Click **Next** and then **Create**.
5. Under the `import UIKit` statement, add `import MapKit`.
6. Update your class declaration to include the following protocol:

   ```
   class MapViewController: UIViewController, MKMapViewDelegate
   ```

Now, let's connect this file with our `UIViewController` and our map view in the storyboard:

1. Add the following after the class declaration:

   ```
   @IBOutlet var mapView: MKMapView!
   ```

2. Open your `Map.storyboard` file.
3. In the Outline view, select the View Controller that contains the map view.
4. Now, in the Utilities panel, select the Identity inspector.

5. Under **Custom Class**, in the **Class** drop-down menu, select `MapViewController` and hit *enter* to connect the View Controller to the class.

6. Now, select the Connections inspector.

7. Under the Outlets section, you will see an empty circle next to `mapView`. Click and drag the outlet to the map view in the View Controller in the Outline view.

We are going to start working with our map, but first, we need to add some things to our `MapDataManager`:

1. Open the `MapDataManager.swift` file in the Navigator panel. Underneath the `import Foundation` statement, add `import MapKit`.

2. Next, add the following method to our `MapDataManager`:

```
func currentRegion(latDelta:CLLocationDegrees,
longDelta:CLLocationDegrees) -> MKCoordinateRegion {
    guard let item = items.first else { return
MKCoordinateRegion() }
    let span = MKCoordinateSpanMake(latDelta, longDelta)
    return MKCoordinateRegion(center:item.coordinate, span:span)
}
```

Before we delve into the particular sections of this function, we need to understand what this function does. When you use a map and drop pins down onto it, you want the map to zoom in to a particular area. To zoom in on a map, you need latitude and longitude. What this method is doing is grabbing the first pin (or annotation) in the array and zooming in on the area:

```
                                A
func currentRegion(latDelta:CLLocationDegrees, longDelta:CLLocationDegrees) -> MKCoordinateRegion {
    guard let item = items.first else { return MKCoordinateRegion() }      B
    let span = MKCoordinateSpanMake(latDelta, longDelta)        C

    return MKCoordinateRegion(center: item.coordinate, span: span)      D
}
```

Let's break down the code:

- **Part A**: Our method has two parameters, both of which are
  CLLocationDegrees. It is just a class that represents a latitude or
  longitude coordinate in degrees:

  ```
  func currentRegion(latDelta:CLLocationDegrees,
  longDelta:CLLocationDegrees) -> MKCoordinateRegion {
  ```

- **Part B**: This guard statement obtains the first item in the array. If there are
  no items in the array, it will just return an empty coordinate region. If there
  are items in the array, it will return the coordinate region:

  ```
  guard let item = items.first else { return
  MKCoordinateRegion() }
  ```

- **Part C**: Here, we are creating an MKCoordinate with the latitude and
  longitude that we passed into the function. MKCoordinateSpan defines a
  span, in the latitude and longitude directions, to show on the map:

  ```
  let span = MKCoordinateSpanMake(latDelta, longDelta)
  ```

- **Part D**: Lastly, we are setting the center and the span of our region and
  returning them so that when the pins drop, the map can zoom in on the
  area:

  ```
  return MKCoordinateRegion(center: item.coordinate, span: span)
  ```

Now, let's set up our MapViewController to display annotations:

1. Open the MapViewController.swift file in the Navigator panel and
   delete both didReceiveMemoryWarning() and prepare() (which has
   been commented out), as we do not need them for our purposes.
2. Directly under our IBOutlet statement, add the following:

   ```
   let manager = MapDataManager()
   ```

3. Then, inside of the class definition, add the following method after
   viewDidLoad():

   ```
   func addMap(_ annotations:[RestaurantItem]) {
       mapView.setRegion(manager.currentRegion(latDelta: 0.5,
   longDelta: 0.5), animated: true)
       mapView.addAnnotations(manager.annotations)
   }
   ```

In this method, we are doing a couple of things. First, we pass annotations through the parameter. When we call `fetch()` and it is completed, it will return the array of annotations. We will pass that array over to `addMap(_ annotations:)` to use. Next, we set the region by obtaining it from our `MapDataManager`, thus setting the latitude and longitude delta. The delta will set our zoom and region for our map. Once we have that, we then pass all of our annotations for the map to display.

Therefore, we need to have our manager fetch the annotations. Add the following method above `addMap(_ annotations:)`:

```
func initialize() {
    manager.fetch { (annotations) in
        addMap(annotations)
    }
}
```

Inside of the `initialize()` method, we are setting the map delegate to the class. In previous chapters, we did this using storyboard; however, you can also do this with code. This line allows us to be notified when the user taps on an annotation or taps the disclosure indicator in the annotation.

Earlier in this chapter, we created a `fetch()` method in the `MapDataManager`, wherein we used a closure block. This closure block requires that we wrap it in curly braces. Once the `completion()` block is called in the manager, everything inside of the curly braces will run. For our purposes in building this app, we are going to have a small number of pins or annotations; therefore, we do not need a completion block. However, if you have 100 or 500 annotations, for instance, a closure block would be more efficient. We will do more with this later so that you can get more practice with closure blocks.

Add `initialize()` inside of `viewDidLoad()` so that everything will run when the view loads.

Before you build, make sure that you add the `MapLocations.plist` file into the `maps` folder. This file is in this book's `assets` folder for this chapter.

Let's build and run the project by hitting the Play button (or use *command + R*):

We now have pins on our map, but we need to update them so that they look more like the ones in our design. Let's learn how to customize the annotations on our map.

Creating custom annotations

If you have ever owned an iPhone and used Apple Maps, you will be familiar with pins. When you have a map inside of your app, having custom pins (annotations) gives your app a bit more polish. Let's create our custom annotations.

Open up `MapViewController` in the Navigator Panel, then inside of the `initialize()` method, add the following:

```
mapView.delegate = self
```

Next, add the following directly under the `addMap(_ annotations:)` method:

```swift
func mapView(_ mapView:MKMapView, viewFor annotation:MKAnnotation) ->
MKAnnotationView? {
    let identifier = "custompin"
    guard !annotation.isKind(of: MKUserLocation.self) else { return
nil }
    var annotationView: MKAnnotationView?
    if let customAnnotationView =
mapView.dequeueReusableAnnotationView(withIdentifier: identifier) {
        annotationView = customAnnotationView
        annotationView?.annotation = annotation
    } else {
        let av = MKAnnotationView(annotation: annotation,
reuseIdentifier: identifier)
        av.rightCalloutAccessoryView = UIButton(type:
.detailDisclosure)
        annotationView = av
    }

    if let annotationView = annotationView {
        annotationView.canShowCallout = true
        annotationView.image = UIImage(named: "custom-annotation")
    }

    return annotationView
}
```

Let's break down this code so we can understand what we are doing. We will break the function down into the following sections:

```
func mapView(_ mapView: MKMapView, viewFor annotation: MKAnnotation) -> MKAnnotationView? {
    let identifier = "custompin"

    guard !annotation.isKind(of: MKUserLocation.self) else {
        return nil
    }

    var annotationView:MKAnnotationView?

    if let customAnnotationView = mapView.dequeueReusableAnnotationView(withIdentifier:
        identifier) {
        annotationView = customAnnotationView
        annotationView?.annotation = annotation
    }
    else {
        let av = MKAnnotationView(annotation: annotation, reuseIdentifier: identifier)
        av.rightCalloutAccessoryView = UIButton(type: .detailDisclosure)
        annotationView = av
    }

    if let annotationView = annotationView {
        annotationView.canShowCallout = true
        annotationView.image = UIImage(named: "custom-annotation")
    }

    return annotationView
}
```

Let's start with A:

- **Part A**: This method will be called on the `mapView.delegate` we set up earlier when annotations need to be placed. We will use this method to grab the annotations before they are placed and replace the default pins with custom pins:

    ```
    mapView(_:viewFor:)
    ```

- **Part B**: Here, we set an identifier, similar to those that we set when using Collection Views and Table Views:

    ```
    let identifier = "custompin"
    ```

- **Part C**: This guard will ensure that our annotation is not the user location. If the annotation is the user location, the `guard` will return `nil`. Otherwise, it will move on through the method:

    ```
    guard !annotation.isKind(of: MKUserLocation.self) else {
        return nil
    }
    ```

- **Part D**: MKAnnotationView is the class name for the pin; here, we create a variable that we can use to set our custom image:

```
var annotationView:MKAnnotationView?
```

- **Part E**: In this statement, we are checking to see whether there are any annotations that have already been created that we can reuse. If so, we point them to the variable we added previously. Otherwise, we create the annotation in the next else statement:

```
if let customAnnotationView =
mapView.dequeueReusableAnnotationView(withIdentifier:
identifier) {
    annotationView = customAnnotationView
    annotationView?.annotation = annotation
}
```

- **Part F**: If there are no annotations to reuse, we create a new MKAnnotationView and give it a callout with a button. A callout is a bubble that appears above the annotation when you tap it to display the title (restaurant name) and subtitle (cuisines) associated with that annotation. If the user selects this callout button, the user is taken to the restaurant detail view:

```
else {
    let av = MKAnnotationView(annotation: annotation,
reuseIdentifier: identifier)
    av.rightCalloutAccessoryView = UIButton(type:
.detailDisclosure)
                annotationView = av
}
```

- **Part G**: Here is where we make sure that our custom annotation will show a callout. We can also set our custom image for our annotation:

```
if let annotationView = annotationView {
    annotationView.canShowCallout = true
    annotationView.image = UIImage(named: "custom-annotation")
}
```

- **Part H**: Once we are finished going through the method, we return our custom annotation to the map. This method is called for every annotation that appears on the map:

```
return annotationView
```

Let's build and run the project by hitting the Play button (or use *command + R*):

We now have custom annotations displaying on our map. Each pin's callout shows the restaurant name as well as the cuisines for the restaurant associated with that particular pin. If you tap on the callout, the restaurant detail disclosure does not yet work. Let's set that up now.

Map to restaurant detail

For us to go to the restaurant detail from the callout, we need to update our app so that our map can also open the restaurant detail. To do this, we must first create a storyboard reference. The project has a few storyboard references in the app already, but let's set up one together.

Creating a storyboard reference

To link to the restaurant detail from the map, we need to create a storyboard reference:

1. Open the `Map.storyboard`, and in the object library (*command + shift + L*), drag a **Storyboard Reference** into the `Map.storyboard` scene:

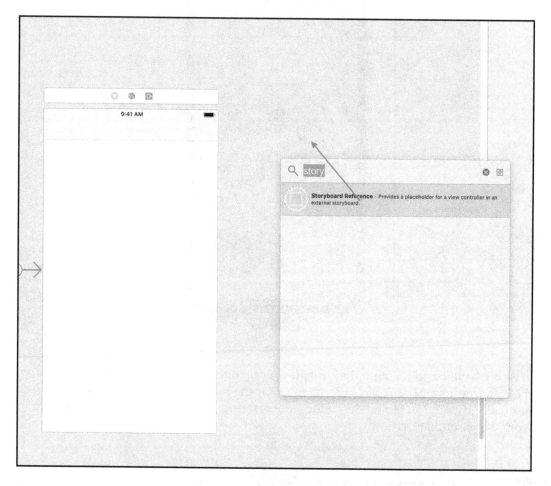

2. Next, select the Attributes inspector in the Utilities Panel, and update the storyboard under **Storyboard Reference** to say `RestaurantDetail`. Then, hit *enter*:

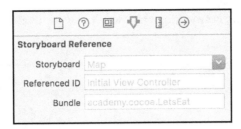

3. Click on *control* and drag from the Map View controller to the storyboard reference we just created and select **Show** on the screen that appears. Note that you can *control* and drag from either the Map View controller in the Outline view or the Map View controller icon in the scene, as shown in the following screenshot:

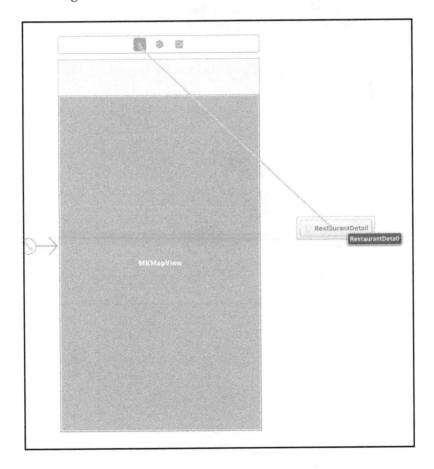

4. Select the segue connecting the Map View controller to the storyboard reference:

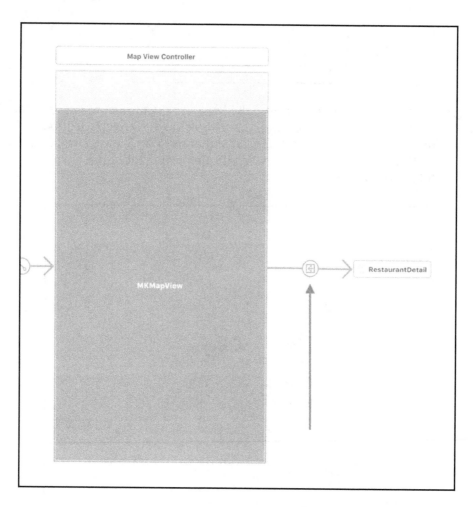

5. In the Attributes inspector, update the **Identifier** under **Storyboard Segue** to say `showDetail`. Then, hit *enter*:

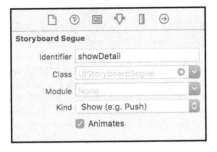

This identifier is what we are going to call whenever the restaurant detail disclosure is tapped. Let's connect our segue next.

Map to restaurant detail

Before we connect our segue, we should create an enumeration (an `enum`, for short) to keep track of our segues. An `enum` is a user-defined data type that consists of a set of related values:

1. Right-click on the `Misc` folder inside the `Common` folder and select **New File**.
2. In the **Choose a template for your new file** screen, select **iOS** at the top and then **Swift File**. Then, hit **Next**.
3. Name this file `Segue` and hit **Create**.
4. Under `import Foundation` in the new file, add the following:

```
enum Segue:String {
    case showDetail
    case showRating
    case showReview
    case ShowAllReviews
    case restaurantList
    case locationList
    case showPhotoReview
    case showPhotoFilter
}
```

We will eventually need all of these segues. Instead of coming back into this file, we will add them all now. Whenever we use a new one, I will refer back to this file. The next thing we need to know is when the user taps the detail disclosure of the callout.

In the `MapViewController.swift` file, add the following delegate implementation under the `addMap(_ annotations:)` method:

```
func mapView(_ mapView: MKMapView, annotationView view:
MKAnnotationView, calloutAccessoryControlTapped control: UIControl) {
    self.performSegue(withIdentifier: Segue.showDetail.rawValue,
sender: self)
}
```

We are using `performSegue()` to call our custom segue. Now, when you tap the annotation and then the callout, you will go to the restaurant-detail view:

```
        mapView.delegate = self

        manager.fetch { (annotations) in
            addMap(annotations)
        }
    }

func addMap( annotations:[RestaurantAnnotation]) {
    mapView.setRegion(manager.currentRegion(latDelta: 0.5, longDelta: 0.5), animated: true)
    mapView.addAnnotations(annotations)
}

func mapView(_ mapView: MKMapView, annotationView view: MKAnnotationView,
    calloutAccessoryControlTapped control: UIControl) {
    self.performSegue(withIdentifier: Segue.showDetail.rawValue, sender: self)
}

func mapView(_ mapView: MKMapView, viewFor annotation: MKAnnotation) -> MKAnnotationView? {
    let identifier = "custompin"

    guard !annotation.isKind(of: MKUserLocation.self) else {
        return nil
    }

    var annotationView:MKAnnotationView?
```

Let's build and run the project by hitting the Play button (or use *command + R*). We can now get to the restaurant detail view from the map.

Passing data to restaurant detail

In the next chapter, we are going to display the data in our restaurant detail. For now, we want to pass the data over to the detail view.

To make this work, we need to update both our `RestaurantDetailViewController` (which we have not created yet) and the `MapViewController`. Let's create the `RestaurantDetailViewController`:

1. Right-click on the new `Restaurant Detail` and select **New File**.
2. In the **Choose a template for your new file** screen, select **iOS** at the top and then **Cocoa Touch Class**. Then, hit **Next**.
3. In the **Options** screen, add the following:

   New file:

   - **Class**: `RestaurantDetailViewController`
   - **Subclass**: `UITableViewController`
   - **Also create XIB**: Unchecked
   - **Language**: `Swift`

6. Click **Next** and then **Create**.
7. Delete everything after the `viewDidLoad()` method, as we do not need all of the other code.

   Your file should now look as follows:

```
//
//   RestaurantDetailViewController.swift
//   LetsEat
//
//   Created by Craig Clayton on 11/15/16.
//   Copyright © 2016 Craig Clayton. All rights reserved.
//

import UIKit

class RestaurantDetailViewController: UITableViewController {

    override func viewDidLoad() {
        super.viewDidLoad()

    }
}
```

8. Next, inside of the class declaration, add the following:

```
var selectedRestaurant:RestaurantItem?
```

9. Then, add the following code inside of `viewDidLoad()`:

```
dump(selectedRestaurant as Any)
```

10. Your file should now look like the following:

```
//
//  RestaurantDetailViewController.swift
//  LetsEat
//
//  Created by Craig Clayton on 11/12/17.
//  Copyright © 2017 Cocoa Academy. All rights reserved.
//

import UIKit

class RestaurantDetailViewController: UITableViewController {

    var selectedRestaurant:RestaurantItem?

    override func viewDidLoad() {
        super.viewDidLoad()
        dump(selectedRestaurant as Any)
    }
}
```

11. Open your `RestaurantDetail.storyboard` file.
12. In the Outline view, select the Table View Controller.
13. In the Utilities panel, select the Identity inspector.
14. Under **Custom Class**, in the **Class** drop-down menu, select `RestaurantDetailViewController` and hit *enter* to connect the View Controller to the class.

    The preceding code is all we need to have in `RestaurantDetailViewController`. Next, we need to update our `MapViewController`.

15. Open the `MapViewController.swift` file.
16. Directly under where we declare our manager, add the following code:

```
var selectedRestaurant:RestaurantItem?
```

17. Then, add the following code into the
    `calloutAccessoryControlTapped()` method above `performSegue`:

    ```
    guard let annotation = mapView.selectedAnnotations.first else
    { return }
    selectedRestaurant = annotation as? RestaurantItem
    ```

Your file should now look as follows:

```
func mapView(_ mapView: MKMapView, annotationView view: MKAnnotationView, calloutAccessoryControlTapped control: UIControl) {
    guard let annotation = mapView.selectedAnnotations.first else { return }     ◄─────────────────
    selectedRestaurant = annotation as? RestaurantItem

    self.performSegue(withIdentifier: Segue.showDetail.rawValue, sender: self)
}
```

18. Next, add the following code after `viewDidLoad()`:

    ```
    override func prepare(for segue: UIStoryboardSegue, sender:
    Any?) {
        switch segue.identifier! {
            case Segue.showDetail.rawValue:
                    showRestaurantDetail(segue: segue)
                default:
                    print("Segue not added")
            }
        }
    ```

You will see an error, but ignore it, as we are going to fix this in the next step.

Whenever we transition with a segue, this method gets called. First, we check for the `showDetail` identifier; if this identifier is called, we want to do something (in this case, get the selected restaurant and pass it to the detail view) before we transition.

Add the following code after the `addMap(_ annotations:)` method:

```
func showRestaurantDetail(segue:UIStoryboardSegue) {
    if let viewController = segue.destination as?
RestaurantDetailViewController, let restaurant = selectedRestaurant  {
        viewController.selectedRestaurant = restaurant
    }
}
```

Here, we are checking to make sure that the segue destination is the
`RestaurantDetailViewController`; if so, we make sure that we have a selected
restaurant. When it is confirmed that the segue destination is the
`RestaurantDetailViewController` and we have a selected restaurant, we use the
`selectedRestaurant` variable that we created in
`RestaurantDetailViewController` and set it to the selected restaurant in
`MapViewController`.

Your file should now look like the following, with the two new methods we just
added:

```
override func viewDidLoad() {
    super.viewDidLoad()

    initialize()
}

override func prepare(for segue: UIStoryboardSegue, sender: Any?) {
    switch segue.identifier! {
    case Segue.showDetail.rawValue:
        showRestaurantDetail(segue: segue)
    default:
        print("Segue not added")
    }
}

func initialize() {
    mapView.delegate = self

    service.fetch { (annotations) in
        addMap(annotations)
    }
}

func addMap(_ annotations:[RestaurantAnnotation]) {
    mapView.setRegion(mapView.currentRegion(latDelta: 0.5, longDelta: 0.5), animated: true)
    mapView.addAnnotations(annotations)
}

func showRestaurantDetail(segue:UIStoryboardSegue) {
    if let viewController = segue.destination as? RestaurantDetailViewController, let restaurant = selectedRestaurant  {
        viewController.selectedRestaurant = restaurant
    }
}
```

Let's build and run the project by hitting the Play button (or using *command* + *R*) and
test whether we can pass data to our `RestaurantDetailViewController`. You
should see the following in your Debug Panel if everything worked:

```
2017-11-12 12:32:42.020113-0500 LetsEat[11094:1811464] Could not inset legal attribution from corner 4
▽ Optional(<LetsEat.RestaurantItem: 0x608000391c60>)
  ▽ some: <LetsEat.RestaurantItem: 0x608000391c60> #0
    - super: NSObject
    ▽ name: Optional("Maria\'s Italian Kitchen - Downtown")
      - some: "Maria\'s Italian Kitchen - Downtown"
    ▽ cuisines: 2 elements
      - "Indian"
      - "Gastropubs"
    ▽ latitude: Optional(34.04934200000001)
      - some: 34.04934200000001
    ▽ longitude: Optional(-118.258174)
      - some: -118.258174
    ▽ address: Optional("615 S. Flower Street")
      - some: "615 S. Flower Street"
    ▽ postalCode: Optional("90017")
      - some: "90017"
    ▽ state: Optional("CA")
      - some: "CA"
    ▽ imageURL: Optional("https://www.opentable.com/img/restimages/19183.jpg")
      - some: "https://www.opentable.com/img/restimages/19183.jpg"
2017-11-12 12:32:45.572309-0500 LetsEat[11094:1811464] [Warning] Warning once only: Detected a case where constraints ambiguously suggest
a height of zero for a tableview cell's content view. We're considering the collapse unintentional and using standard height instead.
```

We now have our `RestaurantDetailViewController`, which is capable of receiving data. In the next chapter, we will display that data. However, before we write any more code, we should organize our code a bit better.

Organizing your code

Earlier, we wrote an extension for our `DataManager`; extensions are useful for adding functionality onto standard libraries, structs, or classes—such as arrays, ints, and strings—or onto your data types.

Here is an example. Let's say that you wanted to know the length of a string:

```
let name = "Craig"
name.characters .count
```

For us to access the count of the string, we would need to access the characters and then get a count.

Let's simplify this by creating an extension:

```
extension String {
    var length: Int {
        return self.characters.count
    }
}
```

With this newly created `String` extension, we can now access the count by writing the following:

```
let name = "Craig"
name.length
```

As you can see, extensions are very powerful by enabling us to add extra functionality without having to change the main class or struct. The `length` property already exists in the `String` class, but I wanted to give you a simplified example of how powerful an extension is and how you can create your own.

Up until now, we have paid very little attention to file structure and more attention to understanding what we are writing. Organizing your code is also very important, which is why we are going to refactor our code. The refactoring will mostly consist of copying and pasting code that you have already written. Extensions can help us organize our code better and stay away from cluttering our View Controllers. Also, we can extend the functionality of View Controllers through extensions. We are going to update four classes: `ExploreViewController`, `RestaurantListViewController`, `LocationViewController`, and `MapViewController`.

Refactoring ExploreViewController

We are going to divide our View Controller into distinct sections using what is known as a `MARK` comment. Let's start with our `ExploreViewController`:

1. In the `ExploreViewController` file, after the last curly brace, hit *enter* a couple of times and add the following code (remember that this should be outside of the class, not inside):

```
// MARK: Private Extension
private extension ExploreViewController {
  // code goes here
}
// MARK: UICollectionViewDataSource
extension ExploreViewController: UICollectionViewDataSource {
  // code goes here
}
```

Here, we are creating two extensions. Our first one will be private and will be where we add any methods that we create that we need for this controller. Our second one is an extension that deals with our `collectionview` data source. Let's keep going for now.

2. We currently have an error because we are using
   `UICollectionViewDataSource` in two places.
   Delete `UICollectionViewDataSource` (including the comma) from the
   class definition at the top of the file:

```
class ExploreViewController: UIViewController, UICollectionViewDataSource {

    @IBOutlet weak var collectionView:UICollectionView!

    let manager = ExploreDataManager()

    override func viewDidLoad() {                                    delete
        super.viewDidLoad()
```

3. Now, let's move all of our `CollectionViewDataSource` methods into our
   extension. You should be moving the following:

```
import UIKit

class ExploreViewController: UIViewController {

    @IBOutlet weak var collectionView:UICollectionView!

    let manager = ExploreDataManager()

    override func viewDidLoad() {
        super.viewDidLoad()

        manager.fetch()
    }

    func collectionView(_ collectionView: UICollectionView, viewForSupplementaryElementOfKind kind: String, at indexPath: IndexPath) -> UICollectionReusableView {
        let headerView = collectionView.dequeueReusableSupplementaryView(ofKind: kind, withReuseIdentifier: "header", for: indexPath)
        return headerView
    }

    func collectionView(_ collectionView: UICollectionView, cellForItemAt indexPath: IndexPath) -> UICollectionViewCell {
        let cell = collectionView.dequeueReusableCell(withReuseIdentifier: "exploreCell", for: indexPath) as! ExploreCell

        let item = manager.explore(at: indexPath)
        if let name = item.name { cell.lblName.text = name }
        if let image = item.image { cell.imgExplore.image = UIImage(named: image) }

        return cell
    }

    func numberOfSections(in collectionView: UICollectionView) -> Int {
        return 1
    }

    func collectionView(_ collectionView: UICollectionView, numberOfItemsInSection section: Int) -> Int {
        return manager.numberOfItems()
    }

    @IBAction func unwindLocationCancel(segue:UIStoryboardSegue) {}
}

// MARK: Private Extension
private extension ExploreViewController {
    // code goes here
}

// MARK: UICollectionViewDataSource
extension ExploreViewController: UICollectionViewDataSource {
    // code goes here    ◄─────────Move all the code marked above to here
}
```

Your file, including the extension, should now look as follows:

```
import UIKit

class ExploreViewController: UIViewController {

    @IBOutlet weak var collectionView:UICollectionView!

    let manager = ExploreDataManager()

    override func viewDidLoad() {
        super.viewDidLoad()

        manager.fetch()
    }


    @IBAction func unwindLocationCancel(segue:UIStoryboardSegue) {}
}
// MARK: Private Extension
private extension ExploreViewController {
    // code goes here
}

// MARK: UICollectionViewDataSource
extension ExploreViewController: UICollectionViewDataSource {
    func collectionView(_ collectionView: UICollectionView, viewForSupplementaryElementOfKind kind: String, at indexPath: IndexPath) -> UICollectionReusableView {
        let headerView = collectionView.dequeueReusableSupplementaryView(ofKind: kind, withReuseIdentifier: "header", for: indexPath)
        return headerView
    }

    func collectionView(_ collectionView: UICollectionView, cellForItemAt indexPath: IndexPath) -> UICollectionViewCell {
        let cell = collectionView.dequeueReusableCell(withReuseIdentifier: "exploreCell", for: indexPath) as! ExploreCell

        let item = manager.explore(at: indexPath)
        if let name = item.name { cell.lblName.text = name }
        if let image = item.image { cell.imgExplore.image = UIImage(named: image) }

        return cell
    }

    func numberOfSections(in collectionView: UICollectionView) -> Int {
        return 1
    }

    func collectionView(_ collectionView: UICollectionView, numberOfItemsInSection section: Int) -> Int {
        return manager.numberOfItems()
    }
}
```

Now, you are probably wondering why we created the `private` extension. Well, one thing that I try to do is keep `viewDidLoad()` as clean as possible. Instead of writing a ton of code inside of `viewDidLoad()`, I like to create an `initialize()` method and call that instead. This way, it's clear to anyone going into my code what I am doing. Let's add the following to our `private` extension:

```
func initialize() {
  manager.fetch()
}
```

```
@IBAction func unwindLocationCancel(segue:UIStoryboardSegue){}
```

Now, we can call `initialize()` inside of `viewDidLoad()`. When you are done, you should see the following:

```
class ExploreViewController: UIViewController {
    @IBOutlet weak var collectionView:UICollectionView!
    let manager = ExploreDataManager()

    override func viewDidLoad() {
```

```
        super.viewDidLoad()
        initialize()
    }
}

// MARK: Private Extension
private extension ExploreViewController {
    func initialize() {
        manager.fetch()
    }

    @IBAction func unwindLocationCancel(segue:UIStoryboardSegue){}
}
```

Now, this might seem like we wrote extra code for nothing, but as your classes grow, you will see the benefit of doing this. Before we clean up the other files, let's look at what the MARK comment does.

Using the MARK comment

Currently, our MARK comment may seem like a useless comment in our code, but it is more powerful than you think. Look at the bottom bar that is located to the right of the Play and Stop buttons in Xcode and look for the last arrow. Mine says No Selection, but if you have your cursor on a method, you might see the following instead:

Click on this last item, and you will see the following:

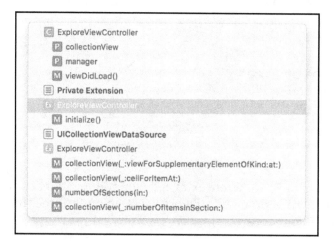

The preceding screenshots show all of your code, divided, just like our file. You can click on any method, and the file will jump right to that method. Even if your file is long and you are looking for a method, you can use this technique to get where you need to be. We are done cleaning up our `ExploreViewController`.

Refactoring RestaurantViewController

We now know our structure, so let's update our `RestaurantListViewController`. Even though we do not currently have anything to put in our `private` extension, we will add it anyway as good practice. As you get more comfortable, only add this when you actually need it:

1. Inside our `RestaurantListViewController`, after the last curly brace, hit *enter* a couple of times and add the following code (remember, this should be outside of the class, not inside):

```
// MARK: Private Extension

private extension RestaurantViewController {}
// MARK: UICollectionViewDataSource

extension RestaurantViewController: UICollectionViewDataSource
{}
```

2. Next, delete the `UICollectionViewDataSource` subclass from the main class.

3. Now, let's move all of our `CollectionViewDataSource` methods into our extension. You should be moving the following:

```swift
import UIKit

class RestaurantViewController: UIViewController, UICollectionViewDataSource {

    @IBOutlet var collectionView:UICollectionView!

    override func viewDidLoad() {
        super.viewDidLoad()
    }

    func collectionView(_ collectionView: UICollectionView, cellForItemAt indexPath: IndexPath) -> UICollectionViewCell {
        return collectionView.dequeueReusableCell(withReuseIdentifier: "restaurantCell", for: indexPath)
    }

    func numberOfSections(in collectionView: UICollectionView) -> Int {
        return 1
    }

    func collectionView(_ collectionView: UICollectionView, numberOfItemsInSection section: Int) -> Int {
        return 10
    }
}

// MARK: Private Extension
private extension RestaurantListViewController {

}

// MARK: UICollectionViewDataSource
extension RestaurantListViewController: UICollectionViewDataSource {          ⟵————— Move all the code marked above to here

}
```

4. Your file, including the extension, should now look as follows:

```swift
import UIKit

class RestaurantViewController: UIViewController {

    @IBOutlet var collectionView:UICollectionView!

    override func viewDidLoad() {
        super.viewDidLoad()
    }
}

// MARK: Private Extension
private extension RestaurantViewController {

}

// MARK: UICollectionViewDataSource
extension RestaurantViewController: UICollectionViewDataSource {
    func collectionView(_ collectionView: UICollectionView, cellForItemAt indexPath: IndexPath) -> UICollectionViewCell {
        return collectionView.dequeueReusableCell(withReuseIdentifier: "restaurantCell", for: indexPath)
    }

    func numberOfSections(in collectionView: UICollectionView) -> Int {
        return 1
    }

    func collectionView(_ collectionView: UICollectionView, numberOfItemsInSection section: Int) -> Int {
        return 10
    }
}
```

We successfully updated our `RestaurantListViewController`.

Next, let's take a look at our `LocationViewController`:

1. Inside of our `LocationViewController`, after the last curly brace, hit *enter* a couple of times and add the following code (remember, this should be outside of the class, not inside):

```swift
// MARK: Private Extension
private extension LocationViewController {}

// MARK: UITableViewDataSource
extension LocationViewController: UITableViewDataSource {}
```

2. Next, remove the `UITableViewDataSource` subclass from the main class.

3. Now, let's move all of our `TableViewDataSource` methods into our extension. You should be moving the following:

```
class LocationViewController: UIViewController {

    @IBOutlet weak var tableView:UITableView!

    let manager = LocationDataManager()

    override func viewDidLoad() {
        super.viewDidLoad()
        manager.fetch()
    }

    func tableView(_ tableView: UITableView, numberOfRowsInSection section: Int) -> Int {
        return manager.numberOfItems()
    }

    func numberOfSections(in tableView: UITableView) -> Int {
        return 1
    }

    func tableView(_ tableView: UITableView, cellForRowAt indexPath: IndexPath) -> UITableViewCell {
        let cell = tableView.dequeueReusableCell(withIdentifier: "locationCell", for: indexPath) as UITableViewCell
        cell.textLabel?.text = manager.locationItem(at:indexPath)

        return cell
    }
}

// MARK: Private Extension
private extension LocationViewController {


}

// MARK: UITableViewDataSource
extension LocationViewController: UITableViewDataSource {
                              ◄─────────────────── Move all the code marked above to here

}
```

Your file, including the extension, should now look as follows:

```
import UIKit

class LocationViewController: UIViewController {

    @IBOutlet weak var tableView:UITableView!

    let manager = LocationDataManager()

    override func viewDidLoad() {
        super.viewDidLoad()
        manager.fetch()
    }
}

// MARK: Private Extension
private extension LocationViewController {


}

// MARK: UITableViewDataSource
extension LocationViewController: UITableViewDataSource {
    func tableView(_ tableView: UITableView, numberOfRowsInSection section: Int) -> Int {
        return manager.numberOfItems()
    }

    func numberOfSections(in tableView: UITableView) -> Int {
        return 1
    }

    func tableView(_ tableView: UITableView, cellForRowAt indexPath: IndexPath) -> UITableViewCell {
        let cell = tableView.dequeueReusableCell(withIdentifier: "locationCell", for: indexPath) as UITableViewCell
        cell.textLabel?.text = manager.locationItem(at:indexPath)

        return cell
    }
}
```

4. Now, just like we did in our `ExploreViewController`, we want to create an `initialize()` method in our `private` extension and update `viewDidLoad()` to call `initialize()`. When you are done, your file should look like mine:

```
class LocationViewController: UIViewController {

    @IBOutlet weak var tableView:UITableView!

    let manager = LocationDataManager()

    override func viewDidLoad() {
        super.viewDidLoad()
        initialize()
    }
}

// MARK: Private Extension
private extension LocationViewController {
    func initialize() {
        manager.fetch()
    }
}
```

We will finish by cleaning up our `LocationViewController`. Finally, let's take a look at our `MapViewController`.

Refactoring MapViewController

We are just about done refactoring our files. The last file we need to refactor is our `MapViewController`. Let's get started:

1. Inside of our `MapViewController`, after the last curly brace, hit *enter* a couple of times and add the following code (remember, this should be outside of the class, not inside):

```
// MARK: Private Extension
private extension MapViewController {}

// MARK: MKMapViewDelegate
extension MapViewController: MKMapDelegate {}
```

2. Next, remove the `MKMapViewDelegate` subclass from the main class and move it into our extension.

3. Now, let's move all of our `MKMapViewDelegate` methods into the
   extension. You should be moving the following:

```
import UIKit
import MapKit

class MapViewController: UIViewController {

    @IBOutlet var mapView: MKMapView!

    let manager = MapDataManager()
    var selectedRestaurant:RestaurantItem?

    override func viewDidLoad() {
        super.viewDidLoad()
        initialize()
    }

    override func prepare(for segue: UIStoryboardSegue, sender: Any?) {
        switch segue.identifier! {
        case Segue.showDetail.rawValue:
            showRestaurantDetail(segue: segue)
        default:
            print("Segue not added")
        }
    }

    func initialize() {
        mapView.delegate = self
        manager.fetch { (annotations) in
            addMap(annotations)
        }
    }

    func addMap(_ annotations:[RestaurantItem]) {
        mapView.setRegion(manager.currentRegion(latDelta: 0.5, longDelta: 0.5), animated: true)
        mapView.addAnnotations(manager.annotations)
    }

    func showRestaurantDetail(segue:UIStoryboardSegue) {
        if let viewController = segue.destination as? RestaurantDetailViewController, let restaurant = selectedRestaurant {
            viewController.selectedRestaurant = restaurant
        }
    }

    func mapView(_ mapView: MKMapView, viewFor annotation: MKAnnotation) -> MKAnnotationView? {
        let identifier = "custompin"

        guard !annotation.isKind(of: MKUserLocation.self) else { return nil }
        var annotationView: MKAnnotationView?

        if let customAnnotationView = mapView.dequeueReusableAnnotationView(withIdentifier: identifier) {
            annotationView = customAnnotationView
            annotationView?.annotation = annotation
        }
        else {
            let av = MKAnnotationView(annotation: annotation, reuseIdentifier: identifier)
            av.rightCalloutAccessoryView = UIButton(type: .detailDisclosure)
            annotationView = av
        }

        if let annotationView = annotationView {
            annotationView.canShowCallout = true
            annotationView.image = UIImage(named: "custom-annotation")
        }

        return annotationView
    }

    func mapView(_ mapView: MKMapView, annotationView view: MKAnnotationView, calloutAccessoryControlTapped control: UIControl) {
        guard let annotation = mapView.selectedAnnotations.first else { return }
        selectedRestaurant = annotation as? RestaurantItem

        self.performSegue(withIdentifier: Segue.showDetail.rawValue, sender: self)
    }
}

// MARK: Private Extension
private extension MapViewController {

}

// MARK: MKMapViewDelegate
extension MapViewController: MKMapViewDelegate {

}
```

⟵————————— Move all the code marked above to here

Your extension should now look as follows:

```
// MARK: MKMapViewDelegate
extension MapViewController: MKMapViewDelegate {
    func mapView(_ mapView: MKMapView, viewFor annotation: MKAnnotation) -> MKAnnotationView? {
        let identifier = "custompin"

        guard !annotation.isKind(of: MKUserLocation.self) else { return nil }
        var annotationView: MKAnnotationView?

        if let customAnnotationView = mapView.dequeueReusableAnnotationView(withIdentifier: identifier) {
            annotationView = customAnnotationView
            annotationView?.annotation = annotation
        }
        else {
            let av = MKAnnotationView(annotation: annotation, reuseIdentifier: identifier)
            av.rightCalloutAccessoryView = UIButton(type: .detailDisclosure)
            annotationView = av
        }

        if let annotationView = annotationView {
            annotationView.canShowCallout = true
            annotationView.image = UIImage(named: "custom-annotation")
        }

        return annotationView
    }

    func mapView(_ mapView: MKMapView, annotationView view: MKAnnotationView, calloutAccessoryControlTapped control: UIControl) {
        guard let annotation = mapView.selectedAnnotations.first else { return }
        selectedRestaurant = annotation as? RestaurantItem

        self.performSegue(withIdentifier: Segue.showDetail.rawValue, sender: self)
    }
}
```

4. Next, let's update our `private` extension by moving the following:

```
import UIKit
import MapKit

class MapViewController: UIViewController  {

    @IBOutlet var mapView: MKMapView!

    let manager = MapDataManager()
    var selectedRestaurant:RestaurantItem?

    override func viewDidLoad() {
        super.viewDidLoad()
        initialize()
    }

    override func prepare(for segue: UIStoryboardSegue, sender: Any?) {
        switch segue.identifier! {
        case Segue.showDetail.rawValue:
            showRestaurantDetail(segue: segue)
        default:
            print("Segue not added")
        }
    }

    func initialize() {
        mapView.delegate = self
        manager.fetch { (annotations) in
            addMap(annotations)
        }
    }

    func addMap(_ annotations:[RestaurantItem]) {
        mapView.setRegion(manager.currentRegion(latDelta: 0.5, longDelta: 0.5), animated: true)
        mapView.addAnnotations(manager.annotations)
    }

    func showRestaurantDetail(segue:UIStoryboardSegue) {
        if let viewController = segue.destination as? RestaurantDetailViewController, let restaurant = selectedRestaurant {
            viewController.selectedRestaurant = restaurant
        }
    }
}

// MARK: Private Extension
private extension MapViewController {
                          ←————————————— Move all the code marked above to here
}
```

When you are done, you should have the following:

```swift
import UIKit
import MapKit

class MapViewController: UIViewController {

    @IBOutlet var mapView: MKMapView!

    let manager = MapDataManager()
    var selectedRestaurant:RestaurantItem?

    override func viewDidLoad() {
        super.viewDidLoad()
        initialize()
    }

    override func prepare(for segue: UIStoryboardSegue, sender: Any?) {
        switch segue.identifier! {
        case Segue.showDetail.rawValue:
            showRestaurantDetail(segue: segue)
        default:
            print("Segue not added")
        }
    }
}

// MARK: Private Extension
private extension MapViewController {
    func initialize() {
        mapView.delegate = self
        manager.fetch { (annotations) in
            addMap(annotations)
        }
    }

    func addMap(_ annotations:[RestaurantItem]) {
        mapView.setRegion(manager.currentRegion(latDelta: 0.5, longDelta: 0.5), animated: true)
        mapView.addAnnotations(manager.annotations)
    }

    func showRestaurantDetail(segue:UIStoryboardSegue) {
        if let viewController = segue.destination as? RestaurantDetailViewController, let restaurant = selectedRestaurant {
            viewController.selectedRestaurant = restaurant
        }
    }
}
```

I did not include the `MKMapViewDelegate` extension because the file is too long. The extension is under our `private` extension. Why did I not move the `prepare()` method? The `prepare()` and `viewDidLoad()` methods are methods that are overrides for `UIViewController` in this case. We want to keep these methods inside of our main class declaration. The more we do this, the clearer it will become.

We've finished cleaning up the four View Controllers. You might be wondering what the benefits of this are. In this project, it may not seem like these updates are very important, because we are not doing a lot in our View Controllers. However, as a project grows, there will be some cases where multiple protocols and delegates are adopted; thus, these updates will be beneficial.

Here is an example:

```
class NewsListingView: UIViewController, NewsListingViewProtocol,
UICollectionViewDelegate, UICollectionViewDataSource,
LiveGameNewsViewDelegate, UIGestureRecognizerDelegate
```

This class is subclassing a View Controller and adopting one protocol, three delegates, and one data source. If you had two methods for each one that you need, you would have 12 functions in your class that would need certain methods. Separating out our code makes it easy to find where things are located.

Summary

In this chapter, we discussed what `MKAnnotations` are and how to add and subclass them so that we can use them on our map. We also learned how to customize our annotations. Our app now takes us from tapping on an annotation to a restaurant detail page. We also learned that extensions help to organize code as well as add functionality without having to change the main class or struct with which we are working.

In the next chapter, we are going to display data on our restaurant list. We will also set up our restaurant detail page to display data.

15
Working with an API

When building iOS apps, data can be the most critical part. Typically, the apps you make require that you get data from an online data source, known as an **Application Programming Interface** (**API**). In the previous chapters, we have only worked with a plist to supply our data. Using a plist bridges the gap to understanding how to work with an API, as you will see shortly. In this chapter, we will work with an API that is in **JavaScript Object Notation** (**JSON**) format. This format is typical, no matter which backend service was used to create the JSON file.

In this chapter, we will cover the following topics:

- What a JSON file is and the different components of this data feed
- Passing data using segues

Creating an API Manager

In this chapter, we will be building an API Manager. This manager will be responsible for anything that has to do with getting data from the internet. When dealing with data online, you will typically get it in a particular format, which you then need to convert into something that your app can read.

What is an API?

A RESTful API is a web service from which an app can receive data. Typically, when you are dealing with APIs, such as YELP, they tend to change often. For our purposes, we want to use static files so that we can work on this project without having to be concerned about changes to the API. Therefore, most of the data we are going to use comes from the `http://opentable.herokuapp.com/` site, which is not managed full-time and does not change often. The site's API, however, is missing some data that we need; therefore, I have updated these files (which are in the project files for this chapter) to include that missing data.

APIs are typically in JSON format, and working with them is similar to working with plists. The transition from one to the other should be pretty seamless. Let's get familiar with the JSON format.

Understanding a JSON file

Before we write any code, we need to take a look at the structure of a simple JSON file. Let's create a new group inside the `Misc` folder in the Navigator panel called `JSON`. Then, we need to drag and drop all of the JSON files found in the project files for this chapter into the new `JSON` folder by clicking on **Finish** in the screen that appears. Lastly, open up the `Charleston.json` file and let's review the first part of it, including the first restaurant listing:

```json
{
    "total_entries": 67,
    "per_page": 25,
    "current_page": 1,
    "restaurants": [
        {
            "id": 147475,
            "name": "Union Provisions",
            "address": "513 King Street",
            "city": "Charleston",
            "state": "SC",
            "area": "South Carolina",
            "postal_code": "29403",
            "country": "US",
            "phone": "8436410821x",
            "lat": 32.790291,
            "lng": -79.93936,
            "price": 2,
            "reserve_url": "http://www.opentable.com/single.aspx?rid=147475",
            "mobile_reserve_url": "http://mobile.opentable.com/opentable/?restId=147475",
            "image_url": "https://www.opentable.com/img/restimages/147475.jpg",
            "cuisines": [
                {
                    "cuisine": "American"
                },
                {
                    "cuisine": "Bar"
                }
            ]
        },
```

This file has four nodes inside it, `total_entries`, `per_page`, `current_page`, and `restaurants`. When you work with a feed, it will split items up into pages so that you are not trying to load all the data at once. This feed tells us that there are 67 total pages with 25 restaurants per page and that we are currently on page one. We do not need the first three nodes in this book since we are just going to load 25 restaurants.

The `restaurant` node, on the other hand, is essential for this book. The restaurant's node is an array of data, recognizable as such by the brackets ([ ]) used in the node. If you review the individual items in the restaurant's node, you will notice that everything needed for our app's name, address, city, and so on, is covered. This structure is the same as that which we saw in the plists earlier in this book. If you look at cuisines, you will notice that it is wrapped inside brackets ([ ]). Again, this is what we had in our plist data previously. We have an idea of what a JSON file looks like; let's see how we can work with it.

Exploring the API Manager file

We just created our `API Manager` folder. Now, let's create the `API Manager` file:

1. Right-click on the `Misc` folder and select **New File**.
2. On the **Choose a template for your new file** screen, select **iOS** at the top. Then, select **Swift File**. Then, hit **Next**.
3. Name this file `RestaurantAPIManager`, and hit **Create**.

We need to define our class definition first; therefore, add the following to the `import` statement:

```
import Foundation

struct RestaurantAPIManager {  (A)
    static func loadJSON(file name:String) -> [[String:AnyObject]] {  (B)
        var items = [[String : AnyObject]]()  (C)

        guard let path = Bundle.main.path(forResource: name, ofType: "json"), let data =
            NSData(contentsOfFile: path) else {  (D)
            return [[:]]
        }

        do {
            let json = try JSONSerialization.jsonObject(with: data as Data, options: .allowFragments) as
                AnyObject

            if let restaurants = json as? [[String: AnyObject]] {  (E)
                items = restaurants as [[String : AnyObject]]
            }
        }
        catch {
            print("error serializing JSON: \(error)")  (F)
            items = [[:]]
        }

        return items  (G)
    }
}
```

- **Part A**: Here, we define the class:

```
struct RestaurantAPIManager {
```

- **Part B**: The `loadJSON()` method is known as a type method because it has the `static` keyword in front of it. Type methods are called using the dot syntax. Static functions cannot be overridden:

```
static func loadJSON(file name:String) -> [[String:AnyObject]]
{
```

The next bullet list explains what we need to write when we want to call the `loadJSON` method inside the `RestaurantAPIManager` file.

- **Part C**: Calling this method will return an array of dictionary objects. If this sounds familiar, it is because our plist data returns the same thing:

```
var items = [[String: AnyObject]]()
```

- **Part D**: On this line, we declare an array of dictionary objects:

```
guard let path = Bundle.main.path(forResource: name, ofType:
"json"), let data = NSData(contentsOfFile: path) else {
    return [[:]]
}
```

- **Part E**: Since we are not loading from the internet, we need to make sure that we call the right filename. If the path is found and there is nothing wrong with the data, we will use the data. Otherwise, we will return an empty array with no dictionary objects.

Here, we are using a `do...catch`. As a reminder, a do-catch statement is used to handle errors by running a block of code. To employ it, we must utilize it with what is known as a try. First, we need to try and serialize or convert the data from the JSON file; if we are successful, we can then access the information inside that file. To obtain the restaurant items in the JSON file (all of which are located inside the restaurant's node), we used `json["restaurants"]`.

Next, we cast this using `as?` as an array of dictionary objects. Also, since our data types are mixed, we used `AnyObject` to accept the dictionary of mixed data types. Finally, we set our data to the array of items. We now have the same structure, and the array of dictionary objects that we had in the `Map` section:

```
do {
    let json = try JSONSerialization.jsonObject(with: data as
Data, options: .allowFragments) as AnyObject
    if let restaurants = json as? [[String: AnyObject]] {
        items = restaurants as [[String : AnyObject]]
    }
}
```

- **Part F**: This `catch` only runs if there is a problem serializing the data from the file. If there is a problem, we will return an empty array with no dictionary objects. Using a do-catch allows for our app to keep running without crashing:

```
catch {
  print("error serializing JSON: (error)")
  items = [[:]]
}
```

- **Part G**: Finally, if all goes well, we return the array of dictionary items back:

```
return items
```

This entire class is built so that we can pass any name we want; it will return data if it finds the file.

Location list

Let's review how our app will work. A user will select a cuisine and location. Then, the location is passed to the Explore view. The user will get restaurants from the selected location, which have been filtered by the selected cuisine.

If this were online, we would pass the location to the API, and the API would return the JSON data. As you can see, we are doing the same thing here. When you eventually deal with an API, the transition to working with online data will be seamless.

Selecting a location

As stated earlier, to get data, we need a location. To get the location, we need to get it from the `LocationViewController`. When a location is selected, we will show a checkmark. We will need this checkmark to update each time a new item is set. Finally, when the **Done** button is tapped, we need to pass this location to `ExploreViewController`.

We need to create a location item that will have both the city and state that we can use and pass around.

Right-click on the **Model** folder inside of **Locations** folder and select **New File**.

Inside the **Choose a template for your new file** screen, select **iOS** at the top. Then, select **Swift** file and name the file `LocationItem`. Hit **Create** and add the following:

```swift
struct LocationItem {
    var state: String?
    var city: String?
}

extension LocationItem {
  init(dict: [String: AnyObject]) {
    self.state = dict["state"] as? String
    self.city = dict["city"] as? String
  }

  var full: String {
    guard let city = self.city, let state = self.state else {
return "" }
    return "\(city), \(state)"
  }
}
```

Here, we are creating a `LocationItem` that is a struct. This struct has two variables, state and city, that are optionals. So far, nothing too crazy. Next, we added an extension that contains a custom `init()` method that passes a dictionary into it. Finally, we created a full variable that will take our city and state and combine it into one string for display purposes. Now that we have our item, let's update our `LocationViewController` next. We need a variable to keep track of the selected location. Add the following inside the `LocationViewController.swift` file, under the constant manager:

```
var selectedCity:LocationItem?
```

Then, we need to create a new extension for `UITableViewDelegate`, as follows. Add the following after our `UITableViewDataSource` extension:

```
//MARK: UITableViewDelegate
extension LocationViewController: UITableViewDelegate {
}
```

As we discussed earlier in this book, delegates supply the behavior. Here, we want a behavior for when the user selects a Table View row, and another behavior for when the user deselects the row. First, let's update our `cellForRowAt` method with the selection behavior in our new extension by adding the following code:

```
func tableView(_tableView:UITableView,
cellForRowAtindexPath:IndexPath) -> UITableViewCell {
    let cell = tableView.dequeueReusableCell(withIdentifier:
"locationCell", for:indexPath) as UITableViewCell
    cell.textLabel?.text = manager.locationItem(at:indexPath).full
    return cell
}
```

Next, let's add the selection behavior in our new extension by adding the following code:

```
func tableView(_ tableView: UITableView, didSelectRowAt
indexPath:IndexPath) {
    if let cell = tableView.cellForRow(at: indexPath) {
        cell.accessoryType = .checkmark
        selectedCity = manager.locationItem(at:indexPath)
        tableView.reloadData()
    }
}
```

Here, we will get the cell of the selected row and set its `accessoryType` to `checkmark`. Then, we will get the location and set it to the `selectedCity` variable. To only see the `checkmark` in our Table View cell, we need to remove the disclosure arrow and gray cell selection. Let's update this by doing the following:

1. Open the `Locations.storyboard` file.
2. Select the `locationCell` Table View in the **Location View Controller**.
3. Select the Attributes inspector in the Utilities panel, and update the **Selection** field from **Gray** to **None**.
4. Next, update the **Accessory** field from **Disclosure Indicator** to **None**.

Adding a Header view

Our **Explore** has a header, and we need to pass data over to it. To do that, we need to create a header class for it:

1. Right-click on the **View** folder inside of **Explore** folder and select **New File**.
2. On the **Choose a template for your new file** screen, select **iOS** at the top. Then, select **Cocoa Touch Class**. Then, hit **Next**.
3. In the options screen that appears, add the following:

   New file:

   - **Class**: ExploreHeaderView
   - **Subclass**: UICollectionReusableView
   - **Also create XIB**: Unchecked
   - **Language**: Swift

4. Click **Next** and then **Create**.
5. Add the following to this file:

```
import UIKit
class ExploreHeaderView: UICollectionReusableView {
    @IBOutlet weak var lblLocation:UILabel!
}
```

6. Next, open the `Explore.storyboard` file and under the Identity inspector in the Utilities Panel, update the **Class** to `ExploreHeaderView`.

Now, let's work on passing data from a location to explore and display the selected location in our header.

Passing a selected location back to Explore View

We need to be able to send the selected city back to our `ExploreViewController`. Therefore, we need a selected city, as well, unwind for the **Done** button inside `ExploreViewController`. First, let's get our selected city to display in our **Explore** view:

1. Add the following variable under the constant manager in our `ExploreViewController.swift` file:

   ```
   var selectedCity:LocationItem?
   var headerView: ExploreHeaderView!
   ```

2. Next, open `Explore.storyboard` and select the **Explore Header View** in the Outline view:

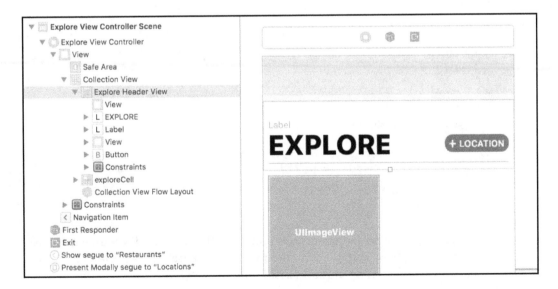

3. Then, select the Connections inspector in the Utilities Panel, and click and drag `lblLocation` from the empty circle under Outlets to the label in the **Explore View Controller Header** scene:

Next, let's unwind our **Done** button in our **Explore View Controller**.

Unwinding our Done button

Earlier in this book, we added an unwind for our **Cancel** button. Now, we need to make it so that our **Done** button can also dismiss the modal, but we also want to capture the selected location when the user is done. Let's add this code next:

1. Open the `ExploreViewController.swift` file again and, in the `private` extension under the `unwindLocationCancel()` function, add the following code:

```
@IBAction func unwindLocationDone(segue:UIStoryboardSegue) {
    if let viewController = segue.source as?
LocationViewController {
        selectedCity = viewController.selectedCity
        if let location = selectedCity {
            headerView.lblLocation.text = location.full
        }
    }
}
```

The code we just added checks the source of the segue. If its source is a class of `LocationViewController`, then we want to grab the selected city and set the `selectedCity` variable inside `ExploreViewController` to that city.

We then use an if...let statement to make sure that selectedCity is not nil; if it isn't, then we set the label in the header to the currently selected city. Now, we need to hook up IBAction.

2. In your UICollectionViewDataSource extension, update collectionView:viewForSupplementaryElementOfKind:atIndexPath: with the following:

```
func collectionView(_ collectionView: UICollectionView,
viewForSupplementaryElementOfKind kind: String, at indexPath:
IndexPath) -> UICollectionReusableView {
    let header =
collectionView.dequeueReusableSupplementaryView(ofKind: kind,
withReuseIdentifier: "header", for: indexPath)
    headerView = header as? ExploreHeaderView
    return headerView
}
```

3. Next, open Locations.storyboard.

4. Now, use *control* and drag from the **Done** button in the **Location View Controller** to **Exit** in the **Location View Controller** scene:

5. When you let go, select `unwindLocationDoneWithSegue:` in the menu that appears:

```
Action Segue
    unwindLocationCancelWithSegue:
    unwindLocationDoneWithSegue:
```

Let's build and run the project by hitting the Play button (or use *command + R*). You should now be able to select a location; when you hit **Done**, the Explore Header view should show you the selected location:

Getting the last selected location

We have a couple of issues that we need to correct under **Select a location**. You will notice that when you click on **Select a location**, you can check multiple locations. We only want the user to be able to select one location. Also, the checkmark next to your selected location disappears if you click on **Done** in **Location View** and then click to choose a location again. We need to set the last selected location so that it is saved when you go back to your location list. We can address these issues at the same time:

1. Open `Explore.storyboard`.
2. Select the segue that is connected to the `LocationViewController`.
3. Then, select the Attributes inspector in the Utilities Panel and set **Identifier** under **Storyboard Segue** to **locationList**. Then, hit *Enter*:

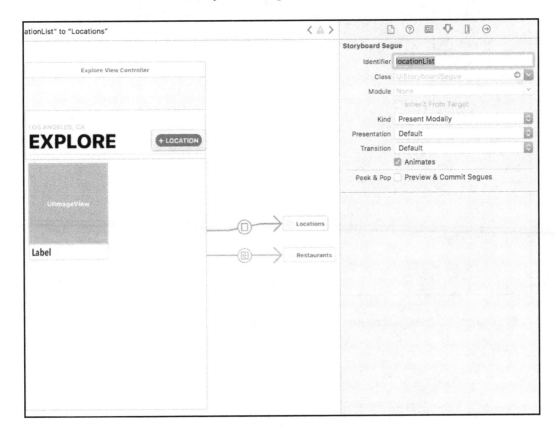

4. Now, select the segue that is connected to the
   `RestaurantListViewController` and set **Identifier** to
   `restaurantList`. Then, hit *enter*:

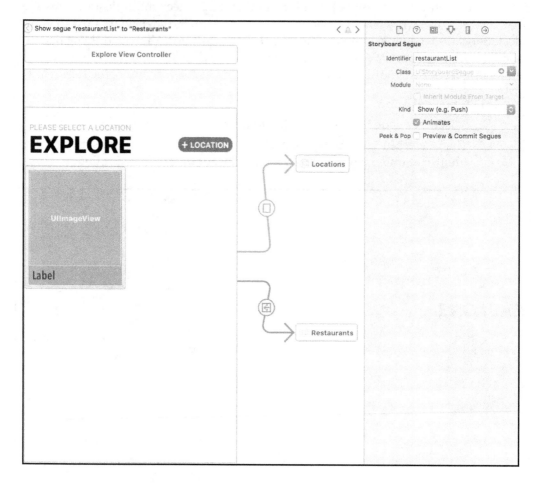

5. Both of these identifiers were added to our `Segue.swift` file.

Right now, we are currently just displaying locations by cities, but we need to also display the state. Our plist, `Locations.plist`, has both a city and state value:

1. Next, open up the `LocationDataManager.swift` file and update the locations array to now be a `LocationItem`:

   ```
   private var locations:[LocationItem] = []
   ```

2. Now, update the `fetch()` method to the following:

   ```
   func fetch() {
       for location in loadData() {
         locations.append(LocationItem(dict:location))
       }
   }
   ```

3. Next, we need to update the `locationItem()` method. Currently, we are returning a `String`, but we want to return the object:

   ```
   func locationItem(at indext:IndexPath) -> LocationItem {
       return locations[index.item]
   }
   ```

4. Finally, let's add the following code before the last curly brace:

   ```
   func findLocation(by name:String) -> (isFound:Bool,
   position:Int) {
       guard let index = locations.index(where: { $0.city == name
   }) else {
           return (isFound:false, position:0) }

       return (isFound:true, position:index)
   }
   ```

This method will allow us to find the location, and then obtain its index position within the array. We will return a tuple, which is a compound type in Swift, meaning that it can hold multiple values. Tuples allow you to combine different data types into one. This method will check the tuple to see whether or not we found the data. If we found the data, then we will use the index position; if not, we will not do anything.

5. Next, we need to check whether or not a previous location was set. Open up the `LocationViewController.swift` file and create the following method after the `viewDidLoad()` method:

```
func set(selected cell: UITableViewCell, at indexPath: IndexPath) {  A
    if let city = selectedCity?.city {  B
        let data = manager.findLocation(by: city)  C
        if data.isFound {  D
            if indexPath.row == data.position {
                cell.accessoryType = .checkmark
            }
            else { cell.accessoryType = .none }
        }
    }
    else {
        cell.accessoryType = .none  E
    }
}
```

Let's break this method down:

- **Part A**: In the parameters of this method, we take in a cell and an index path:

  ```
  set(cell:at)
  if let city = selectedCity?.city
  ```

- **Part B**: Here, we check to make sure that the selected city is set:

  ```
  let data = manager.findLocation(by: city)
  ```

- **Part C**: Then, we call the method we created in `LocationDataManager`, passing the selected city into the manager, and getting back a tuple of data:

  ```
  if data.isFound {
      if indexPath.row == data.position {
          cell.accessoryType = .checkmark
      }
      else { cell.accessoryType = .none }
  }
  ```

- **Part D**: Next, we check to see if data was found in the tuple; if so, we check to see if the selected row is the same as the position in the array. If the row and position are the same, we direct the cell to set its `accessoryType` to a checkmark; otherwise, `accessoryType` will be set to none:

  ```
  else { cell.accessoryType = .none }
  ```

- **Part E**: Finally, if no data is found, we set `accessoryType` to none. Add the following inside `cellForRowAt()` after we set the text for the cell:

```
set(selected: cell, at: indexPath)
```

Build and run the project by hitting the Play button (or use *command + R*). You should see that you can only select one location now. However, after you select the location, if you click on **Done** in the **Location** view and then click to show the locations again, your last selected location will not have been saved. We still need to address this issue, which we will do next.

Passing location and cuisine to the restaurant list

Open the `ExploreViewController.swift` file, and inside the `private` extension, add the following method above the `unwindLocationCancel()` method:

```
func showLocationList(segue:UIStoryboardSegue) {
    guard let navController = segue.destination as?
UINavigationController,
    let viewController = navController.topViewController as?
LocationViewController else {
        return
    }
    guard let city = selectedCity else { return }
    viewController.selectedCity = city
}
```

Our `showLocationList()` method will be called whenever our destination view has a Navigation Controller. Then, it checks to see if the `topViewController` is of the `LocationViewController` class. If either of these two statements are `false`, we do nothing. If both are `true`, we check the `selectedCity`; if it is `nil`, then we also do nothing. If the `selectedCity` has a location, we set the `selectedCity` variable inside the `LocationViewController` to the `selectedCity` in the `ExploreViewController`. Adding this will save the last selected location if we return to the locations list after we selected a location earlier.

We also need to pass the selected city over to the `RestaurantListViewController`. Therefore, add the following variables inside the `RestaurantListViewController.swift` file above your `@IBOutlet var collectionView`:

```
var selectedRestaurant:RestaurantItem?
var selectedCity:LocationItem?
var selectedType:String?
```

While still in the `RestaurantListViewController.swift` file, add the following code under the `viewDidLoad()` method:

```
override func viewDidAppear(_ animated: Bool) {
  super.viewDidAppear(animated)
  print("selected city \(selectedCity as Any)")
  print("selected type \(selectedType as Any)")
}
```

The `viewDidAppear()` method will get called every time we load the View Controller, whereas the `viewDidLoad()` method only gets called once. We can print the `selectedCity` variable to verify that we are passing the location over correctly.

Next, open the `ExploreViewController.swift` file again and, inside, add the following under the `showLocationList()` method:

```
func showRestaurantListing(segue:UIStoryboardSegue) {
    if let viewController = segue.destination as?
RestaurantListViewController, let city = selectedCity,
        let index = collectionView.indexPathsForSelectedItems?.first
{
        viewController.selectedType = manager.explore(at:
index).name
        viewController.selectedCity = city
    }
}
```

We will now check to see if the segue destination is `RestaurantListViewController`, and make sure that `selectedCity` is set in `ExploreViewController`. Next, we need to get the selected `indexPath` of the Collection view. Once we have that, we then get the item from the `ExploreDataManager` at the `index` position.

Finally, we get the name from the item. If we get all of those items back, then we pass the `selectedCity` and `selectedType` variables to the `RestaurantListViewController`. If we do not, then we will display an alert, letting the user know that they need to select a location first. Let's create the three methods that will display such an alert:

1. First, we will create the actual alert. While still in the `ExploreViewController`, add the following code before `unwindLocationCancel()`:

```
func showAlert() {
    let alertController = UIAlertController(title: "Location
Needed", message:"Please select a location.", preferredStyle:
.alert)
    let okAction = UIAlertAction(title: "OK", style: .default,
handler: nil)
    alertController.addAction(okAction)
    present(alertController, animated: true, completion: nil)
}
```

2. Then, we need to check that we have a location; if not, we want to make sure that the user cannot go to the restaurant list. Inside the `ExploreViewController`, add the following method after the `viewDidLoad()` method:

```
override func shouldPerformSegue(withIdentifier identifier:
String, sender: Any?) -> Bool {
    if identifier == Segue.restaurantList.rawValue {
        guard selectedCity != nil else {
            showAlert()
            return false
        }
        return true
    }
    return true
}
```

Here, we check whether the segue equals `restaurantList`. If it does, we check to see if the `selectedCity` variable is set. If we return `true`, then the segue will be performed, and we will go to the restaurant list. If we return `false`, then we display our alert, letting the users know that they need to select a location first.

3. Lastly, we need to show either the location list or restaurant list, depending on whether or not the user chose a location before trying to see the restaurant list. Add the following method after `viewDidLoad()`, and before the `shouldPerformSegue` method we just added:

```
override func prepare(for segue: UIStoryboardSegue, sender:
Any?){
    switch segue.identifier! {
        case Segue.locationList.rawValue:
            showLocationList(segue: segue)
        case Segue.restaurantList.rawValue:
            showRestaurantListing(segue: segue)
        default:
        print("Segue not added")
    }
}
```

The `prepare()` method checks which identifier is called. If it is the location list, then we call the `showLocationList()` method; if it is the restaurant list, then we call the `showRestaurantListing()` method.

Now, build and run the project by hitting the Play button (or use *command + R*). If you try to select a cuisine first, you should not be able to go to the restaurant list. Instead, you should receive an alert, stating that you need to select a location:

If you pick a location, hit **Done**, and then tap the locations list again, you should see that your location is still selected. Now, if you select a cuisine, you should be directed to the restaurant listing and see the selected location printing in the Debug Panel. If you do not see that panel, you can open it using the toggle or *command + shift + Y*:

```
selected city Optional(LetsEat.LocationItem(state: Optional("NC"), city: Optional("Charleston")))
selected type Optional("Bistro")
```

Now that we have the location, we need to check our `RestaurantAPIManager` for data. Therefore, let's update our `print` statement inside the `RestaurantListViewController` by revising the `viewDidAppear()` method so that it does the following:

```
override func viewDidAppear(_ animated: Bool) {
    guard let location = selectedCity?.city, let type = selectedType
    else {
            return
    }

    print("type \(type)")
    print(RestaurantAPIManager.loadJSON(file: location))
}
```

You should now see the type selected, along with an array of dictionary objects, in the Debug Panel:

```
type Bistro
[["state": SC, "city": Charleston, "country": US, "name": Union Provisions, "address": 513 King Street, "lat":
32.790291, "price": 2, "reserve_url": http://www.opentable.com/single.aspx?rid=147475, "long":
-79.93935999999999, "id": 147475, "phone": 8436410821x, "image_url": https://www.opentable.com/img/restimages/
147475.jpg, "mobile_reserve_url": http://mobile.opentable.com/opentable/?restId=147475, "area": South
Carolina, "postal_code": 29403, "cuisines": <__NSArrayI 0x608000232e80>(
{
    cuisine = Pizza;
},
{
    cuisine = Italian;
}
)
], ["state": SC, "city": Charleston, "country": US, "name": McCrady's, "address": 2 Unity Alley, "lat":
32.778, "price": 4, "reserve_url": http://www.opentable.com/single.aspx?rid=3751, "long": -79.92700000000001,
"id": 3751, "phone": 8435770025x1, "image_url": https://www.opentable.com/img/restimages/3751.jpg,
"mobile_reserve_url": http://mobile.opentable.com/opentable/?restId=3751, "area": South Carolina,
"postal_code": 29401, "cuisines": <__NSArrayI 0x6080002311c0>(
{
```

Now that we have our data, let's get that data to display in our `RestaurantListViewController`. To do this, we need to set up our cell, as well as a restaurant data manager. The restaurant data manager, rather than the `RestaurantListViewController`, will be the class that uses our `RestaurantAPIManager`.

Creating our restaurant cell class

Now, we need to create a file so that we can connect to the cell:

1. Right-click on the `Restaurants` folder in the Navigator panel, and create a new group called `View`. Then, right-click the `View` folder and select **New File**.

2. Inside the **Choose a template for your new file** screen, select **iOS** at the top and then **Cocoa Touch Class**. Then, hit **Next**.

3. In the options screen that appears, add the following:

   New file:

   - **Class**: `RestaurantCell`
   - **Subclass**: `UICollectionViewCell`
   - **Also create XIB file**: Unchecked
   - **Language**: `Swift`

4. Click **Next** and then **Create**. Your file should look like the following:

   ```
   import UIKit

   class RestaurantCell: UICollectionViewCell {
   }
   ```

5. Inside the class declaration, add the following:

   ```
   @IBOutlet weak var lblTitle:UILabel!
   @IBOutlet weak var lblCuisine:UILabel!
   @IBOutlet weak var imgRestaurant:UIImageView!
   ```

6. Save the file.

Now that our file is set up, let's work on getting our outlets connected.

Setting up restaurant list cell outlets

We need to set up our `restaurantCell` outlets:

1. Open `Explore.storyboard` and select our `restaurantCell` again in the Outline view.

2. Now, in the Utilities Panel, select the Identity inspector.

3. Under **Custom Class**, in the **Class** drop-down menu, select **RestaurantCell** and hit *enter* to connect the **Cell** to the class.

4. Now, select the Connections inspector.

5. Click on and drag `lblTitle` from the empty circle, which is under Outlets, to the top label in our `restaurantCell`:

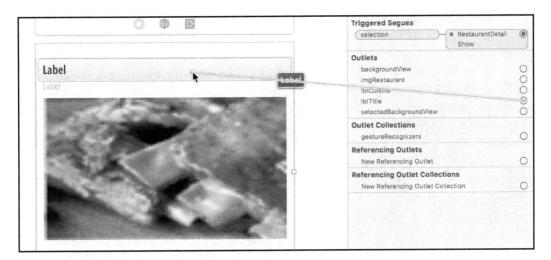

6. Click on and drag `lblCuisine` from the empty circle, which is under Outlets, to the other label in our `restaurantCell`:

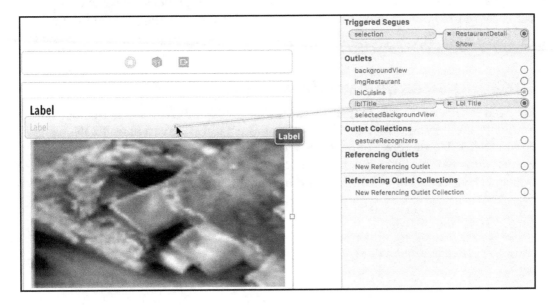

7. Click on and drag `imgRestaurant` from the empty circle, which is under Outlets, to the image in our `restaurantCell`:

Now that we have our `restaurantListCell` outlets set up, let's get some data into our cell. We previously created our `RestaurantItem.swift` file; we will use this in our restaurant list.

Creating a restaurant data manager

We need to create a data manager for our restaurants, but before we do that, we need to update a few things. In Swift 4, we have a more natural way to parse JSON, using what is called **Decodable**. First, we need to update our `RestaurantItem`, but before we get into what this code looks like, our `RestaurantItem` needs to conform to Decodable. Open `RestaurantItem` and update it to include the following:

```
class RestaurantItem: NSObject, MKAnnotation, Decodable {
  var name: String?
  var cuisines:[String] = []
  var latitude: Double?
  var longitude:Double?
  var address:String?
```

```
var postalCode:String?
var state:String?
var imageURL:String?

var title: String? {
  return name
}

var subtitle: String? {
  if cuisines.isEmpty { return "" }
  else if cuisines.count == 1 { return cuisines.first }
  else { return cuisines.joined(separator: ", ") }
}

var coordinate: CLLocationCoordinate2D {
    guard let lat = latitude, let long = longitude else {
  return CLLocationCoordinate2D() }
    return CLLocationCoordinate2D(latitude: lat, longitude: long )
}

enum CodingKeys: String, CodingKey {
      case name
      case cuisines
      case lat
      case long
      case address
      case postalCode = "postal_code"
      case state
      case imageURL = "image_url"
  }
}
```

Our `RestaurantItem` now conforms to Decodable, which can now be used to work with JSON data. The variables in `RestaurantItem` match those variables inside of the JSON files. If your variable is different than the JSON property, you can assign it the property name inside of quotes. We need to create a manager that loads `RestaurantItem` from the location JSON files. Let's create the `RestaurantDataManager` file now:

1. Right-click on the `Restaurants` folder and create a new group called `Model`. Then, right-click the `Model` folder and select **New File**.
2. Inside the **Choose a template for your new file** screen, select **iOS** at the top and then **Swift File**. Then, hit **Next**.
3. Name this file `RestaurantDataManager`, and hit **Create**.

We need to define our class definition first, so add the following under the `import` statement in this new file:

```
class RestaurantDataManager {
}
```

Inside the class declaration, add the following variable:

```
private var items:[RestaurantItem] = []
```

Here, we keep our array `private`, since there is no reason to have to access this outside of the class.

Now, let's add the following three methods:

```
func fetch(by location:String, withFilter:String="All",
completionHandler:() -> Void) {
   var restaurants:[RestaurantItem] = []

   for restaurant in RestaurantAPIManager.loadJSON(file: location) {
         restaurants.append(RestaurantItem(from: restaurant))
   }

   if withFilter != "All" {
         items = restaurants.filter({
$0.cuisines.contains(withFilter) })
   }
   else { items = restaurants }
   completionHandler()
}

func numberOfItems() -> Int {
   return items.count
}

func restaurantItem(at index:IndexPath) -> RestaurantItem {
   return items[index.item]
}
```

The first method here differs from the one we looked at in `ExploreDataManager`, whereas the last two methods here are the same as those in `ExploreDataManager`:

```
import Foundation

class RestaurantDataManager {

    private var items:[RestaurantItem] = []  (A)         (C)                                                                          (B)
    func fetch(by location:String, with filter:String="All", completionHandler:(_ items:[RestaurantItem]) -> Void) {
        if let file = Bundle.main.url(forResource: location, withExtension: "json") {
            do {
                let data = try Data(contentsOf: file)
                let restaurants = try JSONDecoder().decode([RestaurantItem].self, from: data)  (D)
                if filter != "All" {
                    items = restaurants.filter({ ($0.cuisines.contains(filter)) })  (E)
                }
                else { items = restaurants }
            }
            catch {
                print("there was an error \(error)")
            }
        }

        completionHandler(items)  (F)
    }
    (G) func numberOfItems() -> Int {
        return items.count
    }

    (H) func restaurantItem(at index:IndexPath) -> RestaurantItem {
        return items[index.item]
    }
}
```

Let's break these methods down so that we can understand what we are doing:

- **Part A**: This is a private array of `RestaurantItem`:

      private var items:[RestaurantItem] = []

- **Part B**: This function is pretty long; however, we are simply fetching restaurants with a location as a filter. We have a closure block, that will allow us to let the function run until it is complete:

      fetch(location:withFilter:completionHandler)

- **Part C**: In this parameter, we are setting a default. If we do not pass anything into this parameter, it will use `All`; otherwise, it will use whatever we give it:

      with filter:String = "All"

As you type your code, Xcode will provide code hints (choices) that it believes that you might want. When you type this method, Xcode gives you two hints: one that includes the `with:` parameter (that takes a filter), and one that does not:

```
M Void fetch(by: String, completionHandler: ([RestaurantItem]) -> Void)
M Void fetch(by: String, with: String, completionHandler: ([RestaurantItem]) -> Void)
```

- **Part D**: Here, we use Decodable to parse the JSON file and create an array of `RestaurantItem`:

```
do {
    let data = try Data(contentsOf:file)
    let restaurants = try
JSONDecoder().decode([RestaurantItem].self,from:data)
    ...
}
catch {
    print("there was an error \(error)")
}
```

- **Part E**: Inside of the if-statement, we filter the restaurants by cuisine. Since our restaurants have multiple cuisines, we must check each cuisine, which is why we use contains:

```
do {
    ...
    if filter != "All" {
        items = restaurants.filter({ ($0.cuisines.contains(filter)) })
    }
    else { items = restaurants }
}
catch {
    print("there was an error \(error)")
}
```

- **Part F**: This is used to tell our method that we are finished and pass back the restaurant items:

```
completionHandler(items)
```

- **Part G**: This method tells us how many restaurant items we have:

```
numberOfItems()
```

- **Part H**: This method allows us to get the restaurant at the index position at which it is located:

```
restaurantItem(at:)
```

Now we have a greater understanding of our restaurant data manager. We have done a lot of code, and some of it may not make sense to you yet, but as long as you have a basic understanding, then you will be fine.

We now need to update `MapDataManager` to work with the JSON files. Open `MapDataManager` and update `fetch()` to the following:

```
func fetch(completion:( _annotations:[RestaurantItem]) -> ()){
    let manager = RestaurantDataManager()
    manager.fetch(by:"Boston") { (items) in
        self.items = items
        completion(items)
    }
}
```

In this method, we create an instance of `RestaurantDataManager`, and then tell it to fetch Boston. This is hard coded for now, but you could make this dynamic to get a value from the user instead. Now, we need to get the data displaying on our restaurant list. One of the most common things when displaying data is how to handle a Table View or Collection View when there is no data. Some of the filtering we are doing may return no results, so we should handle both cases. We are going to do this next.

Handling no data

It is common to want to create a custom view that you can reuse, but also have a visual representation of it as well. There are two common ways to do this: the first way we will demonstrate now, and the other we will do later in this book. You can create a `UIView` that comes with a **XIB** (pronounced zib or nib). XIBs were the common way to create elements before storyboards, and are still effective today. Let's create one now:

1. Right-click on the `Misc` folder and select **New Group** and call it `No Data`.
2. Then, right-click on the `No Data` folder and create a new file.
3. On the **Choose a template for your new file** screen, select **iOS** at the top. Then, select **Cocoa Touch Class**. Then, hit **Next**.

4. In the options screen that appears, add the following:

New file:

- **Class**: NoDataView
- **Subclass**: UIView
- **Language**: Swift

5. Click **Next** and then **Create**.
6. Next, right-click on the No Data folder again and create a new file.
7. Inside the **Choose a template for your new file** screen, select **iOS** at the top. Then, select **View** under **User Interface**. Then, hit **Next**.
8. Name the file NoDataView and hit **Create**.
9. First, open the NoDataView.swift file and add the following into this file:

```swift
class NoDataView: UIView {
    var view: UIView!
    @IBOutlet var lblTitle: UILabel!
    @IBOutlet var lblDesc: UILabel!

    override init(frame: CGRect) {
        super.init(frame: frame)
        setupView()
    }

    required init?(coder aDecoder: NSCoder) {
        super.init(coder: aDecoder)!
        setupView()
    }

    func loadViewFromNib() -> UIView {
        let nib = UINib(nibName: "NoDataView", bundle: Bundle.main)
        let view = nib.instantiate(withOwner: self, options: nil) [0] as! UIView
        return view
    }

    func setupView() {
        view = loadViewFromNib()
        view.frame = bounds
        view.autoresizingMask = [.flexibleWidth, .flexibleHeight]
        addSubview(view)
    }
```

```
func set(title: String) {
    lblTitle.text = title
}

func set(desc: String) {
    lblDesc.text = desc
}
}
```

Our two `init` methods are required; simply call `setupView()`. The `loadViewFromNib()` method is used to get our XIB file. Our `setupView()` is used to take the NIB and is added to the `UIView()`. Finally, we have two methods that set up our two labels. The first four methods are boilerplate code that you will write every time you want to create a `UIView` with a NIB (XIB) file.

Next, let's get this set up:

1. Open `NoDataView.xib`.
2. Select **Files Owner** in the Outline. Then, open the Identity inspector, update **Class** to `NoDataView` and hit *enter*.
3. Next, in the filter field of the object library, type `label`.
4. Then, drag out two labels into the view.
5. Select one of the labels. Then, in the Attributes inspector, update the following values:

   - **Text**: Add `TITLE GOES HERE` into the empty text field under the text
   - **Color**: `Black`
   - **Alignment**: `Center`
   - **Font**: `Avenir Next Condensed Bold 26`

6. Then, in the Size inspector, update the following values:

   - **Width**: `355`
   - **Height**: `36`

7. Select one of the labels. Then, in the Attributes inspector, update the following values:

  - **Text**: Add TITLE GOES HERE into the empty text field under the text
  - **Color**: Black
  - **Alignment**: Center
  - **Font**: Avenir Next Condensed Regular 17

8. Then, in the Size inspector, update the following values:

  - **Width**: 355
  - **Height**: 21

9. Select both labels and then the Pin icon. Enter the value of the **Height** (this should be checked).

10. Now, with both labels selected, hit the Stack View icon. Alternatively, you can go to **Editor | Embed In | Stack View**.

11. Select the Stack View in the Outline view, and then the Pin icon. Enter the following values:

  - **Right**: 10
  - **Left**: 10

12. Then, select the Align icon. Select the following:

  - **Horizontally in the container**: (this should be checked)
  - **Vertically in the container**: (this should be checked)

13. Select the **Files Owner** in the Outline view.

14. Then, open the Identity inspector and connect lblTitle to the label that says TITLE GOES HERE.

15. Connect lblDesc to the other label.

When you are done, you should see the following:

Finally, let's connect everything. Open the
`RestaurantListViewController.swift` file:

1. Above the `selectedRestaurant` variable, add the following:

   ```
   var manager = RestaurantDataManager()
   ```

2. Next, add the following method inside the `private` extension:

   ```
   func createData() {
       guard let location = selectedCity?.city, let filter =
   selectedType else { return }
       manager.fetch(by: location, with: filter) { _ in
           if manager.numberOfItems() > 0 {
               collectionView.backgroundView = nil
           }

           else {
               let view = NoDataView(frame: CGRect(x: 0, y: 0,
   width: collectionView.frame.width, height:
   ```

```
collectionView.frame.height))
        view.set(title: "Restaurants")
        view.set(desc: "No restaurants found.")
        collectionView.backgroundView = view
    }

    collectionView.reloadData()
  }
}
```

This method checks to see if we have a selected location and a filter. Then, we need to run the fetch method we created earlier. If we have any items, we should make sure that our background view is `nil`. If not, we will create our `NoDataView` and set it to display `No restaurants found`. Finally, we need to reload the Collection View.

3. Next, let's update `collectionView:cellForItemAt:` by adding the following:

```
func collectionView(_ collectionView: UICollectionView,
cellForItemAt indexPath: IndexPath) -> UICollectionViewCell {
    let cell =
collectionView.dequeueReusableCell(withReuseIdentifier:
"restaurantCell", for: indexPath) as! RestaurantCell
    let item = manager.restaurantItem(at: indexPath)
    if let name = item.name { cell.lblTitle.text = name }
    if let cuisine = item.subtitle { cell.lblCuisine.text =
cuisine }
    if let image = item.imageURL {
        if let url = URL(string: image) {
            let data = try? Data(contentsOf: url)
            if let imageData = data {
                DispatchQueue.main.async {
                    cell.imgRestaurant.image = UIImage(data:
imageData)
                }
            }
        }
    }
    return cell
}
```

Here, we are just passing data into our cell. We are displaying the title, cuisine, and the image.

4. Finally, update `-collectionView:numberOfItemsInSection:` to the following:

```
func collectionView(_ collectionView: UICollectionView,
numberOfItemsInSection section: Int) -> Int {
    return manager.numberOfItems()
}
```

5. Build and run the project. You should now see the following, either with data or without:

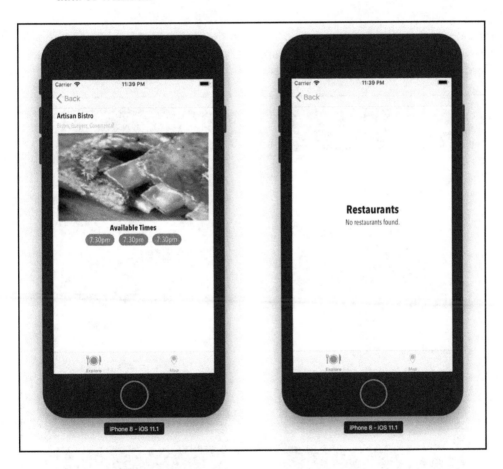

Before we wrap this up, let's add one more thing. When you select a location, display it on this view using the new iOS 11 large titles. Add the following into the private extension under `createData()`, inside of `RestaurantListViewController`:

```
func setupTitle() {
  navigationController?.setNavigationBarHidden(false, animated: false)
  if let city = selectedCity?.city, let state = selectedCity?.state {
    title = "\(city.uppercased()), \(state.uppercased())"
  }
  navigationController?.navigationBar.prefersLargeTitles = true
}
```

Then, call `setupTitle()` after `createData` in the `viewDidAppear()` method. Now, if you build and rerun the project, you should see the selected city. When you scroll, the large title will appear in the title view:

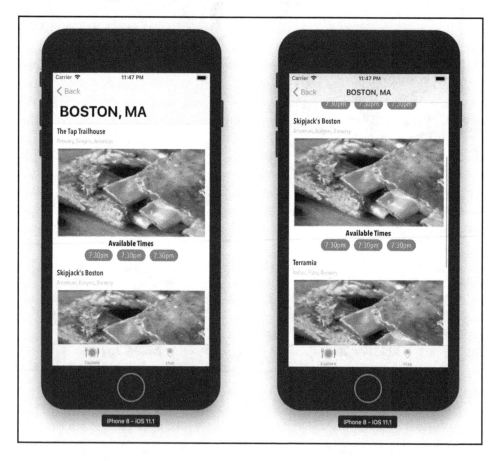

We are done with this chapter; good work! We did a lot, but you should be starting to see this app coming to life.

Summary

Well, we finally have data working on our app. We are not using a service, but if we wanted to, it wouldn't be hard to add it. Working with local JSON files is pretty close to working with an API feed. You should feel confident doing either. One thing I love to do is this: when I know what the feed is like, but I do not want to write that portion yet, I will create static JSON files of the feed and work with those. Using static JSON files allows me to focus on getting the app to where it needs to be, and not get stopped because of the API data layer.

In this chapter, we learned what JSON is and how to use that JSON feed to make data for our app. We also looked at how to pass data using segues.

In the next chapter, we will look at how to display even more data.

16
Displaying Data in Restaurant Detail

Our app is coming together nicely, but we have one more section to do before we can start adding features. We have data in all of our views, except for in our restaurant detail view. In the last chapter, we passed data using segues, and we are going to do this again in this chapter. We have a few other things in this view that we need to set up before we move on to some of the features of the app.

In this chapter, we will cover the following topics:

- Passing data using segues
- Connecting `IBOutlet` to display data
- Displaying one annotation in a map view

Let's set up our `RestaurantDetailViewController` by adding the following:

1. Add the following variables after the class declaration and before the `selectedRestaurant` variable:

```
// Nav Bar
@IBOutlet weak var btnHeart:UIBarButtonItem!

// Cell One
@IBOutlet weak var lblName:UILabel!
@IBOutlet weak var lblCuisine:UILabel!
@IBOutlet weak var lblHeaderAddress:UILabel!

// Cell Two
@IBOutlet weak var lblTableDetails:UILabel!
// Cell Three
@IBOutlet weak var lblOverallRating:UILabel!

// Cell Eight
```

```
@IBOutlet weak var lblAddress:UILabel!
@IBOutlet weak var imgMap:UIImageView!
```

2. Make sure you save the file.

Now that we've created our IBOutlet, we need to connect them:

1. Open the RestaurantDetail.storyboard, select the Restaurant Detail View Controller in the Outline view, and then open the Connections inspector in the Utilities Panel.
2. Now, from the empty circle, click on and drag each of the following variables we just added under Outlets to their respective elements in either the scene or Outline view.
3. The following is an empty circle for imgMap to the map view in the Outline view:

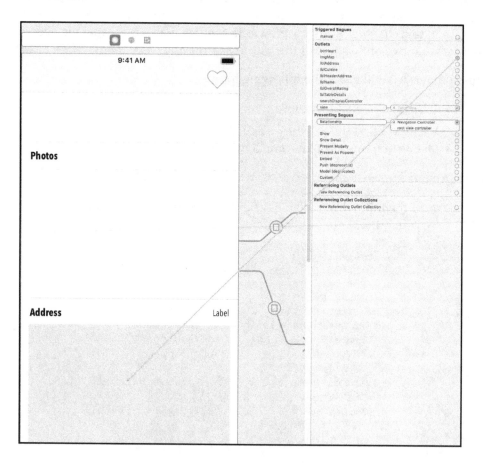

4. The following is an empty circle for `lblAddress` to the address **Label** above the map:

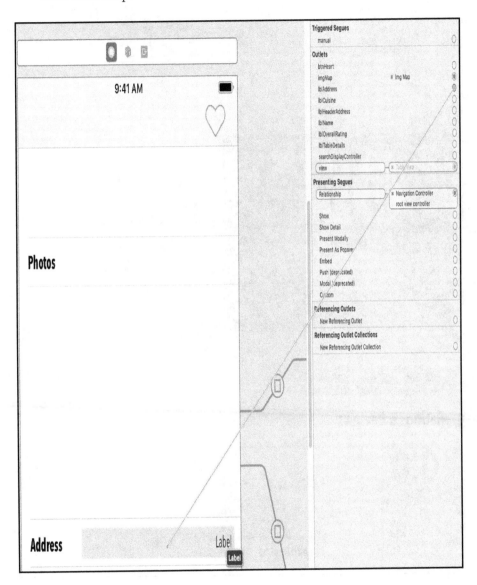

5. The following is an empty circle for `lblOverallRating` to the **Label** inside the **Reviews** cell:

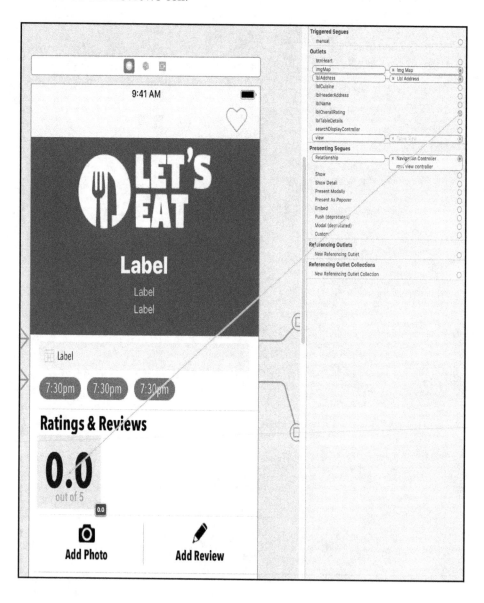

6. The following is an empty circle for `lblTableDetails` to the **Label** under the header in the scene:

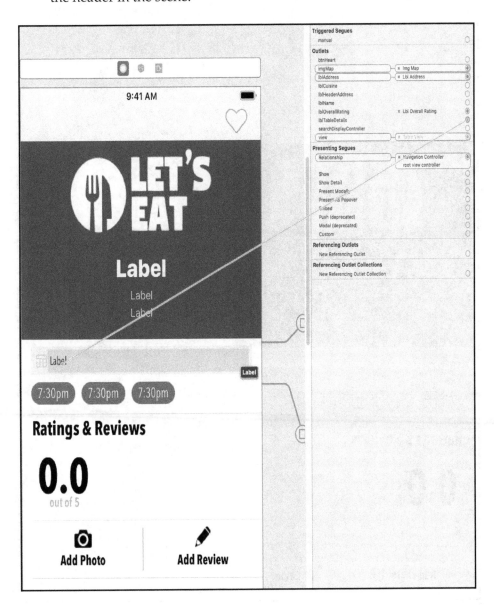

7. The following is an empty circle for `lblName` to the **Label** under the logo in the scene:

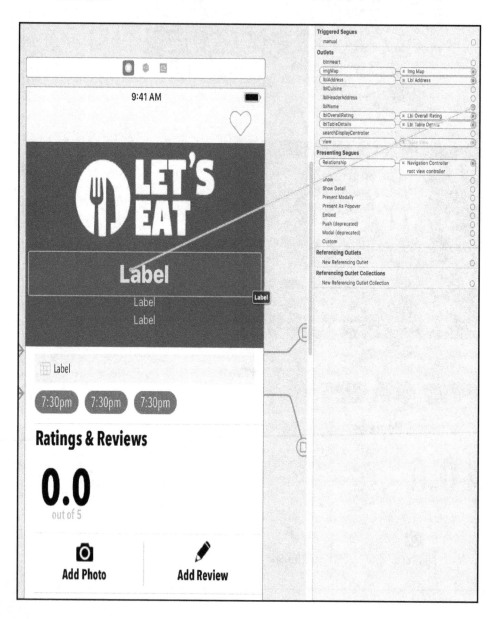

8. The following is an empty circle for `lblCuisine` to the **Label** under `lblName` in the scene:

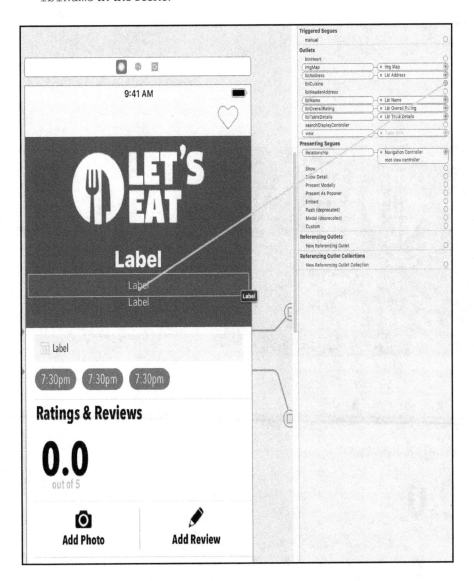

9. The following is an empty circle for `lblHeaderAddress` to the **Label** under `lblCuisine` in the scene:

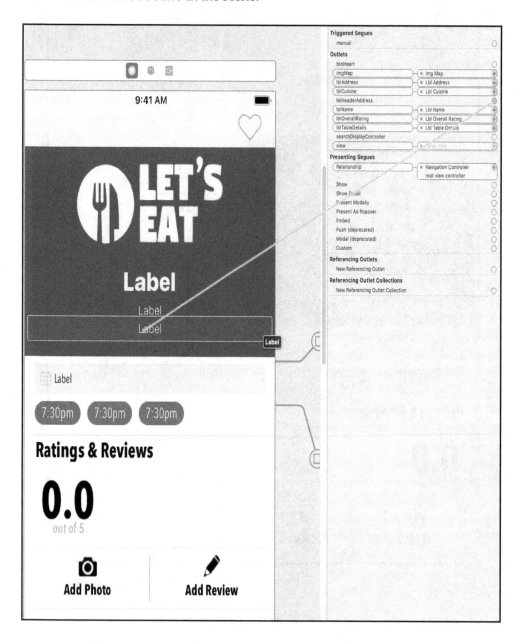

10. Finally, the following is an empty circle for `btnHeart` to our heart button:

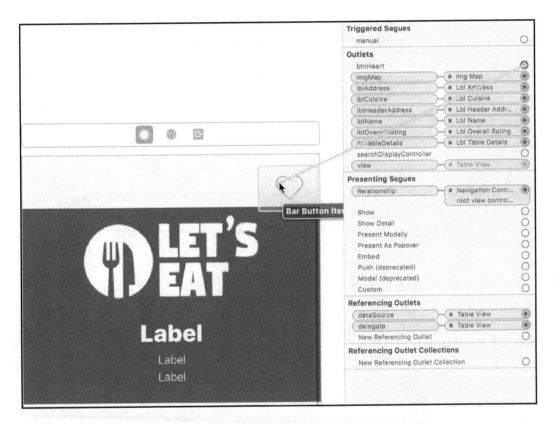

Now that we have everything connected, we can jump into coding and get our detail page displaying data.

Displaying data in our static Table View

Next, we need to create a method that will display all of our data in our labels.

Open the `RestaurantDetailViewController.swift` file and add the private extension after the last curly brace:

```
private extension RestaurantDetailViewController {
    func setupLabels() {
        guard let restaurant = selectedRestaurant else { return }
        if let name = restaurant.name {
```

```
        lblName.text = name
        title = name
    }

    if let cuisine = restaurant.subtitle { lblCuisine.text =
cuisine }
    if let address = restaurant.address {
        lblAddress.text = address
        lblHeaderAddress.text = address
    }

    lblTableDetails.text = "Table for 7, tonight at 10:00 PM"
    }
}
```

This method will now get the data and display it inside our labels. Next, we want to display a map of the restaurant location at the bottom of our Detail view. Now, you might be wondering why we are using an image and not a map. Using a map uses a lot more resources, whereas an image makes things a lot smoother. When you go with this approach, you can always add a button to go to an actual map, but this is a good way to do a snapshot of the map instead of loading a map for every detail.

Let's arrange for an image of a map to display, and also show our custom annotation in the image. Add the following method under the setupLabels() method and before the last curly brace:

```
func createMap() {
    guard let annotation = selectedRestaurant, let long =
annotation.long, let lat = annotation.lat else { return }
    let location = CLLocationCoordinate2D(
        latitude: lat,
        longitude: long
    )

    takeSnapShot(with: location)
}
```

In this method, we get the longitude and latitude and enter the values into a CLLocationCoordinate2D object. We then pass the location to a method called takeSnapShot(with:). We get two errors after we add this. The first one is for CLLocationCoordinate2D, and to get rid of it, we need to import CoreLocation at the top of the file. To get rid of the last one, simply add the following method under the createMap() method:

```
func takeSnapShot(with location: CLLocationCoordinate2D) {
    let mapSnapshotOptions = MKMapSnapshotter.Options()
```

```
var loc = location
let polyLine = MKPolyline(coordinates: &loc, count: 1)
let region = MKCoordinateRegion(polyLine.boundingMapRect)

mapSnapshotOptions.region = region
mapSnapshotOptions.scale = UIScreen.main.scale
mapSnapshotOptions.size = CGSize(width: 340, height: 208)
mapSnapshotOptions.showsBuildings = true
mapSnapshotOptions.showsPointsOfInterest = true

let snapShotter = MKMapSnapshotter(options: mapSnapshotOptions)
snapShotter.start() { snapshot, error in
guard let snapshot = snapshot else {
return
}

UIGraphicsBeginImageContextWithOptions(mapSnapshotOptions.size, true,
0)
snapshot.image.draw(at: .zero)

let identifier = "custompin"
let annotation = MKPointAnnotation()
annotation.coordinate = location

let pinView = MKPinAnnotationView(annotation: annotation,
reuseIdentifier: identifier)
pinView.image = UIImage(named: "custom-annotation")!
let pinImage = pinView.image
var point = snapshot.point(for: location)

let rect = self.imgMap.bounds
if rect.contains(point) {
let pinCenterOffset = pinView.centerOffset
point.x -= pinView.bounds.size.width / 2
point.y -= pinView.bounds.size.height / 2
point.x += pinCenterOffset.x
point.y += pinCenterOffset.y
pinImage?.draw(at: point)
}

if let image = UIGraphicsGetImageFromCurrentImageContext() {
UIGraphicsEndImageContext()
DispatchQueue.main.async {
self.imgMap.image = image
}
}
}
}
```

This method is long, but it allows us to create a map image at the size we need. We then pass all of our settings to our snapshotter to create a picture. Once we have created our image, we can then add our custom annotation to it. Although this requires a lot of code, it is the best way to understand it in its entirety. Here, we would recommend changing the values line-by-line to see how it affects the image. We have more errors, and these are because we need to import `MapKit`.

Now that we have created our functions, we need to call them as follows:

Add the following after the `viewDidLoad()` method in the `RestaurantDetailViewController.swift` file:

```
func initialize() {
    setupLabels()
    createMap()
}
```

This method needs to be called inside your `viewDidLoad()` method. Replace the `dump` statement in the `viewDidLoad()` method with the following:

```
initialize()
```

Now, we have finished with our Restaurant Detail View Controller, but we need to make sure that the selected restaurant is passed over from the restaurant list view. Open `RestaurantListViewController` and add the following code under `viewDidLoad()`:

```
override func prepare(for segue:UIStoryboardSegue, sender:Any?) {
    if let identifier = segue.identifier {
        switch identifier {
        case Segue.showDetail.rawValue:
            showRestaurantDetail(segue:segue)
        default: print("Segue not added")
        }
    }
}
```

Here, we are looking for the `showDetail` segue. When it's called, we call the `showRestaurant()` method. Let's add that method next:

```
func showRestaurantDetail(segue:UIStoryboardSegue) {
    if let viewController = segue.destination as?
RestaurantDetailViewController, let index =
collectionView.indexPathsForSelectedItems?.first {
        selectedRestaurant = manager.restaurantItem(at:index)
        viewController.selectedRestaurant = selectedRestaurant
```

```
        }
    }
```

Let's build and run the project by hitting the Play button (or using *command + R*). When you select a restaurant, you should see all of the restaurant's information on the details page.

Also, you should see that a pin has been dropped at the restaurant's location on the map, which is actually an image:

We are done with the restaurant detail for now, but we still need to be able to show ratings, reviews, and photos. We will work on all of these features in upcoming chapters.

Summary

We now have JSON data loading into our app. As you can see, going from a plist to a JSON file was not a huge step. Our app is now looking more and more like it should be available on the App Store. In the following chapters, we will turn our attention to adding features that you might want to use in your app. These features will enhance the user's experience, and therefore learning them will be invaluable. Even if the features don't seem like something you want or need, it will be beneficial in the long run to understand what they are and how they work.

In the next chapter, you will work with the camera, and learn how to apply filters and save images to the Camera Roll.

17
Foodie Reviews

We are all familiar with reviews, from food reviews to App Store reviews. Seeing reviews for websites and apps is commonplace. In this chapter, we will create a review form that has a custom five-star rating component, which we will then add to it. We will learn about `UIControls` and how powerful they are. We will also look at literals and how to use them in our code.

In this chapter, we will cover the following topics:

- Creating a form that users can use to write a review
- Creating a custom star rating
- Image and color literals

Getting started with reviews

Our review form UI is set up, but we need to make a slight change to it. Right now, we have an image displayed for ratings. We are going to build a custom rating component that we will use in both restaurant details and our Review form.

We will add it to our restaurant details first, and then, when finished, we will add it to the Review form. We want our ratings view to be able to show ratings from zero stars to five stars. We also want the user to be able to select half stars when rating, so it will also need to show half stars.

The first thing we do is start creating our custom `UIControl`. `UIButtons` and `UISwitches` are sub-classes of `UIControls`, and without getting super technical, we are going to create our control:

1. Right-click the `Reviews Form` folder and select **New File**.
2. Inside the **Choose a template for your new file** screen, select **iOS** at the top, and then **Cocoa Touch Class**. Then, hit **Next**.

3. In the options screen that appears, add the following:

New file:

- **Class**: RatingsView
- **Subclass**: UIControl
- **Language**: Swift

4. Click **Next**, and then **Create**.

Now that we have created our file, we want to be able to hook it up to a UIView in the storyboard. Let's do the following:

1. Open up RestaurantDetail.storyboard.
2. You will see an empty UIView next to the **0.0** rating label:

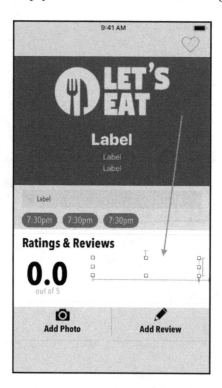

3. Next, select the view. Then, in the Identity inspector, update the **Custom Class** to RatingsView and hit *Enter*.

Now, we can get started. Open up the `RatingsView.swift` file and let's get started.

Displaying ratings in our custom UIControl

Inside the `RatingsView.swift` file, we first need to create all of the variables we will need. Add the following under the class declaration:

```
let imgFilledStar = #imageLiteral(resourceName: "filled-star")
let imgHalfStar = #imageLiteral(resourceName: "half-star")
let imgEmptyStar = #imageLiteral(resourceName: "empty-star")
let shouldBecomeFirstResponder = true
var rating:CGFloat = 0.0
var totalStars = 5
```

If you copy and paste this code, you will have to select each image to see the actual image. If you are having trouble using an image literal, you can use `UIImage(named:)` instead.

We are doing something new in this file. We are using image literals as our variables. If you type `Image Literal` in your file and hit return, you will see a small icon:

Double-click this icon and a modal will appear, which will allow you to select an image:

You can look and find the three images using this window, or you can type everything you see here, and the image will appear. When done, you should see the following:

```
import UIKit

class RatingView: UIControl {

    let imgFilledStar = ★
    let imgHalfStar = ⯪
    let imgEmptyStar = ☆

    let shouldBecomeFirstResponder = true
    var rating:CGFloat = 0.0
    var totalStars = 5
}
```

The first three variables are used for drawing our ratings view. The next variable, `shouldBecomeFirstResponder`, is a variable that lets us respond and handle events as they happen. Next, the rating variable is used for keeping track of our current rating. Finally, we have a variable to keep track of the total number of stars.

Now, let's add our `init` methods:

```
override init(frame: CGRect) {
    super.init(frame: frame)
}

required init?(coder aDecoder: NSCoder) {
    super.init(coder: aDecoder)
}
```

This is just boilerplate code that you need when creating views. There's nothing to explain here other than that you need it. Next, we need to create a few methods that will handle creating our stars. We need three of them for each type of star (full, half, and empty). Add the following after the last curly bracket:

```
private extension RatingsView {
    func drawStar(with frame:CGRect, highlighted:Bool) {
        let image = highlighted ? imgFilledStar :imgEmptyStar
        draw(with: image, and: frame)
    }

    func drawHalfStar(with frame:CGRect) {
        draw(with: imgHalfStar, and: frame)
    }
```

```
        func draw(with image:UIImage, and frame:CGRect) {
            image.draw(in: frame)
        }
    }
```

These methods create a full, half, or empty star. We now need to be able to draw these stars. UIView has a draw method that we can use to draw stars. Before the drawStar(frame:highlighted:) method, add the following method inside the class:

```
override func draw(_ rect: CGRect) {
 let context = UIGraphicsGetCurrentContext()
 context!.setFillColor( colorLiteral(red: 1, green: 1, blue: 1, alpha:
0).cgColor)
 context!.fill(rect)

 let availWidth = rect.size.width
 let cellWidth = availWidth / CGFloat(totalStars)
 let starSide = (cellWidth <= rect.size.height) ? cellWidth :
rect.size.height

 for index in 0...totalStars {
     let value = cellWidth*CGFloat(index) + cellWidth/2
     let center = CGPoint(x: value+1, y: rect.size.height/2)
     let frame = CGRect(x: center.x - starSide/2, y: center.y -
starSide/2, width: starSide, height: starSide)
     let highlighted = (Float(index+1) <= ceilf(Float(self.rating)))

     if highlighted && (CGFloat(index+1) > CGFloat(self.rating)) {
        drawHalfStar(with: frame)
     } else {
        drawStar(with: frame, highlighted: highlighted)
     }
   }
 }
}
```

This is all of the code we'll need to create our stars. Let's break down the code and see what is happening. First, we get a graphics context, and we set its fill color to be clear. We are using a **Color Literal** this time, and this allows us to create colors and see those colors directly in our Swift file.

You can either type `Color Literal` and hit *Enter* or use `UIColor` instead. You will see that a white box has been created for you, and if you double-click this box, you can edit the color, just like you would in the storyboard.

Next, we create three variables: `availWidth`, `cellWidth`, and `starSide`. Since we are using `UIView` in the storyboard, we need to check the size of this container. We then determine the size of each star based on the width and the number of stars. Finally, we calculate the height of the star.

Then, we loop through each star and create them based on the rating value. Our rating can be from 0-5, with increments of `0.5`. We also need to set up the positioning of each star using the center point. Finally, we determine, based on the value, whether the star should be an empty star, a half star, or a full star. This is our setup method. You do not have to get what is going on entirely—you only need to have a basic understanding. The more you code, the more it will start to make sense.

Before we build the project, open `RestaurantDetailViewController`, and add the following `IBOutlet` after `imgMap`:

```
@IBOutlet weak var ratingView: RatingsView!
```

Next, add the following method into the private method:

```
func createRating() {
    ratingView.rating = 3.5
}
```

Then, call the method after `createMap()` in the `initialize()` method.

Next, open `RestaurantDetail.storyboard` and select the Restaurant View Controller. Then, in the Outlet inspector, click and drag `ratingView` to the `UIView`. Let's build and run the project by hitting the Play button (or use *command* + R). When you get to the restaurant details, you will see that we now have 3.5 stars:

This is precisely what we want, but we also need our control to be able to handle touch events.

Adding our touch events

Adding touch events will be used so that the user can change the rating to their desired rating. Open `RatingView`. Let's add the methods we need to get our control to accept touch events. Start by adding the following inside the main class:

```
override var canBecomeFirstResponder: Bool {
 return shouldBecomeFirstResponder
}

override func beginTracking(_ touch: UITouch, with event: UIEvent?) ->
Bool {
    if self.isEnabled {
        super.beginTracking(touch, with: event)
        if (shouldBecomeFirstResponder && self.isFirstResponder) {
            becomeFirstResponder()
```

```
        }
        handle(with: touch)
          return true
    } else {
        return false
    }
}
```

Then, add the following in the private extension:

```
func handle(with touch: UITouch) {
    let cellWidth = self.bounds.size.width / CGFloat(totalStars)
    let location = touch.location(in: self)
    var value = location.x / cellWidth

    if (value + 0.5 < CGFloat(ceilf(Float(value)))) {
        value = floor(value) + 0.5
    } else {
        value = CGFloat(ceilf(Float(value)))
    }

    updateRating(with: value)
}

// Update Rating
func updateRating(with value:CGFloat) {
    if (self.rating != value && value >= 0 && value <=
CGFloat(totalStars)) {
        self.rating = value
        setNeedsDisplay()
    }
}
```

The following code is used to handle touch. First, we need to set the
`canBecomeFirstResponder` variable. Next, we
have `beginTracking(touch:event:)`. In this method, we set whether our control
can accept touch events. If the control is enabled, then we allow touches, and we call
the `handle()` method and pass it the `UITouch` location. Let's discuss the `handle()`
method.

In our handle method, we start with three variables. First, we get the width of the
entire rating view. Next, we get the value of the touch location, and then, finally, we
take the x value of the location and divide it by the width. We then check the value,
figure out whether it is less than `0.5` or greater than `0.5`, and round appropriately.
Last, we update the rating with the value we calculate.

In the `updateRating(value:)` method, we check to make sure that our value is not equal to the current value and whether the value is greater than zero and less than the total number of stars. If these conditions pass, then we set the rating to the new value and call the `setNeedsDisplay()` method. This method makes sure that our control is redrawn.

Open `RestaurantDetailsViewController`. In the `createRating()` method, add the following:

```
ratingView.isEnabled = true
```

We now have a rating, and by setting the rating to 3.5, we should now see 3.5 stars. We also set the `isEnabled` value to `true`, which means that we can touch and change the rating. If we set it to `false`, then the value cannot change. In the restaurant details, we want to turn off the touch, but in the `ReviewFormViewController`, we want that to be enabled. You can play with this, and when done, set the `isEnable` value to `false` and remove the rating.

We will set the rating later in this book when we start saving reviews:

You can now change the rating from 3.5 to 4.5 by tapping on the view. Now that we have this set up, let's get our review form set up.

Setting up the unwind segues

Currently, if you tap the Add Review button, you will see our review form modal. However, currently, you can not dismiss this view. As we have done before, we need to add code that allows us to unwind (dismiss) a View Controller:

1. Open the `RestaurantDetailsViewController.swift` file and add the following into the private extension:

   ```
   @IBAction func unwindReviewCancel(segue:UIStoryboardSegue) {}
   ```

2. Save the file and open the `ReviewForm.storyboard`.

3. Use *control* and drag the **Cancel** button to the exit icon inside of the same View Controller:

4. In the screen that appears, under **Action Segue**, select
`unwindReviewCancelWithSegue`.

If you build and run the project by hitting the Play button (or use *command + R*), you
should now be able to dismiss the **Review Form**.

Creating our ReviewFormController

1. Right-click the `Review Form` folder again and select **New File**.
2. Inside of the **Choose a template for your new file** screen, select **iOS** at the
   top, and then **Cocoa Touch Class**. Then, hit **Next**.
3. In the options screen that appears, add the following:

   New file:

   - **Class**: `ReviewFormViewController`
   - **Subclass**: `UITableViewController`
   - **Also create XIB**: Unchecked
   - **Language**: `Swift`

4. Click **Next**, and then **Create**.

Delete everything after the `viewDidLoad()` method, as we do not need all of the
other code. Next, let's set up our `ReviewFormViewController` by adding the
following after the class declaration:

```
@IBOutlet weak var ratingView: RatingsView!
@IBOutlet weak var tfTitle: UITextField!
@IBOutlet weak var tfName: UITextField!
@IBOutlet weak var tvReview: UITextView!
```

We also need to add a method when our save button is tapped. We can do this by
adding the following code:

```
@IBAction func onSaveTapped(_ sender: Any) {
  print(ratingView.rating)
  print(tfTitle.text as Any)
  print(tfName.text as Any)
  print(tvReview.text)
  dismiss(animated: true, completion: nil)
}
```

Now, let's connect this file with our `UIViewController` and our review form in the storyboard:

1. In the Utilities panel, select the Identity inspector.
2. Under **Custom Class**, in the **Class** drop-down menu, type/select `ReviewFormViewController` and hit *Enter* to connect the View Controller to the class.
3. Now, select the Connections inspector in the Utilities panel.
4. Now, from the empty circle, click and drag each of the variables we just added under Outlets to their respective elements in either the scene or Outline view.
5. Click and drag from the empty circle for `ratingView` to the `UIView` in the storyboard:

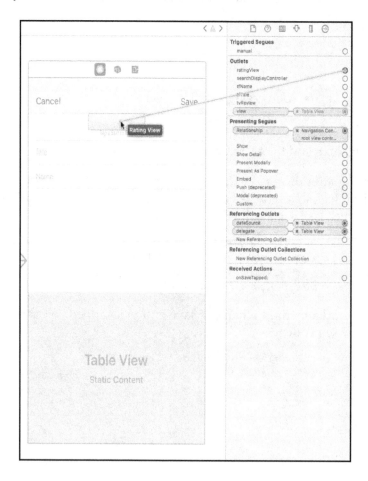

6. Click and drag from the empty circle for `tfTitle` to the `Textfield` in the storyboard:

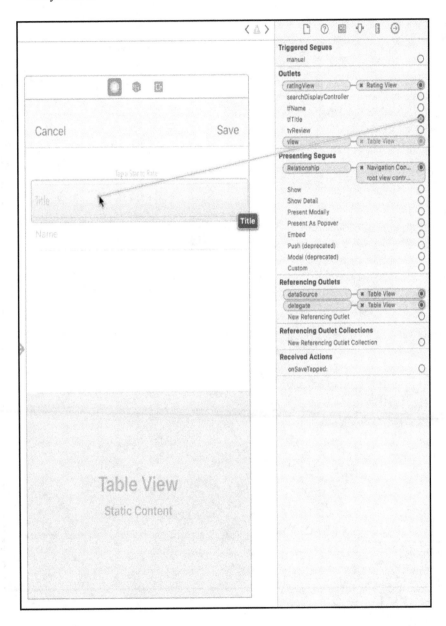

7. Click and drag from the empty circle for `tfName` to the `Textfield` in the storyboard:

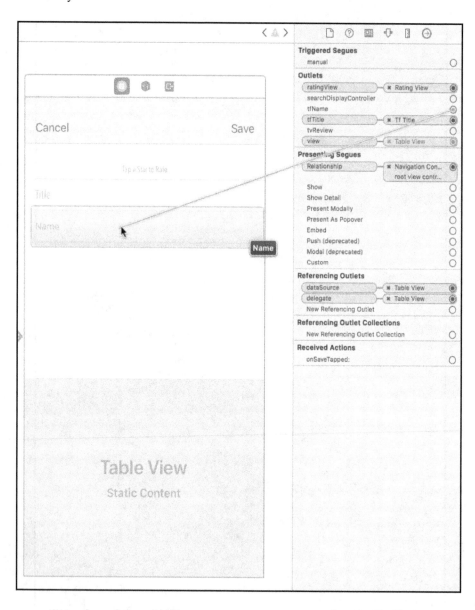

8. Click and drag from the empty circle for `tvReview` to the `Text View` in the storyboard:

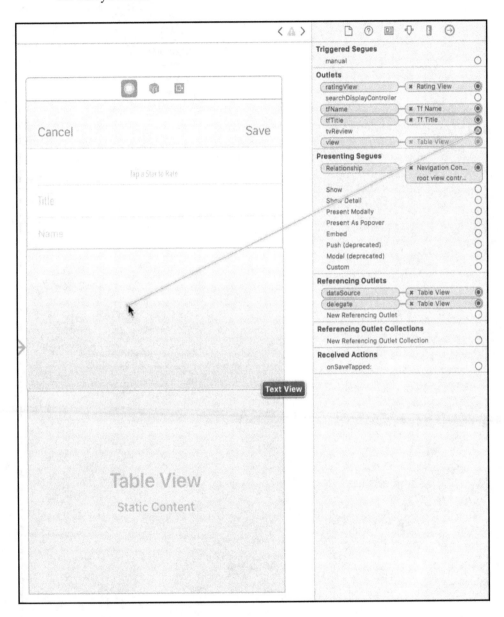

9. Finally, click and drag from the empty circle for `onSaveTapped` to the **Save** button in the Navigation controller:

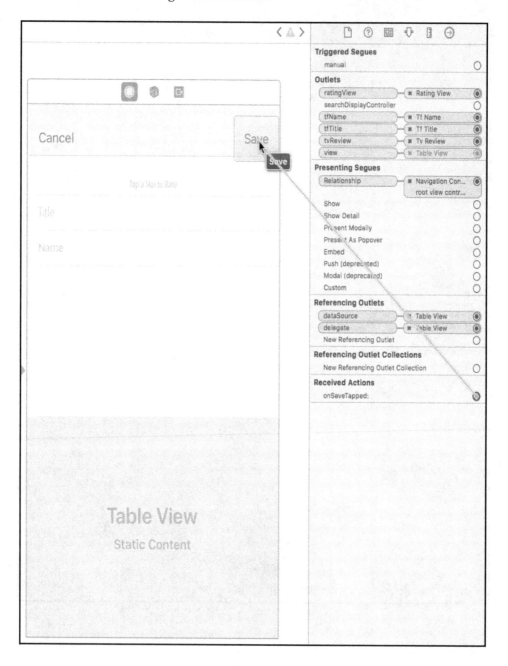

Now that we have an outlet connected to our form, let's build and run the project by hitting the Play button (or use *command + R*). If you go to your form, enter the information and hit save so that you can see that information in your Output panel. Our reviews are now ready to go.

Summary

In this chapter, we created a Review Form using a static table view. We worked with Text View and Text Fields for the first time. We also set up our first custom `UIControl` with our star rating, and we got to use color and **Image Literals**. Literals are a great way to see your image or the color you are working with visually.

In the next chapter, we will work on creating a way to add a photo to a restaurant. We will also learn how to add filters to our photos.

18
Working with Photo Filters

In this chapter, we will focus on creating photos for a restaurant and learn how to use the camera and camera roll. We will give the user the ability to take a picture and apply a filter to that picture. In the next chapter, we will tie the last chapter and this chapter together by completing the work on the Review Form and enable users to save their reviews. We will also learn how to save photos as well.

In this chapter, we will cover the following topics:

- How to use the camera roll to get pictures
- How to use the camera to take pictures and bring them into our app
- How to apply filters to our pictures and get them ready to save to the device

Understanding filters

Based on our design, we know that we are going to need to apply filters to a photo. Instead of just creating an array of filters, we are going to use a plist to load in a set of filters that we want. You can find the `FilterData.plist` file inside this chapter's `asset` folder. Drag and drop this file into the `Model` folder that is inside the `Review` folder. Make sure that `Copy` items, if needed, is checked, and then hit **Finish**.

Let's take a look at the plist and see what it contains:

Key	Type	Value
▼ Root	Array	(10 items)
▼ Item 0	Dictionary	(2 items)
filter	String	None
name	String	None
▼ Item 1	Dictionary	(2 items)
filter	String	CIPhotoEffectMono
name	String	Mono
▼ Item 2	Dictionary	(2 items)
filter	String	CISepiaTone
name	String	Sepia
▼ Item 3	Dictionary	(2 items)
filter	String	CIPhotoEffectTonal
name	String	Tonal
▼ Item 4	Dictionary	(2 items)
filter	String	CIPhotoEffectNoir
name	String	Noir
▼ Item 5	Dictionary	(2 items)
filter	String	CIPhotoEffectFade
name	String	Fade
▼ Item 6	Dictionary	(2 items)
filter	String	CIPhotoEffectChrome
name	String	Chrome
▼ Item 7	Dictionary	(2 items)
filter	String	CIPhotoEffectProcess
name	String	Process
▼ Item 8	Dictionary	(2 items)
filter	String	CIPhotoEffectTransfer
name	String	Transfer
▼ Item 9	Dictionary	(2 items)
filter	String	CIPhotoEffectInstant
name	String	Instant

This list only has 10 of over 170 filters and effects that you can use. If you would like to see a full list of filters, you can find the list at `http://tinyurl.com/coreimage-ios`. Feel free to add, remove, or update any filters. Now that we have seen what our plist looks like, we need to create a model that represents this data. We also need to create a `Manager` class to manage our items. Let's create the model first:

1. Right-click the `Review` folder and create a new group called **Model**. Then right-click the `Model` folder and select **New File**.
2. Inside the **Choose a template for your new file** screen, select **iOS** at the top, and then **Swift File**. Then, hit **Next**.
3. Name this file `FilterItem` and hit **Create**.
4. Next, we need to define our struct; therefore, add the following under the `import` statement:

```
class FilterItem: NSObject {
    let filter:String
    let name:String

    init(dict:[String:AnyObject]) {
        name   = dict["name"] as! String
        filter = dict["filter"] as! String
    }
}
```

The `filter` property will be the class that's passed to apply the filter, and the `name` property will be used as a display.

Let's create our `FilterManager` file next:

1. Right-click the `Photo Filter` folder and select **New File**.
2. Inside of the **Choose a template for your new file** screen, select **iOS** at the top, and then **Swift File**. Then, hit **Next**.
3. Name this file `FilterManager` and hit **Create**.
4. Next, we need to define our class definition; therefore, add the following under the `import` statement:

```
class FilterManager: DataManager {
    func fetch(completionHandler:(_ items:[FilterItem]) ->
Swift.Void) {
        var items:[FilterItem] = []
        for data in load(file: "FilterData") {
            items.append(FilterItem(dict: data))
        }
        completionHandler(items)
```

```
        }
    }
```

This file uses our `DataManager` base class, which converts our plist data into an array of dictionary objects. Once that is complete, we create `FilterItems` from that.

Next, we need to create a file that takes a `FilterItem` and apply a filter to an image. Since we are going to do this in numerous places, it is best to have all of this code in one place. Therefore, we are going to create a file that handles all of this processing for us. Let's create our `ImageFiltering` file:

1. Right-click the `Photo Filter` folder and select **New File**.
2. Inside the **Choose a template for your new file** screen, select **iOS** at the top, and then **Swift File**. Then, hit **Next**.
3. Name this file `ImageFiltering`, and hit **Create**.
4. Update your file to the following:

```swift
import UIKit
import CoreImage

protocol ImageFiltering {
    func apply(filter:String, originalImage:UIImage) ->
UIImage
}

protocol ImageFilteringDelegate:class {
    func filterSelected(item:FilterItem)
}

extension ImageFiltering {
    func apply(filter:String, originalImage:UIImage) ->
UIImage {
        let initialCIImage = CIImage(image: originalImage,
options: nil)
        let originalOrientation =
originalImage.imageOrientation
        guard let ciFilter = CIFilter(name: filter) else {
            print("filter not found")
            return UIImage()
        }
        ciFilter.setValue(initialCIImage, forKey:
kCIInputImageKey)
        let context = CIContext()
        let filteredCIImage = (ciFilter.outputImage)!
        let filteredCGImage =
context.createCGImage(filteredCIImage, from:
```

```
filteredCIImage.extent)
        return UIImage(cgImage: filteredCGImage!, scale: 1.0,
orientation: originalOrientation)
    }
}
```

Let's break down each section so that we can understand what we are doing with this code:

```
import UIKit
import CoreImage
```

`CoreImage` give us access to the image processing we need for filtering:

```
protocol ImageFiltering {
   func apply(filter:String, originalImage:UIImage) -> UIImage
}
```

Creating this protocol allows us to have other classes conform to it, therefore giving us access to the method and allowing us to use it wherever we want:

```
protocol ImageFilteringDelegate:class {
   func filterSelected(item:FilterItem)
}
```

We use this protocol when a filter is selected. When the filter is selected, that data is passed from one View or View Controller to another. The extension has the `apply(filter:originalImage:)` method in it. In this method, we are creating an extension and adding all of the code that we are going to use for applying filters to images.

Creating our filter scroller

After a user selects a photo to use, we present the user with a screen, which contains that image. In the following screenshot, we have a scroller, also known as a `UIScrollView`, which allows us to create content that scrolls either horizontally or vertically. The `UIScrollView` displays an image (thumbnail) with the filter applied to it as well as the name of the filter. This image and name represent our filters visually to our users.

When the user taps on the image, the user will see the selected filter change the primary image. Let's look at an example:

We are now going to create the elements inside the `UIScrollView`. Since we have created a lot inside our storyboard, let's create the `PhotoItem` entirely in code:

1. Right-click the `Model` folder inside of `Review Form` folder and select **New File**.
2. Inside the **Choose a template for your new file** screen, select **iOS** at the top, and then **Swift File**. Then, hit **Next**.
3. Name this file `PhotoItem` and hit **Create**.
4. Update your file to the following:

```swift
import UIKit

class PhotoItem: UIView, ImageFiltering {
}
```

5. Next, add your variables inside of the class declaration:

```
var imgThumb:UIImageView?
var lblTitle:UILabel?
var data:FilterItem?
weak var delegate: ImageFilteringDelegate?
```

Here, we are creating a delegate, which is used to let any class know when something happens. We use this delegate when someone taps on the object itself, which allows us to pass the `FilterItem` data to a delegate class.

You have used this pattern already plenty of times. Table Views and Collection Views both have delegates to which you conform.

6. Now, we need to add our `init` methods. Add the following after your variables:

```
required init?(coder aDecoder: NSCoder) {
    fatalError("init(coder:) has not been implemented")
}

init(frame:CGRect, image:UIImage, item:FilterItem) {
    super.init(frame: frame)
    setDefaults(item: item)
    createThumbnail(image: image, item: item)
    createLabel(item: item)
}
```

Whenever you create a `UIView`, you are required to add this method. If you do not, it gives you an error.

This custom `init()` method allows us to pass data (here, the frame, image, and filter items) when the item gets created. We have a few errors because we have not created the methods that we added to our `init()` method.

7. Next, let's create an extension and add the following methods:

```
private extension PhotoItem {
  func setDefaults(item:FilterItem) {
    data = item
    let tap = UITapGestureRecognizer(target: self,
    action:#selector(thumbTapped))
    self.addGestureRecognizer(tap)
    self.backgroundColor = .clear
  }
```

```swift
    func createThumbnail(image:UIImage, item:FilterItem) {
        if item.filter != "None" {
          let filteredImg = apply(filter: item.filter,
originalImage: image)
          imgThumb = UIImageView(image: filteredImg)
        }
        else { imgThumb = UIImageView(image: image) }

        guard let thumb = imgThumb else {
          return
        }

        thumb.contentMode = .scaleAspectFill
        thumb.frame = CGRect(x: 0, y: 22, width: 102, height: 102)
        thumb.clipsToBounds = true
        addSubview(thumb)
    }

    func createLabel(item:FilterItem) {
        lblTitle = UILabel(frame: CGRect(x: 0, y: 0, width: 102,
height: 22))

        guard let label = lblTitle else {
          return
        }

        label.text = item.name
        label.font = UIFont.systemFont(ofSize: 12.0)
        label.textAlignment = .center
        label.backgroundColor = .clear

        addSubview(label)
    }
}
```

Our `setDefaults()` method is used to create a tap gesture. When the item gets tapped, we call the `thumbTapped` method. We also set the data and the background color of this method.

`createThumbnail(image: item:)` is used to create an image and apply a filter to the image. Then, we need to set its frame and add the image to the View.

With our final method, `createLabel(item:)`, we are creating a label and passing in the name of the filter. Then, we are setting its frame and adding the label to the View. We have two more methods that we need to add to our extension.

8. Add the following after the `createLabel(item:)` method:

```
@objc func thumbTapped() {
   if let data = self.data {
     filterSelected(item: data)
   }
}

func filterSelected(item:FilterItem) {
   delegate?.filterSelected(item: item)
}
```

The `thumbTapped()` method is used to detect taps. When the user taps the item, it calls `filterSelected`.

The `filterSelected(item:)` method is the protocol we created earlier; all we are doing is calling the `delegate` method, `filterSelected`. We will see what happens when the selected filter gets called next.

Our `PhotoItem` is complete; now, we need to work on our cell for our `Filter` collection view.

Creating a filter cell

We already created the cell that we need in the storyboard. However, before we create our View Controller, we need to create a filter cell. This cell is used to display all of the available filters:

1. Right-click the `Photo Filter` folder and select **New File**.
2. Inside the **Choose a template for your new file** screen, select **iOS** at the top, and then **Cocoa Touch Class**. Then, hit **Next**.

3. In the options screen that appears, add the following:

New file:

- **Class**: FilterCell
- **Subclass**: UICollectionViewCell
- **Also create XIB**: Unchecked
- **Language**: Swift

4. Click **Next**, and then **Create**.
5. Update your file with the following:

```swift
class FilterCell: UICollectionViewCell {
  @IBOutlet var lblName:UILabel!
  @IBOutlet var imgThumb: UIImageView!
}

extension FilterCell: ImageFiltering {
  func set(image:UIImage, item:FilterItem) {
    if item.filter != "None" {
      let filteredImg = apply(filter: item.filter,
originalImage: image)
      imgThumb.image = filteredImg
    }
    else { imgThumb.image = image }

    lblName.text = item.name

    roundedCorners()
  }

  func roundedCorners() {
    imgThumb.layer.cornerRadius = 9
    imgThumb.layer.masksToBounds = true
  }
}
```

Our cell is pretty basic: we are setting an image and giving it rounded corners.

6. Open PhotoFilter.storyboard.
7. In the Outline view, select the **Collection View** cell. Then, in the Utilities panel, under the Identity inspector, set the **Custom Class** to **FilterCell**.
8. In the Attributes inspector, set the **Identifier** to **filterCell**.

9. Next, connect your outlets for both `lblName` and `imgThumb`.

10. We need to make sure that we can dismiss our modal when we click the **Add Photo** button. We already added the method we needed, but we need to add this to the storyboard. Use *Control* and drag from **Cancel** to the **Exit** icon:

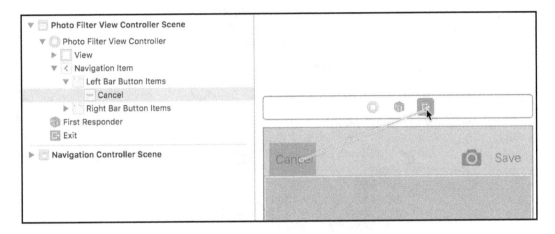

11. In the popup, select `unwindReviewCancelWithSegue:`

We are done with setting up the cell and storyboard. Let's move on to creating our View Controller.

Creating our PhotoFilterViewController

Now, we need to create our `PhotoFilterViewController`:

1. Right-click the `Photo Filter` folder and select **New File**.

2. Inside the **Choose a template for your new file** screen, select **iOS** at the top, and then **Cocoa Touch Class**. Then, hit **Next**.

3. In the options screen that appears, add the following:

New file:

- **Class**: `PhotoFilterViewController`
- **Subclass**: `UIViewController`
- **Also create XIB**: Unchecked
- **Language**: `Swift`

4. Click **Next**, and then **Create**.

When the file opens, delete everything after the `viewDidLoad()` method.

5. Then, add the following:

```
class PhotoFilterViewController: UIViewController {
    var image: UIImage?
    var thumbnail: UIImage?
    let manager = FilterManager()
    var selectedRestaurantID:Int?
    var data:[FilterItem] = []

    @IBOutlet var collectionView: UICollectionView!
    @IBOutlet weak var imgExample: UIImageView!

    override func viewDidLoad() {
        super.viewDidLoad()
        initialize()
    }
}
```

Here, we are setting up our variables and our `initialize()` method. You can ignore the error, as we will fix this next by creating an extension after our class definition.

6. Add the following extension:

```
// MARK: - Private Extension
private extension PhotoFilterViewController {

  func initialize() {
    requestAccess()
    setupCollectionView()
    checkSource()
  }
}
```

We are creating some basic functions that we need. Our first function is our `initialize()` method, which calls three new methods. Let's create those three methods next.

7. Add the following methods after the `initialize()` method:

```
func requestAccess() {
  AVCaptureDevice.requestAccess(for: AVMediaType.video) {
granted in
    if granted {}
  }
}

func setupCollectionView() {
  let layout = UICollectionViewFlowLayout()
  layout.scrollDirection = .horizontal
  layout.sectionInset = UIEdgeInsets(top: 7, left: 7, bottom:
7, right: 7)
  layout.minimumInteritemSpacing = 0
  layout.minimumLineSpacing = 7

  collectionView?.collectionViewLayout = layout
  collectionView?.delegate = self
  collectionView?.dataSource = self
}

func checkSource() {
  let cameraMediaType = AVMediaType.video
  let cameraAuthorizationStatus =
AVCaptureDevice.authorizationStatus(for: cameraMediaType)

  switch cameraAuthorizationStatus {
    case .authorized:
    showCameraUserInterface()
    case .restricted, .denied:
    break
    case .notDetermined:
    AVCaptureDevice.requestAccess(for: cameraMediaType) {
granted in
      if granted {
        self.showCameraUserInterface()
      }
    }
  }
}
```

Our next method, the `setupCollectionView()` method, is the basic setup for our collection view. We are doing something different with `delegate` and `dataSource`. In the previous chapters, we set this up using the Outlet inspector. This time, I am setting them up in code. Either can be done; there is no right or wrong way, but pick one way and stick with it throughout the entire app. I did both for demonstration purposes.

The next method requests user access to their camera or the photo library. The `checkSource()` method, under the case `.notDetermined:` statement, checks whether you are running this on a simulator or on a phone. If you are running it on a simulator, you automatically get the photo library, since there is no camera. If you are on a device, then the user has access to their camera. Now, we need to add two more helper methods. Let's add them first and then discuss them.

8. Add the following methods:

```
func showApplyFilter() {
    manager.fetch { (items) in
        if data.count > 0 { data.removeAll() }
        data = items
        if let image = self.image {
            imgExample.image = image
            collectionView.reloadData()
        }
    }
}

func filterItem(at indexPath: IndexPath) -> FilterItem{
    return data[indexPath.item]
}

@IBAction func onPhotoTapped(_ sender: Any) {
    checkSource()
}
```

The first method, `showApplyFilter()`, is used to create the filter content inside of our collection view. `filterItem(at:)` is used when the user selects a `filter` item. We will pass the index position of the Collection View and create a filter item from it. This item is used to display the currently selected filter in the larger image above our Collection View.

Let's work on getting items displayed in our Collection View. As we have done in the past, we have a few methods that are required for our Collection View to display cells. Add the following extension under our private extension:

```
extension PhotoFilterViewController: UICollectionViewDataSource {
    func collectionView(_ collectionView: UICollectionView,
numberOfItemsInSection section: Int) -> Int {
        return data.count
    }

    func numberOfSections(in collectionView: UICollectionView) -> Int
{
        return 1
    }

    func collectionView(_ collectionView: UICollectionView,
cellForItemAt indexPath: IndexPath) -> UICollectionViewCell {
        let cell =
collectionView.dequeueReusableCell(withReuseIdentifier: "filterCell",
for: indexPath) as! FilterCell
        let item = self.data[indexPath.row]
        if let img = self.thumbnail {
            cell.set(image: img, item: item)
        }
        return cell
    }
}
```

We have done this before, but let's go over the methods again. – `collectionView:numberOfItemsInSection:` is responsible for the number of items in each section. For this collection view, it means the number of filter items we are going to display. Next, we have `–numberOfSectionsInCollectionView:`, which tells our Collection View how many sections we have; in our case, we only have one. Finally, we have `collectionView:cellForItemAtIndexPath:`. This is the method that gets run for every cell we need to create. In this method, we are creating a filter cell.

Now that we have our basic collection view set up, we need to make sure that our Collection View is laid out correctly. Let's add another extension in this file that is responsible for the layout of items for our Collection View. Add the following extension and method after the last extension we just added:

```
extension PhotoFilterViewController:
UICollectionViewDelegateFlowLayout {
    func collectionView(_ collectionView: UICollectionView, layout
collectionViewLayout: UICollectionViewLayout, sizeForItemAt indexPath:
```

```
IndexPath) -> CGSize {
        let screenRect = collectionView.frame.size.height
        let screenHt = screenRect - 14
        return CGSize(width: 150, height: screenHt)
    }
}
```

This extension sets up our cell size and spacing. Save the file. Next, let's hook up our two IBOutlets:

1. Open the `PhotoFilter.storyboard`.
2. Select the View Controller in the Outline view, and then the Identity inspector in the Utilities panel.
3. Under **Custom Class**, in the **Class** drop-down menu, select or type `PhotoFilterViewController` and hit *Enter*.
4. Select the Connections inspector in the Utilities panel.
5. Under Outlets, click and drag from the empty circle of each of the components, `imgExample`, `collectionView`, and `onPhotoTapped:`, to `Image View`, `CollectionView View`, and `Camera Icon (inside Navigation Bar at the top)`, respectively, in the scene. Now, open the `PhotoFilterViewController.swift` file again. Let's add some more code.

   Our Collection View is set up, but we need to add some more code before we can get everything else working. Next, we need to add two more extensions that handle when a user uses the camera and photo library and the second one that is for our custom protocol, which we created earlier. We will need to use `AVFoundation` and `MobileCoreServices` in our app. `AVFoundation` is a framework that gives us access to the camera and `MobileCoreServices` is a framework that gives us access to the filters. At the top of the file, under import `UIKit`, add the following:

   ```
   import AVFoundation
   import MobileCoreServices
   ```

6. Now, let's add the first extension so that we can access the camera and photo library:

   ```
   extension PhotoFilterViewController:
   UIImagePickerControllerDelegate,
   UINavigationControllerDelegate {

       func imagePickerControllerDidCancel(_ picker:
   ```

```
UIImagePickerController) {
      picker.dismiss(animated: true, completion: nil)
   }

   func imagePickerController(_ picker:
UIImagePickerController,  didFinishPickingMediaWithInfo info:
[UIImagePickerController.InfoKey : Any]) {
      let image =
info[UIImagePickerController.InfoKey.editedImage] as? UIImage
      if let img = image {
         self.thumbnail = generate(image: img, ratio:
CGFloat(102))
         self.image = generate(image: img, ratio:
CGFloat(752))
      }
      picker.dismiss(animated: true, completion: {
         self.showApplyFilter()
      })
   }

   func showCameraUserInterface() {
      let imagePicker = UIImagePickerController()
      imagePicker.delegate = self
      #if targetEnvironment(simulator)
         imagePicker.sourceType =
UIImagePickerController.SourceType.photoLibrary
      #else
         imagePicker.sourceType =
UIImagePickerControllerSourceType.camera
         imagePicker.showsCameraControls = true
      #endif
      imagePicker.mediaTypes = [kUTTypeImage as String]
      imagePicker.allowsEditing = true
      self.present(imagePicker, animated: true, completion:
nil)
   }

   func generate(image:UIImage, ratio:CGFloat) -> UIImage {
      let size = image.size
      var croppedSize:CGSize?
      var offsetX:CGFloat = 0.0
      var offsetY:CGFloat = 0.0
      if size.width > size.height {
         offsetX = (size.height - size.width) / 2
         croppedSize = CGSize(width: size.height, height:
size.height)
      }
      else {
```

```
                    offsetY = (size.width - size.height) / 2
                    croppedSize = CGSize(width: size.width, height:
        size.width)
                }
            guard let cropped = croppedSize, let cgImage =
        image.cgImage else {
                    return UIImage()
            }
            let clippedRect = CGRect(x: offsetX * -1, y: offsetY *
        -1, width: cropped.width, height: cropped.height)
            let imgRef = cgImage.cropping(to: clippedRect)
            let rect = CGRect(x: 0.0, y: 0.0, width: ratio,
        height: ratio)
            UIGraphicsBeginImageContext(rect.size)
            if let ref = imgRef {
                UIImage(cgImage: ref).draw(in: rect)
            }
            let thumbnail =
        UIGraphicsGetImageFromCurrentImageContext()
            UIGraphicsEndImageContext()
            guard let thumb = thumbnail else { return UIImage() }
            return thumb
        }
    }
```

The extensions that we created for UIImagePickerControllerDelegate and UINavigationControllerDelegate have two methods that we need to implement. We also have some custom helper methods that we can use. The imagePickerControllerDidCancel: method is called when the user hits the **Cancel** button; therefore, we dismiss the Controller and do nothing.

The imagePickerController:didFinishPickingMediaWithInfo: method is used when we get the image from the Picker once it is dismissed. We set our thumbnail and image values here; then, we apply the generate() method to get them in a smaller size. Finally, we dismiss the Controller and then call showApplyFilter() to add our selected image to our filter view.

showCameraUserInterface() is used to show the camera interface, along with the camera controls. As I mentioned earlier, the code first checks whether you are running the simulator and, if so, shows the photo library. If you are running on a device, you see the camera interface.

The `generate(image:ratio:)` method is what we use to take the images and crop them to the size we need and return an image as a smaller size. The photo library and camera images are quite large. Therefore, if we did not use this method, it would take a long time for UI to go through and do everything we need.

We have one more extension to add, and that is for the custom protocols we created earlier. Add the following extension at the bottom of your `PhotoFilterViewController`:

```
extension PhotoFilterViewController: ImageFiltering,
ImageFilteringDelegate {
    func filterSelected(item: FilterItem) {
        let filteredImg = image
        if let img = filteredImg {
            if item.filter != "None" {
                imgExample.image = self.apply(filter: item.filter,
originalImage: img)
            } else {
                imgExample.image = img
            }
        }
    }
}
```

`filterSelected(item:)` gets the selected filter item and applies the filter to `imgExample`. We have an `if` statement that checks whether the user selected `None` and, if so, shows the image without any filters. We finally need to add one last extension for selecting a filter item. Add the following extension at the bottom of your `PhotoFilterViewController`

```
extension PhotoFilterViewController: UICollectionViewDelegate {
    func collectionView(_ collectionView: UICollectionView,
didSelectItemAt indexPath: IndexPath) {
        let item = self.data[indexPath.row]
        filterSelected(item: item)
    }
}
```

Here were are simply getting the selected filter item and passing it into the newly created method filterSelected(). Before we can run it, we need to get the user's permission to use the camera or access the user's photo library.

Getting permission

Apple requires that, if we use the camera or access the camera roll, we must let the user know that we are doing so and why. If you fail to do this, your code regarding the camera will not work, and your app will be rejected when you submit it. Let's take care of this now.

Open the `Info.plist` file and add the following two keys by hovering over any key and hitting the plus icon for the first key. We will then repeat this for the second key:

- `NSPhotoLibraryUsageDescription`
- `NSCameraUsageDescription`

For each key's value, enter anything you want as an alert that the user will see. In the following example, the value is set as `The app uses your camera to take pictures`:

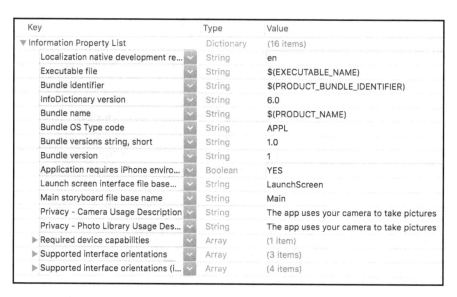

Key	Type	Value
▼ Information Property List	Dictionary	(16 items)
Localization native development re...	String	en
Executable file	String	$(EXECUTABLE_NAME)
Bundle identifier	String	$(PRODUCT_BUNDLE_IDENTIFIER)
InfoDictionary version	String	6.0
Bundle name	String	$(PRODUCT_NAME)
Bundle OS Type code	String	APPL
Bundle versions string, short	String	1.0
Bundle version	String	1
Application requires iPhone enviro...	Boolean	YES
Launch screen interface file base...	String	LaunchScreen
Main storyboard file base name	String	Main
Privacy - Camera Usage Description	String	The app uses your camera to take pictures
Privacy - Photo Library Usage Des...	String	The app uses your camera to take pictures
▶ Required device capabilities	Array	(1 item)
▶ Supported interface orientations	Array	(3 items)
▶ Supported interface orientations (i...	Array	(4 items)

Please make sure that if you are submitting this to the store that you put in the appropriate verbiage. The user, as well as Apple, sees this verbiage. Let's build and run the project by hitting the Play button (or using *command + R*).

You should now be able to get a photo from the photo library or use the camera:

Once you have a photo, the window is dismissed, and you can apply a filter and save it:

We are not saving the photo yet. We will do this in the next chapter.

Summary

In this chapter, we covered a lot of new things. You learned how to use the camera and how to integrate the camera roll when a camera is not available. We used a `UICollectionView` horizontally for the first time so that we could put in a row of images. This chapter had a lot of code, and there may be some parts that were confusing. Review these parts and make sure that you fully understand them. There are numerous things in this chapter that you can reuse in many other apps.

In the next chapter, we will be able to save photos and reviews to restaurants.

Understanding Core Data 19

Our app is coming along nicely, and we are close to wrapping it up. In the previous chapter, we created a restaurant review form, the Create Review form, which allows us to take pictures or use photos from our library. We can apply filters to photos and even add more filters quickly by updating our plist file.

In this chapter, we will finish up working on the Create Review form. We will get the form fully working so that we can save the data that's entered into the form to what is known as Core Data. Core Data is a framework that handles persistent data, using what is known as **Object-Relational Mapping** (**ORM**). We will go much deeper into what Core Data is and how to use it in this chapter.

In this chapter, we will cover the following topics:

- What is Core Data?
- What are `NSManagedObjectModel`, `NSManagedObjectContext`, and `NSPersistentStoreCoordinator`?
- Creating our first Core Data model

What is Core Data?

Let's start by taking a quote directly from Apple:

> *"Core Data is a framework for managing and persisting an object graph."*

Apple does not call Core Data a database, even though, behind the scenes, it saves data to an SQLite file in iOS. Core Data is very hard to explain to someone new to programming or to someone who has come from a different programming language. However, in iOS 10, Core Data has been dramatically simplified. Having a general understanding of what Core Data does and how it works is sufficient for the purposes of this book.

When using the Core Data framework, you should be familiar with the MANAGED OBJECT MODEL, the **MANAGED OBJECT CONTEXT**, and the **PERSISTENT STORE COORDINATOR**. Let's look at a diagram to get a better understanding of how they interact with each other:

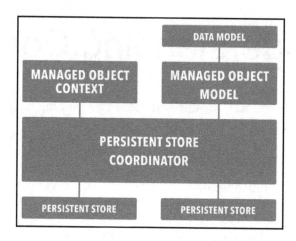

- `NSManagedObjectModel`: The managed object model represents the data model of your Core Data application. It interacts with all of the data models (also known as entities) that you create within your app. This model is known for any relationships that your data may have in your app. It interacts with your data model, as well as with the persistent store coordinator.
  Entities are just objects that represent your data. In our app, since we are going to be saving customer reviews of restaurants, we need to create a review entity.
- `NSManagedObjectContext`: The managed object context manages a collection of model objects, which it receives from the persistent store coordinator. It context is responsible for creating, reading, updating, and deleting models. The context is what you interact with the most.
- `NSPersistentStoreCoordinator`: The persistent store coordinator has a reference to the managed object model, as well as the managed object context. It communicates with the persistent object store. The persistent store coordinator also interacts with an object graph. This graph is where you create your entities and set up relationships within your app.

Core Data is not an easy topic, so you do not need to worry about the finer details. The more you work with Core Data, the easier it becomes to understand it. In this chapter, focus on obtaining a high-level understanding, and the rest will come.

Before iOS 10, you had to create an instance of each of the following: the managed object model, the managed object context, and the persistent store coordinator. Now, in iOS 10, these have been consolidated into what is called `NSPersistentContainer`. We will cover this shortly but, first, we need to create our data model.

Creating a data model

The data model is where you create your app's model objects and their properties. For our project, we only need to create one model object, called **Review**. Let's create a managed object model now:

1. In the Navigator panel, right-click on the `Misc` folder and create a new group, called `Core Data`.
2. Next, right-click this new `Core Data` folder and click **New File**.
3. Inside the **Choose a template for your new file screen**, select **iOS** at the top and then scroll down to the **Core Data** section. From there, select **Data Model**. Then, hit **Next**:

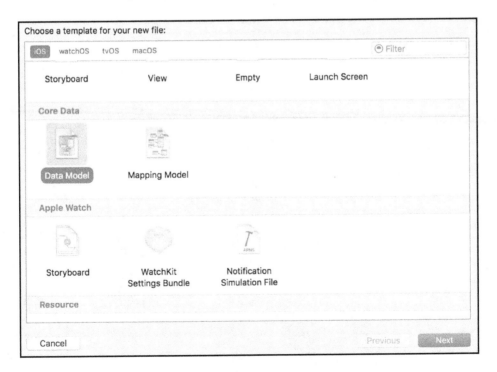

4. Name the file `LetsEatModel` and click **Create**.

5. Click **Add Entity** in the screen that appears:

Then, in the bottom-right corner of the new screen, change the **Editor Style** to **Graph Style**:

In the **Graph Style**, double-click on **Entity** in the box in the middle of the graph to change your entity's name:

6. Update the text to say **Review** and then hit *Enter*.

7. Now that we have our first entity created, let's add our first attribute. Select **Review Entity** and click **Add Attribute** in the bottom-right corner of the screen. The word **attribute** appears under **Attributes** in the box in the middle of the screen:

8. You will see that Xcode shows an error. The reason for this error is that we created an attribute without giving it a type. Let's do that now.

9. Select the word attribute and open your Utilities panel. You will only see three icons: the File inspector, the Quick Help inspector, and the Data Model inspector.

10. Select the last icon, the Data Model inspector and, under **Attribute**, click on the dropdown for **Attribute Type** and change it from **Undefined** to **String**. The error should now disappear.

11. Next, under **Attribute** in the Data Model inspector, change the **Name** from attribute to name and hit *Enter*.

Your first attribute should now look as follows:

We have created our first attribute in the **Graph Style** and now need to set up the rest of our attributes, which we will do in the **Table Style**:

1. Switch the **Editor Style** to**Table Style** and then click **Add Attribute**.
2. Update the attribute to date and set its data type to **Date**. You do not have to do anything in the Data Model inspector for this attribute.
3. Next, select the + button in the **Attributes** section of the **Table Style** screen under the two attributes we just added.
4. Update this third attribute to `customerReview` and set its data type to **String**.
5. Next, add a fourth attribute, named rating, with a data type of **Float**.
6. Now, add a fifth attribute, named `restaurantID`, with a data type of **Integer 32**. When we save reviews, we save them with their `restaurantID`. Whenever we go to a restaurant detail page, we get all of the reviews just for that specific restaurant and then display them. If we do not have any reviews, then we display a default message.

7. Now, add a sixth attribute, named `title`, with a data type of **String**.

8. Lastly, add a seventh attribute, named `uuid`, with a data type of **String** and, under **Attribute** in the Data Model inspector, uncheck the **Optional** checkbox. This attribute is our unique ID for each review.

Your **Attributes** table should now look like the following:

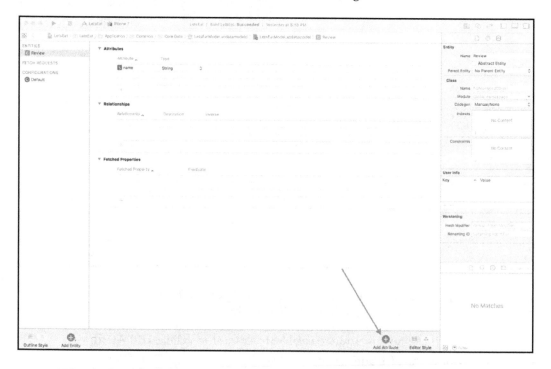

Now that we have our attributes set, we need to do a few more things before we start working on some code.

Entity autogeneration

We could have Xcode create a file for our **Review Entity**; however, if we wanted to add more attributes, we would have to generate more code. Core Data offers the ability to autogenerate our code for us. To take advantage of this feature, follow these steps:

1. In the list of entities in the left-hand panel, select our only **Entity**, **Review**.
2. After you select the entity, select the Data Model inspector in the Utilities panel. You should notice that your Data Model inspector panel has changed from when you were working on your **Attributes**:

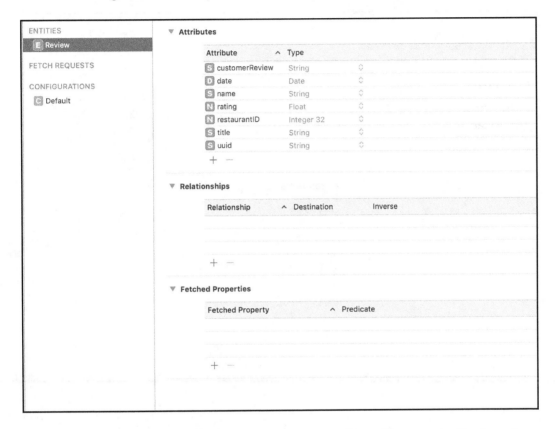

3. Now, hit *command + B* to build the project. This will create the **Review** class that we created in **Core Data**. You will not see the file anywhere, but it will have been created.

Now, we need to create another entity, called `RestaurantPhoto`.

The RestaurantPhoto Entity

Using the same steps as in the previous section, create a photo entity with the following values:

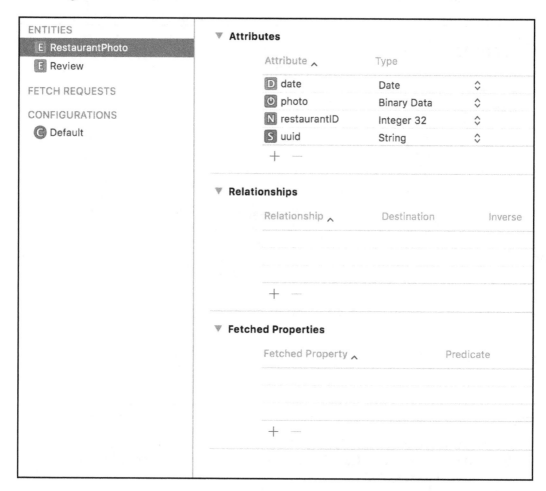

Now, hit *command + B* to build the project; this creates the `Photo` class that we created in **Core Data**.

We cannot just store images in Core Data, as they have to be converted into data first. Therefore, we need take the image that we used in the review and convert it to binary data for Core Data to save. Then, when we pull the review out of Core Data, we will convert it back into an image so that we can display it.

For learning purposes, we are storing images in Core Data. I would stay away from doing this as much as possible, because images can be large and you can quickly fill up the user's storage. If you are using a feed, you can save the URL path to the image instead of the actual image. If the user is not online, then you can display a placeholder in its place.

Review item

We get this new `Review` class back from Core Data when we need to fetch items from it. Instead of passing the `Review` class around, we will create a generic data object that we can use instead.

When I work with stored data, I typically like to have two model objects: one that's used when storing data and another that's generic. In the past, passing around Core Data objects caused a lot of technical issues. These issues were addressed in iOS 10; however, with an overabundance of caution, I typically get the items from Core Data and then convert those objects into a struct.

Let's create this file now:

1. Right-click on the `Model` folder inside of the `Review Form` folder and select **New File**.
2. Inside the **Choose a template for your new file screen**, select **iOS** at the top, and then **Swift File**. Then, hit **Next**.
3. Name this file `ReviewItem` and click **Create**.
4. Update your file to the following:

```
import UIKit

struct ReviewItem {
    var rating:Float?
    var name:String?
    var title:String?
    var customerReview:String?
    var date:Date?
    var restaurantID:Int?
    var uuid = UUID().uuidString

    var displayDate:String {
        let formatter = DateFormatter()
        formatter.dateFormat = "MMMM dd, yyyy"
        guardl let reviewDate = date else { return "" }
        return formatter.string(from: reviewDate Date)
```

```
        }
    }

extension ReviewItem {
    init(data:Review) {
            if let reviewDate = data.date { self.date =
reviewDate }
            self.customerReview = data.customerReview
            self.name = data.name
            self.title = data.title
            self.restaurantID = Int(data.restaurantID)
            self.rating = data.rating
            if let uuid = data.uuid { self.uuid = uuid }
    }
}
```

This file is not doing anything special, other than using a variable to handle dates.

The extension in this file allows us to take the Review from Core Data and map it to a `ReviewItem`. Our custom `init()` method allows us to pass the `Review` object into the `init` parameters.

We need to create another item for the photos that we are saving. This file will have the same basic structure as the `ReviewItem` does. Let's create this file now:

1. Right-click `Controllers` to create a new group called `Photo Reviews`.
2. Right-click the `Photo Reviews` folder and select **New File**.
3. Inside the **Choose a template for your new file screen**, select **iOS** at the top, and then **Swift File**. Then, hit **Next**.
4. Name this file `RestaurantPhotoItem` and hit **Create**.
5. Update your file to the following:

```
struct RestaurantPhotoItem {
    var photo:UIImage?
    var date:NSDate?
    var restaurantID:Int?
    var uuid = UUID().uuidString

    var photoData:NSData {
            guard let image = photo else {
                    return NSData()
            }

            return NSData(data: image.pngData()!)
    }
}
```

```
extension RestaurantPhotoItem {
    init(data:RestaurantPhoto) {
        self.restaurantID = Int(data.restaurantID)
        if let restaurantPhoto = data.photo { self.photo =
UIImage(data:restaurantPhoto, scale:1.0) }
        if let uuid = data.uuid { self.uuid = uuid }
        if let reviewDate = data.date { self.date =
reviewDate }
    }
}
```

The first part of this file is similar to what we did for the review item, except for the `photoData` variable. Since we cannot store an image directly in Core Data, we need to convert it into binary data. The `photoData` variable handles this for us and makes it easier when we save an item to pass `photoData` to Core Data.

Now that we have our `ReviewItem` and `RestaurantPhotoItem`, we need to set up our manager.

Core Data manager

As we have done throughout this book, we are going to create a `Manager` class. This class will be responsible for getting data in and out of Core Data. Let's get started:

1. Right-click the `Core Data` folder in the `Common` folder and select **New File**.
2. Inside the **Choose a template for your new file screen**, select **iOS** at the top, and then **Cocoa Touch Class**. Then, hit **Next**.
3. In the options screen that appears, add the following:

   New file:

   - **Class**: `CoreDataManager`
   - **Subclass**: `NSObject`
   - **Also create XIB**: Unchecked
   - **Language**: `Swift`

4. Click **Next** and then **Create**.

When the file opens, under your `import UIKit`, add the following:

```
import CoreData
```

This import allows us to have access to the Core Data library. Next, inside the class definition, add the following:

```
let container:NSPersistentContainer
```

This constant, which is an NSPersistentContainer, gives us everything we need within a Core Data stack. As we discussed earlier, NSPersistentContainer is composed of three things: a persistent store coordinator, a managed object context, and a managed object model.

You may have noticed an error after adding this variable. The reason for the error is that we have not created an init() method.

Let's add this init() method after the constant we just added:

```
override init() {
    container = NSPersistentContainer(name: "LetsEatModel")
    container.loadPersistentStores { (storeDesc, error) in
        guard error == nil else {
            print(error?.localizedDescription as Any)
            return
        }
    }
    super.init()
}
```

This code is initializing the container and grabbing the managed object model we created earlier. The model is now able to see all of our entities and attributes therein.

Our CoreDataManager needs to do two things for us. We need to be able to add a new ReviewItem and fetch it. When we save a restaurant review, we want to be able to save the review with the restaurant. We do not need to save all of the restaurant information, since we can simply use restaurantID. When we go to restaurant details, we can check Core Data for any reviews for a particular restaurant by using restaurantID. Let's add the following method after our init() method to accomplish this task for us:

```
func fetchReviews(by identifier:Int) -> [ReviewItem] {
    let moc = container.viewContext
    let request:NSFetchRequest<Review> = Review.fetchRequest()
    let predicate = NSPredicate(format: "restaurantID = %i",
Int32(identifier))
    var items:[ReviewItem] = []
    request.sortDescriptors = [
      NSSortDescriptor(key: "date", ascending: false)]
    request.predicate = predicate
```

```
    do {
        for data in try moc.fetch(request) {
            items.append(ReviewItem(data: data))
        }
        return items
    } catch {
        fatalError("Failed to fetch reviews: (error)")
    }
}
```

Let's review this code. Our `fetchReviews(by:)` method takes an ID, and we use this to find reviews for a particular restaurant:

```
let moc = container.viewContext
let request:NSFetchRequest<Review> = Review.fetchRequest()
let predicate = NSPredicate(format: "restaurantID = %i",
Int32(identifier))
```

In the first line, we are creating an instance of the **managed object context** (**moc**). This variable allows us to interact with Core Data. In the next line, we are creating a fetch request. This request is passed to the managed object context and tells it what we need. Finally, we are creating a predicate, which allows us to apply some search parameters. Specifically, we are saying that we want every `ReviewItem` that has the ID that we pass it:

```
request.sortDescriptors = [NSSortDescriptor(key: "date", ascending:
false)]
request.predicate = predicate
```

Here, we are applying a sort descriptor to our request. Instead of getting reviews back in a random order, we sort all of the reviews by date:

```
do {
    for data in try moc.fetch(request) {
        items.append(ReviewItem(data: data))
    }
    return items
} catch {
    fatalError("Failed to fetch reviews: (error)")
}
```

Finally, we are wrapping everything into a do...catch block. When the search occurs, it returns an array of `ReviewItems` or, if there were no `ReviewItems`, an empty array. If there was a problem with your setup, then you will get a fatal error. When the fetch is complete, we then loop through the items and create our `ReviewItems`.

We have added our method to get reviews; we need to do the same for fetching photos. Add the following after the `fetchReviews(identifier:)` method:

```swift
func fetchPhotos(by identifier:Int) -> [RestaurantPhotoItem] {
    let moc = container.viewContext
    let request:NSFetchRequest<Review> =
RestaurantPhoto.fetchRequest()
    let predicate = NSPredicate(format: "restaurantID = %i",
Int32(identifier))
    var items:[RestaurantPhotoItem] = []
    request.sortDescriptors = [NSSortDescriptor(key: "date",
ascending: false)]
    request.predicate = predicate
    do {
        for data in try moc.fetch(request) {
            items.append(ReviewItem(data: data))
        }
        return items
    } catch {
        fatalError("Failed to fetch photos: (error)")
    }
}
```

Everything is the same as what we did to fetch review items, except we are fetching `RestaurantPhoto` items instead. Now, we need to add a method to save our data into Core Data. Let's add the next two methods by adding the following after our `init()` method:

```swift
func addReview(_ item:ReviewItem) {
    let review = Review(context: container.viewContext)
    review.name = item.name
    review.title = item.title
    review.date = NSDate()
    if let rating = item.rating { review.rating = rating }
    review.customerReview = item.customerReview
    review.uuid = item.uuid

    if let id = item.restaurantID {
        review.restaurantID = Int32(id)
        print("restaurant id (id)")
        save()
    }
}

func addPhoto(_ item:RestarauntPhotoItem) {
    let photo = RestarauntPhoto(context: container.viewContext)
    photo.date = NSDate()
```

```
photo.photo = item.photoData
photo.uuid = item.uuid

if let id = item.restaurantID {
        photo.restaurantID = Int32(id)
        print("restaurant id (id)")
          save()
    }
}
```

You will get an error because you have not created the `save()` method yet. Ignore it for now, as we will create that next.

This `addReview()` method takes a `ReviewItem` in the parameters. We convert the `ReviewItem` into a `Review` and then call the `save()` method.

Now, let's add the `save()` method after the `addReview()` method we just created:

```
fileprivate func save() {
    do {
        if container.viewContext.hasChanges {
            try container.viewContext.save()
        }
    }
    catch let error {
        print(error.localizedDescription)
    }
}
```

Once again, we are wrapping everything in a `do...catch` block. Inside of the do, we check to see whether the managed object context has changed. If it has changed, then we call the `save()` method. We have now completed our Core Data manager.

Next, we need to create another manager class. This manager is responsible for making calls to the Core Data manager, similar to how the corresponding manager in the explore manager is responsible for getting data from the plist. This gets us photos and reviews. Let's create this manager file now:

1. Right-click the `Misc` folder and select **New File**.
2. Inside the **Choose a template for your new file screen**, select **iOS** at the top, and then **Cocoa Touch Class**. Then, hit **Next**.

3. In the options screen that appears, add the following:

New file:

- **Class**: ReviewDataManager
- **Subclass**: NSObject
- **Also create XIB**: Unchecked
- **Language**: Swift

4. Hit **Next** and then **Create**. Update your file to the following:

```swift
import Foundation

class ReviewDataManager: NSObject {

    private var reviewItems:[ReviewItem] = []
    private var photoItems:[RestaurantPhotoItem] = []
    let manager = CoreDataManager()

    func fetchReview(by restaurantID:Int) {
        if reviewItems.count > 0 { reviewItems.removeAll() }
        for data in manager.fetchReviews(by: restaurantID) {
            reviewItems.append(data)
        }
    }

    func fetchPhoto(by restaurantID:Int) {
        if photoItems.count > 0 { photoItems.removeAll() }
        for data in manager.fetchPhotos(by: restaurantID) {
            photoItems.append(data)
        }
    }

    func numberOfReviewItems() -> Int {
        return reviewItems.count
    }

    func numberOfPhotoItems() -> Int {
        return photoItems.count
    }

    func reviewItem(at index:IndexPath) -> ReviewItem {
        return reviewItems[index.item]
    }

    func photoItem(at index:IndexPath) -> RestaurantPhotoItem
```

```
            {
                return photoItems[index.item]
            }
        }
    }
```

This manager class is similar to the other managers that we have created so far. In this manager, our fetch method takes an ID in the parameter. This ID represents the `restaurantID` that we use to search for `ReviewItems` in Core Data. If we find any `ReviewItems`, we add them to our array.

Summary

In this chapter, you learned about what Core Data is and how to use it. We also looked at `NSManagedObjectModel`, `NSManagedObjectContext`, and `NSPersistentStoreCoordinator`, and how they work together inside Core Data. Even if they do not make sense to you—they did not work for me the first time—it is all right because it will eventually click. Finally, we created two Core Data models: one for reviews and one for photos.

In the next chapter, we will work on actually saving the data we create, as well as getting it back out. We will take our reviews and photos, and display them inside our restaurant details.

20
Saving Reviews

We are just about done with our app. In this chapter, we will finally start saving reviews and photos in Core Data. We will then learn how to pull data from Core Data and display it in our app. A lot of the setup is already done for us, and most of what we will do is calls methods that we created earlier in this book.

In this chapter, we will cover the following topics:

- Saving items to Core Data
- Fetching items from Core Data
- Displaying items from Core Data in a Table View

Saving reviews

First, we will start saving reviews in Core Data. Open up `ReviewFormViewController.swift` and, above `@IBOutlets`, add the following variable:

```
var selectedRestaurantID:Int?
```

Next, delete all of the print statements inside your `onSavedTapped(:)` method and then add the following:

```
@IBAction func onSaveTapped(_ sender: Any) {

    var item = ReviewItem()
    item.name = tfName.text
    item.title = tfTitle.text
    item.customerReview = tvReview.text
    item.restaurantID = selectedRestaurantID
    item.rating = Float(ratingView.rating)

    let manager = CoreDataManager()
    manager.addReview(item)
```

```
    dismiss(animated: true, completion: nil)
}
```

This code is all we need to save an item in Core Data using `CoreDataManager`. To display reviews for a particular restaurant, we need to save every review with a restaurant identifier. Then, when we go to a certain restaurant, we will use the restaurant identifier to search Core Data to see if there are any saved reviews. We pass this identifier using a segue:

1. Open `RestaurantDetail.storyboard` and select the segue we will use to go to the `ReviewForm`.

2. In the Attributes inspector of the Utilities panel, update **Identifier** under **Storyboard Segue** to say `showReview`. Then, hit *enter*.

3. Next, we need to make sure that, when a user creates a review, we pass `restaurantID` to the **Review Form View Controller**. We need to update our `RestaurantItem` so that it has an ID. Open `RestaurantItem` after `var imageURL:String?` and add the following:

   ```
   var restaurantID:Int?
   ```

4. Next, inside the `CodingKeys:String` enum, add the new case:

   ```
   case restaurantID = "id"
   ```

5. Open `RestaurantDetailViewController.swift` and add this method after the `viewDidLoad()` method (ignore the errors for now):

   ```
   override func prepare(for segue: UIStoryboardSegue, sender:
   Any?) {
       if let identifier = segue.identifier {
           switch identifier {
           case Segue.showReview.rawValue:
               showReview(segue: segue)
           default:
               print("Segue not added")
           }
       }
   }
   ```

The `prepare()` method inside `RestaurantDetailViewController` will check for the `showReview` segue identifier. If successful, it will call the `showReview()` method, which will take you to the Reviews list.

6. Next, add the following method above the `createRating()` method, inside the private extension:

```
func showReview(segue:UIStoryboardSegue) {
    guard let navController = segue.destination as?
UINavigationController,
        let viewController = navController.topViewController
as? ReviewFormViewController else {
            return
    }
    viewController.selectedRestaurantID =
selectedRestaurant?.restaurantID
}
```

7. While we are cleaning up, move the `initialize()` method into the `private` extension.

8. Next, open `ReviewFormViewController`; let's create a `private` extension and move `onSaveTapped(_:)` into it. Then, delete everything inside the method and update the method with the following:

```
private extension ReviewFormViewController {
    @IBAction func onSaveTapped(_ sender: Any) {
        var item = ReviewItem()
        item.name = tfName.text
        item.title = tfTitle.text
        item.customerReview = tvReview.text
        item.restaurantID = selectedRestaurantID
        item.rating = Float(ratingView.rating)

        let manager = CoreDataManager()
        manager.addReview(item)

        dismiss(animated: true, completion: nil)
    }
}
```

Let's make sure that we are passing `restaurantID` by adding a `print` statement inside `ReviewFormViewController`.

9. Inside the `–viewDidLoad()` method, add the following `print` statement:

```
print(selectedRestaurantID as Any)
```

Let's build and run the project by hitting the Play button (or by using *command + R*). You should now be able to see `restaurantID` in the console. You can create a review and, after you save the review, will be brought back to the restaurant detail view. However, we still can't display our reviews in restaurant details. We will work on this later in the chapter. Before we do that, let's look at how we can save photos in Core Data.

Saving photos

Saving reviews was pretty simple, and is virtually no different to saving photos. Our code will be pretty similar to what we had for reviews.
Open `PhotoFilterViewController` and update it with the following:

```
func checkSavedPhoto() {
    if let img = self.imgExample.image {
        var item = RestaurantPhotoItem()
        item.photo = generate(image: img, ratio: CGFloat(102))
        item.date = NSDate() as Date
        item.restaurantID = selectedRestaurantID
        let manager = CoreDataManager()
        manager.addPhoto(item)

        dismiss(animated: true, completion: nil)
    }
}
```

This method will make sure that we have an image and that we can save it to Core Data with its restaurant ID. We need to add a method for when **Save** is tapped. Add the following method inside the private extension:

```
@IBAction func onSaveTapped(_ sender: AnyObject) {
    DispatchQueue.main.async {
        self.checkSavedPhoto()
    }
}
```

Now, when a user taps the **Save** button, this will make sure that an image is saved in Core Data.

 Note: Here, I am using a `DispatchQueue`. This is for UI purposes and might not be needed, but it helps with performance when something is using a lot of resources and locking up the phone.

Before we can save, we need to pass the restaurant identifier to
`PhotoFilterViewController.swift`:

1. Open `RestaurantDetail.storyboard` and select the segue we will use
   to go to the Photo Filter View.
2. In the Attributes inspector of the Utilities panel, update **Identifier** under
   Storyboard Segue to say `showPhotoFilter`. Then, hit *enter*.
3. Inside `RestaurantDetailViewController.swift`, update your
   `prepare` method with the following:

```
override func prepare(for segue: UIStoryboardSegue, sender:
Any?) {
    if let identifier = segue.identifier {
        switch identifier {
        case Segue.showReview.rawValue:
            showReview(segue: segue)
        case Segue.showPhotoFilter.rawValue:
            showPhotoFilter(segue: segue)
        default:
            print("Segue not added")
        }
    }
}
```

4. Next, add the following method after the `showReview()` method
   inside your `private` method:

```
func showPhotoFilter(segue:UIStoryboardSegue) {
    guard let navController = segue.destination as?
UINavigationController,
        let viewController = navController.topViewController as?
PhotoFilterViewController else {
            return
    }

    viewController.selectedRestaurantID =
selectedRestaurant?.restaurantID
}
```

We are passing the restaurant identifier to our photos, and we now have our photos
saved in Core Data. After you save a photo, you are brought back to the restaurant
detail view, but next, we need to display the photos in our **Detail** section.

We are missing one last thing. The photo review and review sections need to pull data from the database for it to be displayed. We need to create a class for each one, so let's start by adding this class:

1. Create a new folder called `Reviews`.
2. Right-click the folder and select **New File**.
3. Inside the **Choose a template for your new file screen**, select **iOS** at the top, and then **Cocoa Touch Class**. Then, hit **Next**.
4. In the options screen that appears, add the following:
   New file:

   - **Class**: `ReviewsViewController`
   - **Subclass**: `UIViewController`
   - **Also create XIB**: Unchecked
   - **Language**: `Swift`

5. Hit **Next** and then **Create**. When the file opens, replace everything with the following code:

```swift
import UIKit
class ReviewsViewController: UIViewController {
    @IBOutlet weak var collectionView: UICollectionView!
    var selectedRestaurantID:Int?
    let manager = CoreDataManager()
    var data: [ReviewItem] = []
    override func viewDidLoad() {
        super.viewDidLoad()
        initialize()
    }

    override func viewDidAppear(_ animated: Bool) {
        super.viewDidAppear(animated)
        setupDefaults()
    }
}
```

6. Next, let's add our `private` extension by adding the following:

```swift
private extension ReviewsViewController {
    func initialize() {
        setupCollectionView()
    }

    func setupDefaults() {
```

```
            checkReviews()
    }

    func setupCollectionView() {
        let flow = UICollectionViewFlowLayout()
        flow.sectionInset = UIEdgeInsets(top: 7, left: 7,
bottom: 7, right: 7)
        flow.minimumInteritemSpacing = 0
        flow.minimumLineSpacing = 7
        flow.scrollDirection = .horizontal
        collectionView?.collectionViewLayout = flow
    }

    func checkReviews() {
        let viewController = self.parent as?
RestaurantDetailViewController
        if let id =
viewController?.selectedRestaurant?.restaurantID {
            if data.count > 0 { data.removeAll() }
            data = manager.fetchReviews(by: id)
            if data.count > 0 {
                collectionView.backgroundView = nil
            }
            else {
                let view = NoDataView(frame: CGRect(x: 0, y:
0, width: collectionView.frame.width, height:
collectionView.frame.height))
                view.set(title: "Reviews")
                view.set(desc: "There are currently no
reviews")
                collectionView.backgroundView = view
            }
            collectionView.reloadData()
        }
    }
}
```

This is the basic setup that we did before. Our checkReviews() method is a bit different, because we first check to see if there are any reviews at all. If there are none, we display a message that says **There are currently no reviews. If there are, we do not display anything**.

7. Next, let's add our Collection View extensions by adding the following to our data source:

```
extension ReviewsViewController: UICollectionViewDataSource {
    func collectionView(_ collectionView: UICollectionView,
numberOfItemsInSection section: Int) -> Int {
        return data.count
    }

    func numberOfSections(in collectionView: UICollectionView)
-> Int {
        return 1
    }

    func collectionView(_ collectionView: UICollectionView,
cellForItemAt indexPath: IndexPath) -> UICollectionViewCell {
        let item = data[indexPath.item]
        cell.lblName.text = item.name
        cell.lblTitle.text = item.title
        cell.lblReview.text = item.customerReview
        cell.lblDate.text = item.displayDate
        if let rating = item.rating { cell.ratingView.rating =
CGFloat(rating) }
        return cell
    }
}
```

8. Next, let's add our Collection View extensions by adding the following to our layout:

```
extension ReviewsViewController:
UICollectionViewDelegateFlowLayout {

    func collectionView(_ collectionView: UICollectionView,
layout collectionViewLayout: UICollectionViewLayout,
sizeForItemAt indexPath:IndexPath) -> CGSize {
        if data.count == 1 {
            let width = collectionView.frame.size.width - 14
            return CGSize(width: width, height: 200)
        }
        else {
            let width = collectionView.frame.size.width - 21
            return CGSize(width: width, height: 200)
        }
    }
}
```

Next, for our Collection View to work, we need to create our cell class and an extension of that class:

1. Right-click the `Reviews` folder and select **New File**.
2. Inside the **Choose a template for your new file screen**, select **iOS** at the top, and then **Cocoa Touch Class**. Then, hit **Next**.
3. In the options screen that appears, add the following:

   New file:

   - **Class**: `ReviewCell`
   - **Subclass**: `UICollectionViewCell`
   - **Also create XIB**: Unchecked
   - **Language**: `Swift`

4. Click **Next** and then **Create**.
5. In this new file, add the following code:

   ```
   @IBOutlet weak var lblTitle: UILabel!
   @IBOutlet weak var lblDate: UILabel!
   @IBOutlet weak var lblName: UILabel!
   @IBOutlet weak var lblReview: UILabel!
   @IBOutlet weak var ratingView: RatingView!
   ```

6. Save the file and open up `RestaurantDetail.storyboard`.

7. Locate the `Container` that was created for `Reviews`:

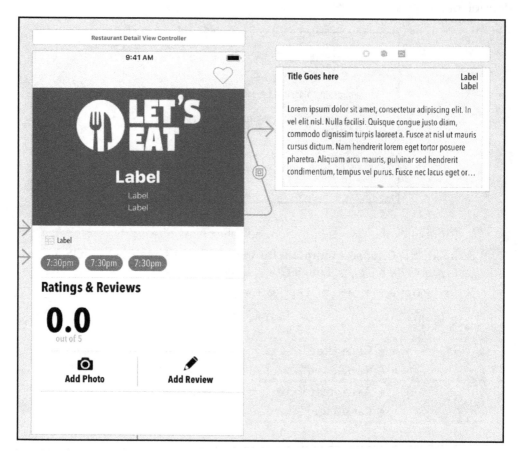

8. Select the cell inside the Collection View. Select the View Controller, and in the Identity inspector, under **Custom Class**, set **Class** to `ReviewsViewController`. Then, hit *enter*.

9. Under Identity inspector, update the class to `ReviewCell`.

10. Select the Collection View, and in the Identity inspector, click and drag from `dataSource` and delegate to the View Controller.

Build and run your project and add a couple of reviews; you should now see reviews appearing in your restaurant details:

We have two more things to update before the end of this chapter. Now that we are saving reviews, we have an overall rating for restaurants. Let's add this next.

Adding an overall rating

To add an overall rating, we need to pull all of the reviews from Core Data, add them all together, and get an average. Let's add a new method to our Core Data manager to handle this. Add the following inside `CoreDataManager.swift`:

```
func fetchRestaurantRating(by identifier:Int) -> Float {
    let reviews = fetchReviews(by: identifier).map({ $0 })
    let sum = reviews.reduce(0, {$0 + ($1.rating ?? 0)})
    return sum / Float(reviews.count)
}
```

In this method, we fetch all of the reviews for a restaurant by their ID. Then, we use the `reduce` method to add them all together, and finally, we calculate the average. Now, let's use this newly created method. Open up `RestaurantDetailViewController.swift`. Under the `selectedRestaurant` variable, add the following:

```
let manager = CoreDataManager()
```

Next, under the `createRating()` method, we just set our rating to `3.5` stars. Update this method to the following:

```
func createRating() {
    if let id = selectedRestaurant?.restaurantID {
        let value = manager.fetchRestaurantRating(by: id)
        ratingView.rating = CGFloat(value)
        if value.isNaN { lblOverallRating.text = "0" }
        else { lblOverallRating.text = "\(value)" }
    }
}
```

Now, our method is checking to make sure that we have a restaurant ID. If we do, then we set the rating for `ratingView`. We also update the overall label to display the average. Build and run your project, and you should now see a rating for restaurants that have one:

We are finished with this chapter, but there is one thing left that we did not do, and that's adding photo reviews. Your challenge is to add photo reviews and get them displayed in the Collection View. We covered everything you'll need in this chapter, and all of the code is the same. If you get stuck, feel free to use the project files that are in the next chapter.

Summary

We covered a lot in this chapter, and we've now finished building our main app's primary functionality. Our app is starting to take shape. We were able to create a Core Data model and can now save reviews to Core Data. We can also display all of the reviews for a restaurant or pull out the last review and display it.

In the next chapter, we will work on putting the final touches to our app to make it more universal. Once we have done that, our main app will be finished, and we'll be able to focus on adding some cool features, such as an iMessage app, notifications, and 3D Touch.

21
Universal

We have spent most of this book focusing on the logic of our app and getting it to work on iPhones. We have not paid much attention to the app working on iPads or other devices. In this chapter, we will look at the app on an iPad, as well as updating it on all iPhone devices. You will be surprised at how much is already working, and that only minor changes will need to be made to get our app to look how we want. We will also take the time to clean up some of our design elements to match the design more closely.

In this chapter, we will cover the following topics:

- Updating our app to be supported on all devices
- Learning about multitasking and how to code for it
- Cleaning up design elements and using global settings

Explore

Let's make some design tweaks before we jump into making our layout work for every device and start to get this app more polished.

Let's compare what we can see on an iPhone 8 with the original design:

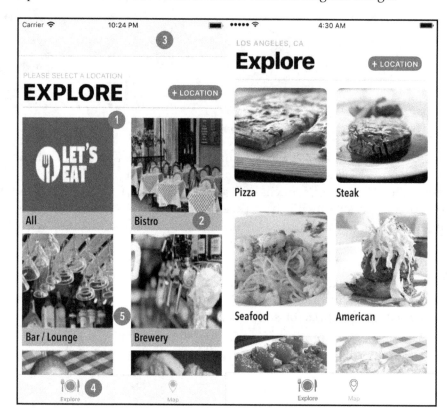

There are a few things we need to fix:

- Implement rounded corners
- Remove the gray background
- The navigation bar is being displayed
- Tab bar color
- Spacing

We will fix all of these, but we will focus on the first four right now. We have rounded corners in our photo filter list. We can implement these here. Open the `ExploreCell.swift` file by hitting *command + shift + O*, type `ExploreCell`, and hit *enter*. Add the following extension:

```
private extension ExploreCell {
    func roundedCorners() {
        imgExplore.layer.cornerRadius = 9
```

```
            imgExplore.layer.masksToBounds = true
        }
    }
```

Add a `roundedCorners()` call inside the `layoutSubviews` method:

```
override func layoutSubviews() {
    super.layoutSubviews()
    roundedCorners()
}
```

Now that we have fixed the first issue, let's fix the second by removing the background color. Open `Explore.storyboard` and select `exploreCell` in the Outline view. Under the Utility panel, in the Attributes inspector, update the **Background** from **LetsEat Dark Grey** to **White Color**. The third issue, being the fact that the navigation bar is displayed, is pretty easy to fix as well. Open the `ExploreViewController.swift` file by hitting *command + shift + O*, type `ExploreViewController`, and hit *Enter*. After `viewDidLoad()`, add the following method:

```
override func viewWillAppear(_ animated: Bool) {
    super.viewWillAppear(animated)
    navigationController?.setNavigationBarHidden(true, animated:
false)
}
```

That is all we need to do; now, every time we go to this view, we will always hide the Navigation bar at the top. Finally, let's update our app so that our tab bar buttons are the correct color. We need to add a new color to our **Color Set** called **LetsEat Red** and set the **Hex** value to D0021B. Open up the `AppDelegate.swift` file at the bottom of the file after the last curly brace, and add the following:

```
private extension AppDelegate {
    func initialize() {
        setupDefaultColors()
    }

    func setupDefaultColors() {
        guard let red = UIColor(named: "LetsEat Red") else { return }
        UITabBar.appearance().tintColor = red
        UITabBar.appearance().barTintColor = .white
        UITabBarItem.appearance()
            .setTitleTextAttributes(
                [NSAttributedString.Key.foregroundColor:
UIColor.black],
                for: UIControl.State.normal)
```

```
        UITabBarItem.appearance()
            .setTitleTextAttributes(
                [NSAttributedString.Key.foregroundColor: red],
                for: UIControl.State.selected)
        UINavigationBar.appearance().tintColor = red
        UINavigationBar.appearance().barTintColor = .white
        UITabBar.appearance().isTranslucent = false
        UINavigationBar.appearance().isTranslucent = false
    }
}
```

Inside `application:didFinishLaunchingWithOptions:`, add the `initialize()` method call. Build and run the project by hitting the Play button (or by using *command + R*):

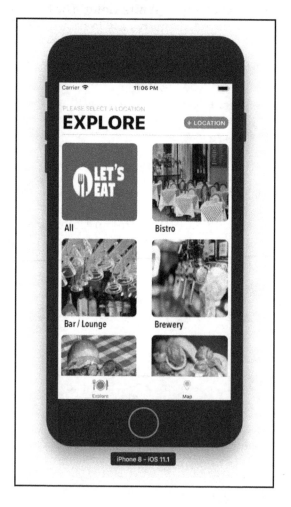

You should now see that we have completed the first four items. Let's address the spacing issue next. Before we do, first, let's switch our device to any iPad. Then, build and run the project by hitting the Play button (or by using *command + R*). You will see that it is not too bad currently, but the spacing is different on each device. So far, we have only set up values that work for one device. However, we need this to work on all devices.

Let's start with `Explore.storyboard`. First, we need to update the Auto Layout for our explore cells. Right now, we have a width set up for our image that needs to be more dynamic:

1. Open up `Explore.storyboard`.
2. Select the image inside the `exploreCell`.
3. Then, in the Utilities panel, select the Attributes inspector and change the **Content Mode** under the **View** section to **Aspect Fill**. Updating this will keep images from looking stretched, while still filling the entire area:

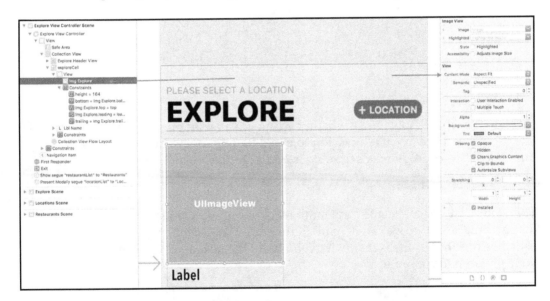

These are the only updates we need to make to our explore cell. Next, we are going to create a file that will let us know which device is being used. We can then use this to set up different looks, depending on the device. Let's create this file:

4. Right-click the `Misc` folder and select **New File**.

5. Inside the **Choose a template for your new file** screen, select **iOS** at the top, and then **Swift File**. Then, hit **Next**.

6. Name this file `Device` and then hit **Create**.

First, we need to update our `import` statement from `import Foundation` to `import UIKit`.

Next, add the following to the `import` statement:

```
struct Device {
    static var currentDevice: UIDevice {
        struct Singleton {
            static let device = UIDevice.current
        }
        return Singleton.device
    }

    static var isPhone: Bool {
        return currentDevice.userInterfaceIdiom == .phone
    }

    static var isPad: Bool {
        return currentDevice.userInterfaceIdiom == .pad
    }
}
```

Our new struct will now tell us whether we are on an iPad or an iPhone. Having a file like this is good because it allows you to avoid having to rewrite the same code. To implement this code, all we need to do is add a snippet of code like the following:

```
if Device.isPhone{ }
```

This statement will make our code more readable; if we need to add any more checks for particular devices, we can do it all in the same file. One more great use of putting code like this into its file is that, when you build the next app, you can add this file to your project and continue.

Next, let's open the `ExploreViewController.swift` file and make some more updates to our code. We need to create a variable that we will use for the spacing we want between items. Add the following before your `viewDidLoad()` method:

```
fileprivate let minItemSpacing: CGFloat = 7
```

Now, we need to create a function to set up some default Collection View values. We also need to create an `initialize()` method to call our setup function. Add the following method call inside of the `initialize()` method:

```
setupCollectionView()
```

Next, add the following inside of the `private` extension after the `initialize()` method:

```
func setupCollectionView() {
    let flow = UICollectionViewFlowLayout()
    flow.sectionInset = UIEdgeInsets(top: 7, left: 7, bottom: 7,
right: 7)
    flow.minimumInteritemSpacing = 0
    flow.minimumLineSpacing = 7
    collectionView?.collectionViewLayout = flow
}
```

This method will make sure that we have seven pixels of spacing all the way around. Finally, we need to create an extension that will let us handle all of the spacing programmatically. After the last curly brace, add the following extension:

```
extension ExploreViewController: UICollectionViewDelegateFlowLayout {
    func collectionView(_ collectionView: UICollectionView, layout
collectionViewLayout: UICollectionViewLayout, sizeForItemAt indexPath:
IndexPath) -> CGSize {
        if Device.isPad {
            let factor = traitCollection.horizontalSizeClass ==
.compact ? 2:3
            let screenRect = collectionView.frame.size.width
            let screenWidth = screenRect - (CGFloat(minItemSpacing) *
CGFloat(factor + 1))
            let cellWidth = screenWidth / CGFloat(factor)

            return CGSize(width: cellWidth, height: 195)
        }
        else {
            let screenRect = collectionView.frame.size.width
            let screenWidth = screenRect - 21
            let cellWidth = screenWidth / 2.0
```

```
                    return CGSize(width: cellWidth, height: 195)
            }
        }

        func collectionView(_ collectionView: UICollectionView, layout
    collectionViewLayout: UICollectionViewLayout,
    referenceSizeForHeaderInSection section: Int) -> CGSize {

            return CGSize(width: self.collectionView.frame.width, height:
    100)
        }
    }
```

Adding `UICollectionViewDelegateFlowLayout` allows us to update our cell item size in code. Let's discuss each part of the extension we just added. The – `collectionView:layout:sizeForItemAtIndexPath:` method is used to set the size of the cell. Inside this method, we are using the struct we created. We are checking to see whether we are using an iPad or an iPhone.

In the if part of the `if...else` statement, we are checking whether the screen is compact or not. If the screen is compact, then we want a two-column grid; otherwise, we want a three-column grid. We are also distributing our items evenly across the width of the screen.

In the else part of the `if...else` statement, we are just setting up a two-column grid on all phones. We get the screen width and then subtract 21, and then we divide the result by 2 to distribute the cells evenly.

Now, build and rerun your project by hitting the Play button (or by using *command* + *R*) and rotate the device. You will see that our layout spacing now updates:

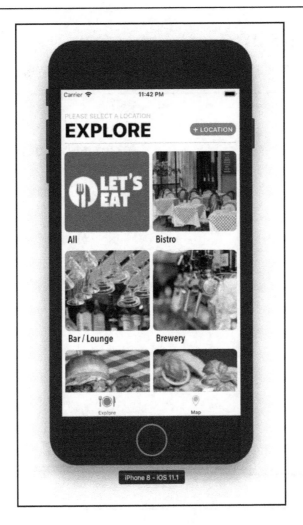

Explore is now complete; let's move on to our locations list.

Location listing

Let's compare our current location listing with the original design:

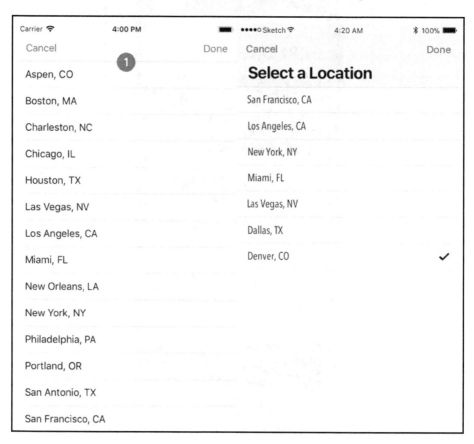

We have one thing that needs fixing: the large title. Updating to large titles is simple. Open up the `LocationViewController` and, inside of the `initialize()` method, add the following code after `manager.fetch()`:

```
title = "Select a Location"
navigationController?.navigationBar.prefersLargeTitles = true
```

In this code, we are setting a new iOS 11 feature, `prefersLargeTitles`, to `true`. If you build and run, you will see that we are good here now. Next, we will direct our attention to the restaurant listing page and go into more detail on the iPad and multitasking.

Restaurant listing

For our restaurant listing page, we want a one-column grid on all phones and a two-column grid on all iPads. If you build and run the project by hitting the Play button (or by using *command + R*) and go to a restaurant listing page, you will see that we need to fix the spacing on the iPad to show two columns correctly:

Let's see how we can fix this. Remember that we still want one column on the iPhone and a grid on the iPad. Open the `RestaurantListViewController.swift` file and add the following above the `createData()` method inside of the private extension:

```
func initialize() {
    createData()
    setupTitle()
    if Device.isPad{ setupCollectionView() }
}
```

You will get an error for the `setupCollectionView()` method. Ignore it for now, as we will fix this shortly. This method checks whether the device is an iPad; if it is, it calls the `setupCollectionView()` method. Next, add the following under the `initialize()` method we just added:

```
func setupCollectionView() {
    let flow = UICollectionViewFlowLayout()
    flow.sectionInset = UIEdgeInsets(top: 7, left: 7, bottom: 7, right:
7)
    flow.minimumInteritemSpacing = 0
    flow.minimumLineSpacing = 7
    collectionView?.collectionViewLayout = flow
}
```

The preceding method is the same as we previously added in the storyboard regarding spacing between items, but here, we are implementing it programmatically.

We have a couple more things that we need to address. First, we are going to have the size of the screen calculated for us programmatically. Just as we did in `ExploreViewController`, we are going to a new extension to handle our Collection View layout. Add the following before your `viewDidLoad()` method:

```
fileprivate let minItemSpacing: CGFloat = 7
```

Now, add the following at the bottom of the file, after the last curly brace:

```
extension RestaurantListViewController:
UICollectionViewDelegateFlowLayout {

    func collectionView(_ collectionView: UICollectionView, layout
collectionViewLayout: UICollectionViewLayout, sizeForItemAt indexPath:
IndexPath) -> CGSize {
        if Device.isPad {
            let factor = traitCollection.horizontalSizeClass ==
.compact ? 2:3
            let screenRect = collectionView.frame.size.width
            let screenWidth = screenRect - (CGFloat(minItemSpacing) *
CGFloat(factor +
1))
            let cellWidth = screenWidth / CGFloat(factor)
            return CGSize(width: cellWidth, height: 325)
        }

        else {
            let screenRect = collectionView.frame.size.width
            let cellWidth = screenRect - 14
```

```
            return CGSize(width: cellWidth, height: 325)
        }
    }
}
```

This code states that, if the device is an iPhone, a one-column grid will be shown; if it is an iPad, a two-column grid will be shown. Now, we need to update our `viewDidAppear()` method. Currently, we are calling both `createData()` and `setupTitle()`. We need to remove both of these calls and call `initialize()` instead. When you are finished, `viewDidAppear()` should look like the following:

```
override func viewDidAppear(_ animated: Bool) {
    super.viewDidAppear(animated)
    initialize()
}
```

Let's build and run the project for the iPad by hitting the Play button (or by using *command + R*):

The two-column grid is what we want for the iPad for our restaurant listing page, but we need to verify that we did not change the one-column grid on the iPhone. Switch the device back to any iPhone simulator and, after building and rerunning the project, you should still see a one-column grid on the iPhone.

There are still issues with the iPad setup. Switch back to the iPad and build and rerun the project by hitting the Play button (or by using *command + R*). You will now see that, every time you update the size of the restaurant listing page, the grid updates as well, to fit the new size. Let's move on to the restaurant detail page.

Updating the restaurant detail page

If you click on a restaurant and go to a restaurant detail page, you should see something similar to the following screenshot:

We do not have much to fix on this screen. If you scroll down to the bottom, you will see that the image we created is not sized correctly. We need to update this so that, depending on the device, we render the appropriate image size. We also need to update the Auto Layout. You can try other device sizes; you should see the same display on all screens:

1. Open `RestaurantDetail.storyboard`
2. Select the image map using the Outline view a1nd, in the Attributes inspector, update **Content Mode** to **Aspect Fill**
3. Now, with the image still selected, select the Pin icon and enter the following values:
   - All values under **Add New Constraints** are set to 0
   - Uncheck the **Constrain to margins** checkbox
   - Click on **Add 4 Constraints**

If you build and run now, you will see that our map fills the area, but our image is stretched. We can leave this but, if this were being submitted, making our image a certain size based on a device would be a much better way of handling this. We are done with cleaning up and making our app ready for the iPad. You should now be able to see how powerful Collection Views are and how they make it easy for you to have a custom look with very little code.

Summary

You now have an app that functions correctly on all devices. You can see how using the Collection View gives your app some variety on different devices with very little code. As you get more and more comfortable with this, you will find other ways to make your app look unique on various devices.

We could submit the app as is right now and it would be perfectly fine, but why not take advantage of some additional features that you can implement?

In the next chapter, we will do just that by creating an iMessage app for our app.

22
iMessages

Text messaging started with just simple text and the creation of emoticon faces using special characters. As smartphones became more commonplace, so did text messaging. Messages are now a significant form of communication for the vast majority of people. People find it easier to respond to a text message than to answer a phone call.

When Apple announced *iMessage* apps and stickers, it took messaging to another level. We had stickers before this announcement, but now we had a fully-integrated system. iMessage does not only allow you to send a sticker to express a feeling or an emotion more effectively than words, you can now use messages to send the basketball score or even play games through text messages.

In this chapter, we are going to create an *iMessages* app. This app will allow the user to look for restaurants and send reservations to others. We will build our UI to look similar to the phone app. To create the *iMessages* app, we need to add a message extension to our app.

We will cover the following topics in this chapter:

- Building a custom message app UI
- Creating a framework
- Sharing code between multiple targets
- Learning how to send a reservation to others

Understanding iMessages

Starting with the UI is always my preferred way to begin building an app, because you can get a feel for what you need to code. We are going to implement a single screen that will be a list of restaurants (accessible by hitting the sticker icon next to where a user writes their message).

The user can choose a restaurant for which they have a reservation and send it via messages to another person. Once that other person receives the message, that person will be able to tap on the reservation and see all of the details.

In a message View Controller, there are two types of presentation styles—compact and expanded:

Apple recommends that you have two different View Controllers for each style. However, since our screen is simple, we will use just one. Keep in mind, however, that if you want to make a more complicated layout, you should use two controllers.

Creating our extension

Let's get started by working on the UI:

1. In the Navigator panel, select the Project navigator and then your project:

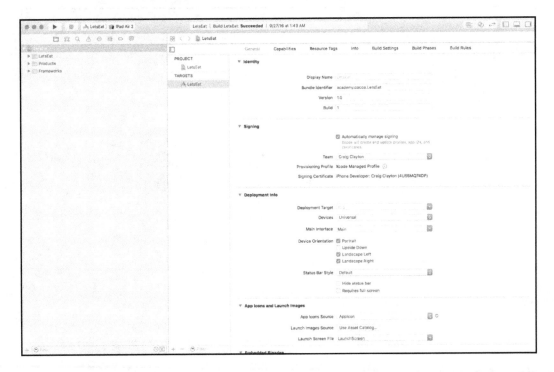

2. In the Standard Editor, locate the **TARGETS** area and then the + (plus button) at the bottom of the **TARGETS** area (if your **TARGETS** area is not displaying, hit the icon highlighted in blue to the left of **General** in the following screenshot):

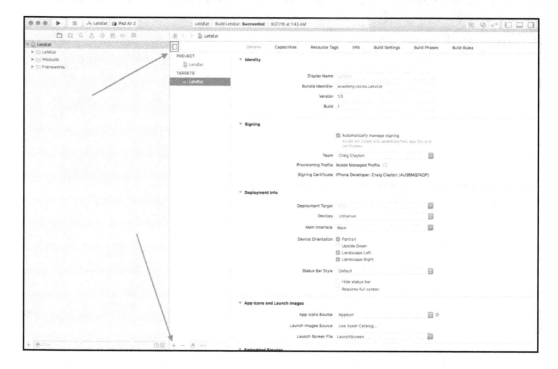

3. Click the + (plus button) and then select **iMessage Extension**:

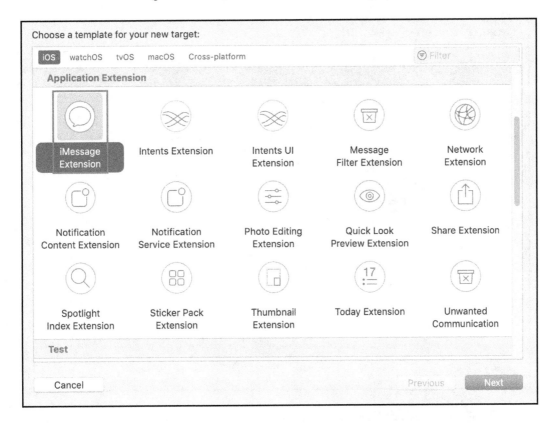

4. Click **Next** and you should see the following screen:

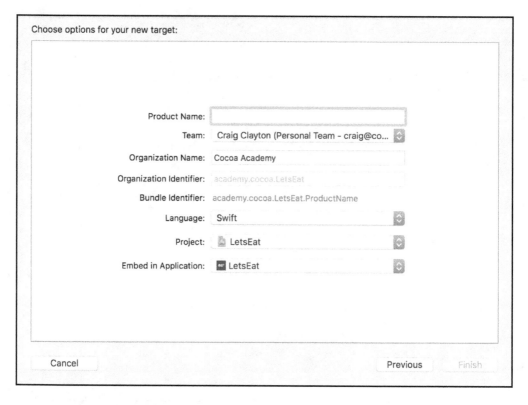

```
Choose options for your new target:

            Product Name:
                    Team:   Craig Clayton (Personal Team - craig@co...
        Organization Name:   Cocoa Academy
    Organization Identifier:   academy.cocoa.LetsEat
        Bundle Identifier:   academy.cocoa.LetsEat.ProductName
                Language:   Swift
                 Project:   LetsEat
      Embed in Application:   LetsEat


    Cancel                              Previous      Finish
```

5. Set the **Product Name** to MessageApp and click **Finish**.

Updating our assets

Next, we need to add the assets that are necessary for our *iMessages* app:

1. In the MessageApp folder in the Navigator panel, select the Assets.xcassets folder.
2. Hit the *Delete* button and then select **Move to Trash** in the screen that appears.
3. Open the project's assets folder downloaded from Packt's website (https://www.packtpub.com/).

4. Open `chapter_22` and drag the `Assets.xcassets` folder into your `MessageApp` folder, inside the Navigator panel. Don't do this in Xcode; you will need to open this up in Finder, just like we did at the beginning of the book.

5. In the options screen that appears, ensure that **Copy items if needed** and **Create groups** are both selected, and then select **Finish**.

6. Grab `MainInterface.storyboard` and replace it with the one in your assets folder from Packt's website.

If you open the `Assets.xcassets` folder, you will see that you now have an icon and two other image assets that you will need for your *iMessages* app. If you open up `MainInterface.storyboard`, you will see the following:

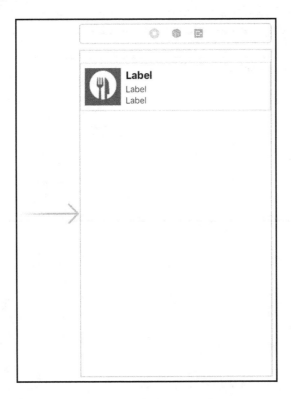

Your storyboard is set up! Now let's look at how to get data into your iMessage app and display it.

Creating a framework

Since all of our code for data was created in our iOS app, it does not make sense to rewrite it for our *iMessages* app. We can create what is known as a framework to share our data between our iOS and iMessage apps.

Using frameworks along with app extensions allows us to put shared code in one place. That means less code and more efficiency, because you will not need to update code in multiple places when you have to make a change. Let's get started with creating our framework:

1. In the Navigator panel, select the Project navigator and then your project.
2. Find the **TARGETS** area and click on the + button at the bottom of that area.
3. Under the **iOS** tab, scroll to the bottom to **Framework & Library**, select **Cocoa Touch Framework**, and then hit **Next**:

4. Under **Product Name**, type `LetsEatDataKit` and then hit **Finish**.

You should now see the following folder and files in the `Products` folder in your Navigator panel:

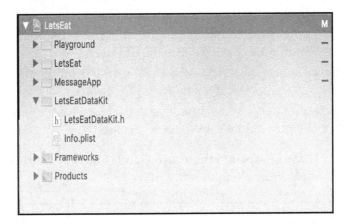

5. Select the `LetsEatDataKit` target and ensure that, under **Deployment Info**, your **Deployment Target** is set to `12.0` and above. Also, make sure that **App Extensions (Allow app extension API only)** is checked:

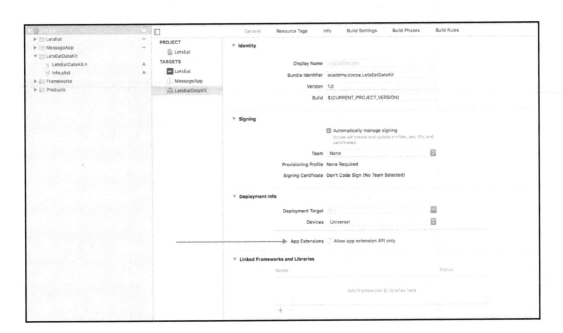

6. Right-click the `LetsEatDataKit` folder in the Navigator panel and create a new group named `Restaurant`.

7. From your *Let's Eat* app, drag the `RestaurantDataManager.swift` file from the `Restaurant` folder inside the `Model` folder into the newly-created `LetsEatDataKit` folder's `Restaurant` folder.

8. Drag the `RestaurantItem.swift` file from the `Map` folder inside the `Model` folder into the `LetsEatDataKit` folder's `Restaurant` folder.

9. Drag the `RestaurantAPIManager.swift` file from the `Misc` folder into the `LetsEatDataKit` folder's `Restaurant` folder.

10. Drag the entire `JSON` folder from inside the `Misc` folder into the `LetsEatDataKit` folder's `Restaurant` folder.

When you have completed these steps, you should have the following files in your `LetsEatDataKit` folder:

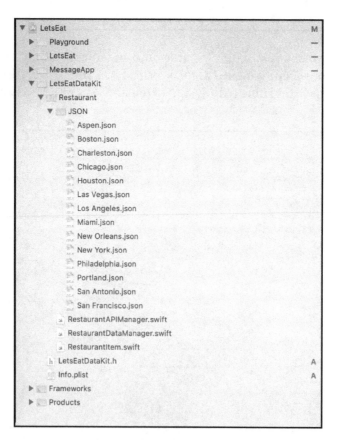

11. Open the `JSON` folder you just moved and, in the `Restaurant` folder, select the `Aspen.json` file.

12. In the Utilities panel, select the File inspector and locate the **Target Membership** section:

13. To set the target of this file not only to your app but also to your MessageApp and LetsEatDataKit, check MessageApp and LetsEatDataKit under **Target Membership**. Therefore, your *Let's Eat* app, MessageApp, and LetsEatDataKit should all be checked:

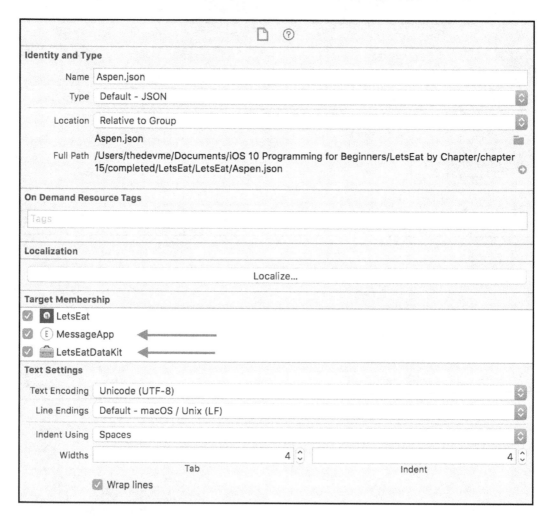

14. Select each JSON file inside of the json folder and update all of the files so that they are all targeted to LetsEat, MessageApp, and LetsEatDataKit. Doing this means that all three targets will be able to access these JSON files.

15. Select each of the remaining three files inside the `LetsEatDataKit` folder's `Restaurant` folder and update them so that each one is targeted to `LetsEatDataKit` only. Doing this means that only your framework will be able to see these files.

16. Change your target from `MessageApp` to `LetsEatDataKit`:

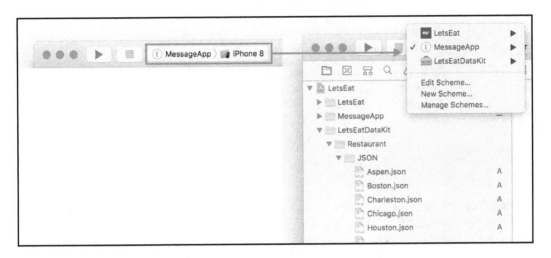

Hit *command* + *B* to build the app without running it, and your build should be successful as long as you updated the target of all of your files.

Now, switch back to the *Let's Eat* app and hit *command* + *B*. You may notice some errors. Basically, we moved `restaurantItem`, Restaurant Manager, and `RestaurantAPIManager` out of the main project and into the framework, so our app does not know where these files are now. Let's fix that by doing the following:

1. Inside the `MapViewController.swift` file, add the following `import` at the top of the file:

    ```
    import LetsEatDataKit
    ```

2. We need to update our `RestaurantItem`. We need to make this file public so that other files see it. Inside of the `RestaurantItem.swift` file, update your struct declaration to add `public` before the class so that it looks like the following:

    ```
    public class RestaurantItem
    ```

3. Open your `RestaurantItem` class and update it, each of the following variables, and the `init()` method with `public` access:

```
public class RestaurantItem: NSObject, MKAnnotation, Decodable
    public var name: String?
    public var cuisines:[String] = []
    public var latitude: Double?
    public var longitude:Double?
    public var address:String?
    public var postalCode:String?
    public var state:String?
    public var imageURL:String?
    public var restaurantID:Int?
    public var title: String?
    public var subtitle: String?
    public var coordinate: CLLocationCoordinate2D
    public enum CodingKeys: String, CodingKey
```

4. Save the file and your `RestaurantItem` errors will disappear.

We still have more minor updates to make. We need to make both `RestaurantAPIDataManager` and `RestaurantDataManager` public as well. Let's start with `RestaurantAPIDataManager` and update the following `struct` and method with `public` access:

```
public struct RestaurantAPIManager {
    public static func loadJSON(file name:String) ->
[[String:AnyObject]]
```

Next, update the class and each of the following methods inside `RestaurantDataManager` with `public` access:

```
public class RestaurantDataManager {
    public func fetch(by location:String, withFilter:String="All",
completionHandler:() -> Void)
    public func numberOfItems() -> Int
    public func restaurantItem(at index:IndexPath) -> RestaurantItem
```

We also need to make our `init()` method for our `RestaurantDataManager` class `public`; so, after the class declaration, add the following:

```
public init() {}
```

Having this `init()` method allows us to write the following:

```
let manager = RestaurantDataManager()
```

When we make it `public`, we are calling the `init()` method when we have `RestaurantDataManager()`.

Now, change the target to `LetsEatDataKit` and build it again by hitting *command + B*. The build should be successful again at this point. If you open the `MapViewController` file, you should see that all of the errors are fixed in this file.

However, we still have more errors to address inside `MapDataManager`, `LocationViewController`, `RestaurantListViewController`, `ExploreViewController`, `RestaurantDetailViewController`, and `MessagesViewController`. Therefore, inside each of these three files, add the following at the top of each file in the `import` statement section:

```
import LetsEatDataKit
```

Next, hit *command + B* again, and there should be no errors inside of any of these three files, or in your entire project.

Now, if you switch the target back to your *Let's Eat* app and build and run it by hitting the Play button (or by using *command + R*), you should see that everything is working as expected. We can now start using this data in our *iMessages* app. Before we move on, I want to explain why you would want to do this. It is good practice to adhere to the DRY (don't repeat yourself) principle. You do not want to have to recreate files you already have. This will become more evident when you need to update this file and you only have to do it once instead of multiple times in multiple places.

Connecting your message cell

Now that we have our files in order, we can start connecting everything. Earlier, we created our cell, and now we need to create a cell class with which to connect it:

1. Right-click the `MessageApp` folder in the Navigator panel and select **New File**.
2. Inside the **Choose a template for your new file screen**, select **iOS** at the top, and then **Cocoa Touch Class**. Then, hit **Next**.

3. You will now see an options screen. Please add the following in the new file section:

- **Class**: `RestaurantMessageCell`
- **Subclass**: `UICollectionViewCell`
- **Also create XIB**: Unchecked
- **Language**: `Swift`

4. Click **Next** and then **Create**.

5. In the new file, add the following inside of the class declaration:

```
@IBOutlet var lblTitle:UILabel!
@IBOutlet var lblCity:UILabel!
@IBOutlet var lblCuisine:UILabel!
```

6. Save the file and then open `MainInterface.storyboard` in the `MessageApp` folder in the Navigator panel.

7. In the Outline view, select the **Collection View Cell**.

8. Select the Identity inspector in the Utilities panel. Under **Custom Class** in the **Class** drop-down menu, select **RestaurantMessageCell** and hit *enter*.

9. Switch to the Attributes inspector in the Utilities panel, update the identifier to `restaurantCell`, and then hit *Enter*.

10. Switch to the Connections inspector in the Utilities panel, and click and drag from the empty circle next to each outlet listed to the corresponding `UILabel` in the screen shown in the following screenshot:

```
A.  lblTitle
B.  lblCity
C.  lblCuisine
```

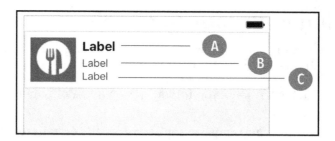

We now have our cell set up. Let's continue getting our *iMessages* app working.

Showing restaurants

We will display a list of restaurants, just like in our app, but we will not be doing the entire interface. Most of this code will be familiar to you, as we have used it before:

1. Open up the `MessagesViewController.swift` file in the Navigator panel and add the following code inside of the class declaration:

```
@IBOutlet var collectionView: UICollectionView!
let manager = RestaurantDataManager()
var selectedRestaurant:RestaurantItem?
```

2. Set up the Collection View defaults. Add the following method inside a `private` extension:

```
private extension MessagesViewController {

    func setupCollectionView() {
        let flow = UICollectionViewFlowLayout()
        flow.sectionInset = UIEdgeInsets(top: 7, left: 7,
bottom: 7, right: 7)
        flow.minimumInteritemSpacing = 0
        flow.minimumLineSpacing = 7
        collectionView.collectionViewLayout = flow
        collectionView.delegate = self
        collectionView.dataSource = self
    }
}
```

The first method we have done a few times just setting up our Collection view. The `createMessage()` method is where we set up our message for a message. Once we are done with the message, we insert into the Message.

You will see errors once you add the preceding code. Ignore them for now, as we will fix them shortly. Create an `initialize()` method that will set up the Collection View and fetch our data.

3. Add the following method above the `setupCollectionView()` method:

```
func initialize() {
    setupCollectionView()
    manager.fetch(by: "Chicago", completionHandler: { _ in
        self.collectionView.reloadData()
    })
}
```

Since this tab does not contain a location list, we will just pass a city in manually. Here, we use Chicago, but you can change it to any city of your choice.

4. Call the `initialize()` method inside the `viewDidLoad()` method, so that your `viewDidLoad()` method now looks as follows:

```
override func viewDidLoad() {
    super.viewDidLoad()
    initialize()
}
```

5. Let's create another extension for our Collection View delegates and data source. After the last curly bracket in the `MessagesViewController.swift` file, add the following `extension` declaration:

```
extension MessagesViewController:UICollectionViewDelegate,
UICollectionViewDataSource, UICollectionViewDelegateFlowLayout
{
}
```

6. Let's add all of the methods we need to get our Collection View showing data. Add the following inside your extension (which will get rid of the earlier errors):

```
func numberOfSections(in collectionView: UICollectionView) ->
Int {
    return 1
}

func collectionView(_ collectionView: UICollectionView,
numberOfItemsInSection section: Int) -> Int {
    return manager.numberOfItems()
}

func collectionView(_ collectionView: UICollectionView,
cellForItemAt indexPath: IndexPath) -> UICollectionViewCell {
```

```
let cell =
collectionView.dequeueReusableCell(withReuseIdentifier:
"restaurantCell", for: indexPath) as! RestaurantMessageCell
    let item = manager.restaurantItem(at: indexPath)
    if let name = item.name { cell.lblTitle.text = name }
    if let address = item.address { cell.lblCity.text =
address }
    if let cuisine = item.subtitle { cell.lblCuisine.text =
cuisine }

    return cell
}

func collectionView(_ collectionView: UICollectionView, layout
collectionViewLayout: UICollectionViewLayout, sizeForItemAt
indexPath: IndexPath) -> CGSize {
    let cellWidth = self.collectionView.frame.size.width - 14

    return CGSize(width: cellWidth, height: 78)
}
```

You should be very familiar with what we just added. We are setting up our Collection View data source as well as making sure our cells have a spacing of 14 pixels (7 on each side).

Lastly, before we build our app, we need to connect our Collection View in the storyboard:

1. Open up `MainInterface.storyboard` in the `MessageApp` folder in the Navigator panel
2. Select **Message View Controller** and then the Connections inspector in the Utilities panel
3. Under **Outlets**, click and drag from the empty circle next to `collectionView` to the **Collection View** in your scene

Let's change the target *Message App* and build and run our *iMessages* app by hitting the Play button (by using *command + R*). Your app should look similar to the following after clicking the stickers button. It might take a while to load when first launching:

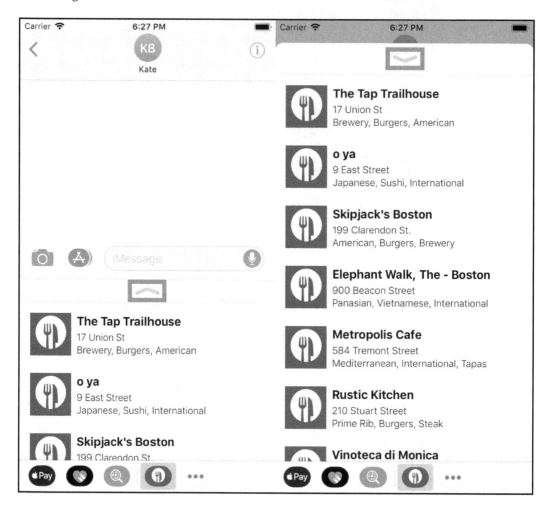

Hitting the arrow (highlighted by the red boxes) will change the screen from compact mode to expanded mode and back again. Now that we have our restaurants displaying, we need to be able to send restaurant reservations to other people. Let's add that next.

iMessage crashing

This may or may not happen to you, but if you just tried to launch the app and it crashed, there is a fix for this:

1. In the simulator, open the `Messages` app
2. Select **Kate**
3. Click on the icon with three dots:

4. Click **Edit**:

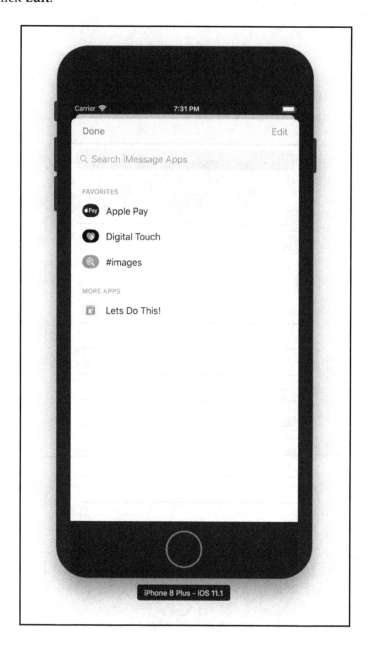

5. Click the switch for `MessageApp`:

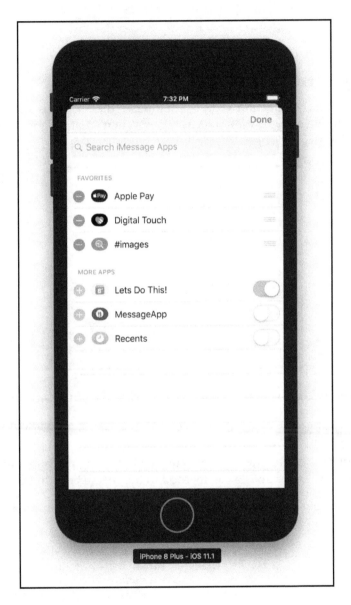

6. Click **Done**.

Build and rerun the app, and you should be fine. This error is an Apple bug, and performing these steps is the only way to fix this issue. Let's move on to sending reservations.

Sending reservations

We need to set up our Collection View so that, when the user taps on a cell, it will add the reservation to the conversation in iMessages. When creating a message to send, we can set the following things:

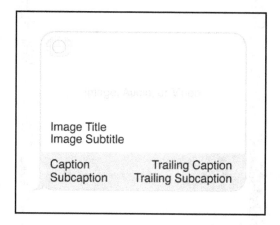

We will use everything but **Trailing Caption** and **Trailing Subcaption**.

1. Open `MessagesViewController` in the `MessageApp` folder in the Navigator panel.
2. In your main class declaration, add the following method after the `setupCollectionView()` method in the `private` extension:

```
func createMessage(with restaurant:RestaurantItem) {
    if let conversation = activeConversation {
        let layout = MSMessageTemplateLayout()
        layout.image = UIImage(named: "restaurant-detail")
        layout.caption = "Table for 7, tonight at 10:00 PM"
        layout.imageTitle = restaurant.name
        layout.imageSubtitle = restaurant.cuisine
        let message = MSMessage()
        message.layout = layout
        message.url = URL(string: "emptyURL")
        conversation.insert(message, completionHandler: {
(error: Error?)  in
```

```
        if error != nil {
                print("there was an error (error)")
        }
        else {
                self.requestPresentationStyle(.compact)
        }
    })
    }
}
```

In this method, we are setting up MSMessage. We'll check for an active conversation first. If true, we'll then set up our layout. Here, we are just using an image from our assets to create an image background (we could have also used a video, for example). Also, we set the caption to Table for 7, tonight at 10:00PM. This allows the receiver to see all of the relevant information for the reservation. Next, we set the restaurant name as the image title and the restaurant's cuisine as the image subtitle. Then, we create an instance of MSMessage, pass it the layout we created, and give it a URL (which, in our case, is just an empty string, since we don't have a URL). Finally, we insert the message into the conversation. We need to make sure that, when we want to send a message, we are in compact mode; otherwise, the user will think that the app does not work.

Lastly, we just need to add the code that calls our createMessage() method. Add the following method in your extension, before the last curly bracket:

```
func collectionView(_ collectionView: UICollectionView,
didSelectItemAt indexPath: IndexPath) {
    selectedRestaurant = manager.restaurantItem(at: indexPath)
    guard let restaurant = selectedRestaurant else { return }
    createMessage(with: restaurant)
}
```

Here, we are checking for when the user taps a cell; then, we get selectedRestaurant and pass it to our createMessage() method.

Let's build and run the project by hitting the Play button (or by using *command + R*). Select a restaurant and you will now see a message with the selected restaurant in the message area:

You can see that, with a little bit of work, you can add a nice *iMessages* app to your app.

Summary

In this chapter, we looked at how to add an *iMessages* app to our app. We also created a framework that allowed us to use data in both our apps without having to duplicate code. We looked at what is involved in creating an `MSMessage` and how we can pass `MSMessageTemplateLayout` to an `MSMessage`. We now know that we can also send embedded videos, as well as images, when we send messages. Also, we can now send reservations through the *iMessages* app with relevant data for a reservation.

In the next chapter, we will go back to our *Let's Eat* app and learn how to work with in-app notifications.

23
Notifications

Notifications were first launched in 2009 and are a staple of the iOS system. Whether from your favorite app or a text message, you have encountered a notification at some point while using a smartphone. Pre-iOS 10, if you had to work with notifications in iOS, you had two types of push notifications: remote (from a server) and local.

iOS 10 made changes to notifications that simplified them, but also made them more robust. In iOS 10, there is now one notification that covers both remote and local notifications, which is excellent for those who have worked with them in the past. Concerning breadth of functionality, notifications now allow you to embed rich media (such as images, video, and audio), and also have custom UI content.

In this chapter, we are going to learn how to create basic notifications, as well as notifications with embedded images. After we look at both of these examples, we'll look at how to create a custom UI for our notifications.

In this chapter, we'll cover the following topics:

- Learning how to build basic notifications
- Learning how to embed images into notifications
- Learning how to build a custom notification UI

Starting with the basics

Let's begin by getting our app to send us basic notifications. Inside of our restaurant details page, we have three buttons that all say **7:30 PM**, which currently don't do anything. We are going to update those buttons so that, when you tap on one of them, it creates a restaurant reservation notification. If this were a real reservations app, we would want to store these reservations. When the reservation date and time nears, we would then post a notification to the user as a reminder. Doing all of that is outside the scope of this book, so we will address creating a restaurant reservation notification.

Getting permission

Before we can send any notifications, we must get the user's permission. Therefore, open the `AppDelegate.swift` file and add the following method after the `didFinishLaunchingWithOptions()` method:

```
func checkNotifications() {
    UNUserNotificationCenter.current().requestAuthorization(options:
[.alert, .sound, .badge]) { (isGranted, error) in
        if isGranted {
            print("Notifications permissions granted.")
        } else {
            print("Notifications permissions denied.")
        }
    }
}
```

This method checks for the user's authorization. If the user has not been asked, it displays a message to the user for permission to use notifications. When you add this method, you will get an error. The reason for this error is that we need to `import UserNotifications`. At the top of the file, under `import UIKit`, add the following:

```
import UserNotifications
```

Next, the method we just added needs to run inside of the `initialize()` method. Add the following after `setupDefaultColors()`:

```
checkNotifications()
```

Your `initialize()` method should now look like the following:

```
func initialize() {
    setupDefaultColors()
    checkNotifications()
}
```

Build and run the project by hitting the Play button (or using *command + R*), and you should see the following message:

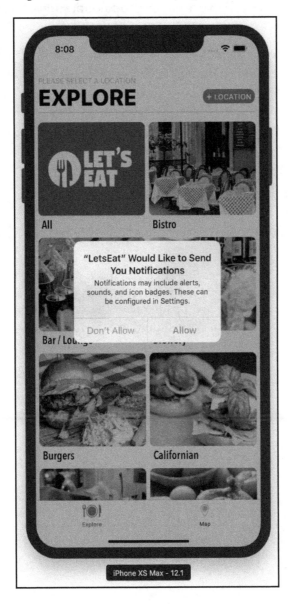

Setting up notifications

Now that we have permission, we need to set up notifications. We will start setting up our buttons:

1. Open the `RestaurantDetailViewController.swift` file.

2. At the top of the file, under `import UIKit`, add the following:

   ```
   import UserNotifications
   ```

3. Add the following method after our `@IBAction func unwindReviewCancel(segue: UIStoryboardSegue) {}` method and before the last curly bracket of our class file:

   ```
   @IBAction func onTimeTapped(sender: UIButton) {
   }
   ```

4. Save the file, and you will see an empty circle appear next to this new `@IBAction`.

5. Open the `RestaurantDetail.storyboard` for which we are going to use the time buttons for our notifications. Select each button. In the Attributes inspector, update the text inside of `eachbutton` to display **9:30pm**, **10:00pm**, and **10:30pm**. You should get the following:

6. Select `RestaurantDetailViewController` and then select the Connections inspector in the Utilities panel. Under `Received Actions`, you should see `onTimeTappedWithSender`, which we added earlier:

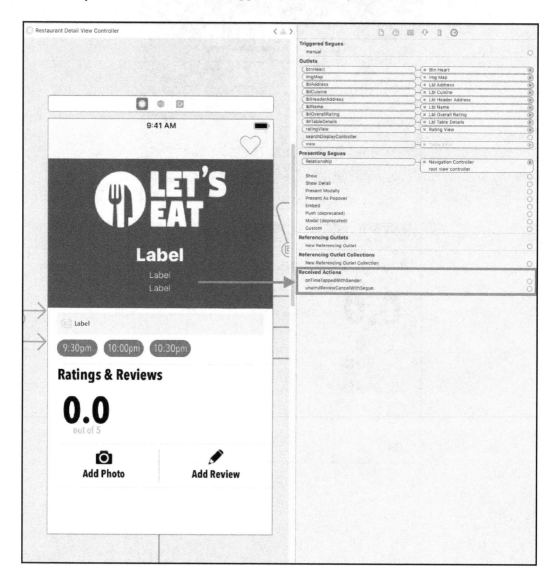

7. Click and drag from the empty circle next to `onTimeTappedWithSender` to the first button (marked **9:30pm**) in the restaurant detail scene:

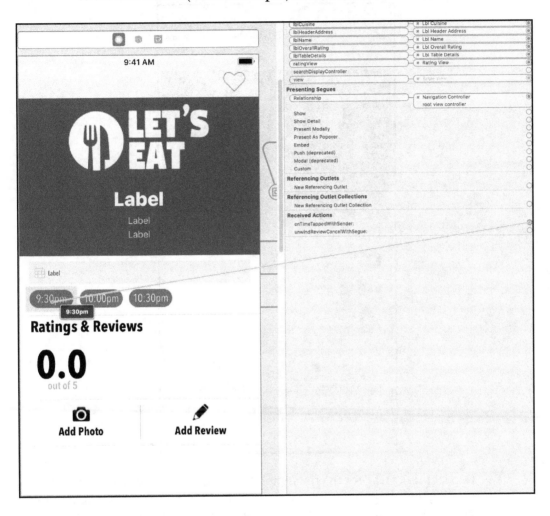

8. In the prompt, select **Touch Up Inside**:

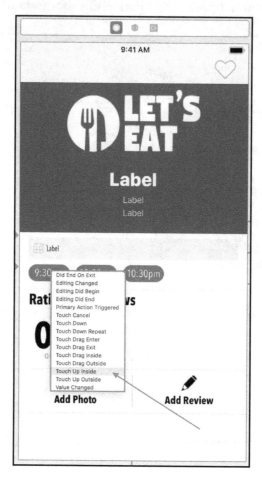

9. Repeat these steps for the remaining two buttons (**10:00pm** and **10:30pm**), clicking and dragging the same circle (now filled) to each of the remaining buttons in the scene and then choosing **Touch Up Inside** for each prompt that follows.

10. Open `RestaurantDetailViewController.swift`; this is where we need to get the time from inside of the buttons and pass them to our notifications. Add the following method after the `onTimeTapped()` method:

```
func showNotification(sender:String?) {
    print(sender as Any)
}
```

11. Inside of the `onTimeTapped()` method, add the following:

```
showNotification(sender: sender.titleLabel?.text)
```

We are now passing the time value to our `showNotification()` method. Build and run the project by hitting the Play button (or using *command + R*). You should now see the time of each selected button in the console.

Showing notifications

Now that we are showing a time, let's show our notification, along with the time selected:

1. Inside of the `showNotification()` method, delete the print statement and add the following:

```
let content = UNMutableNotificationContent()

if let name = selectedRestaurant?.name {
    content.title = name
}

if let time = sender {
    content.body = "Table for 2, tonight at \(time)"
}

content.subtitle = "Restaurant Reservation"
content.badge = 1

let trigger = UNTimeIntervalNotificationTrigger(timeInterval:
5, repeats: false)
let identifier = "letsEatReservation"
let request = UNNotificationRequest(identifier: identifier,
content: content, trigger: trigger)

UNUserNotificationCenter.current().add(request,
withCompletionHandler: nil)
```

Here, we are creating a notification content object. In this object, we are going to set the title, the body, the subtitle, the badge, and the sound.

2. Before the `showNotification()` method, add the following method:

```
func setupNotificationDefaults() {
    UNUserNotificationCenter.current().delegate = self
}
```

This method is our `delegate` method for notifications. We get an error for our `delegate`, because we have not yet implemented the required functions.

3. Create an extension at the end of this file, after the last curly bracket. You may already have an extension in this file for our map if you tackled any challenges, if so, add this new extension after the last curly bracket of that `Map` extension. In either case, add the following code:

```
extension RestaurantDetailViewController:
UNUserNotificationCenterDelegate {
    func userNotificationCenter(_ center:
UNUserNotificationCenter, willPresent notification:
UNNotification, withCompletionHandler completionHandler:
@escaping (UNNotificationPresentationOptions) -> 'Void) {
        completionHandler([.alert, .sound])
    }
}
```

4. Call the `setupNotificationDefaults()` method inside of our `initialize()` method. Your updated `initialize()` method should now look like as follows:

```
func initialize() {
    setupLabels()
    setupMap()
    setupNotificationDefaults()
}
```

5. Build and run the project by hitting the Play button (or using *command + R*). Open a restaurant detail page, tap the time button, and wait two seconds. You should see the following:

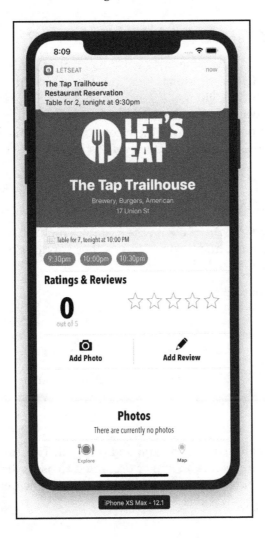

We just implemented a basic notification; however, we can do so much more. Next, let's get an image inside of our notification.

Customizing our notifications

Now that we understand how to set up a basic notification, let's get into some more features that we can offer. Some of these features were introduced in iOS 11 and some were introduced in iOS 12. I will make sure that I note which features are from which OS. The first feature I want to talk about is a new iOS 12 feature. Deliver quietly allows users to have more control over their notifications, but Deliver quietly only sends notifications to the Notification Center. Let's look at how this works.

Deliver quietly (iOS 12 feature)

Open `AppDelegate`. In the `checkNotifications()` method, you currently have three options: .alert, .sound, and .badge. Update these options by adding .provisional. When you are done, you should have the following:

```
func checkNotifications() {
    UNUserNotificationCenter.current().requestAuthorization(options:
[.alert, .sound, .badge, .provisional]) { (isGranted, error) in
        if isGranted {
            print("Notifications permissions granted.")
        } else {
            print("Notifications permissions denied.")
        }
    }
}
```

For this to work, we need to delete the app and re-run it. This time, when you rerun it, you will notice that the user is no longer promoted to use notifications. Proceed to a restaurant detail, and this time when you tap the time in the detail, you will notice that you no longer get notifications.

If you leave the app and go to the Notification Center (swipe down from the upper left corner of the phone), you will see the notification there instead:

Deliver quietly is a great feature if you want to get your users using notifications by getting them to show up in the Notification Center by default. There, the user can customize these notifications themselves in the settings. We are done with this feature, so delete the app and remove the .provisional from the request, as we will be moving forward along the normal route. Rerun your app and you should see the notification permission message again:

The next feature I want to look at is embedding images into your notifications. This feature was introduced in iOS 10. Before we can embed an image, we need a test image. In the Misc folder of the Navigator panel, create a new group, called Images. Then, in the project folder for this book, open the asset folder for this chapter and drag the image assets into the Images folder that we just created.

Embedding images (iOS 10 feature)

Next, let's embed our images. First, return to the
RestaurantDetailViewController.swift file and, in the showNotification()
method we created, remove the following code:

```
let trigger = UNTimeIntervalNotificationTrigger(timeInterval: 5,
repeats: false)
let identifier = "letsEatReservation"
let request = UNNotificationRequest(identifier: identifier, content:
content, trigger: trigger)
UNUserNotificationCenter.current().add(request, withCompletionHandler:
{ error in
    // handle error
})
```

Replace the deleted section of code with the following code:

```
guard let imgURL = Bundle.main.url(forResource: "sample-restaurant-
img@3x", withExtension:"png") else { return }
let attachment = try! UNNotificationAttachment(identifier:
"letsEatReservation", url:imgURL, options:nil)

content.attachments = [attachment]

sendNotification(with:content)
```

In this code, we are getting the image URL from our project and creating an
attachment. We attach the rich media (here, an image) to the notification and send it.
Next, let's add the sendNotification() method:

```
func sendNotification(with content:UNNotificationContent) {
    let uuid = UUID().uuidString
    let trigger = UNTimeIntervalNotificationTrigger(timeInterval:2,
repeats:false)
    let request = UNNotificationRequest(identifier:uuid,
content:content, trigger:trigger)
    UNUserNotificationCenter.current().add(request,
withCompletionHandler: nil)
}
```

Build and rerun the project by hitting the Play button (or using *command + R*). When you get to a restaurant detail page, tap the time button and wait five seconds. You should now see a thumbnail image in the notification:

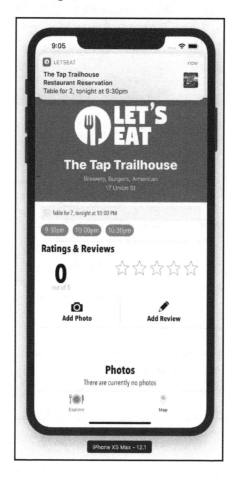

Also, if you click and pull down on the notification, you should see the following:

Thus far, we have been receiving notifications while inside the app. If you want to test notifications outside of the app, take the following steps (you might have to update your timer from two to five seconds if it is too quick): build and run the project by hitting the Play button (or using *command + R*). When you get to a restaurant detail page, tap the time button and then immediately hit *command + shift + H*. This takes you out of the app, and you will then see the following:

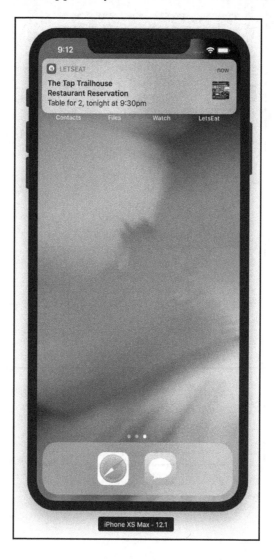

If you click and pull down on the notification, you will see the following:

Our notifications are looking good, but you really cannot do anything with them. It would be nice to confirm your reservation with a yes or no, for example. We need to add some buttons for the notifications to do this.

Adding buttons

Before we add any more String values, it is a good practice to eliminate as many strings from your app as you can. Adding this file will not only eliminate strings, but it also keeps you from accidentally typing in the wrong value. For example, we could easily misspell identifier. Therefore, it is a protective measure to have it in an enum. Let's add a new file:

1. Right-click the Misc folder and select **New File**.
2. Inside of **Choose a template for your new file screen**, select **iOS** at the top and then choose **Swift File**. Then, hit **Next**.
3. Name this file Identifier and hit **Create**:

   ```
   enum Identifier:String {
       case reservationCategory
       case reservationIdentifier = "letsEatReservation"
   }

   enum Option:String {
       case one = "optionOne"
       case two = "optionTwo"
   }
   ```

We only need to add a few things to add buttons to our notifications. First, we need to update our restaurant detail:

1. Inside the RestaurantDetailViewController.swift file, add the following into the showNotification() method after content.badge = 1:

   ```
   content.categoryIdentifier =
   Identifier.reservationCategory.rawValue
   ```

2. We will use this to create our button options for our notification. Open the AppDelegate.swift file. After the checkNotifications() method, add the following code:

   ```
   func permissionGranted() {

       let optionOne = UNNotificationAction(identifier:
   Option.one.rawValue, title: "Yes", options:     [.foreground])
       let optionTwo = UNNotificationAction(identifier:
   Option.two.rawValue, title: "No", options: [.foreground])
       let category = UNNotificationCategory(identifier:
   Identifier.reservationCategory.rawValue, actions: [optionOne,
   ```

```
    optionTwo], intentIdentifiers: [], options: [])

    UNUserNotificationCenter.current().setNotificationCategories([
    category])
    }
```

3. In this function, we are setting up two actions: one for yes, and one for no. We are creating a category and setting it to our notification category, which defines the type of notification that we want to use. Add `self.permissionGranted()` inside the if statement:

```
func checkNotifications() {
    UNUserNotificationCenter.current().requestAuthorization(options:
        [.alert, .sound, .badge, .provisional]) { (isGranted, error) in

        if isGranted {
            print("Notifications permission granted.")
            self.permissionGranted()
        } else {
            print("Notifications permission denied.")
        }
    }
}
```

4. We need to write code to handle when we receive a notification. Return to the `RestaurantDetailViewController.swift` file and add the following inside of your new extension for notifications after the `willPresent()` method:

```
func userNotificationCenter(_ center:
UNUserNotificationCenter, didReceive response:
UNNotificationResponse, withCompletionHandler
completionHandler: @escaping () -> Void) {
    if let identifier = Option(rawValue:
response.actionIdentifier) {
            switch identifier {
            case .one :
                    print("User selected yes")
            case .two:
                    print("User selected no")
            }
    }
    completionHandler()
}
```

5. Build and run the project by hitting the Play button (or using *command + R*). When you get the notification and pull down on it, you will see that you now have button options:

Inside of our `didReceive()` method, we are printing out what the user selected, but you can choose whatever `print` statement you like.

When you receive multiple notifications, they are displayed one after another. However, we can actually group them together instead. Let's see how grouped notifications work.

Grouped notifications (iOS 11)

To get grouped notifications, we just need to give our notifications a thread ID inside
of the `RestaurantDetailViewController.swift` file. Inside the file, add the
following code after `content.categoryIdentifier =
Identifier.reservationCategory.rawValue`:

```
if let id = selectedRestaurant?.restaurantID {
    content.threadIdentifier = "\(id)"
}
```

Rerun the app, and when you get to a restaurant detail, tap the time button a few
times and then swipe down from the upper-left corner to access your Notification
Center. You should see grouped notifications now:

With grouped notifications, you can customize the summary text as well as the hidden text. Hidden text is the text that is shown to users when they do not want to see the information inside of the notification. Let's update the summary text as well as the hidden text next.

Summary and hidden text (iOS 12)

Open the `AppDelegate` file and let's add a couple of things to the `permissionGranted()` method. Add the following under the let `optionTwo` constant:

```
// Add this under optionTwo
let hiddenRestaurantPlaceholder = "%u new restaurant invites."
let summaryFormat = "%u more restaurant invites for %@"
```

Next, delete the let category constant and replace it with the following:

```
let category =
UNNotificationCategory(identifier:Identifier.reservationCategory.rawVa
lue, actions:[optionOne,optionTwo], intentIdentifiers: [],
hiddenPreviewsBodyPlaceholder: hiddenRestaurantPlaceholder,
categorySummaryFormat: summaryFormat, options:[])
```

Your `permissionGranted()` method should now look like the following:

```
func permissionGranted() {

    let optionOne = UNNotificationAction(identifier:
Option.one.rawValue, title: "Yes", options:      [.foreground])
    let optionTwo = UNNotificationAction(identifier:
Option.two.rawValue, title: "No", options: [.foreground])
    let hiddenRestaurantPlaceholder = "%u new restaurant invites."
    let summaryFormat = "%u more restaurant invites for %@"
    let category =
UNNotificationCategory(identifier:Identifier.reservationCategory.rawVa
lue,actions:[optionOne,optionTwo],intentIdentifiers:[],hiddenPreviewsB
odyPlaceholder: hiddenRestaurantPlaceholder, categorySummaryFormat:
summaryFormat, options:[])

    UNUserNotificationCenter.current().setNotificationCategories([category
])
}
```

Build and run the app again. Hit the time button in restaurant details a few times and pull down on the Notification Center. You will now see that your summary text has been customized:

Next, go to the Settings app in the simulator, scroll down to the *LetsEat* app, and select it:

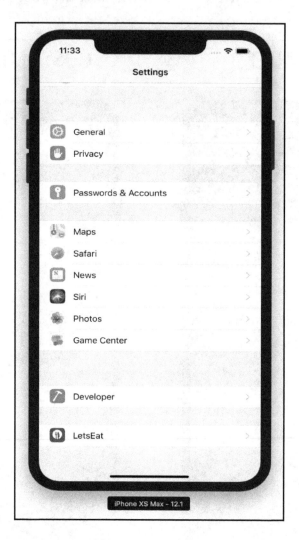

Select **Notifications** | **Show Previews**, and then select **Never**:

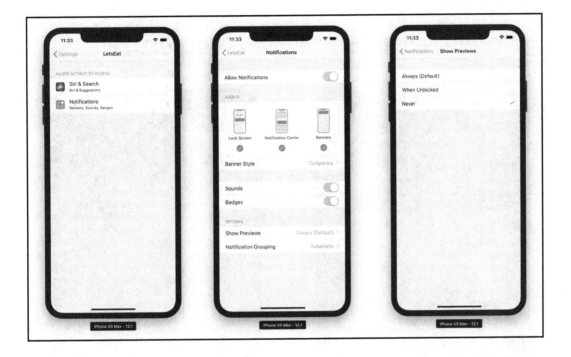

Finally, go back to the Notification Center; you will see that your notifications have changed to hidden and are now displaying our custom summary text:

So far, we have looked at how to create basic notifications as well as notifications with images embedded in them. Next, we can take our app a step further by adding our custom UI to our notifications.

Custom UI in notifications

To add custom UI to our notifications, we need to add an extension. Let's get started by doing the following:

1. In the Navigator panel, select the Project navigator and then your project.
2. At the bottom of the **TARGETS** area, click the + button.
3. Select **Notification Content Extension** under **Application Extension** and then click **Next**:

4. In the options screen that appears, set **Product Name** to `LetsEatNotificationExtension` and click **Finish.**

Now that our extension has been created, we need to be able to use it:

1. Open the `info.plist` file in the `LetsEatNotificationExtension` folder.
2. Tap the `NSExtension` disclosure arrow to open up that key.
3. Tap the disclosure arrow to open `NSExtensionAttributes`, under which you can see `UNNotificationExtensionCategory`:

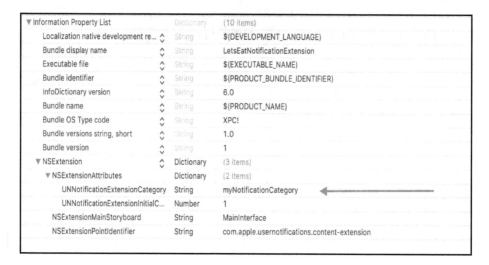

This category is the category of the notification we set previously.

4. Update `myNotificationCategory` to `reservationCategory`.

Save the file and switch your target back to the *Let's Eat* app. Build and run the project by hitting the Play button (or using *command* + *R*). This time, instead of seeing our custom image, we now have the following:

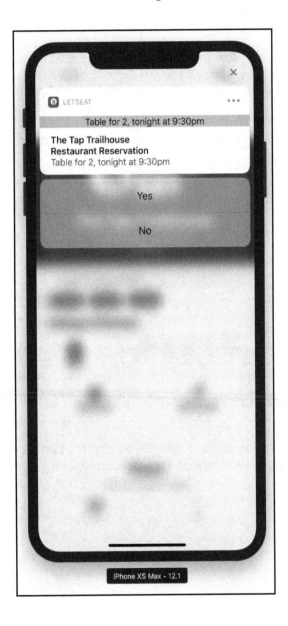

You might have noticed something slightly off when you pulled down on the notification. The notification starts out large and then shrinks down. Inside of your `Info.plist` file, there is a property, `UNNotificationExtensionInitialContentSizeRatio`, that is currently set to 1. Changing it to 0.25 makes this less noticeable.

Currently, this custom notification is showing us the custom and default content together. We can fix this by returning to our `Info.plist` inside of `LetsEatContentExtension`.

Inside of `NSExtensionAttributes`, add a new item, called `UNNotificationExtensionDefaultContentHidden`, and set the type as **Boolean** and the value to **YES**:

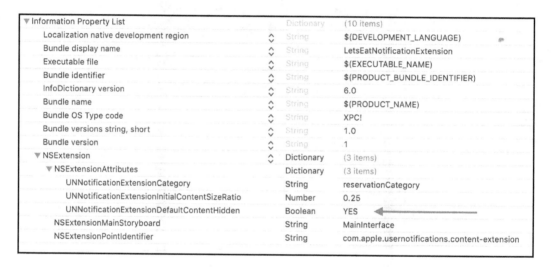

Save the file and build and run the project by hitting the Play button (or using *command + R*). Once you pull down on the notification, you will see that the default content is hidden:

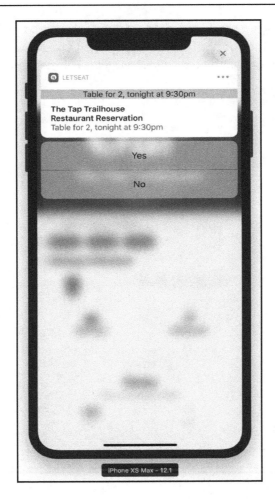

You can now update `MainInterface.storyboard` inside of your `LetsEatContentExtension` folder. In iOS 12, you can now add custom buttons into your storyboard for users to interact with. This is outside the scope of this book, but we have covered a lot of what you need already.

Custom Notification Settings (iOS 12)

The last thing I want to cover is Custom Notification Settings. This feature is really good if you have an app that has buttons to toggle different notification settings off and on. Apple now lets users go directly from the Settings app and launch their custom settings page.

Before we get into this, in the `assets` folder for this chapter, drag and drop the `Settings` folder into the `Controllers` folder. When you are done, you should see the following (make sure that on the *LetsEat* target is selected):

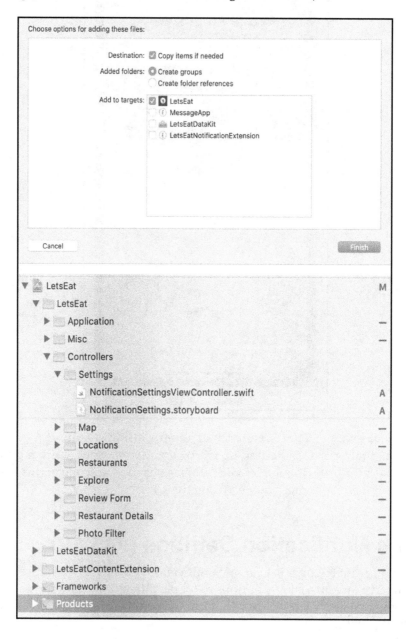

There is nothing special about the settings folder; it is just a screen with text. Let's look at how we can set it up. Open the `RestaurantDetailViewController.swift` file; in the `UNUserNotificationCenterDelegate` extension, add the following method:

```
func userNotificationCenter(_ center:UNUserNotificationCenter,
openSettingsFor notification: UNNotification?) {
    let storyboard = UIStoryboard(name:"NotificationSettings",
bundle:nil)
    let vc = storyboard.instantiateViewController(withIdentifier:
"NotificationSettingsNavController")
    self.present(vc, animated:true, completion:nil)
}
```

Next, open `AppDelegate`. In the `checkNotifications()` method, you currently have three options: `.alert`, `.sound`, and `.badge`. Update these options by adding `.providesAppNotificationSettings`. When you are done, you should have the following:

```
func checkNotifications() {
    UNUserNotificationCenter.current().requestAuthorization(options:
[.alert, .sound, .badge, .providesAppNotificationSettings]) {
(isGranted, error) in
        if isGranted {
            print("Notifications permissions granted.")
            self.permissionGranted()
        } else {
            print("Notifications permissions denied.")
        }
    }
}
```

Now, rerun the app and then go to the restaurant detail. Once you are in the restaurant detail, exit the app, go to the *LetsEat* app settings inside of the Settings app, and select **Notifications**. You will now see a new link:

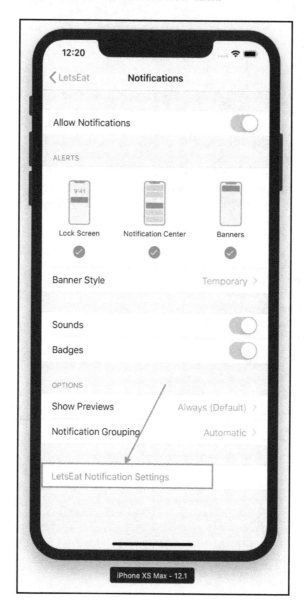

Next, tap the **LetsEat Notification Settings** button. You will be sent back to the LetsEat app and the settings page will launch:

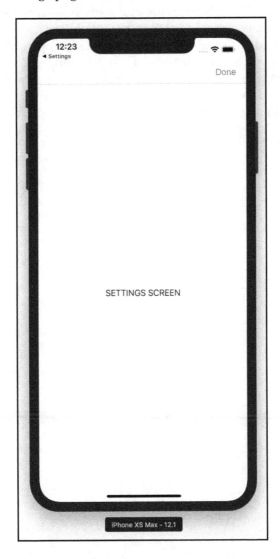

For this example to work, you must go to the restaurant detail page before you go to settings. In a real-world application, you would want to set this up inside of your `AppDelegate` so that no matter where the user is in the app, the settings page will open.

Summary

Notifications since iOS 10 are getting more and more powerful every year, and give you the flexibility to create rich custom content with very little work. In this chapter, we learned how to build basic notifications, as well as grouped notifications, and added a custom summary and hidden text. Then, we stepped it up a bit by adding embedded images into our notifications. We briefly looked at how to add a custom notification using an extension. Finally, we looked at launching Custom Notification Settings from the settings app into our app.

In the next chapter, we will look at SiriKit and look at how we can integrate it into our app.

24
SiriKit

Last year, Apple announced the addition of a new framework called **SiriKit**. This framework allows developers to leverage Siri in their apps. For the last year, SiriKit has been slowly adopted by developers. This year, Apple added even more supported domains. In this chapter, we are going to add SiriKit support to our app.

My original goal was to have Siri set up restaurant reservations, but unfortunately, Apple software requires this feature to be done using MapKit. Using MapKit is not the real issue, though. The real problem is that you have to work with Apple to get this setup, so we can not make restaurant reservations using Siri directly. If you are working on an app that needs this feature, then you need to contact Apple support. In this chapter, we are going to set up the framework so that we can request money from someone. The setup for SiriKit is quite similar, so once you are comfortable with this chapter, you should not have a problem working through the others. Please note that to use SiriKit, you must have a developer license to do this chapter. Apple has made changes to what non-account holders have access to and SiriKit is one of them.

We will cover the following topics in this chapter:

- Working with Siri Shortcuts
- Understanding SiriKit
- Working with SiriKit extensions
- Working with SiriKit UI extensions

Using Siri Shortcuts

In iOS 12, Apple introduced Siri Shortcuts. Siri Shortcuts are a way to create shortcuts to your app for your users. For example, let's say a user, every Tuesday, makes the same date night reservation with his wife at her favorite restaurant. Instead of having to go through all the steps each time, we can make this easier. Let's see how this works.

Open up your `Info.plist` file and add `academy.cocoa.LetsEat.reservation-activity-type` to `NSUserActivityTypes`. Make sure that you are in `Info.plist` for the app and not one of the other targets:

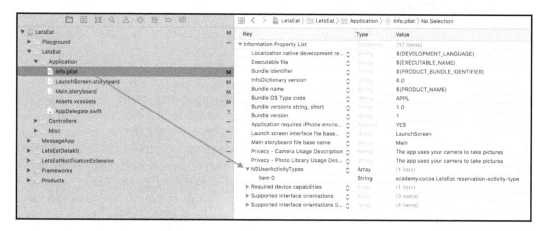

Now that we have our `Info.plist` set up, let's add some code. Open up the `RestaurantDetailViewController.swift` file and the following imports:

```
import Intents
import CoreSpotlight
import CoreServices
```

Next, add the following method after:

```
func setupReservation(with description: String) {
    let reservationActivity = NSUserActivity(activityType:
"academy.cocoa.LetsEat.reservation-activity-type")
    reservationActivity.isEligibleForSearch = true
    reservationActivity.isEligibleForPrediction = true

    if let name = selectedResaurant?.name {
        reservationActivity.title = "Reservation for 2 at \(name) at
\(description)"
```

```
    }
    reservationActivity.suggestedInvocationPhrase = "Restaurant
Reservation"
    reservationActivity.userInfo = ["Key":"Value"]
    let attributes =
CSSearchableItemAttributeSet(itemContentType:kUTTypeItem as String)
    let date = Date()
  let dateFormatter = DateFormatter()
    dateFormatter.dateFormat = "EEEE, MMM d, yyyy"

    attributes.contentDescription = dateFormatter.string(from: date)
    attributes.thumbnailData = UIImage(named:"mexican")?.pngData()
    reservationActivity.contentAttributeSet = attributes
    self.userActivity = reservationActivity
    self.userActivity?.becomeCurrent()
}
```

This method creates a reservation activity. NSUserActivity is great for opening your app through shortcuts. If you want advanced controls, you will want to use Intents, which we will cover later in this chapter.

The suggestedInvocationPhrase variable is used to give the user an idea about what phrase they should set for the Siri voice shortcut. We will also attach an image to the suggestion; in a real-world application, you would want to make this dynamic and change based on the suggestedInvocationPhrase, but that is beyond the scope of this book.

Now, add the setupReservation() method inside of the if statement of if let time = sender, since we need to pass the time to our reservation method:

```
if let time = sender {
    content.body = "Table for 2, tonight at \(time)"
    // New line
    setupReservation(with: sender)
}
```

Finally, before you launch the simulator, go to **Settings** | **Developer** and scroll all the way down, and make sure that both the options under **Shortcuts Testing** are enabled, as shown here:

Now, launch the app, go to a restaurant's details, and hit a time similar to what we did for notifications. Once the notification appears, exit the app and go to your search by swiping right; in the search, type reservation and you will see our Siri suggestion:

Siri voice shortcut

If you want to add a Siri voice shortcut, open the Settings app in the simulator and select Siri. Simply press the + button to add your shortcut as a Siri voice shortcut. This shortcut will quickly launch your app using Siri. With some advanced code, you can take this farther by sending the user to the correct detail page. This code is beyond the scope of the book, but you are at a good starting point for this. Next, let's discuss SiriKit and work with Intents. Please note that in order to continue with this chapter, you will need to have a developer account. You can get more information about this here: `https://developer.apple.com/support/app-capabilities/`.

Understanding SiriKit

We first need to understand how Siri interacts with our app before we get started. Have a look at how it works through this diagram:

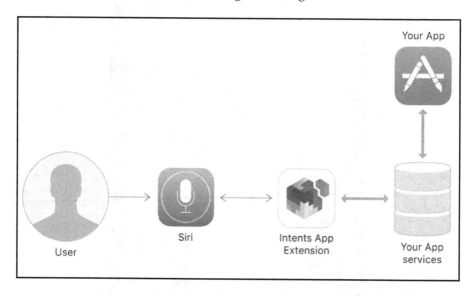

A user interacts with Siri to compose a request. Siri takes the request and looks through the intents for the requesting app. If the app is not found, Siri lets you know. If the app is located, but cannot do what was requested, Siri will notify you that the request cannot be made at this time. If the app can handle the intent, it will pass the information to your app. Your app does what it needs to do with that information and reports back to Siri. If the app needs further information, it lets Siri know what to request until the app has everything it needs or the user cancels the request.

Supported intents

As of iOS 11, Apple currently supports the following intents:

- VoIP calling (initiate calls and search the user's call history)
- Messaging (send messages and search the user's received messages)
- Payments (send payments between users or pay bills)
- Lists and notes (create and manage notes and to-do list items)
- Visual codes (convey contact and payment information using Quick Response (QR) codes)
- Photos (search for and display photos)
- Workouts (start, end, and manage fitness routines)
- Ride booking (book rides and report their status)
- Car commands (manage vehicle door locks and get the vehicle's status)
- CarPlay (interact with a vehicle's CarPlay system)
- Restaurant reservations (create and manage restaurant reservations with help from the *Maps* app)

This API requires you to work with Apple Maps before your app can use it. For information on how to get started, go to `http://mapsconnect.apple.com`.

We are going to use the Payment intent, which allows us to send payments between users or pay bills. When we are done, we can just say *"Hey Siri! Send $100 to Jason Clayton for dinner last night using LetsEat."* We can hook this up to any banking system, but at the moment, we have everything else set up for this. Let's get started.

Enabling Siri's capabilities

The first thing we need to do is enable SiriKit:

1. In Xcode, go to your app and select the **LetsEat** target:

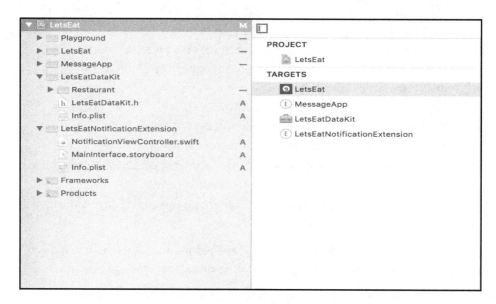

2. Next, click on the **Capabilities** tab:

3. Then, hit the switch for Siri to switch it to **ON**:

4. You should see the following when you are done:

5. You need a working developer account to do the following steps. Otherwise, you will see errors when trying to follow along. Next, we need to add a new target to our project. At the bottom of the **TARGETS** section, you should see a + button:

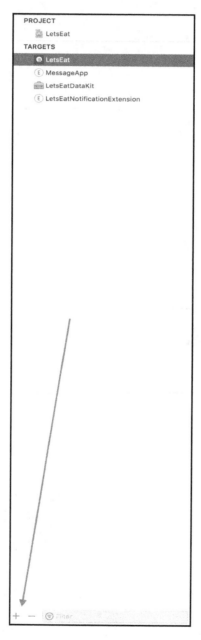

6. Click the **+** button and you will see the following screen:

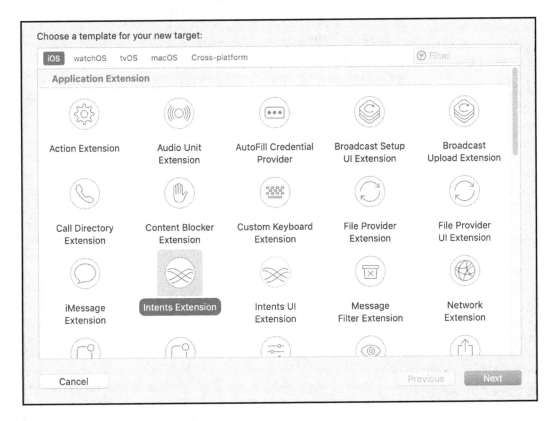

7. Next, select **Intents Extension** under the **iOS** tab. Then, hit **Next**.

8. In the **Options** screen that appears, there are some fields to fill out or choose from. Add the following to the **Options** screen and then hit **Next**:

- **Product Name**: MakePayment
- **Team**: Must have a team
- **Organization Name**: Your name/company name
- **Organization Identifier**: Your domain name in reverse order
- **Language**: Swift
- **Include UI Extension**: Checked
- **Project**: LetsEat
- **Embed in Application**: LetsEat

You should see the following:

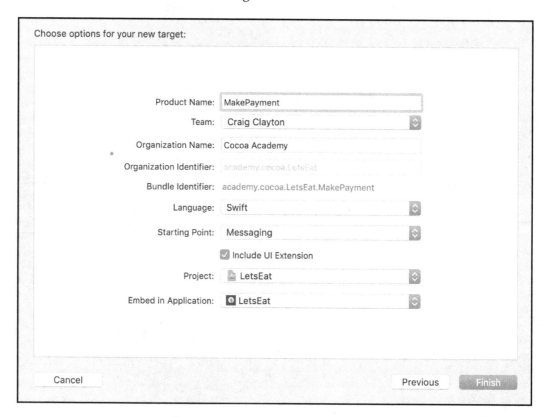

When you have finished, we will have two extensions that have been added to our project: the `MakePayment` and `MakePaymentUI` extensions. These extensions are what we will use to add SiriKit to our project. We need to edit these extensions so that they can accept payments:

1. Open the `MakePayment` folder and select the `Info.plist` file.
2. Open all of the disclosure arrows under `NSExtension`. When they are all open, you should see the following:

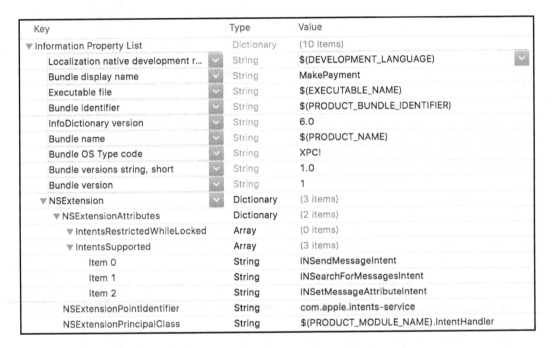

Key	Type	Value
▼ Information Property List	Dictionary	(10 items)
Localization native development r…	String	$(DEVELOPMENT_LANGUAGE)
Bundle display name	String	MakePayment
Executable file	String	$(EXECUTABLE_NAME)
Bundle identifier	String	$(PRODUCT_BUNDLE_IDENTIFIER)
InfoDictionary version	String	6.0
Bundle name	String	$(PRODUCT_NAME)
Bundle OS Type code	String	XPC!
Bundle versions string, short	String	1.0
Bundle version	String	1
▼ NSExtension	Dictionary	(3 items)
▼ NSExtensionAttributes	Dictionary	(2 items)
▼ IntentsRestrictedWhileLocked	Array	(0 items)
▼ IntentsSupported	Array	(3 items)
Item 0	String	INSendMessageIntent
Item 1	String	INSearchForMessagesIntent
Item 2	String	INSetMessageAttributeIntent
NSExtensionPointIdentifier	String	com.apple.intents-service
NSExtensionPrincipalClass	String	$(PRODUCT_MODULE_NAME).IntentHandler

Currently, the app is set up to use the **Send Message** intent, but we want to use the **Send Payment** intent.

3. Under `IntentsSupported`, delete `Item 1` (`INSearchForMessagesIntent`) and `Item 2` (`INSetMessageAttributeIntent`):

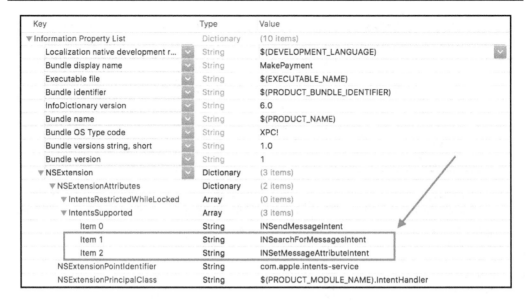

4. Now, for `Item 0`, change `INSendMessageIntent` to `INSendPaymentIntent`.

5. Under `IntentsRestrictedWhileLocked`, add `INSendPaymentIntent` by clicking the + button:

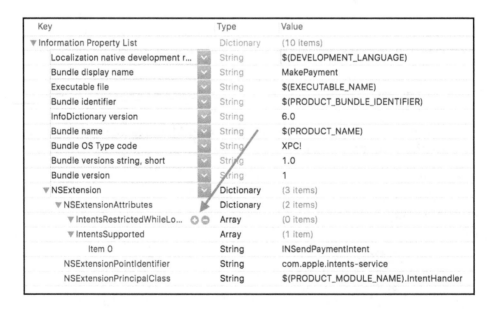

6. When finished, you should see the following:

Key	Type	Value
▼ Information Property List	Dictionary	(10 items)
Localization native development r...	String	$(DEVELOPMENT_LANGUAGE)
Bundle display name	String	MakePayment
Executable file	String	$(EXECUTABLE_NAME)
Bundle identifier	String	$(PRODUCT_BUNDLE_IDENTIFIER)
InfoDictionary version	String	6.0
Bundle name	String	$(PRODUCT_NAME)
Bundle OS Type code	String	XPC!
Bundle versions string, short	String	1.0
Bundle version	String	1
▼ NSExtension	Dictionary	(3 items)
▼ NSExtensionAttributes	Dictionary	(2 items)
▼ IntentsRestrictedWhileLocked	Array	(1 item)
Item 0	String	INSendPaymentIntent
▼ IntentsSupported	Array	(1 item)
Item 0	String	INSendPaymentIntent
NSExtensionPointIdentifier	String	com.apple.intents-service
NSExtensionPrincipalClass	String	$(PRODUCT_MODULE_NAME).IntentHandler

7. Next, open up `Info.plist` in the `MakePaymentUI` folder, open all the disclosure arrows under `NSExtension`, and change `INSendMessageIntent` under `IntentsSupported` to `INSendPaymentIntent`:

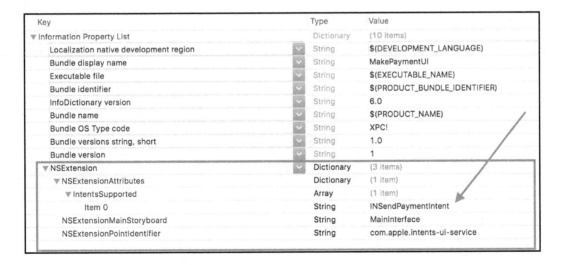

Key	Type	Value
▼ Information Property List	Dictionary	(10 items)
Localization native development region	String	$(DEVELOPMENT_LANGUAGE)
Bundle display name	String	MakePaymentUI
Executable file	String	$(EXECUTABLE_NAME)
Bundle identifier	String	$(PRODUCT_BUNDLE_IDENTIFIER)
InfoDictionary version	String	6.0
Bundle name	String	$(PRODUCT_NAME)
Bundle OS Type code	String	XPC!
Bundle versions string, short	String	1.0
Bundle version	String	1
▼ NSExtension	Dictionary	(3 items)
▼ NSExtensionAttributes	Dictionary	(1 item)
▼ IntentsSupported	Array	(1 item)
Item 0	String	INSendPaymentIntent
NSExtensionMainStoryboard	String	MainInterface
NSExtensionPointIdentifier	String	com.apple.intents-ui-service

We have finished setting up our plist. Whenever we access something, we always have to ask permission, just like we did earlier when we accessed the user's photos. In the `Info.plist` file of the *LetsEat* app, we need to update our plist to let users know that we need access for Siri and our reasoning. Add the `NSSiriUsageDescription` key.

For the key value, enter anything you want as an alert that the user sees. In the following example, the value is set as `This app uses Siri to send payments.`:

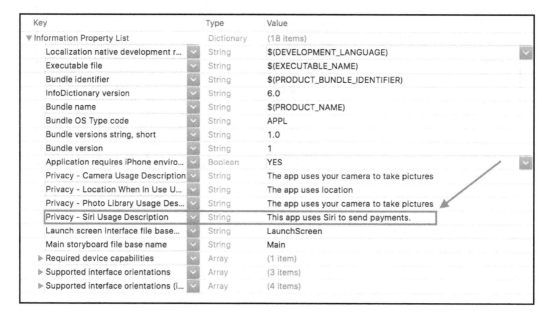

Now, inside of `AppDelete`, add the following import after `import UIKit`:

```
import Intents
```

Next, after `setupDefaultColors()`, add the following method:

```
func requestSiriPermissions() {
    INPreferences.requestSiriAuthorization({ (status) in
        print(status)
    })
}
```

Then, in your `initialize()` method under `checkNotifications()`, add `requestSiriPermissions()`.

Adding this asks the user for permission to use Siri. Now, if you are going to use this in a real app, I would say that you should add a **Settings** section where users can use a switch to turn Siri on or off. You do not want to force users to use something without really giving them a reason. In iOS, once you ask a user for permission and they decline, they have to go into the **Settings** section. If you want to ask, then it is better to have another dialog box that asks for permission; if they say yes, then run the request, and if the users say no, then you do nothing. This way, you do not have to force your users to go to their phone's settings to turn this feature on. Now that we have our permissions set up, we need to create users that we can send money to.

Creating users

When using SiriKit, it needs to have an `INPerson` object. An `INPerson` object is used by Siri to send users things—money, in our case. Let's create this new file:

1. Right-click the `Misc` folder and select **New File**.
2. Inside of the **Choose a template for your new file** screen, select **iOS** at the top and then **Swift**. Then, hit **Next**.
3. Save the file as `RestaurantContact`.
4. Click **Create**.
5. Add the following code to this file:

```
import Intents

struct RestaurantContact {
    let name: String
    let email: String
    static func allContacts() -> [RestaurantContact] {
        return [
            RestaurantContact(name: "Jason Clayton", email:
"jason@mac.com"),
            RestaurantContact(name: "Joshua Clayton", email:
```

```
"joshua@texas.edu"),
            RestaurantContact(name: "Teena Harris", email:
"teena@gmail.com")
        ]
    }
    func inPerson() -> INPerson {
        let formatter = PersonNameComponentsFormatter()
        let handle = INPersonHandle(value: email, type:
.emailAddress)
        if let components =
formatter.personNameComponents(from: name) {
            return INPerson(personHandle: handle,
nameComponents: components, displayName:
components.familyName, image: nil, contactIdentifier: nil,
customIdentifier: nil)
        }
        else {
            return INPerson(personHandle: handle,
nameComponents: nil, displayName: nil, image: nil,
contactIdentifier: nil, customIdentifier: nil)
        }
    }
}
```

Here, we are creating contacts that we can use to ask Siri to send money. We have set up three people to accept payment at this time: Jason Clayton, Joshua Clayton, and Teena Harris. When we request with Siri, these are the names that it looks for to see if the person exists. If the name is not in this list, Siri lets you know that the name is not found. This list can have any name you wish to have, so if you want to change the names to something else, you can do that now. Just make sure that when we get to the requesting section, you change the name there as well. Our `inPerson()` method is just formatting into a format that SiriKit needs to be able to read the object.

Next, update the Target Membership for this file to also include `MakePayment`:

We now need to add code that runs when the Send Payment intent is invoked.

Updating our intent handler

We can now finally add our code that runs when the **Send Payment** intent is invoked. Open the `IntentHandler` class inside of the `MakePayment` extension folder. After the import intents line deletes everything else from this file, add the following code:

```
class IntentHandler: INExtension{
    override func handler(for intent: INIntent) -> Any {
        if intent is INSendPaymentIntent {
            return SendMoneyIntent()
        }
        return self
    }
}
```

Here, we are creating a custom intent handler. When the intent is to send payment, we want to run our `SendMoneyIntent` class. We need to create this file next. In the same file direction under the `IntentHandler` class, add the following:

```
class SendMoneyIntent: NSObject, INSendPaymentIntentHandling {
    func handle(intent: INSendPaymentIntent, completion: @escaping
(INSendPaymentIntentResponse) -> Void) {
        if let person = intent.payee, let amount =
intent.currencyAmount {
            //handle payment
            print("person \(person.displayName) - amount
\(String(describing: amount.amount))")
            completion(INSendPaymentIntentResponse(code: .success,
userActivity: nil))
        }
        else {
            completion(INSendPaymentIntentResponse(code: .failure,
userActivity: nil))
        }
    }

}
```

In this class, the `handle()` method responds to a `SendPaymentIntent`. We are printing the person's display name and amount. We pass a completion block here, but in real production code, you would run whatever API you are using to verify the payment. Add the following inside of the `SendMoneyIntent` under the `handle()` method:

```
func resolvePayee(for intent: INSendPaymentIntent, with completion:
@escaping (INPersonResolutionResult) -> Void) {
    if let payee = intent.payee {
        let contacts:[RestaurantContact] =
RestaurantContact.allContacts()
        var result: INPersonResolutionResult?
        var matchedContacts:[RestaurantContact] = []
        for contact in contacts {
            print("checking existing: (contact.name) -
(payee.displayName)")
            if contact.name == payee.displayName {
                matchedContacts.append(contact)
            }
            switch matchedContacts.count {
                case 0:
                    print("no matches")
                    result = .unsupported()
                case 1:
```

```
                        print("best matched")
                        let person = matchedContacts[0].inPerson()
                        result = INPersonResolutionResult.success(with:
person)
                    default:
                        print("more than one match")
                        let person:[INPerson] = matchedContacts.map {
contact in
                            return contact.inPerson()
                        }
                        result =
INPersonResolutionResult.disambiguation(with: person)
                }
            }
            completion(result!)
        } else {
            completion(INPersonResolutionResult.needsValue())
        }
    }
}
```

In this method, we are getting the payee's information and checking to see if the person matches one of our contacts. We are looping through the contacts and looking for a match. When completed, we return the result to Siri. If the user is not found, then Siri will tell you that the person is not found. If Siri finds the person, then `PaymentIntent` continues. Lastly, inside of the `IntentViewController`, update the `desiredSize` variable to the following:

```
var desiredSize: CGSize {
    return CGSize(width: self.desiredSize.width, height: 150)
}
```

Here, we are setting the size of the UI to a `height` of `150`. Let's look at how we can test this.

Testing Siri

We can test Siri on a device or in the simulator. If you want to test on a device, just change the target to the `MakePayment` target and plug in your iOS 12 device. If you want to test this in the simulator, you have two options. First, you can run the app and Siri in the simulator. At this point, you can hold down the power button and say `Send $100 to Jason Clayton for dinner last night using LetsEat` (or you use the name of whomever you added to the contacts we created earlier). Option two is that you can enter text that you want to display each time.

To set up this text, every time you run the app, select the `MakePayment` scheme:

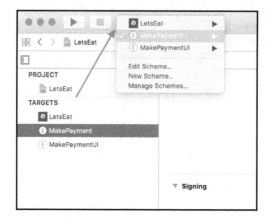

1. Hit the **Scheme** dropdown again and select **Edit Scheme...**:

2. Then, under **Siri Intent Query**, put in the desired text, such as `Send $100 to Jason Clayton for dinner last night using LetsEat`, and then hit **Close**:

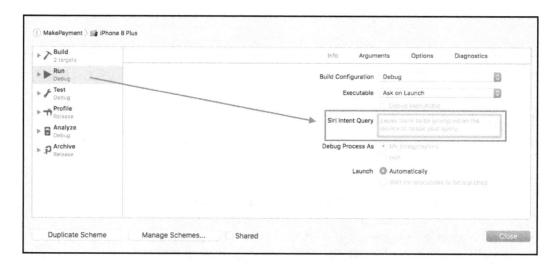

Remember that we have the `MakePayment` scheme. Run the `MakePayment` scheme. The first thing that will happen is that Siri will ask you for permission:

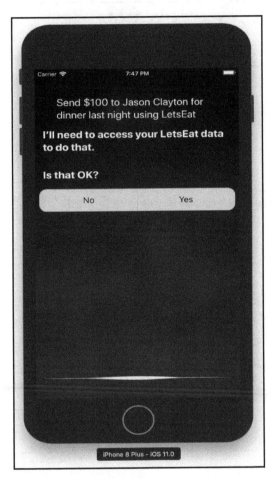

3. When you accept, Siri will show you your request and ask if you have received it:

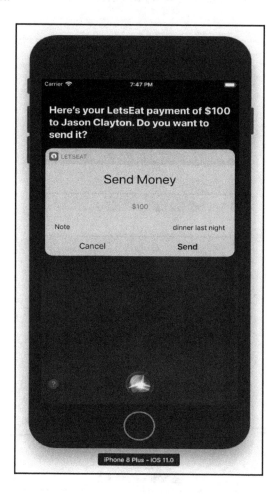

When you accept, you will see that your money's been sent. In our example, we are not sending money, so this step will always go through:

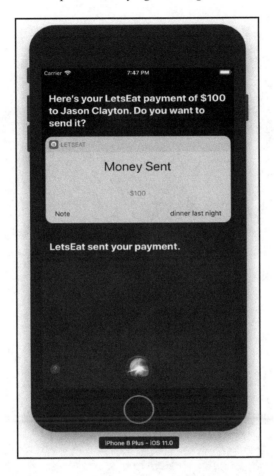

Note that the reason Siri is asking for permission is that we are running Siri first, instead of the app. If we ran the app, we would get the following:

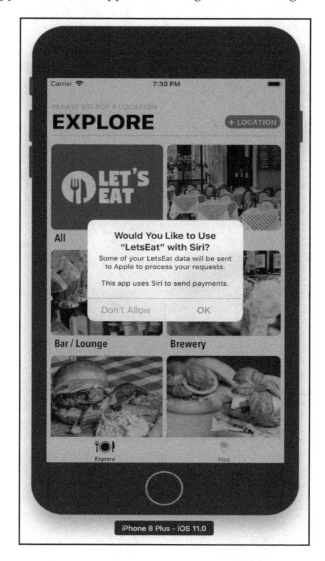

We are now done. We did not do anything with our UI, but you can add anything you want to your UI, such as a logo, a view or display to show to the payee, or whatever you decide. Have fun with it and make it your own.

Summary

In this chapter, we looked at how to integrate Siri into our app. Even though Siri is limited to specific intents, we can still find unique ways to use it, such as using it for messaging, notes, and lists. The overall setup for each intent is the same—the only difference is what you do once the intent hits your app. In the next chapter, we will look at how to distribute our app to others for testing, as well as how to submit our app to the App Store.

25
Beta and Store Submission

Over the course of this book, we've come a long way, from learning about Xcode to how to build an entire app. This process would not be complete, however, without actually learning how to submit the app to the App Store. This process may seem like a lot when doing it for the first time, but it becomes more natural and even second nature after a while.

When I submitted my first app, I was extremely nervous. I remember the relief I felt after submitting the app, but I was soon repeatedly checking the site and my inbox for that approval email. I'd heard many stories of people who spent a lot of time working on an app only to have it rejected; these fears are understandable, but know that Apple wants you to succeed. Even if your app gets rejected (and my first one did), it's not necessarily a bad thing.

My first app was a sports app, and it was rejected for two reasons. First, in Apple's eyes, the logo for my app was too similar to the NFL logo. To address this, I just made a generic logo with the initials of the app. Second, the quality of my images was considered not up to standard; therefore, I obtained better images. I then resubmitted my app, and within a couple of days, my app was approved. It is almost a certainty that you will encounter rejections, even if you have been doing this for a while. Take comfort in the fact that you can address any issues with your app and resubmit it for approval from the App Store.

In this chapter, we will cover everything you need to know about getting your app into the App Store. In Xcode 10, a lot of things are done for you behind the scenes; however, the goal of this chapter is to show you how you can set up things on your own. You will need a developer account to follow along with these steps. Go to `https://developer.apple.com/programs/` if you would like to purchase a developer account.

We will cover the following topics in this chapter:

- Creating a bundle identifier
- Generating a certificate signing request

- Creating production and development certificates
- Creating production and development provisioning profiles
- Creating an App Store listing
- Making the release build and submitting to the App Store
- Conducting internal and external testing

This chapter is set up for you to use as you need it. It is not meant for you to follow in order, as with the other chapters in this book. For example, you may need to create a bundle identifier and then need to know how to add external testers. Use this chapter as a resource for when you need to do one of these tasks.

Creating a bundle identifier

When we created our project, we talked about the bundle identifier (also known as your App ID). This bundle identifier is used to identify your app, and therefore must be unique. Let's proceed with the following steps:

1. Log in to your Apple developer account, and you will see the following screen:

2. Click **Certificates, IDs & Profiles**.
3. Then, under **IDs**, click **App IDs**:

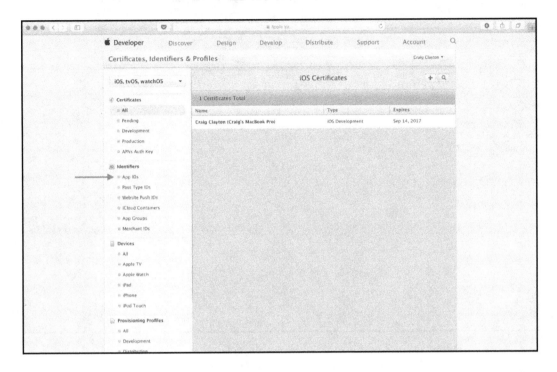

4. Click on the + button at the top right of the screen:

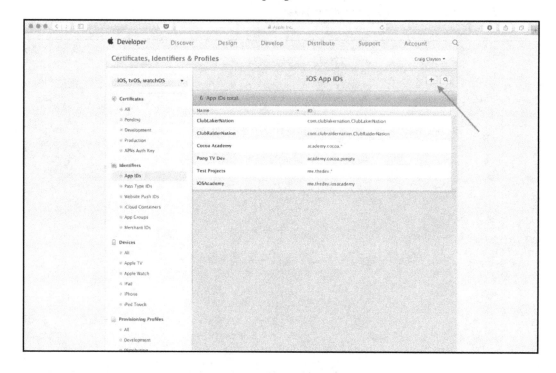

5. The **Registering an App ID** screen will appear, as follows:

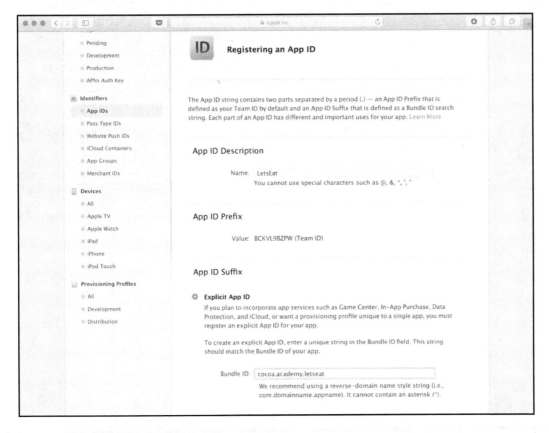

6. In the top part of the **Registering an App ID** screen, as seen in the preceding screenshot, add the following:

- **Name**: Update this field under **App ID Description** as `LetsEat`.
- **Explicit App ID**: This field under **App ID Suffix** should be selected.
- **Bundle ID**: This field under **App ID Suffix** should be filled with your details.

Make sure that the **Bundle ID** follows the standard naming convention: `com.yourcompanyname.letseat`. Your **Bundle ID** should be the same ID that you set up when we created the project. For example, mine is `cocoa.academy.letseat`.

7. Next, in the bottom part of the **Registering an App ID** screen, shown as follows, select the **App Services** that the app requires and then click **Continue**.

Our project does not have any **App Services**, but this is where you would set them if a future app required them:

If you later decide to add **App Services**, you can do so inside of Xcode. You would select the project under **Targets**, then select the **Capabilities** tab and modify it as necessary:

After verifying your App ID information, click **Register**:

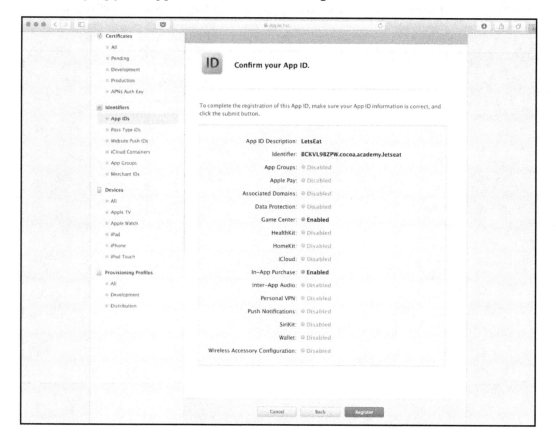

Your App ID has now been created. Now, let's look at what certificates are and how to use them.

Creating a certificate signing request

Whenever you work on a project, you will need to create a **certificate signing request** (**CSR**). You generate this certificate on your computer. Let's create one certificate for production (for the App Store) and one certificate for development (for building locally):

1. Open **Keychain Access** (which you can find by clicking on the search icon in the upper-right corner of your menu bar and typing `Keychain Access`):

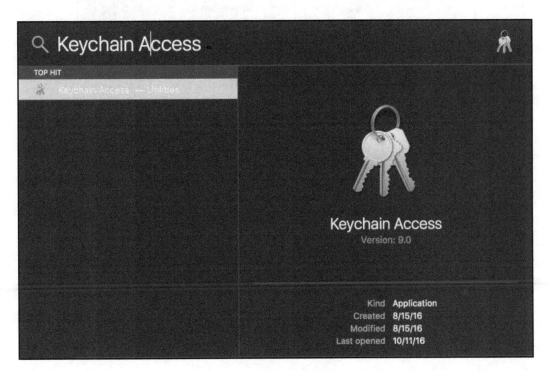

2. In the menu bar, while in **Keychain Access**, select **Keychain Access** | **Certificate Assistant** | **Request a Certificate From a Certificate Authority...**:

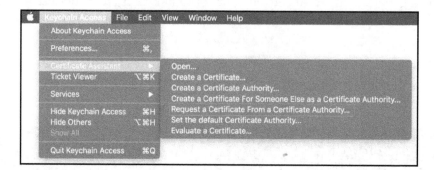

3. Enter your email address for **User Email Address** and the app name for **Common Name**, and then select **Saved to disk** under **Request is**:

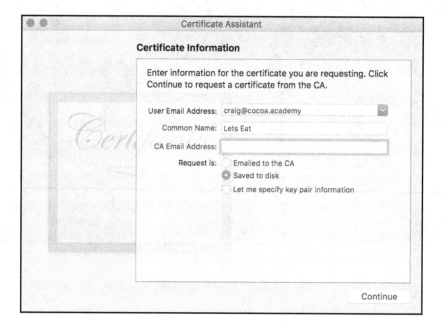

4. Then, click **Continue**.

5. In the screen that appears, enter the certificate name, select a save location, and click **Save**, as follows:

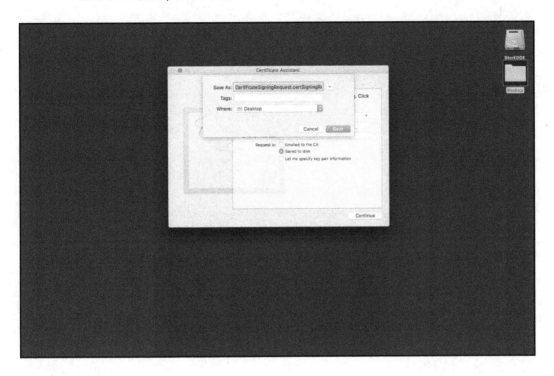

6. Click **Done**, export the certificate, and save it to your computer:

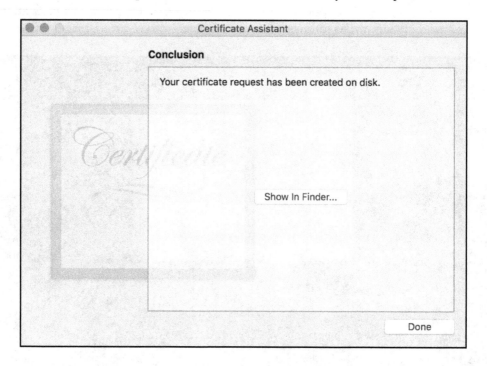

Creating production and development certificates

We need to create production and development certificates. Production certificates are used for the App Store, while development certificates are used to verify that you are a team member who allows apps signed by you to launch on a device. Remember that Xcode 9 can now handle this for you, but knowing the process is still useful. Let's start by creating a production certificate first:

1. Log in to the Apple developer account, and you will see the following screen:

2. Click **Certificates, IDs & Profiles**, and then under **Certificates**, select **All**.
3. Click on the + button at the top right of the screen:

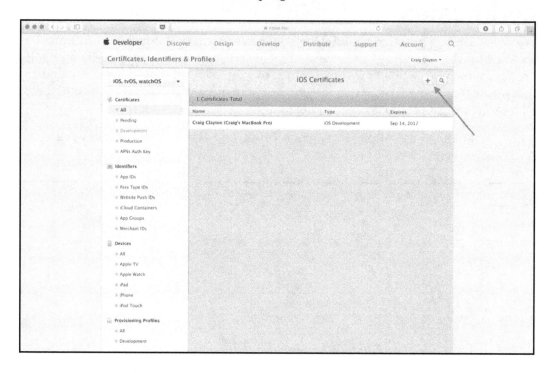

4. On the screen that appears, select **App Store and Ad Hoc** under **Production** and then click **Continue**:

5. The following screen then lists the steps required for creating a CSR file (which we have already created). Click **Continue**:

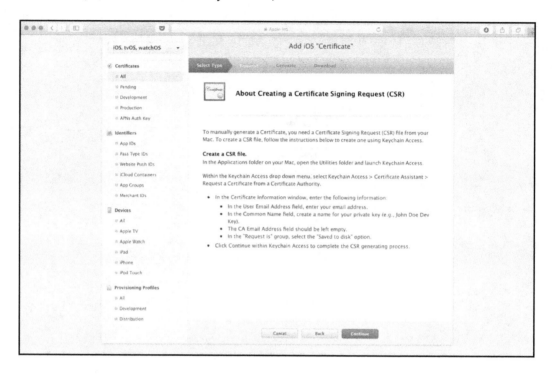

6. Upload the CSR created earlier by selecting **Choose File** under **Upload CSR file**, selecting the certificate file you saved, and clicking **Open**. Then, click **Continue**:

7. Next, download the certificate:

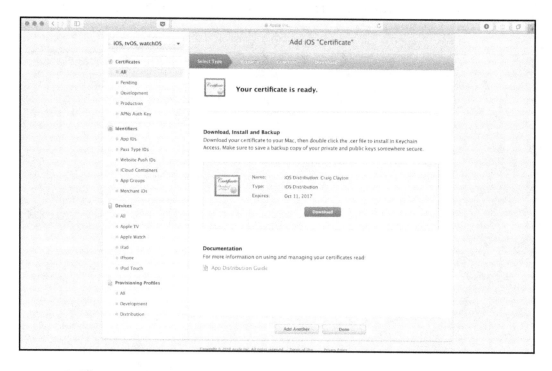

8. Then, install the downloaded certificate by double-clicking it.

For the development certificate, you will need to repeat these steps, except in the step where you choose the type of certificate you need, instead of selecting **App Store and Ad Hoc** under **Production**, you will select **iOS App Development** under **Development**. All the other steps will be the same.

Creating a production provisioning profile

Now, let's create a production provisioning profile, which is used for distributing your application. Xcode 9 creates these for you, but again it is still good to know how to do it:

1. Log in to the Apple developer account, and you will see the following screen:

2. Click **Certificates, IDs & Profiles**, and under **Provisioning Profiles**, select **All**.

3. Click on the + button at the top right of the screen:

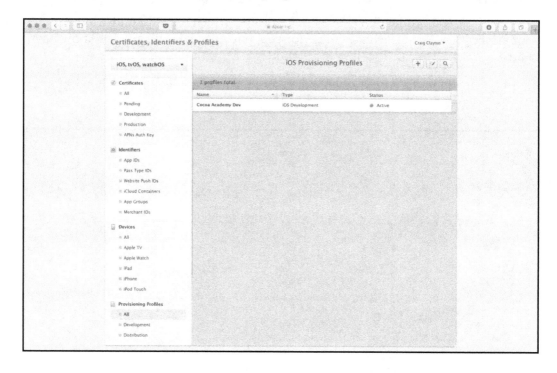

4. Select **App Store** under **Distribution** and then click **Continue**:

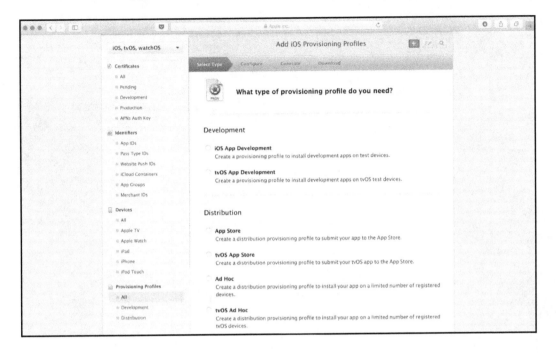

5. Select the **Bundle ID** created earlier and then click **Continue**:

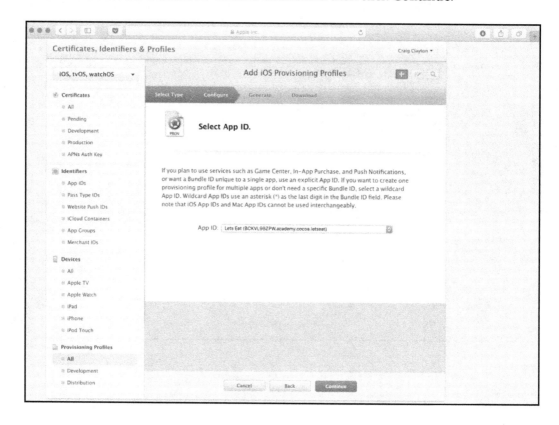

6. Next, select the certificate created earlier and then click **Continue**:

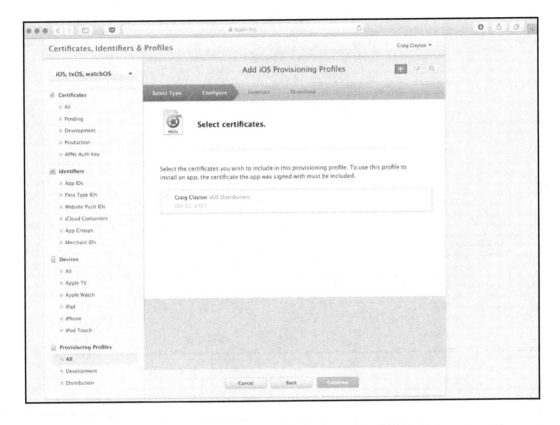

7. Next, enter the **Profile Name**, **Lets Eat Prod**, and click **Continue**:

8. Download the profile:

9. Install the downloaded profile by double-clicking it.

Creating a development provisioning profile

Now, let's create a development provisioning profile, which is used for building apps on your device using Xcode:

1. Log in to the Apple developer account.
2. Click **Certificates, Identifiers & Profiles**.
3. Next, under **Provisioning Profiles**, click **All**.
4. Then, click on the + button at the top right of the screen.
5. Next, select **App Store** under **Distribution** and then click **Continue**.
6. Select the **Bundle ID** created earlier and click **Continue**.
7. Next, select the certificate created earlier and then click **Continue**.
8. Enter the **Profile Name**, Lets Eat Dev, and click **Continue**:

9. Select the devices you wish to use or choose **Select All**:

10. Download the profile:

11. Install the downloaded profile by double-clicking it.

Creating an App Store listing

Next, we are going to create the App Store listing:

1. Log in to your iTunes account (`https://appstoreconnect.apple.com`) and select **My Apps**:

2. Click on the + button at the top left of the screen:

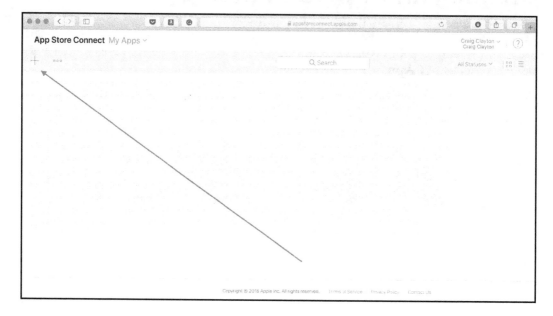

3. Select **New App**:

4. Enter your app details and then hit **Create**:

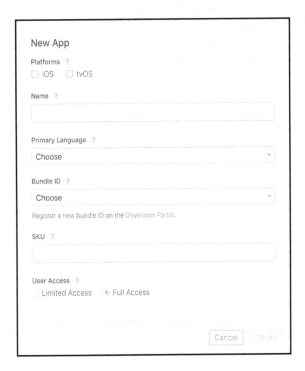

The app will now be listed in your iTunes account.

Creating an archive build

When you submit your app to the App Store, you need to create an archive. This archive will also be used for internal and external testing, which we will address shortly. When your archive is complete, you will upload it to the App Store. Let's create an archive now:

1. Open Xcode, select the project, and enter the following information:

   - Under **Identity**, update the **Version** and **Build numbers** to 1.1 and 2, respectively.
   - Under **Signing**, ensure **Automatically manage signing** is checked.

- Under **Signing**, select **Team**.
- For minor builds, you want to increment your **Version number** by 0.1 and your **Build number** by 1. In some instances, developers make their **Version numbers** three digits (for example, 1.1.2). This is all based on your business and how you want to handle **Version numbers**. If you are performing a major update, then you typically increment your **Version number** by 1:

2. Select **Generic iOS Device** as the build destination:

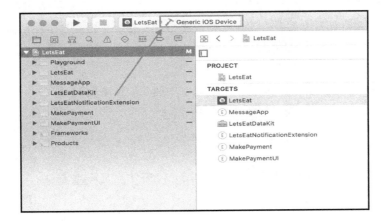

3. Update your `Info.plist` by adding `ITSAppUsesNonExemptEncryption`, making its type `Boolean`, and setting its value to `NO`. The value should be `NO` unless you are using some special encryption. Since our app does not have special encryption, we will set our value to `NO`.

4. Select **Product | Archive**:

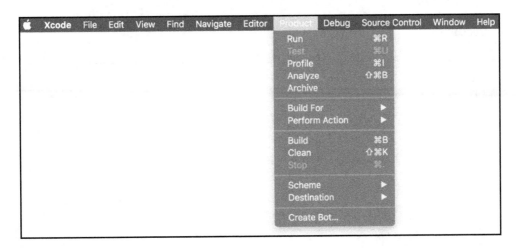

5. On the **Archives** tab on the screen that appears, select your **Development Team** and then hit **Choose**:

6. Your IPA file will now be created, so now click **Upload**:

7. You will see uploading begin, as shown in the following screenshot:

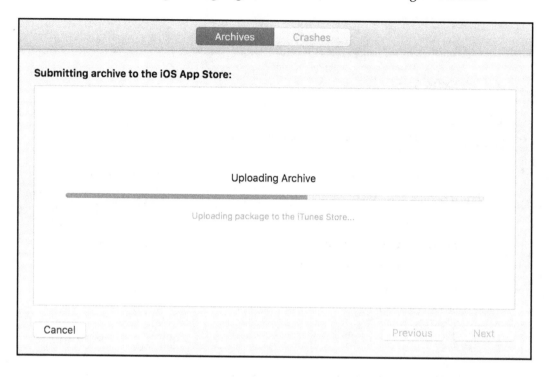

8. Then, when your upload is successful, you will see the following:

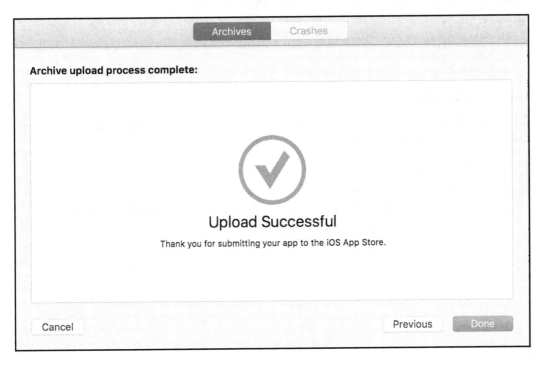

9. You will receive an email when your app is either approved or rejected. If rejected, once you fix the issues, you can resubmit it in the same manner by updating the archive and following the steps laid out previously.

Internal and external testing

Internal and external testing use what is known as **TestFlight**. The *TestFlight* app can be downloaded from the App Store. Let's look at how to create each type of testing.

Internal testing

Internal testing does not go through a review process. You can only send builds to up to 25 testers for internal testing. Let's begin:

1. Log in to your iTunes Account and select **My Apps**.
2. Select your *Let's Eat* app and then *TestFlight*.
3. On the left side of the page, select **Internal Testing**, and then on the right side of the page, click **Select Version to Test**:

4. Then, select the version you want to test and click **OK**:

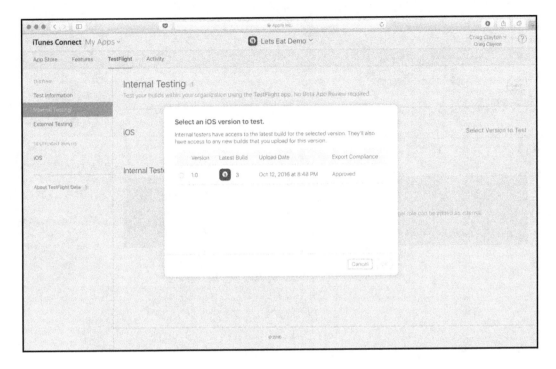

5. You will now see the following screen:

6. Finally, click the + button next to **Internal Testers** and add your **Internal Testers**:

External testing

External testing may or may not go through a review process, but with external testing, you can have up to 2,000 testers. For external testing, follow these steps:

1. Log in to your iTunes account and select **My Apps**.
2. Select your *Let's Eat* app and then *TestFlight*.
3. On the left side of the page, select **External Testing**.

4. Next, on the right side of the page, click **Add Build to Test**, select your build, and hit **OK**:

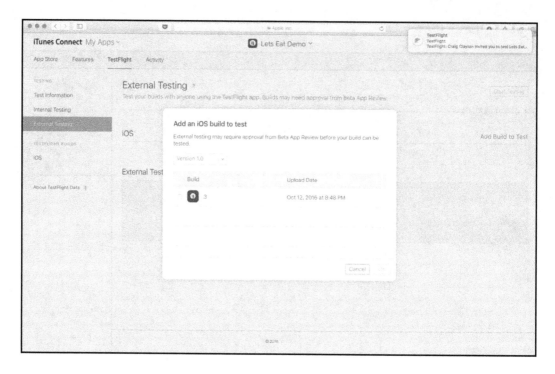

5. Finally, click the + button next to **External Testers** and add your external testers:

6. When you are done adding testers, click the **Start Testing** button and you will see the following screen. You will need to provide the information requested:

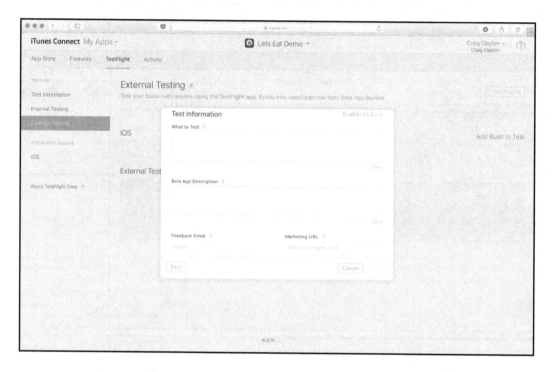

7. Next, submit your app to Apple for review; you will receive an email when it is either approved or rejected. If rejected, once you have fixed the issues, you can resubmit it in the same manner by updating the archive and following the steps laid out previously.

Summary

You have now completed the entire process of building an app and submitting it to the App Store. If you have gone from beginning to end, congratulate yourself, because it is genuinely a big feat.

At this point, all you can do is wait for Apple to review your project. The next week or so will be the most nerve-wracking (at least it was for me). Don't worry if your app gets rejected, because it happens to the most experienced of developers and is often fixable. Apps can be rejected for minor reasons that are easy to fix; however, you do not want to work for months on a project and miss something big that Apple will never approve. So, do your research regarding what is and is not acceptable to Apple. When you submit your apps to the App Store, please reach out to me on Twitter (`@thedevme`) to let me know—I would love to see what you have built.

Other Books You May Enjoy

If you enjoyed this book, you may be interested in these other books by Packt:

Mastering iOS 12 Programming - Third Edition
Donny Wals

ISBN: 9781789133202

- Build a professional iOS application using Xcode 10 and Swift 4.2
- Use AutoLayout to create complex layouts that look great on every device
- Delve into advanced animations with UIViewPropertyAnimator and UIKit Dynamics
- Enhance your app by using instruments and building your own profiling tools
- Integrate iMessage, Siri, and more in your app through app extensions
- Train and use machine learning models with Core ML 2 and Create ML
- Create engaging augmented reality experiences with ARKit 2

Swift Game Development - Third Edition
Siddharth Shekar

ISBN: 9781788471152

- Deliver powerful graphics, physics, and sound in your game by using SpriteKit and SceneKit
- Set up a scene using the new capabilities of the scene editor and custom classes
- Maximize gameplay with little-known tips and strategies for fun, repeatable action
- Make use of animations, graphics, and particles to polish your game
- Understand the current mobile monetization landscape
- Integrate your game with Game Center
- Develop 2D and 3D Augmented Reality games using Apple's new ARKit framework
- Publish your game to the App Store

Leave a review - let other readers know what you think

Please share your thoughts on this book with others by leaving a review on the site that you bought it from. If you purchased the book from Amazon, please leave us an honest review on this book's Amazon page. This is vital so that other potential readers can see and use your unbiased opinion to make purchasing decisions, we can understand what our customers think about our products, and our authors can see your feedback on the title that they have worked with Packt to create. It will only take a few minutes of your time, but is valuable to other potential customers, our authors, and Packt. Thank you!

Index

CPSIA information can be obtained
at www.ICGtesting.com
Printed in the USA
LVHW102333150819
627877LV00005B/71/P